Sushil • Edward A. Stohr
Editors

The Flexible Enterprise

Springer

Editors
Sushil
Department of Management Studies
Indian Institute of Technology Delhi
Hauz Khas, New Delhi, India

Edward A. Stohr
Professor and Director of the BI&A Progr
Stevens Institute of Technology
Hoboken, New Jersey, USA

ISBN 978-81-322-2898-1 ISBN 978-81-322-1560-8 (eBook)
DOI 10.1007/978-81-322-1560-8
Springer New Delhi Heidelberg New York Dordrecht London

Softcover reprint of the hardcover 1st edition 2014

Printed on acid-free paper

Springer is part of Springer Science+Business Media (www.springer.com)

Preface

The need for enterprise flexibility is apparent in an era of rapidly advancing technology, increasing competition, and globalization. Flexibility can be thought of as an ability of the enterprise to quickly and efficiently respond to market changes and to bring new products and services to the market place with fast speed. Beyond this definition, a truly flexible enterprise should proactively change the market through its ability to create entirely new and innovative products and services.

The proposed book is intended to provide a conceptual framework of "Flexible Enterprise" supported by researches/case applications in various types of flexibilities exhibited by a flexible enterprise.

This book presents selected, reviewed, and updated papers of GLOGIFT 08 conference and some recent developments on the theme of Flexible Enterprise. These are organized in the form of an edited volume that can serve as a good reference material in the area of creating and managing flexible enterprises.

"GLOGIFT 08," an International Conference with the theme "Flexible Enterprise for Global Business," was held at Stevens Institute of Technology, Hoboken, New Jersey, USA. It was an effort to provide a global forum for practitioners, policy makers, teachers, researchers, and learners to share their practical experiences, knowledge, and insight in the evolution, formulation, and implementation of strategies and models for flexible enterprises to meet the changing requirements of global business. The objective of the conference was to provide a knowledge-sharing platform for dissemination of research and experiential findings through empirical study, qualitative modeling, case studies, new concepts, and state-of-the-art studies.

The selected papers from a variety of issues concerning the planning and operation of a flexible enterprise are organized into the following four parts:

I. Enterprise and Strategic Flexibility
II. Organizational Flexibility
III. Business Process and Information Systems Flexibility
IV. Operations Flexibility

Part one, on enterprise and strategic flexibility, comprises of six chapters. The first one introduces the concept of a flexible enterprise. It defines enterprise flexibility and its cornerstones such as strategic flexibility, organizational flexibility, financial flexibility, marketing flexibility, manufacturing flexibility, and information systems flexibility. The basic purpose and best practices of each type of flexibility in an enterprise are outlined. Finally, it provides an outline of a flexibility maturity model of an enterprise. The next chapter discusses the architectures that contribute in creating enterprise flexibility with special emphasis on service-oriented architecture. A review of various prominent definitions of strategic flexibility is presented in the next chapter. Strategic flexibility is considered as managing confluence of continuity and change that is illustrated in the context of e-governance in another contribution in this part. This provides an illustration of the novel framework of flowing stream strategy. The next contribution is yet another application-based study that illustrates the relationship of various types of flexibility with performance measures as competitiveness of the enterprise. Finally, an evolving framework of flexible strategy game-card is presented as a strategic performance management system, and its theoretical roots are traced.

The second part of the book, on organizational flexibility, consists of five chapters. The first chapter, in this part, is on architecting flexible organizations. It describes the dimensions of organizational flexibility and various types of contracts in an organization which are illustrated by a few examples. The next chapter deals with flexibility dynamic of a typical organization that is conceptualized as "system of systems." It deliberates on the effects of outsourcing on flexibility of such a loosely coupled organization with a case study of yellow cabs of New York City. Another dimension of organizational flexibility is intuitive flexibility that helps in creating order out of disorder, which is dealt with case illustrations in the next chapter. Another conceptual contribution on flexible organization is in the area of knowledge creation and application. This highlights the power of connecting the knowledge dots. The last contribution in this part uses grounded theory to identify flexibility and controllability parameters that would be exhibited by a flexible organization.

The business process and information systems flexibility is the subject matter of part three. It consists of five chapters; the first one is dealing with agile systems migration across next-generation life cycle boundaries. The business process management is further developed in another chapter dealing with workflow breakthroughs. The issue of modular computing technologies is covered in the next contribution in order to develop flexible business process management. The rapid deployment approach through flexible system design is discussed in the context of e-clinical research in yet another chapter. Finally, a review on information systems flexibility is provided to bring out conceptual models and research issues.

Part four, on operations flexibility, covers four chapters on manufacturing, supply chain, and marketing flexibilities. The first chapter in this part deals with virtual cellular system as a source of manufacturing flexibility. The manpower flexibility issues in lean manufacturing are reviewed in the next chapter. The manufacturing operations are extended to bring out perception on supply chain flexibility in the third chapter in this part. Finally, a unique framework of marketing flexibility is evolved through an inductive study of practices being followed in a number of case situations.

Flexible Systems Management

Volume 1

Series Editor

Sushil

For further volumes:
http://www.springer.com/series/10780

We take this opportunity to thank all the authors and reviewers whose efforts have made it possible to create this volume. Special thanks are due to Rejani Raghu who helped at various stages in communicating with authors and reviewers and also provided support in word processing and formatting the manuscript.

It is hoped that this volume on "The Flexible Enterprise" will generate enough interest in the readers to further evolve and enrich the paradigm of flexible systems management.

Sushil
Edward A. Stohr

Contents

Contributors

Jainarine Bansee The University of Trinidad and Tobago, Pt. Lisas, Trinidad and Tobago, West Indies

Anilkumar Bhate Stevens Institute of Technology, Hoboken, NJ, USA

Bibhushan JDA Software, Bangalore, India

John T. Boardman Stevens Institute of Technology, School of Systems and Enterprises, Hoboken, NJ, USA

Boppana V. Chowdary The University of the West Indies, St Augustine, Trinidad and Tobago, West Indies

Rick Dove Stevens Institute of Technology, Hoboken, NJ, USA

Ozgur Erol Stevens Institute of Technology, School of Systems and Enterprises, Hoboken, NJ, USA

S. Jimmy Gandhi California State University, Northridge, CA, USA

Alex Gorod University of Adelaide, Adelaide, Australia

Kuldeep Kumar College of Business Administration, Florida International University, Miami, FL, USA

Babu Lal Bharat Heavy Electricals Limited (BHEL), New Delhi, India

Arnab Mitra KPMG, Gurgaon, India

Joseph Morabito Stevens Institute of Technology, Hoboken, NJ, USA

S. Nasim Faculty of Management Studies and Research, AMU, Aligarh, India

Ramaraj Palanisamy Schwartz School of Business and IS, St. Francis Xavier University, Antigonish, NS, Canada

Brig R.C. Pathak Imperial College of Engineering and Research, Wagholi, Pune, India

H.D. Patil Imperial College of Engineering and Research, Wagholi, Pune, India

Anuj Prakash The Hong Kong Polytechnic University, Hung Hom, Hong Kong, China

MaryAnne Rizk Stevens Institute of Technology, Hoboken, NJ, USA

Norman Roberts Business School, The University of Western Australia, Crawley, Australia

Ira Sack Stevens Institute of Technology, Hoboken, NJ, USA

Brian Sauser University of North Texas, Denton, USA

Manoj Kumar Sharma JSS Academy of Technical Education, Noida, UP, India

Nripendra Singh Jaypee Business School, JIIT University, Noida, India

T.P. Singh Symbiosis Institute of Technology, Symbiosis International University, Pune, India

Gary J. Stockport Business School, The University of Western Australia, Crawley, Australia

Garry Turkington Paradigm Shift International, Columbia, MD, USA

Bharat Wadhwa Indian Institute of Technology Delhi, Hauz Khas, New Delhi, India

Minhong Wang Division of Information & Technology Studies, The University of Hong Kong, Hong Kong, China

Neetu Yadav Department of Management Studies, Indian Institute of Technology Delhi, Hauz Khas, New Delhi, India

Robert Zotti Stevens Institute of Technology, Hoboken, NJ, USA

Part I
Enterprise and Strategic Flexibility

Chapter 1
The Concept of a Flexible Enterprise

Sushil

1 Introduction

The handling of paradoxes and strategic dilemmas is a major concern in the modern day organizations. One major strategic dilemma is that whether to move ahead on the lines of continuity or to initiate change for progress. The traditional strategic management thinking went for an "either-or" framework, that is, to choose either continuity or change. Conventionally, under the stable environment, the strategic thinkers as well as practitioners preferred the strategic route of continuity. But the forces of competition and globalization have proven to be dominant to let the strategic choice heavily tilted towards change in the last two decades. Both continuity and change have a lot of promise to offer for the growth of the enterprise and opening new vistas of opportunities and possibilities, and it is a challenge to strategically leverage each one of the opposing forces together. The postmodern management thinking, in general, is tilted towards a "both-and" approach rather than the conventional "either-or" one. The paradigm of flexibility in general and strategic flexibility in particular provides the philosophical basis and acts as fountainhead for channelizing the flowing stream strategy framework (Sushil 2005, 2012a). This chapter first clarifies the concept of flexibility in general terms and then builds the concept of flexible enterprise.

Flexibility has multiple connotations as per the situation; some of the important ones are adaptiveness to the changes in the environment, adjustment to situation, agility in action, amiability in relationships, autonomy in functioning, balance in competing opposites, broadening of mind, compromising for betterment, and contingency in planning. It also implies customizing solutions, elasticity under tension, freedom of thought and expression, informal attitude, liberalization from controls,

Sushil (✉)
Department of Management Studies, Indian Institute of Technology Delhi,
Vishwakarma Bhawan, Shaheed Jeet Singh Marg, New Delhi 110016, India
e-mail: sushil@dms.iitd.ac.in; profsushil@gmail.com

Sushil and E.A. Stohr (eds.), *The Flexible Enterprise*, Flexible Systems Management,
DOI 10.1007/978-81-322-1560-8_1, © Springer India 2014

localness in organization, openness in thinking, resilience in implementation, responsiveness to customers' requirements, variability in parameters and specifications, mobility in transactions, and versatility in solutions and operations. This is only a representative list, and many more connotations of flexibility can be identified and added to it (Sushil 1997, 1999).

2 Flexibility in Management

The concept of flexibility is multidimensional in nature. To grasp and explain such a multidimensional concept, the concept of paradox/continuum is used. A paradox is in the form of a pair of polar opposites: a thesis and an antithesis, forming a continuum from the thesis to the antithesis, for example, above–below, light–dark, and male–female. In the organizational context, some leading paradoxes or dichotomies are centralization–decentralization, continuity–change, stability–dynamism, and so on. If we treat the thesis as rigidity, then can we say that the antithesis is flexibility? Is flexibility the opposite of rigidity? These are the basic questions that would clarify the concept of systemic flexibility (Sushil 2000a). A review of flexibility on multiple fronts is provided by Sharma et al. (2010).

By simply moving from the thesis to the antithesis, we need not necessarily bring flexibility; rather the system may lose its identity if pushed to extreme antithesis. For example, if an organization with high degree of centralization opts for the antithesis, that is, extreme decentralization, it may lead to disintegration or fragmentation of the organization as was experienced by HP and Motorola who ultimately opted for recentralization. HP, prior to merger of Compaq, adopted restructuring to recentralize it from a number of divisions to four divisions only: two on the front end for corporate and individual customers and two on the back end for computers and peripherals. A flexible organization would be a "collective," bimodal or multimodal organization having centralization and decentralization at the same time and changing their degree over time as per the requirement.

"Flexibility is the exercise of free will or freedom of choice on the continuum to synthesize the dynamic interplay of thesis and antithesis in an interactive and innovative manner, capturing the ambiguity in systems and expanding the continuum with minimum time and efforts." (Sushil 1999)

This definition of systemic flexibility involves three keywords:

i. Options
ii. Change mechanisms
iii. Freedom of choice

Hence, in order to define flexibility in any area, we can identify the following:

- What is the range of "options" created in the process or system?
  These can be mapped on the continuum ranging from the thesis to the antithesis.

- What types of "change mechanisms" or dynamic syntheses are created for continuous renewal and adaptation?
  These can be listed down according to the process or system under consideration.
- What are the domains of "freedom of choice" of participating actors?

These can be identified in terms of various actors involved in the problem context.

Let us take the example of a flexible organization on the following continuum.

Centralization -------------------------- Decentralization

Options: A rigid organization would choose the extremes, whereas a flexible organization will have a range of options from centralization to decentralization at the same time. It may have:

- Highly centralized financial control systems
- Highly localized cross-functional teams to respond to customer requirements

Change: The flexible organization may create organizational architectures to learn, renew, and adapt over time such as:

- Cross-functional teams with distributors and customers
- Dialogue projects
- Quality circles
- Suggestion schemes
- Knowledge management systems
- Service-oriented architecture

Freedom of choice: The flexible organization creates a set up to provide more external freedom to managers and releases their internal freedom (from biases) by creating a learning organization. They may have freedom to choose their projects, teams, approach, and tools.

It may be further noted that there are various types of flexibilities in an enterprise, such as strategic flexibility, organizational flexibility, financial flexibility, manufacturing flexibility, information systems (IS) flexibility, marketing flexibility, operational flexibility, and technology management flexibility. Under each category, there are many types of flexibilities. For example, the manufacturing flexibility encompasses product flexibility, process flexibility, volume flexibility, routing flexibility, tooling flexibility, labor flexibility, static flexibility, dynamic flexibility, and so on (Sushil 2000b).

Similarly, financial flexibility would incorporate outlay flexibility, investment flexibility, flexible budgets, and flexible exchange rates to hedge the risk and uncertainty around. The organizational flexibility deals with flexible structure and flexible work processes like flexi-time and flexi-place.

Depending upon the variety and speed combination, the flexibility could be of four types, namely, static flexibility (low variety-low speed), operational flexibility (low variety-high speed), structural flexibility (high variety-low speed), and strategic flexibility (high variety-high speed) (Volbreda 1998). The flexibility dimensions provided by e-Education industry are shown in Table 1.1.

Table 1.1 Flexibility dimensions provided by the e-Education industry

Dimension of flexibility	External flexibility (for outside world, competitors, and customers)	Internal flexibility (internal management and employees)
Adaptiveness	Adapting to the global standards of IT Education	Adapting to flexible hierarchies in the organization in the new business model
Responsiveness	Responsiveness to customer's needs of "anytime, anywhere" education	Responsiveness to individual employees' needs to have a better quality of life
Elasticity	Expanding markets – domestic as well as global	Elasticity in the definition of roles and responsibilities of key managers (focus on innovation and stretch)
Agility	Faster change in education contents and style	Faster hiring and firing too

3 Enterprise Flexibility: A Conceptual Framework

"Enterprise flexibility means creating ***options*** at various levels in the enterprise, developing ways and means of ***change*** across the range of options, and providing ***freedom of choice*** to various actors in the enterprise to make this change happen with minimum time and efforts" (Sushil 2001a). Select continua of enterprise flexibility are given below.

Select Continua of Enterprise Flexibility

Centralization	________________	Decentralization
Bureaucracy	________________	Adhocracy
Hierarchy	________________	Network
Formal	________________	Informal
Closed Systems	________________	Open Systems
Monolithic	________________	Plural
Procedure	________________	Innovation
Specialization	________________	Multiskilling
Simple	________________	Complex
Continuity	________________	Change
Gradual	________________	Radical

The enterprise triangle of Strategy-Structure-Systems (SSS) is shown in Fig. 1.1, which is used as the basis for developing the concept of a flexible enterprise.

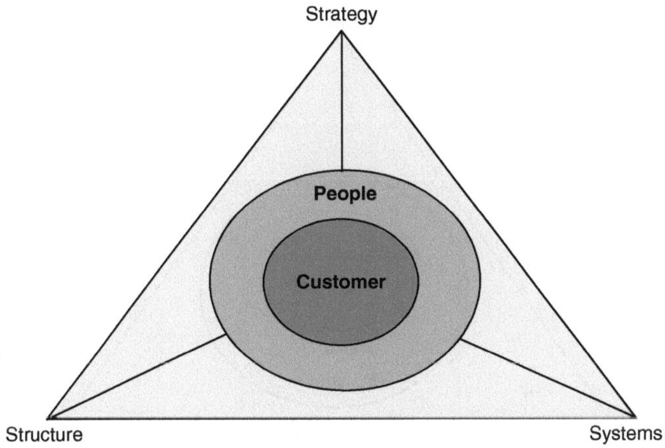

Fig. 1.1 The enterprise triangle

Let us take the example of enterprise flexibility in terms of the options created by **Maruti Suzuki** to withstand the competitive pressures so far, as given below:

- A large range of models aimed at both the domestic and the export markets.
- Product variants to suit the needs of customer groups.
- Product range covers a broad spectrum of market segments starting from economy to luxury segment.
- Continuous upgradation of products to offer "value for money" to the customers.
- Extensions of brand from "economy" to "economy with style."

The crucial make or buy decisions have been made by **Tata Motors** keeping in mind various aspects:

- Global shopping has brought off the shelf products without a premium for customization.
- Changes can be made by using Tata Motors in-house capabilities.
- It sourced design from Italy (IDEA) and engine from France (*Institut Francais de Petrol)* and integrated them using its engineering skills.
- The assembly line was imported from Nissan, Australia (second hand) and modified to suit local requirements.
- Target costing was employed to contain component costs.
- Innovative logistic management techniques (optimum container size to hub, daily delivery to factory) are being used.
- It acquired Jaguar to induct technology in that segment.

The situation-actor-process (SAP) model (Sushil 2001b, c) of the enterprise triangle is shown in Fig. 1.2. In this model, customer represents the situation, people act as actor, and SSS are the process dimensions. The options field in terms of actions to create enterprise flexibility on different dimensions is exhibited in Table 1.2.

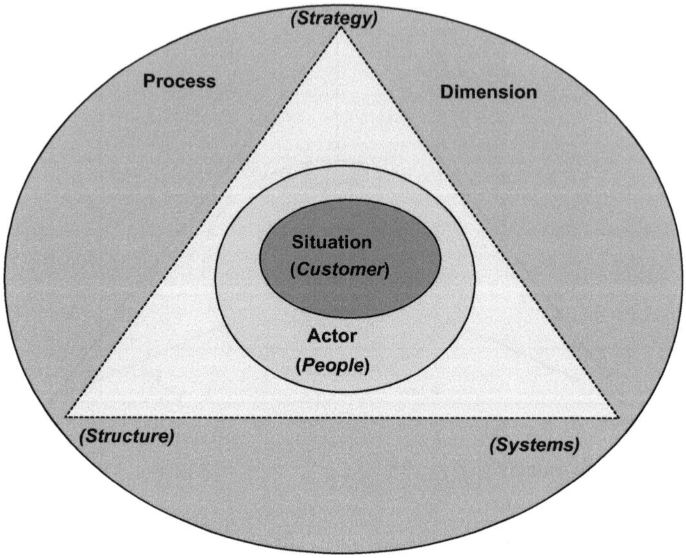

Fig. 1.2 SAP model of enterprise triangle

Table 1.2 Actions to create enterprise flexibility in different dimensions

Strategy	Structure	Systems	People
Shared vision	Fluid and flexible structure	Process-oriented systems	Learning environment
Entrepreneurial strategies	Flatter and networked organization	Knowledge-based learning systems	Multiskilling
Dynamic balancing of paired opposites	Informal organization	Customer-oriented systems	Empowerment
SAP–LAP (situation-actor-process–learning-action-performance) paradigm	Localness and collective organization	Self-organizing teams	Cultural diversity
Open environment	Open communication	Systems balancing paradoxes	Innovation culture
Paradoxical strategies	Enlightened organization	Systems thinking	Creative tension
Flowing stream strategy for managing continuity and change			Flexible work practices

The enterprise triangle is used as a base to identify various types of flexibilities in the enterprise. The strategy dimension relates with strategic flexibility, the people and structure dimensions connote the organizational flexibility, and the systems dimension relates with a variety of flexibilities in different systems such as financial flexibility, IS flexibility, marketing flexibility, and manufacturing flexibility as

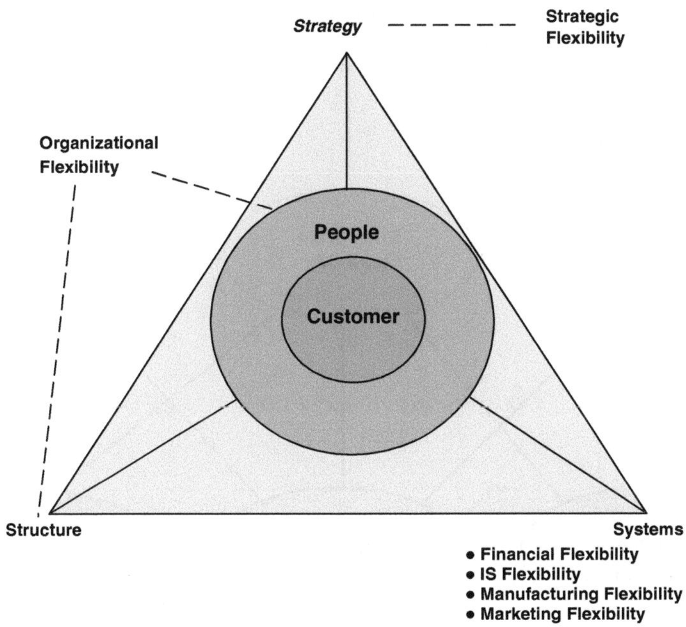

Fig. 1.3 Types of flexibility in enterprise triangle

shown in Fig. 1.3. The different types of flexibilities act as cornerstones of creating a flexible enterprise, as shown in Fig. 1.4 (Sushil 2000b). The hierarchy of various types of flexibilities is shown in Fig. 1.5. In the subsequent sections, definitions, purpose, and best practices of various types of flexibilities in an enterprise are summarized.

3.1 Strategic Flexibility

The *strategic flexibility* provides transformational capability in terms of perpetual renewal of the enterprise as well as dynamic balancing of the paradoxical strategic options. This provides openness, focus, change, and resilience in the strategy formulation and implementation like a flowing stream. The case-let of Hero Group of Industries in India is discussed below highlighting strategic flexibility exhibited on various fronts.

Hero Group

- Hero Group displayed strategic flexibility in making earnest attempt to give real-time fast response to changing environment (customers' needs and competitors' moves), and there was continuous interaction between environmental turbulence and strategy

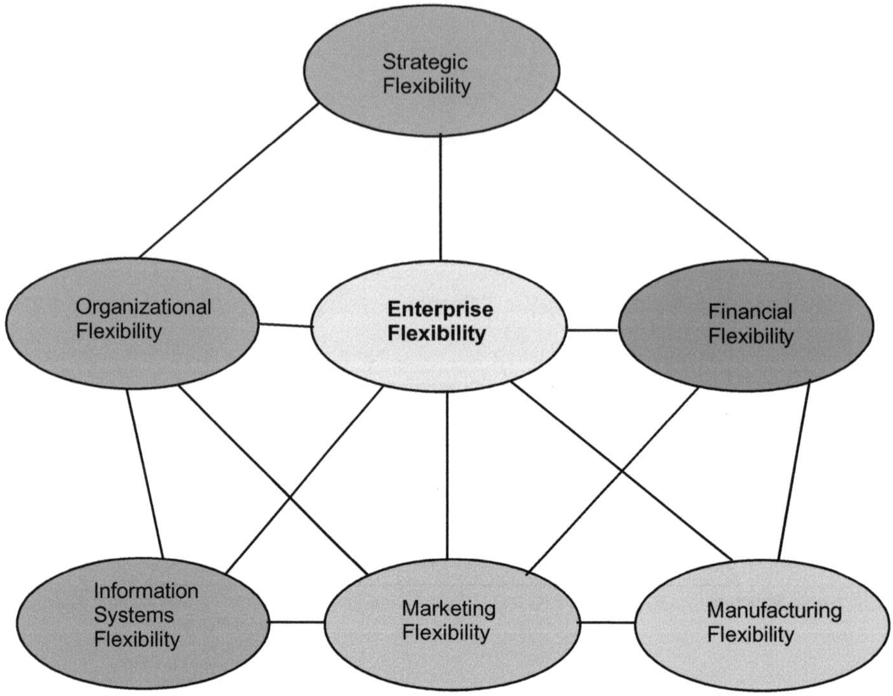

Fig. 1.4 Cornerstones of enterprise flexibility

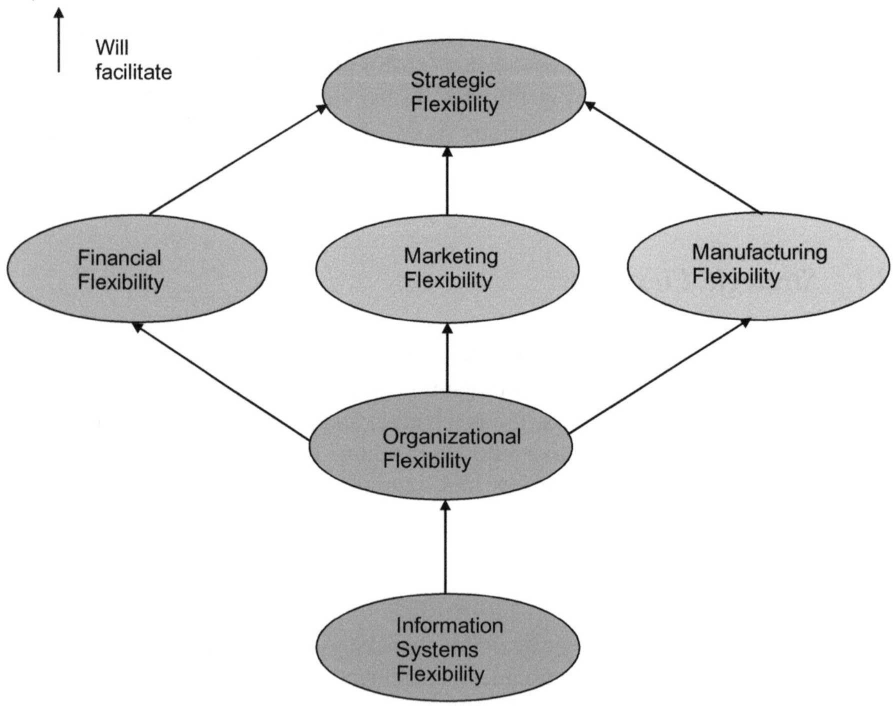

Fig. 1.5 Hierarchy of flexibilities in an enterprise

formulation and Hero's responsiveness to environmental change. It also required reframing of strategies at several stages, which are mentioned as under:

- Hero Group hived off the engine making unit of Hero Motors to another joint venture Hero Briggs and Stratton. This resulted in conversion of fixed costs to variable costs, which has reduced break-even point of Hero Motors, which would in turn give boost to bottom line. This strategy can be called organizational restructuring.
- It established exclusive dealerships in the south, the biggest moped market and one where Hero had negligible presence. This strategy aimed at increasing marketing efforts in new territory to follow the leader – TVS Suzuki.
- Hero planned to go beyond mere consolidation. Hero tied up with BMW to sell high-end bikes. It was a radical experiment. A company, which was operating in high volume, low value markets wanted to venture in a high value, low volume business. This is a clear evidence of adaptability and flexibility of Hero to move to diagonally opposite ends of product and market matrix.
- For starting new venture of scooters, the logic was that moped market was crowded with several players, but scooters market had an overwhelming presence of only two players – Bajaj and LML – along with TVS-Suzuki's Spectra. This strategy implies charting into new market with new product having some synergy with existing product lines – motorcycles and mopeds.
- It established Hero MotoCorp after the joint venture with Honda was over and developed collaboration with European partners for technology.

Purpose

To generate growth and renewal capabilities under an environment of complexity and chaos enabling management of strategic paradoxes, such as managing confluence of continuity and change.

Best Practices

- Incorporating emergence in the planning
- Entering into new market spaces
- Managing confluence of continuity and change (flowing stream strategy)
- Redefining the enterprise and the industry
- Reinventing strategy
- Creating strategic architecture
- Developing scenario planning
- Evolving the shared vision
- Entering into alliances and strategic networks
- Strategically changing the scope by mergers and acquisitions
- Corporate restructuring
- Developing new business models and implementing e-business architecture
- Building innovative products and services
- Redefining bases of customer value
- Quick launch of new products and services
- Providing new knowledge-based services

- Retaining existing customers and entering new markets
- Building existing core competencies and acquiring new competencies

3.2 *Organizational Flexibility*

The *organizational flexibility* is the change making capability of the organization (without sacrificing vital areas of continuity) in its structure, processes, people, and culture, so as to carry more than one option on the same continua at the same time and to dynamically interplay across the organizational options.

Purpose

To provide change preparedness, learning, and adaptation for organizational transformation.

Best Practices

- Creating ambidexterity in organization
- Creating empowerment and localness of decision-making
- Developing multiskilling across the organization
- Institutionalizing organizational learning
- Leading management of change
- Creating innovative culture
- Working through self-organizing cross-functional teams
- Organizational restructuring
- Reengineering business processes
- Becoming a total quality organization
- Downsizing and delayering the organization
- Designing a network and virtual organization
- Implementing dialogue projects and suggestion schemes
- Acquiring, sharing and storing the knowledge
- Integration and interconnectedness for creating a boundaryless organization
- Disaggregating and reaggregating the value chain
- Cross-cultural management
- Experimenting flexi-time, flexi-place, and telecommuting

3.3 *Financial Flexibility*

The *financial flexibility* can be defined as exercise of freedom of choice within the framework of Government monetary and fiscal policy, capital market regulations, investors' risk-return preferences, and corporate strategy to evolve the financial processes with versatility, adaptiveness, and transparency so as to have better resonance with the business environment.

Purpose

To generate more financial options and change across these options under turbulence so as to enhance financial performance and minimize risk.

Best Practices

- Defining a range for financial ratios
- Account for multiple future financial options and compute modified discounted cash flow incorporating alternative options
- Generating new instruments by integration of debt and equity
- Implementing flexible interest rates
- Flexible exchange rates
- Planning flexible budgets
- Following activity-based costing
- Venture capital financing to promote entrepreneurship
- Providing multiple dividend options
- Developing a flexible capital structure

3.4 Information Systems Flexibility

The *information system flexibility* is the capacity of the information systems to change or to adapt and adjust in response to new conditions, demands, or circumstances both within and outside the enterprise. It is composed of both systemic flexibility (flexible for organization requirements) and usage flexibility (flexible for usage) (Palanisamy and Sushil 2003; Palanisamy 2012).

Purpose

To make the information system more active, knowledge intensive, and intelligent to enable organizational change and generate competitive advantage.

Best Practices

- Designing flexible architecture
- Designing network-based IS
- Utilizing the power of Internet
- Using client server architecture
- Introducing e-business architecture
- Implementing integrated IS within and beyond the enterprise
- Enterprise resource planning
- Supply chain management
- Customer relationship management
- Providing an environment for end-user computing
- Distributed and parallel processing

- Experiencing virtual reality/video conferencing
- Implementing knowledge tone applications
- Providing higher connectivity, compatibility, and upgradability
- Building artificial intelligence in IS
- Implementing knowledge-based decision support and management support systems
- Involving users in planning, analysis, and design of IS
- Utilizing the convergence of technologies effectively
- Implementing mobile applications

3.5 *Manufacturing Flexibility*

The *manufacturing flexibility* is the ability of the manufacturing systems to change or adapt to both external and internal conditions with minimum time and efforts (Sharma and Sushil 2002).

Purpose

To be able to manufacture as per the changing customer requirements with agility and at a low cost so as to gain competitive advantage by reducing the cycle time.

Best Practices

- Implementing flexible manufacturing technology, such as CNC machines, flexible manufacturing systems, automated guided vehicles, and robotics
- Implementing manufacturing resource planning and enterprise resource planning systems
- Enhancing labor flexibility
- Integrating just in time manufacturing and TQM
- Carrying out R&D for manufacturing innovation
- Making job rotation and multiskilling a routine
- Designing flexible manufacturing cells and using group technology
- Integrating IT for computer integrated manufacturing
- Building artificial intelligence in manufacturing systems
- Effective supply chain management

3.6 *Marketing Flexibility*

The *marketing flexibility* is the capability to cater to changing customer needs, handling multiple market segments, and balancing global and local requirements to gain sustainable competitive advantage.

Purpose

To be able to market as per changing customer needs with sustainable competitive advantage over the competitors as well as creating new markets making the competitors irrelevant.

Best Practices

- Flexible pricing to suit the customer
- Direct marketing – minimizing the channels
- Flexible and innovative product designs
- Integrating products and services into solutions
- Creating an ecosystem of applications around the products
- Blue ocean strategy to create new market spaces
- e-Marketing
- Marketing through social networks
- Responsiveness to customer complaints
- Outsourcing customer interface processes
- Integrating R&D personnel with marketing teams

4 Case Studies

4.1 Marketing and Logistics Flexibility in Dell

Dell initiated a direct marketing system on Internet for its personal computers (PCs), which is well established. This model exhibited multiple types of flexibilities. The first and foremost is the *marketing flexibility* that provides the insight about changing customer needs through the options exercised by the customers on the website while ordering the PCs. It also provided *logistics flexibility* to customers to track the progress of the order, which is now followed in most of the e-commerce applications. Further, the model is implemented through a boundaryless organization of Dell, component suppliers, and FedEx as the courier company that reflects *organizational flexibility*. In order to meet the deadlines for supply, at times the components are received and assembled at the FedEx site and dispatched directly to the customers. In this process, the organizational boundaries of various partners get dissolved.

4.2 Manufacturing Flexibility in Honda

Honda introduced its model Civic-2001 worldwide. It wanted to introduce it simultaneously in the trio of the developed world, that is, the USA, Europe, and Japan. In order to shift from the existing model to the new model, the jigs and fixtures were to be subjected to retooling, which used to take a week's time for set up. In order to reduce this time for change over, *manufacturing flexibility* was created by introducing robots in place of jigs and fixtures. This changed the concept from retooling to retraining or reprogramming of robots that could be done overnight in place of a week. Thus, the manufacturing flexibility resulted in reduction of setup time for quick shifting of models from the same line and also manifested in huge cost savings for Honda.

4.3 Learning Issues for the Case Company ABC

A case study of a new IT company in Indian context (ABC) was done to analyze unusually high degree of flexibility provided in the enterprise. The name is changed for the sake of confidentiality. The learning issues for the case company are presented both in the form of critique and advantages of providing high degree of flexibility.

Critique

- In absence of clearly defined policies, there was a state of confusion among employees who are relatively new in the company. Since jobs were not clearly defined, each consultant is told to find/create his/her own position in the company, initially it created a lot of anxiety.
- Consultants coming from other environments usually find it difficult to adjust as it is difficult to believe such a system is possible. These consultants are used to basic handholding. They expect someone will be supervising their work, and when they do not find anyone above them, it becomes uneasy.
- People normally take this philosophy as a stunt. Since the organization is new, the management is facing a Herculean task in convincing the employees that it means what it says. Whereas, all those who want to join the organization have a looming suspicion in their mind that there must be some catch.
- Perceived loss of authority for aspiring consultants may be a barrier for entry for some good consultants. The no hierarchy philosophy of the organization creates an embarrassing situation for senior members of the industry where they cannot *order* anybody to do a job. In this system, they have to convince the other person that by doing that job, it is going to help all concerned.
- A slight over commitment can be very costly. As it has been proved, in such a scenario, the consultant's expectations grow exponentially. Since each one of them is empowered and sees a chance of growth. In such a scenario, if the consultants are not made aware of various constraints and barriers to growth, they might develop a distorted understanding of the situation and become frustrated.
- Investment in training and development of personnel is higher to begin with. The time that an individual takes to adjust into the environment is added to the learning curve of the individual. Till a consultant is comfortable in the environment, the output of that consultant is not optimum, and there is an apparent lack of initiative from within.

Advantages

- Long-term gains
  After initial period of confusion and state of indecision, when a consultant collects enough evidence that company means what it says, the commitment level of each consultant increases. As there is a scope for acquiring new skills, consultants enter into a long-term relationship with the organization.
- Positive contribution from all employees
  The thinking and attitude of workforce turn positive. Consultants take pain to ensure that organization's values and beliefs are not being exploited. Each consultant is ready to help another in many possible ways.
- Timely and correct feedback
  As the entire group observes, including management, consultant gets timely feedback about his/her performance and where should he/she focus.
- Equal distribution of workload
  As the system is open, project manager is only a functional responsibility and most of the work is divided by a combined opinion of the team, the work load is not only uniform but is also balanced on the basis of the skill level of individuals.
- A healthy environment for work
  A good and open working environment has been provided, where management supports all new ideas and encourages the spirit of innovation and entrepreneurship. Problems and shortcomings are identified by the group and sorted out without intervention of management. Management only observes and is perceived as a monitoring authority. The environment promotes a healthy competition among the employees which is reflected in performance and the quality of work produced.
- It is easy to implement a new policy as everybody feels the need of it. Since all decisions are taken involving each employee, it becomes easy for management to implement a new policy or procedure.

5 Creating a Flexible Enterprise

According to SSS model of the enterprise, a flexible enterprise can be created by regenerating the strategy, restructuring the organization, reengineering the systems, reawakening the people, and recreating the culture as shown in Fig. 1.6. The flexible business designs are created by changing value drivers, creating operational excellence, continuous innovation excellence, generating strategic options, and integrating operations and systems. The new business models would create a flexible enterprise in terms of enhanced "options" to both the customers and the enterprise operations, quicker "change mechanisms" to adapt and synthesize options, and more "freedom of choice" to all concerned.

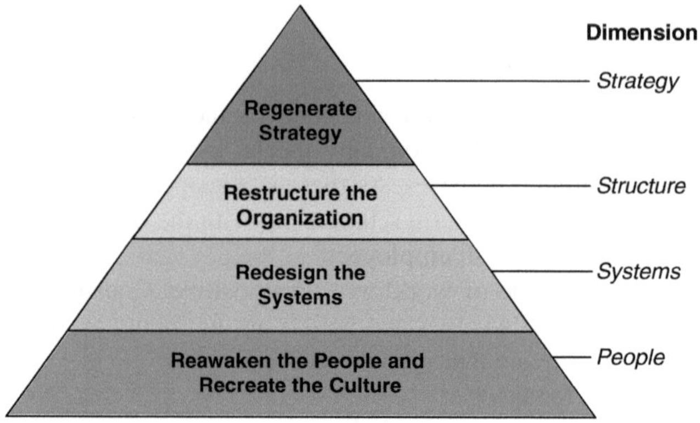

Fig. 1.6 Transforming the enterprise with flexibility

5.1 Flexible Business Designs

The flexible business design demands expansion of the economic model as building digital brands around customer experiences is expansive. It demands to go for a number of different sources of revenue and adopting several different economic models to succeed.

- **Priceline**, for example, combines the "retail" and "media" models and therefore enjoys economies that are vastly superior to those of other travel agencies, both on- and off-line. Applying the retail model, the company aggregates suppliers of travel services, such as airlines. Applying the media model, it "monetizes" its audience to third party advertisers by suggesting products and services to its customers.
- **Dell** also combines two models: the "made-to-order manufacturing" and "do-it-yourself" models. The company offers computer shoppers an unparalleled choice of features and permutations. In addition, its on-line menu and instructions guide consumers through a selection process that is speedier and less prone to error than one handled by live customer service representatives. For Dell, the superior process is also less costly (Kalakota and Robinson 2000).

5.2 Changing Value Drivers

In the new competitive business, the traditional definition of value is challenged. Though price remains an important factor in the new business models, certain new value drivers have gained prominence, namely, speed, convenience, personalization, and experience.

- Speed
- Convenience
- Personalization
- Experience
- Price
- Service excellence

Value Drivers

Cost → Speed and convenience

Ease of use → Self-service

- A significant example of service excellence is "**American Express**" which has moved to e-business design from the traditional design. The key trends in this case are shifting from a product focus to a customer focus and changing the rigid and functionally oriented systems to flexible and integrated service applications.

5.3 Operational Excellence

There is a shift taken place from a low-cost framework to provision of high-quality customized solutions with speed and at reasonable price. An excellent example here is the case of **Dell**, which has followed a "build-to-order" business design.

Low cost → Customized solutions

5.4 Continuous Innovation Excellence

Some enterprises have shifted the focus of innovation from functional efficiency to outsourcing or acquisition. **Cisco Systems** effectively depicts the new model of continuous innovation organized around networks and interdependencies of partners.

Functional efficiency → Outsourcing/Acquisition

5.5 *Strategic Options*

Flexibility is created in enterprises via a variety of new strategic initiatives so as to adapt and respond to global change and competition. In the flexible design, the customer comes first, and the competencies, both in-house and outsourced, are developed to meet the changing customer needs.

- The processes adopted in **Microsoft** are flexible for all kinds of product development, be it operating systems or browser development or even for that matter e-commerce applications. Microsoft adopts a flexible approach towards its new products and leaves place for future solutions to be plugged in. The Internet Explorer is one such product that elucidates this approach. To counter Sun Microsystems Java language and Java enabled browsers for display of colorful and active graphics, Microsoft had changed the rules of the competition by making browser engines that were plug-and-play. So, it was easy for Microsoft to handle this external challenge as the browsers could be made Java enabled with a simple add on module.

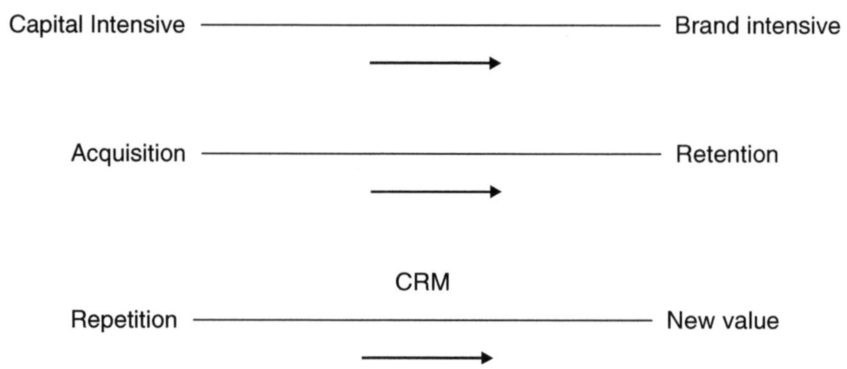

It manages both the continuity and change forces simultaneously and balances the enterprise as well as customer factors as per the flowing stream strategy crystal (Sushil 2005, 2012b)

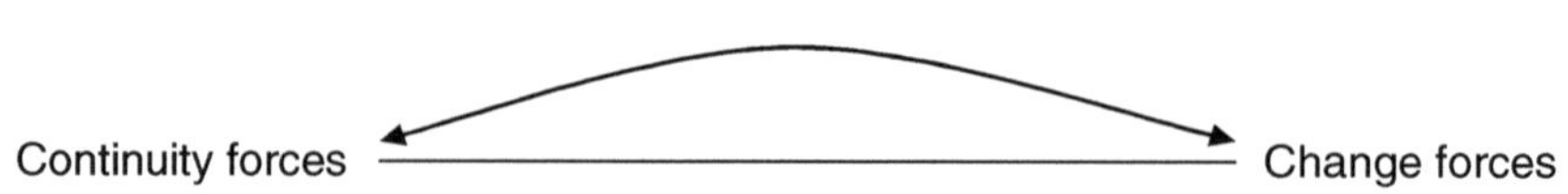

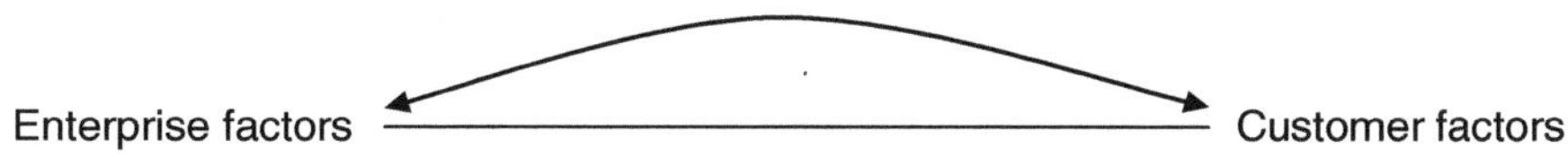

5.6 *Integrating Operations and Systems*

A significant duality in the working of enterprises is of customization vs. integration. The flexible e-business enterprise is bimodal and is able to generate value by both customization and integration.

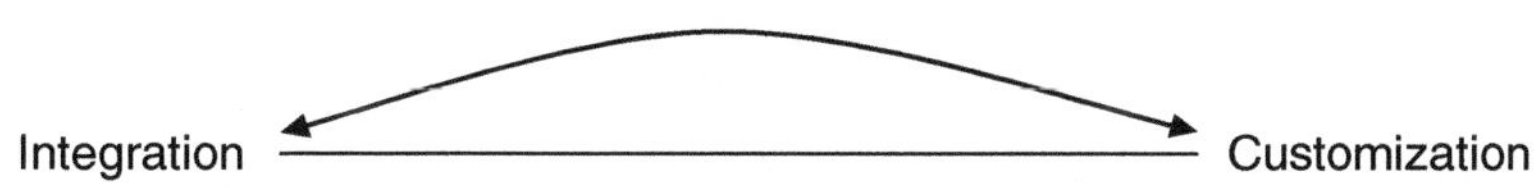

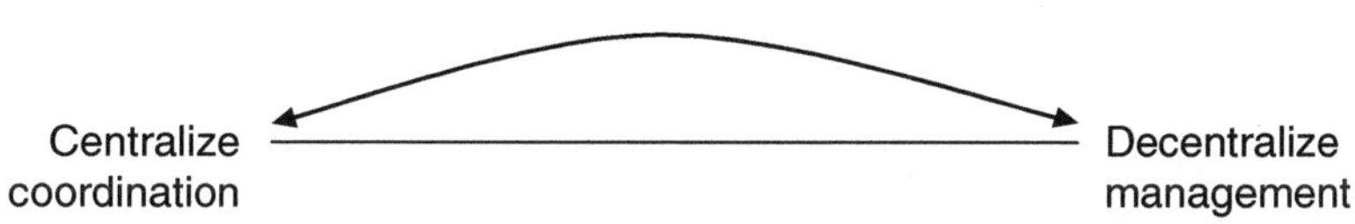

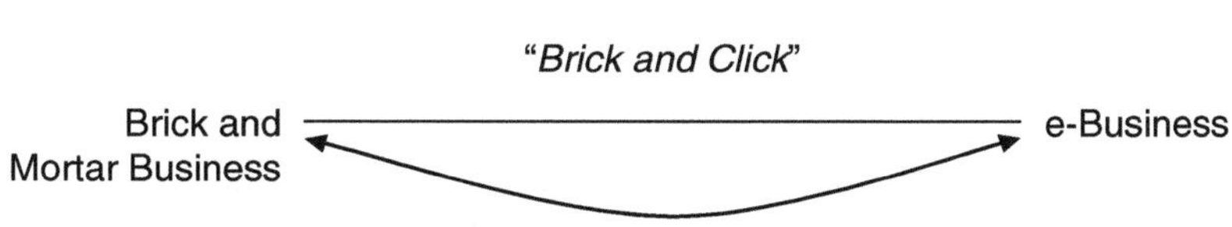

5.7 *Future Enterprise*

The future flexible enterprise would be a synthesis of the thesis and the antithesis on multiple planes taking the "both-and" approach rather than the "either-or" approach.

Reatual (Real as well as Virtual)

Enterprise

Real ———————————— Virtual

Glocal (Global as well as Local)

Strategy

Global ———————————— Local

Technople (Technology as well as People)

Transformation

Technology ———————————— People

5.8 SAP–LAP Model of Enterprise Transformation

The SAP model of enterprise flexibility consists of a situation that is transforming actors that exercise freedom of choice and processes that are adaptive in nature. The SAP–LAP model (Sushil 2000c, 2001c) of enterprise transformation in terms of critical questions is given below.

Situation

- What are the key *external drivers* of enterprise transformation?
- What are the key *internal drivers* of enterprise transformation?
- What are the *enablers/inhibitors* of enterprise transformation?

Actor

- What are the *worldviews* of the key actors about transformation?
- Have the relevant *cross-functional teams* been developed?
- Have the actors been facilitated and motivated for *collective learning* and *knowledge sharing?*

Process

- What are the *key business processes* that need to be transformed?
- How the business processes can be transformed using *new technology* to create a *new business model?*
- Which business processes can be *outsourced* to reinvent the enterprise?

Learning

- What are the *key drivers* of change demanding transformation of the enterprise?
- Are the actors *prepared* for accepting and working to support transformation?
- What is the *purpose* of enterprise transformation?

Action

- How to *imbibe new technology* in the business processes to transform them?
- How to change the *mindset* of actors?
- How to *reinvent* the strategies and *redesign* the systems?

Performance

- In what way transformation will affect the *customer value*?
- On what fronts *speed* will be affected?
- Which *enterprise factors* will be influenced by transformation?

6 Flexibility Maturity Model

As flexibility is emerging to be a major business excellence dimension, it is imperative that maturity models of enterprises should define flexibility of various types at different maturity levels. This will facilitate organizations to chart out their roadmap for creating or enhancing flexibility in order to become more competitive and to effectively manage risk of uncertainty in business environment.

A typical flexibility maturity model (Sushil 2012c) could have multiple maturity levels of flexibility in organizations. According to situation-actor-process (SAP) framework, it may treat situation as the driving force and cope with it by flexibility on the fronts of actors as well as processes. An organization may climb the maturity of flexibility from operational to strategic on one hand and organization centric to value network orientation on the other. Various possible maturity levels could range from lower to higher maturity in terms of flexibility in individual processes at operational level, flexibility in interaction of processes, flexibility in actors, strategic flexibility, and flexibility at operational as well as strategic levels in the whole value network as shown in Fig. 1.7.

At the lowest level of flexibility maturity, an organization is expected to create options and change mechanisms separately in various operational processes. This would facilitate generation of numerous types of flexibilities such as operations flexibility, manufacturing flexibility (Honda by way of using robots), marketing flexibility (Unilever), financial flexibility (ICICI), and human resources flexibility (GE). This becomes the start point of journey of flexibility maturity for any organization.

The next higher level would work towards interaction of flexibilities in various processes by creating flexibility at the interfaces. For example, how flexibility in marketing interfaces with flexibility in manufacturing, how technological flexibility is linked with financial flexibility, and how flexibility in human resource management processes would help in creating a flexible supply chain. Many such interactions among business processes would pave the way for a flexible enterprise. Interaction of two or more processes would open up multiple frontiers of enterprise flexibility.

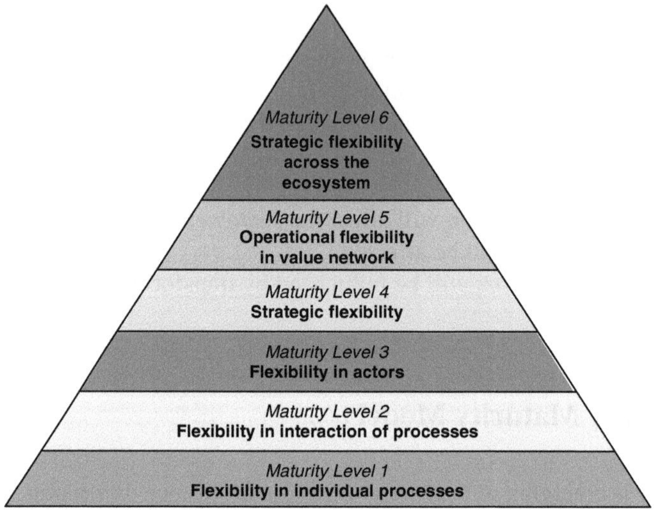

Fig. 1.7 A typical flexibility maturity model

At the next higher level of flexibility maturity, the issues related with actors or stakeholders would become pertinent. At this level, it is expected to link processes with actors (stakeholders) and thus intend to address sustainability and vitality of organizations. In order to effectively implement flexibility in processes and their interactions, flexibility capability is to be nurtured in various actors in terms of openness, questioning worldviews or mental models, responsive actions, learning orientation, flexible leadership, and many more actor-related dimensions.

The flexibility ladder takes the next step to strategic level. At this level, an organization would exhibit strategic flexibility to manage paradoxes; the most prominent one is that of "confluence of continuity and change" addressed by flowing stream strategy (Sushil 2012d). Some other strategic paradoxes could be globalization–localization, expansion–diversification, exploitation–exploration, and many more. This is the highest maturity level in the organizational context, beyond which flexibility in the value network is to be defined. This is reflected by many leading corporations such as Apple (exploring new technologies in convergence to existing ones), Microsoft (cannibalization), IBM (from products to solutions), and Nokia (creating options).

Further, the organization should transcend flexibility to operations in the whole value network. This would enable creating processes and systems to enhance flexibility of interactions with partners such as supply chain flexibility. If the organizational processes are flexible, but the processes in the rest of the value network are comparatively rigid, the whole response would be constrained. In order to effectively practice flexibility in business, operations in the entire value network should have flexibility alignment. This can be facilitated a great deal through developments in information and communication technologies. For example, direct marketing by

Dell through e-route has enhanced logistic, marketing, and organizational flexibilities of all partners in the network.

Finally, it should strive to inculcate strategic flexibility across the ecosystem of business encompassing all possible stakeholders (both near and far) in the star model. This would enhance performance not only of the firm but also of all stakeholders in the ecosystem such as society, environment, customers, government, media, and interfacing industries. This has been reflected by Apple, Nokia, Ford, and other technology-intensive organizations.

7 Conclusion

In order to deal with the dynamic and turbulent business situation, the enterprise is supposed to be flexible on the fronts of strategy, structure, systems, people, and culture. A flexible enterprise can be created by adopting the framework of flowing stream strategy for managing the continuity and change hand in hand. The continuity and change need to be synthesized at the level of strategy, structure, systems, people, and culture. The key channels for such integration are divert, shift, partition, and integrate (Sushil 2012a, d). The flexible enterprise has to evolve in its flexibility maturity over a period of time.

A flexibility maturity model can act as a guiding framework for organizations to enhance their performance, ability to manage risk, and meeting requirements of uncertain business in a more viable manner. Though the baseline flexibility maturity model presented above is hierarchical in nature, the next-generation models would cut across boundaries of levels and creating a web of feedback and learning interactions across these levels.

References

Kalakota R, Robinson M (2000) E-Business: roadmap for success. Addison-Wesley, Reading

Palanisamy R (2012) Building Information Systems Flexibility in SAP-LAP Framework: A Case Study Evidence from SME Sector. Glob J Flex Syst Manag 13(1):57–74

Palanisamy R, Sushil (2003) Achieving organizational flexibility and competitive advantage through information systems flexibility: a path analytic study. J Inf Knowl Manag 2(3):261–277

Sharma OP, Sushil (2002) Issues in managing manufacturing flexibility: a review. Glob J Flex Syst Manag 3(2&3):11–29

Sharma M, Sushil, Jain PK (2010) Revisiting flexibility in organizations: exploring its impact on performance. Glob J Flex Syst Manag 11(3):51–68

Sushil (1997) Flexible systems management – an evolving paradigm. Syst Res Behav Sci 14(4):259–275

Sushil (1999) Flexibility in management, Global Institute of Flexible Systems Management. Vikas Publishing House, New Delhi

Sushil (2000a) Systemic flexibility. Glob J Flex Syst Manag 1(1):77–80

Sushil (2000b) Cornerstones of enterprise flexibility: strategic, organizational, financial, information systems and manufacturing flexibilities, Global Institute of Flexible Systems Management. Vikas Publishing House, New Delhi
Sushil (2000c) SAP-LAP models of inquiry. Manag Decis 38(5):347–353
Sushil (2001a) Enterprise flexibility. Glob J Flex Syst Manag 2(4):53–58
Sushil (2001b) SAP – LAP framework. Glob J Flex Syst Manag 2(1):51–55
Sushil (2001c) SAP – LAP models. Glob J Flex Syst Manag 2(2):55–61
Sushil (2005) A flexible strategy framework for managing continuity and change. Int J Glob Bus Competitiveness 1(1):22–32
Sushil (2012a) Flowing stream strategy: leveraging strategic change with continuity, Springer, New Delhi
Sushil (2012b) Making flowing stream strategy work. Glob J Flex Syst Manag 13(1):25–40
Sushil (2012c) Flexibility maturity model: possibilities and directions. Glob J Flex Syst Manag 13(2):75–76
Sushil (2012d) Flowing stream strategy: managing confluence of continuity and change. J Enterp Transform 2(1):26–49
Volbreda H (1998) Building the flexible firm: how to remain competitive. Oxford University Press, Oxford

Chapter 2
Creating Enterprise Flexibility Through Service-Oriented Architecture

Ozgur Erol, Brian Sauser, and John T. Boardman

1 Introduction

Today enterprises must be capable to adapt to changing business requirements of fast-paced and competitive business environment. This requires a shift from a disintegrated and closed enterprise structure to a more dynamic and flexible enterprise structure. Integration – within the enterprise and across enterprises – facilitates this dynamic and flexible structure by combining processes, systems, and technologies and enables information and resource sharing. Integration facilitates successful operation of a single integrated enterprise, an extended enterprise, or a virtual enterprise. Alignment of processes, systems, and technologies is a critical step to realize enterprise flexibility (Strnadl 2006). This also requires an enterprise architecture which supports a dynamic and flexible enterprise structure. Enterprise architecture provides common view of the primary resources of any enterprise (people, processes, systems, and technology) and how they integrate to provide the primary drivers of the enterprise.

The concept of service-oriented architecture (SOA) is widely accepted software architecture approach which promises the design and implementation of flexible systems and facilitates the change of business processes quickly. SOA leverages the alignment of business and information technology. Although SOA has its roots in software architecture, from a broader perspective the concept has also been applied at the business level (Cherbakov et al. 2005; Bieberstein et al. 2006). In this chapter, we discuss our perspective on SOA as a style of enterprise architecture design and, ultimately, a way of structuring the enterprise.

O. Erol (✉) • J.T. Boardman
School of Systems and Enterprises, Stevens Institute of Technology,
Castle Point on Hudson, Hoboken, NJ 07030, USA
e-mail: oerol@stevens.edu; john.boardman@stevens.edu

B. Sauser
University of North Texas, Denton, USA
e-mail: bsauser@unt.edu

Sushil and E.A. Stohr (eds.), *The Flexible Enterprise*, Flexible Systems Management,
DOI 10.1007/978-81-322-1560-8_2, © Springer India 2014

Based on the available literature, we provide the benefits of SOA and its impact on creating enterprise flexibility. First section of this chapter provides an overview of the challenges of enterprises we encounter in today's business environment. In this section, we discuss the relative concepts of enterprise integration and architecture, emerging enterprise structures such as extended enterprises and virtual enterprises and the enterprise integration challenges. This section is followed by our view on enterprise flexibility and what flexibility means for enterprises. Next, we provide a literature review on service-oriented architecture. In this section, we also discuss the concept of service orientation and its application at enterprise level. In the next two sections of this chapter, we present our theoretical model based on the attributes of SOA and their impact on enterprise flexibility. We provide our definition of enterprise flexibility and how it relates to use of service-oriented architecture. This chapter concludes with a brief discussion on the relevance and potential implication of our model to the practice of SOA and enterprise flexibility.

2 Emerging Challenges of Enterprises

Enterprises are complex and highly integrated systems (Nightangale and Rhodes 2004; Boardman and Sauser 2008). Enterprises consist of people, processes, information, and supporting technologies, with interdependencies and interrelationships across their boundaries (Nightangale and Rhodes 2004; Swarz and Derosa 2006). The enterprises need to be managed not only for their internal operations, but more importantly for many relations to the different environments in which they are operating. Today, these environments are changing rapidly, and the need for relevant information becomes very important in the decision-making processes at all levels of enterprise management. Fluctuations in market demands, technology evolution, and changing regulations require flexible enterprise operations, capable of reacting to those changes. Enterprises need to acquire and share relevant and current information within their boundaries and across enterprises. The changing business requirements and the fast-paced and competitive business environment surrounding enterprises requires a shift from a disintegrated and closed enterprise structure to a more dynamic and flexible enterprise structure. Integration within the enterprise and across enterprises facilitates this dynamic and flexible structure by combining processes, systems, and technologies and enables information and resource sharing.

Adaptation to market changes in a timely fashion requires flexible organizations and the ability to establish partnerships. One of the major challenges for enterprises today is to be able to structure their processes to accommodate cooperation between partners providing the right core competencies at the right time in the form of extended or virtual enterprise structures.

Another major challenge for organizations is the need for integration of enterprise information systems. Today enterprises heavily depend on the information systems (IS) that are responsible for running almost all business processes (Cummins 2002). Originally, organizations focused on developing heterogeneous applications – as widely known as stovepipe applications to support their business processes (Cummins

2002; Lee et al. 2003; Gold-Bernstein and Ruh 2004). However, due to changing business environment, the business processes evolved, and new processes required new applications and data. As a result, organizations are reinforced to form a functional orientation within their information systems, resulting disparate "islands of applications" in which individual systems remained disconnected from other systems (Lam 2007). These heterogeneous applications have become obsolcte and have not served the needs of modern enterprise business solutions such as e-business, supply chain, and customer relationship management which require integration of information and processes within the different parts of the enterprise and across its business partners. The concept of integration of information systems and processes within the enterprise and across enterprises has become one of the critical challenges for modern enterprises.

Enterprise integration facilitates enterprise-wide connectivity of people, processes, applications, and technologies with the goal of improving efficiency, flexibility, and agility. It ensures that the right people and the right processes have the right information at the right time (Brosey et al. 2001). Enterprise integration enables the successful communication between data, applications, processes, people, and enterprises. It helps an organization to establish a technology infrastructure that seamlessly links its complex business applications into a homogenous system so that the processes and the data can be shared across the company (integrated single enterprise), with business partners and customers (extended enterprise) (Kosanke et al. 1999; Brosey et al. 2001; Smith et al. 2002; Venkatachalam 2006).

An enterprise architecture "is a set of descriptive representations (i.e. models) that are relevant for describing an Enterprise such that it can be produced to management's requirements and maintained over the period of its useful life" (Zachman 1987). An enterprise architecture provides a common view of the primary resources of any enterprise (people, processes, and technology) and how they integrate to provide the primary drivers of the enterprise.

Enterprise architecture is a coherent whole of principles, methods, and models that are used in the design and realization of the enterprise's organizational structure, business processes, information systems, and infrastructure (Ortiz et al. 2004). Enterprise architecture integrates different architectural domains such as product, process, technology architecture, application, and information architectures (Jonkers et al. 2006).

Enterprise architectures can be used as a tool for engineering. The enterprise architecture defines guides of the information required, and it complements enterprise methodologies. A methodology defines the steps that the different persons in a company must follow in order to generate that pieces of knowledge and fill the enterprise architecture (Ortiz et al. 2004). Enterprise architectures can also be used as a management tool. Following the engineering phase, a manager could visualize the relationships between any artifact hold at different levels within the enterprise architecture (relationship between processes, resources, information, strategy, and information systems).

Enterprise architecture provides some advantages (Brown 2007) including readily available documentation of the enterprise, ability to unify and integrate business processes across the enterprise, ability to unify and integrate data across the enterprise and to link with external partners, increase agility to business change, and maximized reuse of enterprise models.

3 Enterprise Flexibility

Flexibility provides competitive advantage to enterprises. Enterprise flexibility is defined as the ability of enterprise to adapt to changing requirements of its environment and its stakeholders with minimum time and effort (Sushil 2006). In order to achieve flexibility, enterprise-wide processes can easily be changed across the enterprise to satisfy the emerging requirements. The systems and the information technology infrastructure which support these processes should be easily changed.

In most cases, enterprises concentrate on making individual business processes more efficient. While having efficient processes is very important, enterprise flexibility requires a comprehensive view across the enterprise and its environment including its suppliers, partners, and customers. To create systems and support enterprise processes across the enterprise needs the ability to use and integrate existing systems and processes (Weske 2007). This will provide flexibility to allow the enterprise to easily adapt and bring together new systems to support new business requirements. Aside from the enterprise flexibility that comes from the ability to integrate people, processes, and information across the enterprise, the information technology infrastructure must also be made simpler and more manageable. This requires a well-defined enterprise architecture and overall architectural approach which support flexibility throughout the enterprise-wide processes and applications (Anaya 2005).

4 Service-Oriented Architecture

4.1 Concept of Service-Oriented Architecture

Service-oriented architecture (SOA) promises the design and implementation of flexible systems that facilitate the change of business processes quickly. A SOA-based approach also supports alignment of information technology (IT) and business processes.

SOA is a technology initiative which requires a software architecture approach where basic element of design and development is a service (Kumar et al. 2007). SOA simplifies the development of enterprise applications as modular, reusable business services that are easily integrated, changed, and maintained. SOA facilitates aligning existing information technology infrastructure and systems to achieve end-to-end enterprise integration by removing redundancies, generating collaboration tools, and streamlining IT processes. By adopting an SOA approach and implementing it using supporting technologies, companies can build flexible systems that implement changing business processes quickly and make extensive use of reusable components (IBM 2005). SOA supports an information environment built upon loosely coupled, reusable, standards-based services. It promotes data interoperability rather than application interoperability (Erl 2007).

In service-oriented architecture, main design element is "services." Applications communicate with each other in such architectures through services. Services are self-describing components, which can be recognized by client applications through look up from a registry. The client application and the service provider communicate via standard protocols and exchange information using standard data formats (Brahe 2007).

4.2 *Service Orientation at the Enterprise Level*

Previous section discussed service-oriented architecture from a technology viewpoint and defined it as application architecture. Even though SOA is a technology initiative for many organizations, from a broader perspective the concept of service orientation can also be applied at business level (Cherbakov et al. 2005; Bieberstein et al. 2006). From a business perspective, SOA can be used as a style of enterprise architecture design and, ultimately, a way of structuring the enterprise. It enables a service-oriented enterprise architecture by allowing the business define enterprise workflows around reusable business services.

Service orientation, in theory, is based on the concept of wrapping applications with well-defined interfaces, so that the applications can be turned to a set of "services." "Services" are network-enabled components with well-defined interfaces that are implementation independent (Yang and Lu 2005). The wrapping process creates an abstraction layer that hides all the complex details of the application, as a result the "services" can be integrated with any other application easily. The integration of the applications will not depend on the language, operating system, or database the application uses. Interfaces which describe the services are the most critical part of the service-orientated approach (Cousins and Casanova 2004). Service orientation promotes the creation of highly accessible, loosely coupled, reusable, business-oriented services which can be fully integrated using standards (Bieberstein et al. 2006). Increased interoperability, increased business and technology domain alignment, increased return on investment, and increased organizational agility are benefits of service orientation.

4.3 *Creating Enterprise Flexibility in Enterprises*

In the previous sections, we discussed the related concepts which provide a foundation for our model to create enterprise flexibility using service-oriented architectures.

Our model intends to explain the relationship between enterprise flexibility and the attributes of service-oriented architectures.

We define enterprise flexibility as the ability of enterprise to adapt to changing business and stakeholder requirements more efficiently, easily, and quickly. In this definition, we emphasize efficiency, agility, and adaptability. Efficiency is related to optimal use of resources. Agility is related to timely and faster response to rapidly changing business requirements. Adaptability is the ability of an enterprise to respond to the changing business requirements and to change its business processes. Adaptability is related to integration of new and existing systems and processes. Enterprise flexibility requires the integration of business processes and systems within the enterprise and across the partners of the enterprise. Alignment of business processes and information technology is also an enabling factor for enterprise flexibility which requires a simple and manageable enterprise architecture.

5 Theoretical Model

Our model suggests two key enablers for enterprise flexibility. First enabler is the capability of an enterprise to connect people, processes, and information in a way that allows enterprise to become more flexible and responsive to the dynamics of its environment, stakeholders, and competitors. This requires integration within the enterprise and across the partners, suppliers, and customers of the enterprise.

Second enabler is alignment of information technology and business goals. This requires simplification of the underlying technology infrastructure and creation of a consolidated view of, and access to, all available resources in the enterprise. This can be achieved with well-defined enterprise architecture. Enterprise architecture provides a common view of relationship between processes, resources, information, strategy, and information systems. It provides ability to integrate business processes and data across the enterprise and with external partners and ability to respond to changing business requirements rapidly.

Table 2.1 summarizes our model which we explain the relationship between the attributes of service-oriented architecture (SOA) and enterprise flexibility. In this table, we list the attributes of SOA, business outcome of each attributes, and each attribute's impact on agility, efficiency, and adaptability. Our model suggests that enterprise flexibility can be obtained as a result of agility, efficiency, and adaptability as shown in the table.

6 Conclusion

In this chapter, we introduced our theoretical model based on concepts of enterprise flexibility and service-oriented architectures. Service orientation, at application architecture level, has already been discussed in various literatures to be beneficial

Table 2.1 SOA and creating enterprise flexibility

		Enterprise flexibility = f(agility, efficiency, adaptability)		
Attributes of service-oriented architecture (SOA)	Business outcome	Agility	Efficiency	Adaptability
SOA enables the development of applications as reusable and modular business services	Applications which are developed as reusable and modular services make them easy to be integrated, changed, and maintained	Agility is obtained as a result of timely response to the changing business requirements	Reusable services provide cost savings	Applications which are developed reusable and modular services can easily be changed to support emerging business needs and requirements
SOA as an application architecture promotes loose coupling. Loose coupling is an attribute of systems, referring to an approach of designing interfaces to reduce the interdependencies across modules or components	This approach minimizes the interdependencies between applications. Adding new applications or modules or replacing modules and changing operations within individual business processes do not impact the other applications or modules	The risk of unanticipated changes due to a change in another business application will be minimized. This will enable faster modifications to business application resulting in agility	Due to minimized risk and time of change, efficiency will obtained	Enterprise will respond to changing business requirement maximizing its adaptability. Adaptability, efficiency, and agility will result in higher enterprise flexibility
SOA enables reusability of existing applications	Rather than developing applications from scratch, companies can utilize existing functionality and create new solutions by assembling component applications from existing and new technology	This attribute enables rapid deployment of new solutions	Use of existing functionality provides cost savings	Enterprise can respond to changing business needs, resulting in higher enterprise flexibility

(continued)

Table 2.1 (continued)

		Enterprise flexibility = f(agility, efficiency, adaptability)		
Attributes of service-oriented architecture (SOA)	Business outcome	Agility	Efficiency	Adaptability
SOA promotes development and use of standards-based services. Standard-based services leverage the integration of new and existing applications and enterprise integration	Use of standards provides interoperability between applications and systems, regardless of their technology or location. As a result, lower cost and shorter time to market will be obtained	Shorter development and integration of applications will increase the agility	Lower cost of application development and deployment due to support of universal standards will increase the efficiency	Shorter time to market, shorter integration times will enable the faster response to emerging business requirements. Obtained agility and efficiency will result in higher enterprise flexibility
SOA requires use of self-contained services. Having self-contained services means the state of each service does not depend upon the state of another service	SOA speeds time through parallel development. Since each service is self-contained and does not depend upon the state of another service, subsystems can be developed independently	This provides faster development or modification of subsystems. Agility increases	Through the use of resources optimally, efficiency is increased	Faster and efficient response to new business requirements increases the adaptability of the enterprise, resulting in higher enterprise flexibility
SOA requires the use of wrapping applications with well-defined interfaces. This process turns applications that can be turned into a set of services. The wrapping process creates an abstraction layer that hides all the complex details of the applications	As a result, the services can be integrated with any other application easily. The integration of the applications will not depend on the language, operating system, or database the application uses	Easy integration of applications enables faster response to business changes. New applications can be implemented and integrated rapidly into existing systems without interoperability problems	This will help to economic use of existing and legacy systems. The economic life of legacy systems will be longer which will provide cost savings	Ease of integration with new and existing systems will increase the ability of enterprises to respond to new business requirements efficiently and rapidly. Higher enterprise flexibility will be obtained

in obtaining agility, efficiency, and flexibility. We will further investigate the use of service orientation as a style of enterprise architecture design and, ultimately, a way of structuring the enterprise. Our next step will be to develop an enterprise architecture framework. This framework will apply the concept of service orientation at the enterprise level and can be used to increase an enterprise's ability to respond and adapt to emerging business requirements and challenges.

References

Anaya VOA (2005) How enterprise architectures can support integration. IHIS'05, ACM, New York

Bieberstein N, Bose S, Fiammante M, Jones K, Shah R (2006) Service Oriented Architecture (SOA) compass – business value, planning, and enterprise roadmap, Pearson. IBM Press, Lebanon

Boardman J, Sauser B (2008) Systems thinking: coping with 21st century problems. CRC Press/ Taylor & Francis, Boca Raton

Brahe S (2007) BPM on top of SOA: experiences from the Financial Industry. In: Business process management. Springer, Berlin/Heidelberg

Brosey WD, Neal ER, Marks DF (2001) Grand challenges of enterprise integration. IEEE, Antebes-Juan Ies Pins

Brown A (2007) The value of enterprise architecture, Zachman Institute for Framework Advancement (ZIFA) www.zifa.com

Cherbakov L, Galambos G, Harishankar R, Kalyana S, Rackham G (2005) Impact of service orientation at the business level. IBM Syst J 44:653–678

Cousins P, Casanova I (2004) Service-oriented integration: a strategy brief. IONA Technologies, USA

Cummins FA (2002) Enterprise integration: an architecture for enterprise application and systems integration. Wiley, New York

Erl T (2007) SOA principles of service design. Prentice Hall, Upper Saddle River

Gold-Bernstein B, Ruh W (2004) Enterprise integration: the essential guide to integration solutions. Addison-Wesley, Boston

IBM (2005) The solution designer's guide to IBM on demand business solutions. IBM Redbooks, IBM, New York

Jonkers HLM, Ter Doest H, Arbab F, Bosma F, Wieringa RJ (2006) Enterprise architecture: management tool and blueprint for the organization. Inf Syst Front 8:63–66

Kosanke K, Vernadat F, Zelm M (1999) Cimosa: enterprise engineering and integration. Comput Ind 40:83–97

Kumar S, Dakshinamoorthy V, Krishnan MS (2007) Does SOA improve the supply chain? An empirical analysis of the impact of SOA adoption on electronic supply chain performance. 40th Hawaii international conference on system sciences, Waikoloa

Lam W (2007) Information systems integration and enterprise application integration adoption: a case from financial services. J Inf Syst Educ 18:149–158

Lee J, Siau K, Hong S (2003) Enterprise integration with ERP and EAI. Commun ACM 46:54–60

Nightangale DJ, Rhodes DH (2004) Enterprise systems architecting: emerging art and science within engineering systems, MIT engineering systems symposium, Tang Center – Wong Auditorium, MIT Press, Cambridge, MA

Ortiz A, Anaya V, Franco D (2004) Deriving enterprise engineering and integration frameworks from supply chain management practices. International Conference on Enterprise Integration and Modelling Technology (ICEIMT'04), Toronto, Canada

Smith D, O'brien L, Kontogiannis K, Barbacci M (2002) Enterprise integration. Architect (SEI Interactive News) 4Q 5(4):1–12
Strnadl CF (2006) Aligning Business and IT: the Process-Driven Architecture Model. Inf Syst Manag 23:67–77
Sushil (2006) Enterprise flexibility. Glob J Flex Syst Manag 2:53–58
Swarz RS, Derosa JK (2006) A framework for enterprise systems engineering processes, 19th international conference on software & systems engineering and their applications, ICSSEA 2006, Paris
Venkatachalam AR (2006) A holistic perspective on enterprise integration. J Inf Technol Case Appl Res 8:1–6
Weske M (2007) Business process management: concepts, languages, architectures. Springer, Berlin
Yang HM, Lu FV (2005) Integrating inter- and extra-enterprise applications using web services. Rev Bus 26:3–9
Zachman J (1987) A framework for information systems architecture. IBM Syst J 26:276–292

Chapter 3
Defining Strategic Flexibility

Norman Roberts and Gary J. Stockport

1 Introduction

The topic of this chapter is strategic flexibility. Strategic flexibility has been considered by previous research in strategic management, economics, organization theory, and marketing. Consequently, there is a diverse range of definitions about this term (Genus 1995). This chapter examines the historical development of the term from the 1970s to recently. It synthesizes the literature review and concludes with its own definition.

2 Strategic Flexibility: Conceptually

Strategic flexibility is probably closest to the common understanding of flexibility – the ability to do something other than originally intended.

The conceptualization of strategic flexibility has been described and studied by numerous authors. The notion of strategic flexibility that is probably the closest to an everyday understanding of flexibility is the ability to do something other than that which had been originally intended (Evans 1991).

Conceptually, strategic flexibility suggests the ability to take some action in response to external environmental changes (Evans 1991; Buckley 1997) and thus can be viewed as a strategic capability (Bahrami 1992). Strategic flexibility is the ability to precipitate intentional changes and adapt to environmental changes through the continuous rethinking of current strategies, asset deployment, and investment strategies (Evans 1991; Bahrami 1992; Sanchez 1995). Consequently, strategic flexibility can be conceptualized in two ways: firstly, with regard to the

N. Roberts (✉) • G.J. Stockport
Business School, The University of Western Australia,
35 Stirling Highway, Crawley, WA 6009, Australia
e-mail: robern04@student.uwa.edu.au; gary.stockport@uwa.edu.au

Sushil and E.A. Stohr (eds.), *The Flexible Enterprise*, Flexible Systems Management,
DOI 10.1007/978-81-322-1560-8_3, © Springer India 2014

variation and diversity of strategies and, secondly, to the degree at which companies can rapidly shift from one strategy to another (Slack 1983; Nadkarni and Narayanan 2004).

Hitt conceptualizes strategic flexibility "...as the capability of the company to proact or respond quickly to changing competitive conditions and thereby develop and/or maintain competitive advantage" (Hitt et al. 1998, p. 26). Aaker and Mascarenhas (1984) focus on substantial environmental uncertainty creating the need for strategic adaptation.

Sanchez (1995) suggests that the company's strategic flexibility is jointly depending on the inherent flexibility of the resources available to the company (resource flexibility) and on the company's flexibility in applying those resources to alternative courses of action (coordination flexibility). Evans (1991) suggests strategic flexibility is a function of the event that impacted on the company, by necessity instead of choice, being used to denote the company's deliberate or emerging capabilities to maneuver offensively or defensively.

Other terms that offer a similar conceptualization include the terms "strategic maneuverability" (Klingen 1975), "organizational flexibility" (Volberda 1996), and "dynamic capabilities" (Teece et al. 1997). Aaker and Mascarenhas (1984) argued "organizational flexibility" was a strategic option that could be exercised by an organization and define "organizational flexibility" as "...the ability of the organization to adapt to substantial, uncertain, and fast occurring environmental changes that have a meaningful impact on the organization's performance" (Aaker and Mascarenhas 1984, p. 74). The more recent studies about strategic flexibility in strategic management research mostly applied the concept within the context of product competition (Sanchez 1995, Schilling and Steensma 2001; Worren et al. 2002; Raynor and Leroux 2004).

3 Strategic Flexibility (1970s)

Some early research about strategic flexibility includes Gotcher (1977) who suggested that long range planning required flexibility. Eppink (1978) related the term "adaptiveness" as the ability of the organization to respond to unforeseen change. He added "...Flexibility can be seen as a characteristic of an organization that makes it less vulnerable to unforeseen external changes or puts it in a better position to respond successfully to such a change" (Eppink 1978, p. 42). Eppink (1978) argued strategic flexibility was necessary to compensate for strategic changes in the "indirect" environment of the company that reached it via the components of its "direct" environment. He suggested such changes required a high degree of unfamiliarity and could therefore be very dynamic and urgent.

In 1975, Klingen described "strategic maneuverability" as "...the extent to which strategic behaviour may be realized" (Klingen 1975, p. 11). "Strategic maneuverability" was seen to be determined by a company's freedom of movement, its environment, and the quality of strategic control within the company. Based on this view, a company's freedom of movement could vary from sector to sector.

4 Strategic Flexibility (1980s)

Despite the more specific definitions of strategic flexibility outlined earlier, the term has been widely used in the General Management literature. In 1980, Porter's seminal work "Competitive Strategy" was published, and he took a more deterministic view of strategy that still "dominates" the strategic management literature today. Porter (1980) refers to "strategic choice" where the company has a finite selection of strategies to choose from, based upon study of its external environment. Porter (1980) also strongly supports a "single best option" approach to strategy. This was based upon the need to make strategic choices between options having varying degrees of strategic and financial risk (Porter 1985).

Harrigan (1986) extends Porter's argument to consider how a company may not be able to take advantage of all of the strategies that it is able to identify. This view does not change any of the fundamental assumptions Porter made about the nature of competition and the way in which companies interact with their environment to gain a sustainable competitive advantage. Sustained competitive advantage exists when competitors are unable to duplicate the benefits of the strategy (Barney 1991; Barney 2001).

Strategic flexibility relates to both the internal and external environment of a company. Suggesting a broader view than earlier work such as Klingen (1975), Anderson (1985) argues that strategic flexibility is about a company's ability to restructure itself internally as well as its relationship with the external environment including competition originating from almost anywhere, even from outside a company's industry.

5 The 1990s Onward

As mentioned earlier, definitions often suggest that strategic flexibility means the ability to take some action in response to environmental changes (Evans 1991; Buckley 1997). Sanchez (1995) identified "resource flexibility" and "coordination flexibility" as capabilities contributing to strategic flexibility. Strategic flexibility also came to be viewed as a capability. As a capability, strategic flexibility is influenced by internal and external conditions of the company.

5.1 Strategic Flexibility: Externally

The environment can include external factors such as regulatory, economic, political, and social changes affecting the company's primary and secondary task environments (Achrol and Kotler 1999). A more deterministic strategy approach indicated that changes in the company's environment resulted in the reassessment of strategy among a given array of strategic alternatives (Porter 1980, 1985; Harrigan 1986; Parnell 1994, 2003). Thus, strategic choice was based on how a company evaluated its position in the environment. Porter's identification of low cost, differentiation, and focus as to generic strategies for achieving sustainable competitive advantage (Porter 1980, 1985) is the basis of many strategy studies.

5.2 *Strategic Flexibility: Internally*

Burnes (1992) identified three types of strategy according to the level of strategic decision making. Firstly, Corporate Level Strategy was described as being concerned with the direction, composition and coordination of the various business units within a large and diversified organization. Then, Business Level Strategy related to the operation and direction of individual business units within a group of companies. Finally, Functional Level Strategy related to individual business functions.

Strategic flexibility internally within an organization usually has three levels of strategy analysis: high level, organizational direction; medium level, organizational structure; and low level, organizational operations.

This internally driven strategic flexibility split into three levels is similar to Krinjnen's (1979) division of the strategic decision-making process into the strategic level (strategic policy, economic, social goals, and product market mix), the organizational level (organizational structure, decision making, and communication processes), and, finally, the operational level (production volumes). Sanchez (1995) argued that two critical components of strategic flexibility were "resource flexibility" and "coordination flexibility," which are both controlled from a company's internal environment. This conceptualization of strategic flexibility implies an inward focus on the company's internal environment, and different strategic options are possible depending on the nature of the change and the internal company influence.

The resource-based view focuses on those assets and capabilities that provide competitive advantage. Earlier contributions on strategic flexibility suggested that strategic flexibility depended jointly on what has been termed resource flexibility and the company's flexibilities in applying those resources to alternative courses of action (Sanchez 1995; Pauwels and Matthyssens 2004). The resource-based view of sustainable competitive advantage recognized the importance of the difference between companies based upon their resource endowments.

Within the competence-based view of the company, strategic flexibility characterizes the ability to respond advantageously to a changing environment. The competence-based view of the company came to the forefront of strategic management literature with Prahalad and Hamel's "Core Competence" (Prahalad 1990). Core competences were identified as "...the collective learning in the organization, especially how to coordinate diverse production skills and integrate multiple streams of technologies". This differs from the resource-based view, which focuses on those assets and capabilities that produce a sustainable competitive advantage (strategic assets).

There have been variations in both the application and meaning of strategic flexibility.

6 Defining Strategic Flexibility

The various definitions of strategic flexibility have tended to reflect the different perspectives taken by strategic management researchers. Consequently, there are differences in both the meaning and application of the term. Nevertheless, strategic flexibility provides a means by which companies can become more successful, and this suggests that companies select, develop, and modify strategic choices in order to cope with a continually changing environment. Thus, strategic flexibility can be described as the strategic choices available to a company and the company's ability to take advantage of those choices.

From the previous discussion, it is clear that the term strategic flexibility has no commonly agreed definition. That is why, as mentioned earlier, the various definitions of strategic flexibility by different researchers relate to a number of different perspectives (See Table 3.1).

Based upon the above, it is clear that any definition of strategic flexibility must combine both the external and internal perspectives. Therefore, for the purpose of this chapter, strategic flexibility is about:

- The ability to manage strategic risk
- The ability to respond to environmental change, i.e., both opportunities and threats
- The ability of a company to use its resources in both a proactive and a reactive way

Combining the above, this chapter defines strategic flexibility as "…a company's ability to manage strategic risk through its ability to respond to both opportunities and threats in its environment through using its resources in both a pro-active and a reactive way."

7 Conclusion

This chapter has presented a review of the literature about the term strategic flexibility. It has considered research which has conceptualized the term, and the chapter has also presented a historical discussion. Broadly, there have been two distinct approaches or perspectives to define strategic flexibility: external and internal. The definition presented in this chapter has attempted to "unify" these two approaches in order to provide a common platform for strategic management researchers as well as for researchers from other academic disciplines such as economics, organization theory, and marketing. Consequently, it is suggested that this chapter adds to our general understanding of strategic flexibility.

Table 3.1 Strategic flexibility definitions

Author and year	Definitions
Ansoff (1965)	"Flexibility can be measured by two proxy-objectives: external flexibility achieved through a diversified pattern of product-market investments, and internal flexibility through liquidity of resources" (p. 65); "not putting all of one's eggs in a single basket" (p. 65)
Eppink (1978)	"Flexibility makes an organization less vulnerable to or better able to respond successfully to, unforeseen environmental changes" (p. 10). "Flexibility can be seen as a characteristic of an organization that makes it less vulnerable to unforeseen external changes or puts it in a better position to respond successfully to such a change" (p. 42)
Aaker and Mascarenhas (1984)	"The ability of the organization to adapt to substantial, uncertain and fast-occurring (relative to required reaction time) environmental changes that have meaningful impact on the organization's performance" (p. 74)
Harrigan (1985)	"The ability of firms to reposition themselves in a market, change their game plans, or dismantle their current strategies when the customers they serve are no longer as attractive as they once were" (p. 1)
Kogut (1985)	"Flexibility is gained by decreasing the firm's dependence on assets already in place" (p. 27)
Galbraith(1990)	"The ability to shift or replicate core-manufacturing technologies quickly and effectively between different facilities, both domestically and internationally" (p. 56)
Evans (1991)	"Capability to modify strategies" (p. 77)
Bahrami (1992)	"The ability to precipitate intentional changes, to continuously respond to unanticipated changes, and the ability to adjust to unexpected consequences of predictable changes" (p. 36)
Hayes and Pisano (1994)	"The capability to switch gears-from, for example, rapid product development to low cost-relatively quickly and with minimal resources" (p. 78)
Das and Elango (1995)	"The ability of an organization to respond to changes in the environment in a timely and appropriate manner with due regard to competitive forces in the marketplace" (p. 62)
Upton (1995)	"Whether one is referring to products, production volumes or manufacturing processes, flexibility is about increasing range, increasing mobility, or achieving uniform performance across a specific range" (p. 76)
Lau (1996)	"Strategic flexibility refers to a firm's ability to respond to uncertainties by adjusting its objectives with the support of its superior knowledge and capabilities" (p. 11)

Lei et al. (1996)	"Strategic flexibility suggests that firms will need to become more adept at responding to competitor moves while engaging in opportunistic searches for under-served or unlocated market segments and niches" (p. 512)
Sanchez and Heene (1997)	"The condition of having strategic options that are created through the combined effects of an organizations co-ordination flexibility in acquiring and using flexible resources" (p. 71)
Buckley and Casson (1998)	"Ability to reallocate resources quickly and smoothly in response to change" (p. 23)
Hitt et al. (1998)	"The capability of the firm to proact or respond quickly to changing competitive conditions and thereby develop and/or maintain competitive advantage" (p. 27)
Matusik and Hill (1998)	"A firm's ability to respond quickly to changing market conditions" (p. 682)
Volberda (1996)	"Flexibility is the degree to which an organization has a variety of managerial capabilities and the speed at which they can be activated, to increase the control capacity of management and improve the controllability of the organization" (p. 361)
Volberda (1998)	"A firm has to develop flexible capabilities for speed and surprise. These capabilities derive from broad knowledge bases, generalisable resources, and core competencies that can be applied in various ways" (p. 89)
Volberda and Rutges (1999)	"Strategic flexibility or non-routine steering capacity consists of managerial capabilities related to the goals of the organization or the environment" (p. 103)
Young-Ybarra and Wiersema(1999)	"The flexibility to modify the alliance and the flexibility to exit the alliance relationship when the alliance is performing poorly" (p. 440)
Grewal and Tansuhaj (2001)	"Strategic flexibility represents the organizational ability to manage economic and political risks by promptly responding in a proactive or reactive manner to market threats and opportunities" (p. 72)
Johnson et al. (2003)	"The firm's intent and capabilities to generate firm-specific real options for the configuration and reconfiguration of appreciably superior customer value propositions" (p. 77)
Shimizu and Hitt (2004)	"Strategic flexibility can be defined as an Hitt organization's capability to identify major changes in the external environment (e.g., introduction of disruptive technologies), to quickly commit resources to new courses of action in response to change, and to recognize and act promptly when it is time to halt or reverse such resource commitments" (p. 45)
Combe and Greenley (2004)	"Is used to denote the ability of the firms to respond and successively adapt to environmental change" (p. 1458). "The extent to which new and alternative options in strategic decision making are generated and considered" (p. 1458)

References

Aaker DA, Mascarenhas B (1984) The need for strategic flexibility. J Bus Strategy 5(2):74–83
Achrol RS, Kotler P (1999) Marketing in the network economy. J Market 63:146–164
Anderson G (1985) Planning for restructured competition. Long Range Plann 18(1):21–29
Ansoff I (1965) Corporate strategy. McGraw-Hill, New York
Bahrami H (1992) The emerging flexible organization: perspectives from Silicon Valley. Calif Manage Rev 34(4):33–52
Barney JB (1991) Firm resources and sustained competitive advantage. J Manage 17(1):99–120
Barney JB (2001) Resource-based theories of competitive advantage: a ten year retrospective on the resource-based view. J Manage 27(6):643–650
Buckley A (1997) Valuing tactical and strategic flexibility. J Gen Manage 22(3):74–79
Buckley PJ, Casson MC (1998) Models of the multinational enterprise. J Int Bus Stud 29(1):21–44
Burnes B (1992) Managing change: a strategic approach to organizational development and renewal. Pitman Publishing, London
Combe IA, Greenley GE (2004) Capabilities for strategic flexibility: a cognitive content framework. Eur J Mark 38(11/12):1456–1480
Das TK, Elango B (1995) Managing strategic flexibility: key to effective performance. J Gen Manage 20(3):60–75
Eppink DJ (1978) Planning for strategic flexibility. Long Range Plann 11(4):9–15
Evans JS (1991) Strategic flexibility for high technology manoeuvres: a conceptual framework. J Manage Stud 28(1):69–89
Galbraith CS (1990) Transferring core manufacturing technologies in high-technology firms. Calif Manage Rev 32(4):56
Genus A (1995) Walls and bridges: towards a multi-disciplinary approach to the concept of flexibility. Technol Anal Strateg Manage 7(3):287–306
Gotcher JW (1977) Strategic planning in European multinationals. Long Range Plann, London 10(5):7–13
Grewal R, Tansuhaj P (2001) Building organizational capabilities for managing economic crisis: the role of market orientation and strategic flexibility. J Mark 65(April):67–80
Harrigan KR (1985) Strategic flexibility: the economics of strategic planning. Lexington Books, Lexington
Harrigan KR (1986) Matching vertical integration strategies to competitive conditions. Strateg Manage J 7:535–555
Hayes RH, Pisano GP (1994) Beyond world class: the new manufacturing strategy. Harv Bus Rev 72(1):77–84
Hitt MA, Keats BW, DeMarrie SM (1998) Navigating in the new competitive landscape: building strategic flexibility and competitive advantage in the 21st century. Acad Manage Exec 12(4):22–42
Johnson JL, Lee RP, Saini A, Grohmann B (2003) Market- focused strategic flexibility: conceptual advances and an integrative model. J Acad Mark 31(1):74–89
Klingen DJS (1975) Company strategy: a managerial approach. Saxon House, Westmead
Kogut B (1985) Designing global strategies: profiting from operational flexibility. Sloan Manage Rev 27(1):27–38
Lau RSM (1996) Strategic flexibility: a new reality for world-class manufacturing. SAM Adv Manage J 61(5):11–15
Lei D, Hitt MA, Goldhar JD (1996) Advanced manufacturing technology: organizational design and strategic flexibility. Organ Stud 17(3):501
Matusik SF, Hill CWL (1998) The utilization of contingent work, knowledge creation, and competitive advantage. Acad Manage Rev 23(4):680–697
Nadkarni S, Narayanan VK (2004) Strategy frames, strategic flexibility and firm performance: the moderating role of industry clockspeed. Academy of Management Proceedings, New Orleans

Parnell JA (1994) Strategic consistency versus flexibility: does strategic change really enhance performance? Am Bus Rev 12(2):22–29
Parnell JA (2003) Five critical challenges in strategy making. SAM Adv Manage J 68(2):15–22
Pauwels P, Matthyssens P (2004) Strategic flexibility in export expansion: growing through withdrawal. Int Mark Rev 21(4/5):496–510
Porter M (1980) Competitive strategy: techniques for analyzing industries and competitors. The Free Press, New York
Porter M (1985) Competitive advantage: creating and sustaining superior performance. The Free Press, New York
Prahalad CKAHG (1990) The core competence of the corporation. Harv Bus Rev 68(3):79–91
Raynor ME, Leroux X (2004) Strategic flexibility in R&D. Res Technol Manage 47(3):27–32
Sanchez R (1995) Strategic flexibility in product competition. Strateg Manage J 16:135–159
Sanchez R, Heene A (1997) Strategic learning and knowledge management. Wiley, Chichester
Schilling MA, Steensma HK (2001) The use of modular organizational forms: an industry-level analysis. Acad Manage J 44(6):1149–1168
Shimizu K, Hitt MA (2004) Strategic flexibility: organizational preparedness to reverse ineffective strategic decisions. Acad Manage Exec 18(4):44–59
Slack N (1983) Flexibility as a manufacturing objective. Int J Oper Prod Manag 3(3):4–13
Teece DJ, Pisano G, Shuen A (1997) Dynamic capabilities and strategic management. Strateg Manage J 18(7):509–533
Upton DM (1995) Flexibility as process mobility: the management of plant capabilities for quick response manufacturing. J Oper Manag 12(3, 4):205–224
Volberda HW (1996) Towards the flexible form: how to remain vital in hypercompetitive environments. Organ Sci 7(4):359–387
Volberda HW (1998) Building the flexible firm: how to remain competitive. Oxford University Press, Oxford, UK
Volberda HW, Rutges A (1999) FARSYS: a knowledge-based system for managing strategic change. Decis Support Syst 26(2):99–123
Worren N, Moore K, Cardona P (2002) Modularity, strategic flexibility and firm performance: a study of the home appliance industry. Strateg Manage J 23(12):1123–1140
Young-Ybarra C, Wiersema M (1999) Strategic flexibility in information technology alliances: the influence of transaction cost economics and social exchange theory. Organ Sci 10(4):439–459

Chapter 4
Flexible Strategy Framework for Managing Continuity and Change in E-Government

S. Nasim and Sushil

1 Introduction

The current era of compulsive change has driven organizations to focus excessively on "change and transformation," and government is no exception. However, despite immense focus on change, the record of change success is startlingly low, both in business organizations (Kotter 1995; Beer and Nohria 2000) and in the context of e-government projects (Heeks 2003; Ruth and Doh 2007). This calls for the need to explore the emerging alternatives beneath and beyond change (Sturdy and Grey 2003).

Reviews on organizational change literature have reiterated the fact that "managing change is invariably managing paradoxes" (Nasim and Sushil 2011). As a result, various approaches to managing such dualities and paradoxes have emerged as a possible solution for enhancing change outcomes. One such approach that seems to have gained considerable attention recently calls for "managing continuity and change concurrently" for better change outcomes (Brown and Eisenhardt 1997; Huy 2002; Leana and Barry 2000; Sturdy and Grey 2003; Sushil 2005; Graetz and Smith 2009).

The domain of e-government, on one hand, calls for radical changes embracing new technologies and processes, while "government," as an entity, on the other hand, is largely driven by rules, norms, and laws strengthening forces of continuity. This had led researchers to explore the context of e-government from the dual perspective of managing continuity and change. Based on experts' opinion, researchers have concluded that the e-government domain is highly affected by both continuity and change forces and have even identified these forces (Nasim and Sushil 2010).

S. Nasim (✉)
Faculty of Management Studies and Research, AMU, Aligarh, India
e-mail: saboohinasim@gmail.com

Sushil
Department of Management Studies, IIT Delhi, New Delhi, India
e-mail: sushil@dms.iitd.ac.in; profsushil@gmail.com

Sushil and E.A. Stohr (eds.), *The Flexible Enterprise*, Flexible Systems Management, DOI 10.1007/978-81-322-1560-8_4, © Springer India 2014

Further studies have also explored the hierarchical relationships among these forces and have suggested possible linkage with the performance factors (Nasim 2011).

This chapter is divided into five sections. The first section introduces the theme of this chapter followed by the background literature on managing continuity and change, in general, and also in the context of e-government domain. The third section presents the hierarchical modeling of continuity and change forces affecting e-government performance in India. Further, in the fourth section, the flexible strategy framework is proposed and illustrated with the help of a case project from the e-government domain in India, followed by the concluding section.

2 Background Literature

Continuity and change in strategy discourses have been traditionally treated as mutually exclusive, as an either–or situation. Till 1970s and 1980s when the environment was relatively stable and the pace of change was comparatively slow, organizations focused on "incremental strategies" (Quinn 1978, 1980) with greater thrust on continuity. The organizations used to form strategies so as to survive and grow by maintaining continuity in their business domain. However, in the last two decades, the waves of change have compelled businesses to evolve a more "flexible approach" (Volberda 1998; Sushil 2000) for managing change and transformation.

Despite plethora of literature on strategic change and transformation, the voyage of change has not been smooth enough for a large number of leading organizations with strong legacy – who have actually ended up in greater turbulence and chaos. This has given rise to a growing interest in the concept of "confluence of change and continuity" (Sushil 2005), i.e., managing continuity and change simultaneously. Apparently it may seem paradoxical, but there is ample research evidence of application of such a concept in spheres like corporate governance, organizational identity, and industrial relations.

Continuity, Change, and Management Rhetoric

An analysis of management literature on change and transformation reveals that restructuring discourse is highly dependent on the rhetoric of "turbulent times". Authors demonstrate the gap between managerial rhetoric and business reality. Eccles et al. (1992) point out that management writers and practitioners talked of turbulence and transformative changes even in the supposedly past and less competitive context of the 1950s. They further demolish the rhetoric of Drucker and Tofler for making the same stirring announcements of impending change in nearly all their writings spanning decades. Huczynski (1993) observed that all the gurus gained the currency for their relevance to the changing times. Thompson and Davidson, too, strongly refute the claims of such managerial rhetoric and state that there is no paradigm shift or complete break as these modern gurus ably demonstrate. Bureaucracies continue to evolve and develop new forms of hierarchy, rules, and control. They further establish that it is in fact important to retain a sense of "continuity." Several other researches too have pointed to the need for both "change and continuity" in organizations (Ashforth and Mael 1996; Barney et al. 1998; Collins and Porras 1994; Eisenhardt 2000; Pettigrew 1985).

Strategic Change Versus Continuity

The organizations must realize that people are not Chameleons – they cannot change stripes and colors at the drop of a hat (Hart 1993). Most people have past accomplishments of which they are proud of and valuable strengths to bring forward. If they feel they are being told those things are to be discarded, they will not support the change efforts. According to Tannenbaum and Hanna (1985), changes in organizational identity have been experienced as painful and have been resisted by organizational members. Stability in organizational identity is seen as providing members with psychological anchors in times of change (Gustafson and Reger 1995). It has also been established that sense of sameness over time is necessary for psychological health (Albert and Whetten 1985; Shamir 1990). Christensen and Cheney (2000) indicate that spokespersons need to show that organizations are stable yet responsive entities with an inspiring history and a reliable presence. Thus, every organization needs some stability or continuity for if everything about an organization were to be always in flux, it would be crippled by chaos (Volberda 1998). Yet some aspects of the organization must change so that it can survive and even exploit the shifts and turns of the environment.

Continuity and Change: A Case of Confluence

Leana and Barry (2000) argue that tension between stability and change is inevitable and is a part of organizational life. Others suggest that change leadership must balance continuity and change (Burke and Trahant 2000; Pettigrew et al. 2001). Bianco and Schermerhorn (2006) reiterate that organizational leadership should allow for coexistent states of both "continuity and change." Strangelman (1999) demonstrates this through his case study on British Rail that many reform-minded managers and policy makers (who understand the emotive and political importance of nostalgia) deploy nostalgia as a proactive change-directed discourse rather than as reactionary force. Sturdy and Grey (2003), elaborating on how to manage continuity and change, state that "continuity and change be managed not as alternative states but as co-existent ones." They further add that it is imperative for managers today to embrace stability and learn to manage continuity if they want to survive. What can be a better testimony than the statement of a CEO cum change agent of a 125-year-old retail giant in his narration on the transformation of his company (Sears Roebuck and Co.) in which he admits that "Managing change and continuity simultaneously – is a task far more delicate than managing change alone." Martinez (1997) further suggests the questions to be posed in order to identify the elements of continuity or things to be preserved. Further, a revisit to the organizational change literature reiterates that "managing change is invariably managing paradox," especially the paradox of managing the confluence of both continuity and change forces (Luscher and Lewis 2008; Nasim and Sushil 2011).

2.1 Strategic Framework for Managing Continuity and Change

Though hosts of management writers have emphasized the need for managing "change and continuity," very few of them have actually attempted to present a framework for doing so. Mintzberg's (1988) notion of "reconciling change and continuity" in strategy making represents one of the earliest thinking on how to manage the two forces. In his excerpts on "Crafting Strategy," Mintzberg, however, proposed that the reconciliation between change and continuity forces should be done alternatively, a departure from the current thinking calling for concurrent management of the forces.

Volberda's (1997) "Paradox of Flexibility" emphasizes the need of an organization to manage change and continuity simultaneously via the flexibility route. Huy (2002) suggested an inductive model to resolve the tension between continuity and change at the micro/individual level. Drawing from "Systems thinking," Burchell and Kolb (2006) too emphasized the need to change and the need for stability to create sustainable organizations for future. The "Flowing Stream Strategy framework" for managing continuity and change, as put forward by Sushil (2005, 2012a, b, c), provides a detailed approach to "consciously manage the vital and desirable areas of continuity along with change." Graetz and Smith (2009) have recently proposed a "dualities aware perspective" as a potential way forward in balancing the contradictory forces of continuity and change.

Since the "Flowing Stream Strategy" approach is quite comprehensive and provides methodological details, it has been used as a basic approach for proposing the flexible strategic framework for managing continuity and change in e-government domain in this chapter. Thus, it becomes imperative to delve a little deeper into this approach and is explained in the next subsection.

Flowing Stream Strategy Approach

This approach rests on the philosophy that the strategic management of change could be better leveraged with a clear understanding of continuity of the organization (Sushil 2005, 2012a). The metaphor of a "flowing stream" is proposed by the author for depicting the management of continuity and change concurrently. According to him, organizations are acted upon by both forces of change and forces of continuity which need to be balanced concurrently, just like a flowing stream which exhibits continuity (being a stream) and change (as characterized by continuous flow of water) at the same time. While the major forces for change largely emanate from change situations, the "continuity forces" are generally linked with the actors and processes and hold back an organization from change by creating inertia in the current business domain (Sushil 2005). The continuity and change forces, however, would be different for different contexts and would vary across domains.

2.2 *Managing Change and Continuity in E-Government*

ICT, in general, and Internet in particular, has ushered in new horizons for both the government and the governed, subjecting the domain of e-government to continual change (Stojannovic et al. 2006). However, despite the impressive growth of e-government in making information and services available to people, the intra-governmental changes have been slow, ad hoc, and plagued by poor planning, inadequate application of strategic management principles, and weak leadership (Moon 2002; Sundberg and Sandberg 2006). Researchers have consistently highlighted that e-government is more of an organizational change issue and that the need for managing constant change is central to e-government research (Li 2003; Gupta et al. 2004; Rose and Grant 2010).

E-Government in India

Paradoxically, India, recognized as a leading power in information technology, has a poor e-government index. Far behind in the overall e-government performance, its global ranking has fallen from 87 in 2005 to 125 in 2012. The e-government readiness index too has registered a decline from 0.40 in 2005 to 0.38 this year lagging behind countries like Sri Lanka and Maldives (UN E-government Readiness Report 2005, 2012). With massive investments made by the government in these projects and with dismal success rate (15–17 %) (World Bank 2004; Suri 2005), it becomes all the more important to explore approaches that may enhance the outcomes of such projects.

An integrated nationwide implementation of e-government in India has been launched with NEGP (National E-Governance Plan) providing the way forward. Previous studies and researches in e-government in Indian context not only suggest the significance of managing change in the domain (Kumar 2005; Suri 2009), but also highlight the issues and gaps in planning and implementation (Suri 2009), which are largely due to the presence of continuity forces like culture. Further, a comprehensive review of e-government literature undertaken by researchers, with the objective of identifying change and continuity forces, resulted in seven forces of change (*Globalization, New Opportunities, Pressures of Good Governance, Stakeholders' Needs and Expectations, New Technology, The E-platform, Government Policies and Legislation, and Public–Private Partnership)* and five forces of continuity (*Large Number and Heterogeneity of Citizen Base, Established*

Traditional Infrastructure, Existing Process of Service Delivery, Legacy Databases, and Existing Culture) (Nasim and Sushil 2010). A detailed explanation of these forces and their references is provided in Appendices 1 and 2.

3 Modeling Continuity, Change, and Performance in E-Government

Continuity and change forces being newer constructs, their relationship with the performance variable in the e-government domain, as assumed in the Flowing Stream Strategy framework, did not have strong evidence from e-government literature. Hence, it was deemed important to undertake a preliminary exercise to verify that the forces of continuity and change, as identified from the literature, do lead to better project performance, before proceeding for case-based illustration of the framework in the next section. For this, a qualitative method of interpretive structural modeling (ISM) based on the expert's views has been used to verify the proposed relationships between forces of change, continuity, and e-government performance. Subsequent subsections provide a brief introduction to the methodology followed by the preliminary model developed broadly depicting the hypothesized relationship among the variables.

3.1 Introduction to ISM Methodology

Identification of structure within a system is of great value in dealing effectively with the system and better decision-making. Interpretive structural modeling (ISM) is defined "as a process that transforms unclear and poorly articulated mental models of systems into visible, well-defined models useful for many purposes" (Saxena et al. 2006). ISM methodology helps to impose order and direction on the complex relationships among elements of system. The philosophical basis and the subsequent conceptual and analytical details have been provided by Warfield (1973, 1974). The user of this technique with the help of experts identifies and interprets the relationship between a complex set of factors. After a series of iterations, a hierarchical structure of relationship among the variables is extracted and depicted in the form of a digraph.

For a complex problem, like the one under consideration, where an attempt is made to study continuity and change management – a new frontier, and that too in a new domain like e-governance, ISM technique is bound to add clarity and value in developing conceptual constructs. This methodology has been adopted to obtain a structural hierarchy of relationship between the factors affecting (change or continuity) e-governance in Indian context and their relationship with e-government performance. The steps involved in using ISM technique for the context defined above may be enumerated as follows:

i. Forces driving change and continuity in e-government domain are identified by undertaking literature review.
ii. A contextual relationship among the factors is established (by taking cues from the experts).
iii. A structural self-interaction matrix (SSIM) is developed indicating pair-wise relationship among factors.
iv. From the SSIM matrix, reachability matrix is derived and is then checked for transitivity of relationship among factors.
v. The reachability matrix as obtained in the above step is partitioned further to obtain various levels/hierarchy of factors.
vi. Based on the levels identified in the above step, a digraph is prepared which is then converted into an ISM.
vii. In the end, the ISM model is checked for any inconsistency and eventually interpreted in the context defined.

3.2 Hierarchy of Continuity and Change Forces Affecting Performance

As a result of the iterations of the final reachability matrix, the hierarchy of continuity and change forces affecting "performance" in e-government domain is depicted in Fig. 4.1, and its interpretations are discussed as follows.

Interpretations

As depicted in the Fig. 4.1, the hierarchy of forces affecting e-government performance in India, the forces at the top are interpreted to be more dependent ones and are driven by the forces at the lower end of the hierarchy. It includes both the forces driving change in favor of e-government and the continuity forces.

A closer look at the hierarchical model indicates that forces of continuity are affecting e-government more than the forces of change as they are mostly clustered at the bottom. The most critical forces driving change in e-government domain in India are globalization and stakeholders' needs and expectations leading to new opportunities and new technologies enhancing pressures for good governance, resulting in greater proliferation of e-business/e-platform, public–private partnership, and government policies and legislations finally leading to better performance of e-government projects.

Some of the continuity factors that have emerged out to be significantly affecting e-government are large citizen base, existing culture, existing physical infrastructure, and traditional system of service delivery. Eventually, all the continuity forces lead to better e-government performance. Since all these continuity forces are at the lower level of hierarchy, there seems to be more of an indirect relationship with the performance factors as compared to the change forces which are mostly clustered in the middle and at the top. This perhaps points out the possibility of change forces mediating the relationship between continuity forces and performance factors.

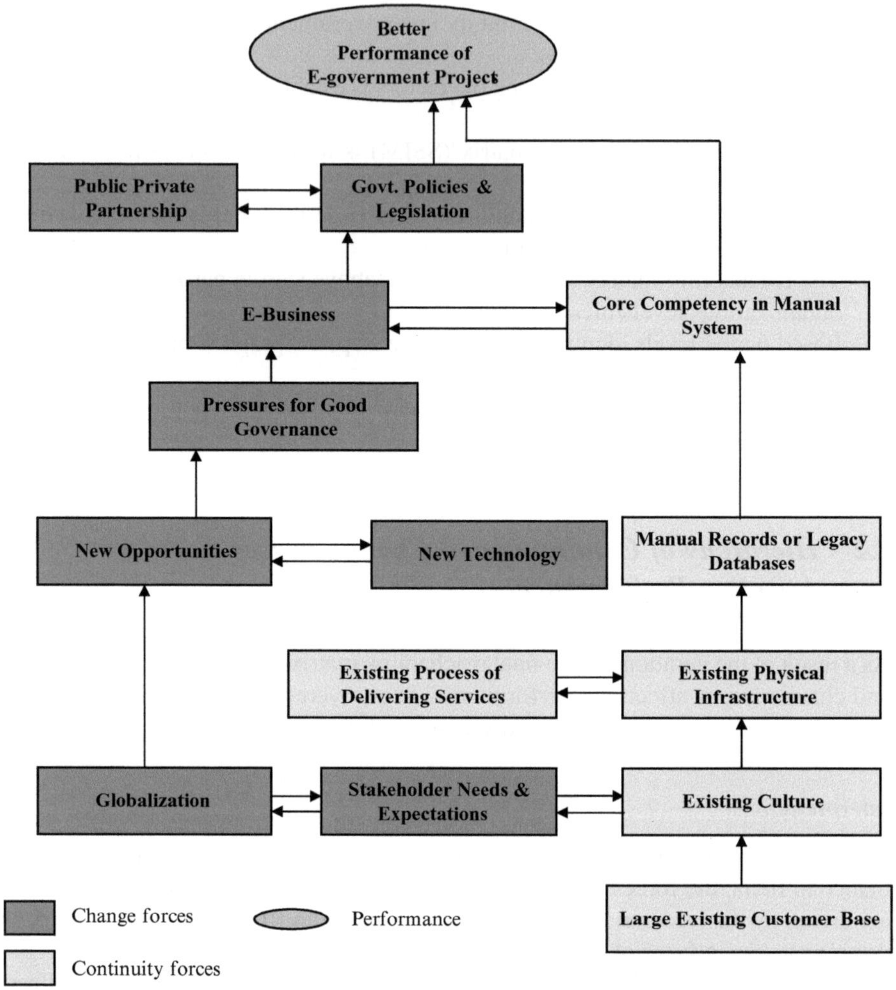

Fig. 4.1 Hierarchy of factors driving change and continuity in e-government in India

Having modeled the continuity, change, and performance factors, it seems imperative to present the flexible strategy framework for managing the continuity and change forces for better outcomes.

4 Flexible Strategy Framework for Managing Continuity and Change in E-Government Domain

As against the popular notion of e-government being change centric – calling for radical change – a more incremental approach is recommended taking into consideration the legacies or the inertia of the pre-e-government era. Drawing predominantly from the Flowing Stream Strategy, the following flexible strategic framework may be proposed to resolve the paradox of continuity and change in e-government:

- Implementers of e-government projects should identify the key factors driving change and also the critical factors obstructing positive change in the context of a specific project.
- Continuity–change template should be developed for each project, facilitating a deeper understanding of the factors in consultation with experts in the field. Higher weights may be assigned to more critical factors affecting the project, and the scores may be used further to map the project on the continuity–change matrix.
- Given the fast pace of change in e-government context, it is expected that both forces of continuity of change will be high in almost all projects, thus calling for a strategy managing the confluence of these factors.
- "Flowing Stream Strategy" (Sushil 2012c) is recommended for strategic management of confluence of continuity and change in e-government domain, the methodology for which includes:
  - VDB (Vital, Desirable, and Burdensome) analysis of continuity forces.
  - Impact analysis of change forces affecting the e-government project.
  - Assess and landscape the performance factors relevant for the e-government project.
  - Suggest strategic actions for improving low performance areas by leveraging continuity with change forces.

The flexible strategy framework for the e-government domain, as proposed above, can be further depicted in Fig. 4.2.

Methodology for Case Illustration

In order to illustrate the flexible strategy framework proposed above, a case-based approach is used. A mission mode Government-to-Citizen (G2C) project called Online Filing of RTI Complaint and Appeal (also known as CIC online) has been selected to demonstrate the Flowing Stream Strategy methodology as it had been rated high on both continuity and change forces. The inputs for analyzing the case have been elicited from the key planners and implementers of the case project, as a part of the doctoral research at IIT Delhi (Nasim 2010). The continuity, change, and performance factors used in case analysis are derived from the literature (Refer Appendices 1 and 2).

4.1 Case Background: Online Filing of RTI Complaint and Appeal (CIC Online)

RTI Complaint and Appeal System (also referred to as Chief Information Commission-CIC online) is a nonprofit initiative under the National Portal of India project and aims to bring the ICT benefits in the government functioning so as to

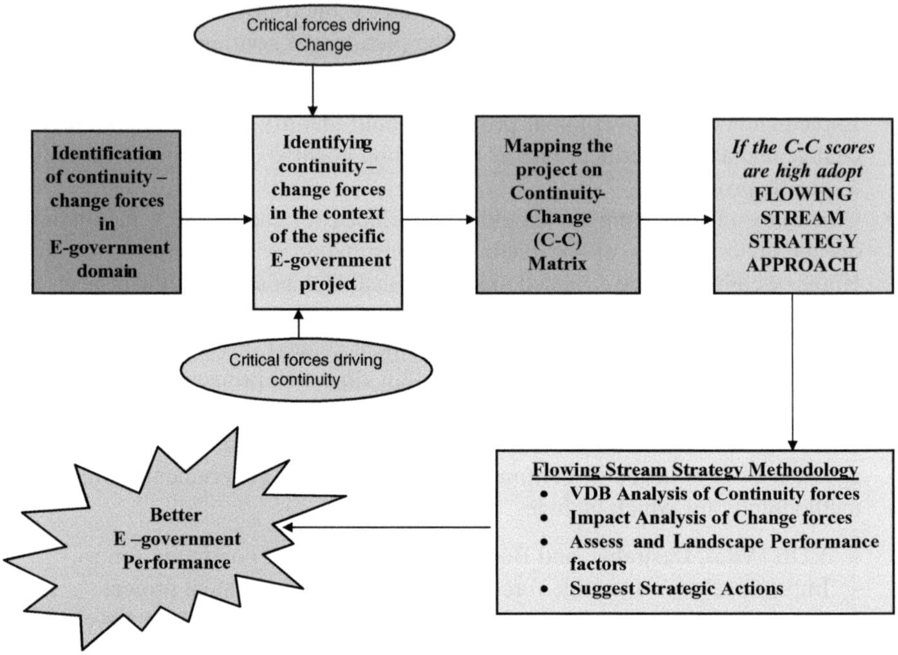

Fig. 4.2 Proposed flexible strategy framework for managing continuity–change

effectively disseminate information to the citizens as per the landmark Indian Right to Information Act (RTI), 2005. The hallmark of the RTI Act, 2005, is that the citizens can have access to information, which so far has been under the control of public authorities (PA), in order to promote transparency and accountability in the matters concerning the public authorities in particular and the government in general. The online filing of RTI complaint and appeal has, thus, institutionalized the convergence of ICT with the Right to Information Act, 2005 in India.

Project Scope and Coverage

Implementation of the initial 3 years (2005–2008) of RTI Act revealed that there is a huge gap between demand and supply side of information. This may largely be attributed to the poor records management, lack of automation, and the inefficient usage of the computerization in the government organizations. Given these problems, it was envisaged to enable the RTI complaint and second appeal process through an ICT-based system providing equal opportunity to the citizens at large. The portal (http://rti.india.gov.in) has nationwide content coverage in terms of information on the complaint and second appeal, which facilitates its target audience and beneficiaries that include the citizens of India of all age groups and demographic backgrounds, the Ministries, Departments and associated offices, Central Government offices, Legislative and Judicial Institutions of government, and public sector enterprises/organizations.

Project Stakeholders and Timeline

This project is a key initiative driven by Central Information Commission and National Informatics Centre in accordance with the National e-Governance Plan (NeGP), which sought to acquire the key benefits of ICT and deliver the RTI system over the digital network for the citizens. The key project stakeholders include representatives of Central Public Authorities (Public bodies falling under the jurisdiction of central government), citizens of India (including the nonresident Indians), and the Civil Society Organizations. While the front-end RTI Complaint and Appeal System had been operational since July 2008 as envisaged, the back end migrated to the new system (with consolidated database) fully by December 2008. All the project timelines were successfully adhered to as planned by the team.

The Front-End Process (Citizen Module)

This front-end module facilitates the citizens to submit their complaints and/or second appeals to the CIC online. A citizen can visit the site http://rti.india.gov.in, fill up the desired form, and submit his/her complaint/appeal online. A choice is made available to the visitor either to submit the form at one go or save the form as a draft mode for final submission at a later date. Once it is finally submitted, the complainant/appellant is prompted by the system to take a print out of the filled form, sign the form, and send the signed form to the CIC in view of requirements of the rule framed under the Act for further processing of the petitions. While generating a hard copy, the system also generates a unique registration number, which can also be used by the citizens for further correspondence or tracking the status of the complaint/appeal online. While filling the forms, information regarding priority category, if any, is also being captured to help CIC dispose the petitions within stipulated period as laid down in the RTI Act. The citizens can access this module by visiting http://cic.gov.in and the National Portal as well.

Major Back-End Process and Technology Architecture

The back-end module aligns on the deliverables at the office end in compliance with the provisions regarding time schedules enacted in the RTI Act. A total of 12 stages have been devised with multiple substages/options to proceed through the life cycle of a complaint/appeal. All actions or decisions taken by the respective officials at different stages in the process flow of complaints/appeals are captured. It also facilitates auto-generation of hearing notices, electronic dispatch of the decisions through e-mail to the concerned stakeholders. This system not only facilitates easy tracking of cases but also monitors the workflow for speedy disposal of cases. This module also assists in generating various documents like official notes, daily cause list, disposal reports, and generation of designer reports comprising of various dynamic queries which may be used by various statutory organizations and by the parliament as an indicator for monitoring the implementation of RTI Act as mandated.

The RTI Complaint and Appeal System is hosted in the Internet Data Centre of NIC and leverages upon the National Portal of India infrastructure with a primary objective of ensuring 24×7×365 support, scalable, secure, accessible, manageable, and highly reliable systems. Disaster Recovery Center, NIC infrastructure allows for a robust physical and technical environment. The Data Centre is ISO 27001 (Information Security Management System) certified with a disaster recovery center at Hyderabad. The project management team comprised of team members from CIC and NIC with a dedicated project manager, system architect, software developers, and implementation support professionals. Secretary, CIC lead the overall team and the Joint Registrar held the responsibility of the entire coordination so as to ensure the completion of the project as scheduled. The Chief Information Commissioner and Information Commissioners provided useful guidance whenever required.

User Experience and Feedback

Online applications have been showing increasing trend as against the conventional mode of filing applications. Since the status of the cases at various stages is available in public domain, request for information at CIC is showing a decreasing trend. Prior to launch of this system, only basic information could have been generated. But now reports on much diverse information are being generated for use by the policy makers in drawing future roadmap regarding RTI implementation in the country. There are several users whose observations and experiences are on record:

- One of the users has filed more than 100 appeals/complaints since the inception of the commission. More than 60 % of all have been filed online. With the help of the features of this module (customer feedback), he used to send emails for classifying the nature of the petitions and requesting for clubbing the similar matters. This has resulted into speedy disposal of most of his cases.
- Civil Society Organizations have made considerable amount of pressure on the government of the day to appoint more numbers of the Information Commissioners by only following the monthly disposal and pendency figures.
- At another occasion one of the appellants brought to the notice of the commission that one of its important orders stand unimplemented by the public authority and this he could do by just following the status of that case.
- Most of the public authorities are following the module to see as to how many appeals/complaints have been filed against them and make themselves prepared well in advance for appearance or the disposal of the cases.
- In yet another case, the complainant filed a case online and left for USA. He kept on checking the status, and when his case came up for hearing, he sent a mail to the commission requesting to hear him through video conference and was accordingly heard.

4.2 VDB Analysis of Continuity Forces

The forces of continuity have been found to be significantly high in the context of CIC online project, the aggregate score for continuity force being 4.14. Out of the

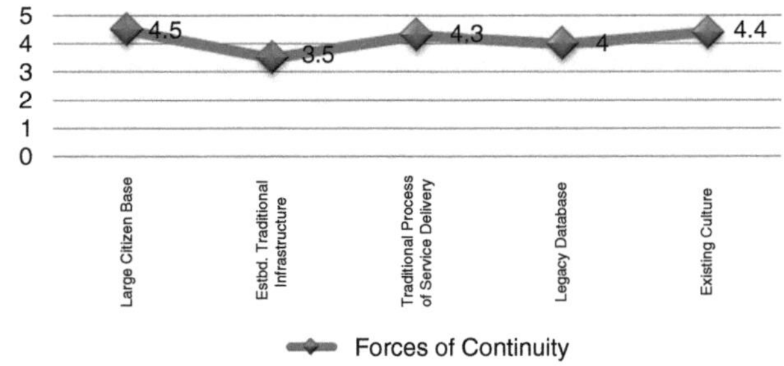

Fig. 4.3 VDB analysis of continuity forces (CIC online)

five continuity forces, three have been identified as vital, one desirable, and one does not seem to be very relevant for this case (Refer Fig. 4.3). The vital continuity forces include large and heterogeneous citizen base, existing process of service delivery, and the existing culture. The critical nature of these continuity forces has made them vital rather inevitable continuity forces.

In the context of all e-government projects, addressing the needs of the citizen base is indispensable, irrespective of size. However, in this case context, this continuity force becomes vital given their strategic response. Being web based, it is not only accessible 24×7, but is also more inclusive due to its accessibility in Hindi language and to people who are physically challenged. Further, some of the states have taken the initiative of setting call centers to facilitate the access to the illiterate masses. The *Jaankari* project of the state of Bihar has been recently awarded for such an innovation promoting the inclusivity of the RTI project. The continuity force of "traditional process of service delivery," though partly burdensome, is critical due to its legal nature. Thus, while most part of the traditional process is facilitated by law, some obstructive part of the law like rigid mode of payment (check, draft, cash) is to be reviewed for speedy delivery of service. Further, the cultural (issues though very resistive initially) are paving way for easier implementation of the project and hence act as a vital force to leverage on for effective outcome.

The continuity force of "legacy data base" does not pose much of a problem as its migration has been enforced by law, though technological issues of file noting do obstruct the workflow. The continuity force of "established traditional infrastructure" does not directly affect the CIC (Chief Information Commission) which is a body constituted recently after the enactment of RTI Act in 2005. However, the public authority, with whom the CIC office coordinates, is definitely faced with the issue of utilizing or leveraging the traditional infrastructure for facilitating information dissemination.

4.3 *Impact Analysis of Change Forces*

As explained before, the inputs regarding the extent of impact of change forces were taken from the case experts on the basis of pre-designed templates.

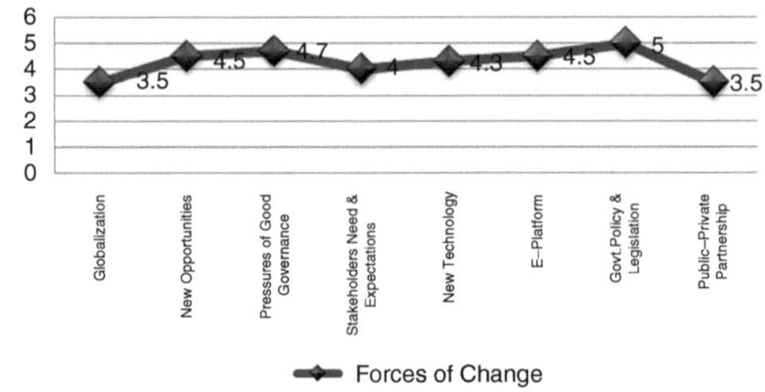

Fig. 4.4 Impact analysis of change forces (CIC online)

An analysis of the impact of change forces in the context of CIC online project reveals that five of these forces, namely, perceived new opportunities, pressures of good governance, new technology, e-platform, and government policies and legislation, have significantly high impact on the project, while globalization and public–private partnership have modest impact (Fig. 4.4).

Discussion on Impact Analysis

The force of "globalization," as per the key officials of the case project, does not seem to have a direct impact on this project as the Indian RTI Act is more comprehensive and stringent compared to the information laws of even the developed nations (like Canada, and the USA). According to them, it is the information dissemination drive within the country pioneered by the RTI Act that has been the major imperative for the project. Adding on to this force has been the "pressures of good governance" and the "perceived new opportunity" related to the "new technology" which acted as the driving force for the project. Such pressures and the lookout for opportunity and new technology-related option were in turn triggered by a huge number of pending cases in just 3 years of enactment of the Act. The proliferation of the e-platform in the country too added on to the imperative to go online. The public–private partnership, however, has little impact as the technical implementation is handled by NIC (National Informatics Centre) – the technical wing of the government, thus, requiring minimal intervention from the private sector unlike the other cases.

4.4 Strategic Factor Assessment and Landscaping

As indicated earlier, this section deals with assessment of the project and citizen-related performance factors (drawn from literature), based on the opinion of the key officials of the project, as depicted in Fig. 4.5. Further, these factors are used for landscaping against the aspired level of service to highlight the areas of improvement.

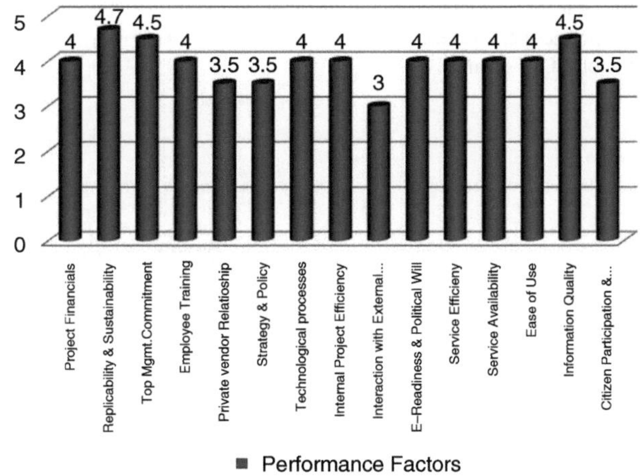

Fig. 4.5 Strategic factor assessment (CIC online)

Strategic Factor Assessment

An analysis of the scores attributed by the case officials to the project and citizen factors indicates that project deliverables are comparatively lower than the citizen-related factors.

Given the project factors, the case project stands out in terms of replicability and sustainability followed by top management commitment. Factors like project financials translating into cost and time saving, project's technological process and architecture, and employee training and involvement have had a fair score of 4 indicating some room for future improvement. The factors requiring attention, however, include the process of strategy and policy and the interaction with and awareness among the external stakeholders like NGOs and Civil society organization, which seem to be rather weak in this project context. Lack of adequate awareness and the limited interaction with such external stakeholder groups have been highlighted in the secondary data sources as well. Private vendor relationship has not been accorded much score given the limited role played due to their involvement of NIC in technical implementation of the project.

As regards the citizen-related performance factors, the contribution to information quality and transparency has been scored the highest. The other factors related to service efficiency, i.e., cost and time savings to the citizens, ease of use, and availability, have been scored well. The only concern area is the citizen participation which is rather low and seems to be largely a fallout of low level of awareness as indicated in the project factors.

Landscaping Performance Factors

Inputs from the experts were obtained regarding their perception of the current status of the project as compared to the aspired level with respect to the performance parameters for both the project- and citizen-related factors.

Fig. 4.6 Strategy landscape for project performance factors (CIC online)

Fig. 4.7 Strategy landscape for citizen performance factors (CIC online)

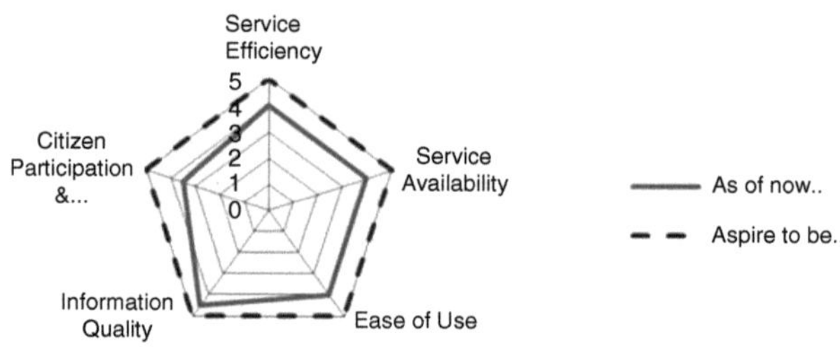

As evident from Fig. 4.6, project factors like "interaction with external stakeholders" and the "strategy and policy" require greater intervention for aspired level of performance exhibiting the maximum gap between the current and aspired levels. The rest of the factors also provide scope for improvement in future, if strategized.

As depicted in Fig. 4.7, the performance factor related to "information quality" does stand out almost reaching the aspired level. There is, however, considerable scope for improvement in the rest of the citizen-related factors, specifically "citizen participation" which is quite behind the aspired level.

4.5 *Strategic Actions Suggested: LAP (Learning–Action–Performance) Synthesis*

In order to synthesize the key learnings and suggest strategic actions to attain the aspired level of performance for the project deliverables, the background information on the case and the subsequent analysis of the case have been utilized. Table 4.1 summarizes the strategic actions suggested for performance factors with low scores only. The practitioners may adopt the same approach for strategizing ahead for better performing strategic factors in order to sustain their performance.

Table 4.1 Strategic actions suggested for low performing factors for CIC online project

S. No.	Strategic factor with low performance scores(≤3)	Learnings from case analysis (Key predictors for the strategic factor)	Strategic actions suggested for aspired level of performance (score: 5)
1	Interaction with external stake holders (EXST) *(Project-related performance factor)*	The influence of the change forces "pressures of good governance" (PGG) has important bearing for this strategic factor Internal project/business efficiency (BSEF) also affects it positively Technological process (TECH) may affect through internal project/business efficiency (BSEF)	Integrate the change force of "pressures of good governance" (PGG) with the right kind and level of technological processes enhancing project efficiency thus strengthening the interactions with external stakeholders
2	Strategy and policy in place (STGP) *(Project-related performance factor)*	Cultural (CUL) forces have negatively affected the strategy and policy for the project Project factors like employee training (ETNG) and technological process (TECH) have a positive effect on STGP Change forces like new technology (NTG) and pressures for good governance (PGG) indirectly affect through the project factors of ETNG and TECH	Delineate the negative aspects of the cultural forces (e.g., public authorities) and leverage or integrate it with suitable employee training and the technological process
3	Citizen participation and empowerment (CTP) *(Citizen-related performance factor)*	This citizen factor is directly affected by one continuity force of culture (CUL) and three project factors like internal project efficiency (BSEF), e-readiness (ERED), and interactions with external stakeholders (EXST) as per the empirical model Efficiency, either at the back end or in service delivery, is a strong predictor of citizen participation. Both being average in this case, low rating of CTP is expected	Strengthen the efficiency of the project and integrate it with positive cultural forces (CUL) as part of the strategy and policy for the project may enhance CTP
4	Private vendor relationship (PVR) *(Project-related performance factor)*	"Established traditional infrastructure" (ETIN) strongly affects private vendor relationship. Since CIC online being a newly conceived project, this link has not found to be very relevant While CIC may not have inherited established infrastructure, the public authorities do confront this issue	While NIC (National Informatics Centre) has successfully implemented the project at the CIC level, to address the problem of traditional form of data storage and retrieval at the public authority level, PPP mode may be recommended to further provide a boost to the project

5 Conclusion

This chapter reiterates the need for a flexible approach for managing the confluence of continuity and change in e-government domain. Drawing from change, strategy, and e-government literature, it proposes a flexible strategy framework for managing such a confluence. A hierarchical modeling of continuity and change forces establishes their relationship with e-government performance, at the outset. Later, a step-by-step demonstration of the proposed strategic framework is undertaken with the help of a case study from e-government domain in India. Most of the continuity and change forces that were found to be significant as per the hierarchical model were also found to be valid in the specific context of the select CIC online case project. Further, based on the insights from the case analysis, strategic actions were suggested for strategic factors with comparatively low performance ratings.

This chapter not only proposes the strategic framework for managing e-government projects for better change outcomes but also illustrates with real case example, thus, providing a roadmap for the practitioners in the domain. From academic perspective, it attempts to add value by proposing a new strategic framework for the domain besides demonstrating the use of techniques like ISM and Flowing Stream Strategy approach.

References

Albert S, Whetten DA (1985) Organizational identity. Res Organ Behav 263–295
Ashforth BE, Mael FA (1996) Organizational identity and strategy as a context for the individual. In: Baum JA, Dutton JE (eds) Advances in strategic management 13:19–64
Barney J et al (1998) A strategy conversation on the topic of organizational identity. In: Whetten DA, Godfrey PC (eds) Identity in organizations: building theory through conversations. Sage, Thousand Oaks, pp 99–168
Beer M, Nohria N (2000) Cracking the code of change. Harv Bus Rev 78:133–141
Bianco AT, Schermerhorn J Jr (2006) Self regulation, strategic leadership and paradox in organizational change. J Organ Change Manag 19(4):457–470
Brown SL, Eisenhardt K (1997) The Art of continuous change: linking complexity theory and time-paced evolution in relentlessly shifting organizations. Adm Sci Q 42:1–34
Burchell N, Kolb DG (2006) Stability and change for sustainability. Univ Auckl Bus Rev 8(2):32–41
Burke WW, Trahant B (2000) Business climate shifts: profiles of change makers. Butterworth Heinman, Boston
Christensen LT, Cheney G (2000) Self-absorption and self-seduction in the corporate identity game. In: Schultz M, Hatch MJ, Larsen MH (eds) The expressive organization: linking identity, reputation and the corporate brand. Oxford University Press, New York, pp 246–270
Collins JR, Porras JI (1994) Built to last. Harper Collins, New York
Eccles RG, Nohria N, Berkley JD (1992) Beyond the hype: rediscovering the essence of management. HBS Press, Boston
Eisenhardt KM (2000) Paradox, spirals, ambivalence: the New language of change and pluralism. Acad Manage Rev 25:703–705
Graetz F, Smith ACT (2009) Duality theory and organizing forms in change management. J Change Manag 9(1):9–25
Gupta MP, Kumar P, Bhattacharya J (2004) Government online. TMH, New Delhi

Gustafson LT, Reger RK (1995) Using organizational identity to achieve stability and change in high velocity environments. Acad Manag Best Pap Proc 8(1):464–468

Hart ER (1993) Designing process based organization. Plann Rev 21(5)

Heeks R (2003) Most e-Government for development projects fail: how can risks be reduced? Analyzing e-Government research: perspectives. IDPM working paper no.16.,http://idpm.man.ac.uk/publications/wp/igov/index.shtml. Accessed Dec 2007

Huy QN (2002) Emotional balancing of organizational continuity and radical change: the contribution of middle managers. Adm Sci Q 47:31–69

Huczynski A (1993) Management gurus. Routledge, London

Kotter JP (1995) Leading change: why transformation efforts fail? Harv Bus Rev 72(2):59–67

Kumar P (2005) A study of effectiveness and change management dimensions of e-Governance. Ph.D. thesis, Indian Institute of Technology, Delhi

Leana CR, Barry B (2000) Stability and change as simultaneous experiences in organizational life. Acad Manage Rev 25:753–759

Li F (2003) Implementing e-Government strategy in Scotland: current situations and emerging issues. J Electron Comm Organ 1(2):44–65

Luscher LS, Lewis MW (2008) Organizational change and managerial sensemaking: working through paradox. Acad Manage J 51(2):221–240

Martinez CA (1997) Transforming the legacy of sears. Strat Leader 25(4):30–35

Mintzberg H (1988) Crafting strategy. The McKinsey Quarterly Summer:71–90

Moon MJ (2002) The evolution of e-Government among municipalities: rhetoric or reality? Public Adm Rev 62(4):424–433

Nasim S (2010) Strategic management of continuity and change: a study of select in e-government projects in India, Doctoral Thesis, Department of Management Studies, IIT Delhi

Nasim S (2011) Total interpretive structural modeling of continuity and change forces in e-government. J Enterprise Transform 1(Special Issue 2):147–168

Nasim S, Sushil (2010) Managing continuity and change: a new approach to strategizing in e-government. J Trans Gov People Process Pol 4(4):334–368

Nasim S, Sushil (2011) Revisiting organizational change: exploring the paradox of managing continuity and change. J Change Manag 11(2):185–206

Pettigrew A (1985) The awakening giant: continuity and change in ICI. Blackwell, Oxford

Pettigrew AM, Woodman RW, Cameron KS (2001) Studying organizational change and development challenges for future research. Acad Manage J 44:697–713

Quinn JB (1978) Strategic change: logical incrementalism. Sloan Manag Rev Fall:7–21

Quinn JB (1980) Strategies for change. Irwin, Illinois

Rose WR, Grant GG (2010) Critical issues pertaining to planning and implementation of e-government initiatives. Gov Inform Q 27(1):26–33

Ruth S, Doh S (2007) Is e-government ready for prime time? IEEE Internet Comput 11(2):80–82. doi:10.1109/MIC.2007.42

Saxena JP, Sushil, Vrat P (2006) Policy and strategy formulation-an application of flexible systems methodology. GIFT Publishing, New Delhi

Shamir B (1990) Calculations, values, and identities: the sources of collectivistic work motivation. Hum Relat 43:313–332

Stojannovic L, Stojannovic N, Apostolou D (2006) Change management in e-government: onto Gov case study. Electron Gov Int J 3(1):74–82

Strangelman T (1999) The nostalgia of organization and the organization of nostalgia: past and present in the contemporary railway industry. Sociology 33(4):725–746

Sturdy A, Grey C (2003) Beneath and beyond organizational change management: exploring alternatives. Organization 10:651–662

Sundberg HK, Sandberg KW (2006) Towards e-government: a survey of problems in organizational processes. Bus Process Manag J 21(2):146–161

Suri PK (2005) Strategic insights into an e-governance project: a case study of AGMARKNET based on SAP-LAP framework. Global J Flexible Syst Manag 6(3–4):39–48

Suri PK (2009) Strategic insights into e-governance planning and implementation: a study of select agriculture related projects. Doctoral Thesis, DMS, IIT Delhi
Sushil (2000) Systemic flexibility. Global J Flex Syst Manag 1(1):77–80
Sushil (2005) Flexible strategy framework for managing continuity and change. Int J Global Bus Competitiveness 1(1):22–32
Sushil (2012a) Flowing stream strategy: managing confluence of continuity and change. J Enterprise Transform 2(1):26–49
Sushil (2012b) Making flowing stream strategy work. Global J Flexible Syst Manag 13(1):25–40
Sushil (2012c) Flowing stream strategy: leveraging strategic change with continuity. Springer, New Dehli
Tannenbaum R, Hanna RW (1985) Holding on, letting go, and moving on: understanding a neglected perspective on change. In: Tannenbaum R, Margulies, Massarik F (eds) Human systems development. Jossey-Bass, San Francisco, pp 95–121
UN E-government Survey Report (2005, 2012), http://www.unpan.org
UN E-government Survey Report (2012) Accessed from http://ww.unpan.org
Volberda HW (1997) Building flexible organization for fast moving markets. Long Range Plann 30(2):169–183
Volberda HW (1998) Building the flexible firm: how to remain competitive. Oxford University Press, Oxford
Warfield JN (1973) Assault on complexities, vol 3, Battelle Monograph. Battelle Memorial Inst, Columbus
Warfield JN (1974) Structuring complex systems, vol 4, Battelle Monograph. Battelle Memorial Inst, Columbus
World Bank (2004) World Bank Official: e-Governance failures abound. World Bank Archives http://www.worldbank.org
www.ciconline.gov.in
www.rti.india.gov.in
www.worldbank.org

Chapter 5
Managing Competitiveness Through Flexibility in Telecom Industry of India: A Policy Perspective

Manoj Kumar Sharma

1 Introduction

Globalization and liberalization are the major factors in enhancing the dynamics of national policy making. These two factors are also responsible for creating pressures on enhancing innovations in products and services leading to competitiveness in any sector of economy and creating more competing organization for market share in their industry sector.

Globalization with reference to telecom sector also brings many international and cross-border regulatory issues and a requirement for multilateral regulatory forums. For example, IT-enabled services, international financial services, and e-commerce entail the transfer of data across borders, and these activities raise the issue inter alia of privacy (ITU-2007). The sheer volume of data transfer is itself a challenge but the OECD (http://www.oecd.org) notes two additional risks related to, firstly, secondary uses of personal data and, secondly, information security breaches.

In 1983, the ITU established the independent Commission for Worldwide Telecommunication Development, also known as Maitland Commission, to recommend ways in which the expansion of the telecommunications across the world could be stimulated. In 1984, the Commission, after studying the earlier works by ITU, OECD, the World Bank, and other international agencies, published "*Missing Link*," which embodied its conclusions and recommendations. The Commission's study of the role of telecommunications persuaded its members that "telecommunications can increase the efficiency of economy, commercial and administrative activities, improve the effectiveness of social and emergency services and distribute

M.K. Sharma (✉)
Department of Management Studies, JSS Academy of Technical Education (JSS Mahavidyapeethata), Noida, UP, India

Faculty of Management, Mahamaya Technical University (MTU Noida), Noida, UP, India
e-mail: hod.dms@jssaten.ac.in; dean.fm@mtu.ac.in

Sushil and E.A. Stohr (eds.), *The Flexible Enterprise*, Flexible Systems Management,
DOI 10.1007/978-81-322-1560-8_5,

Table 5.1 Digital economy shift

From	To
Industrial society; centralized control or regulation, from regulators or monopolies in telecom; significant market powers of incumbents, conglomerates, and MNCs	Information society with a knowledge-driven digital economy, deregulated or privatized telecom, and industry-led self-regulation and power of individual users' fingertips over convergence of ICT, especially in the advent of Internet; share the markets with micro-, small-, and medium-sized entrepreneurs especially in the era of e-business or e-commerce; and almost "instant global village" connected by various technologies and services

Source: Dr. Eun-Ju Kim, ITU (2001)

the social, cultural and economic benefits of the process of development more equitable throughout a community and a nation" (ITU 1984).

The visible paradigm shift in digital economy took shape in the following format given above Table 5.1.

The argument forwarded by Rugman (2006): "Globalization is a myth. As currently understood, it does not exist. Far from taking place in a single global market, most business activity by large international firms takes place within regional blocks. Government regulations, transportation costs and cultural differences divide the world into the triad of North America, Europe, and Asia-Pacific – an extension of the three large economic hubs at its core: the United States, the European Union and Japan. Within these blocks rival multinational enterprises compete for regional market share and so contribute to economic efficiency" (Rugman 2006). But in telecom sector being service industry in nature, it does not discriminate the various sectors of economy. It serves all the sectors of the economy in a similar manner as the services provided by telecom sector to various categories of customers – those who need these telecom services because of faster mode and cost-effectiveness of communication arising due to business process fulfillment and long-distance separation of organizations separated around the globe, i.e., demand driven. Therefore in whatever formats globalization occurs in any country, it does not alter the configuration of telecom service delivery and always enhances the growth of telecom sector as it becomes the common denominator for all the industrial sector's growth enabler.

Within the Asia Pacific region, various voice usage patterns exist among consumers of voice communication services. Generally, there has been a preference shown for mobile communication over fixed-line communication, and as a result, customers have been shifting their subscriptions and usage. Also, in certain regions, particularly where price is an issue, a preference for the use of mobile data services over voice calling has become apparent. This increasing demand for mobile communication services can be attributed to the flexibility and mobility that is characteristic of these technologies as well as the value-added services that have become incorporated into the offerings of mobile providers.

The main theme of this chapter is that flexibility need not be only considered in processes but throughout the enterprise in people, processes, and technology in various forms of flexibilities. Based on the framework presented in this chapter, we convey that flexibility incorporation is required for enhancing competitiveness.

1.1 The Need of Liberalization or Competition

- To provide customers with more choices of technologies and services (flexibility/freedom of choice) with quality and affordable prices (flexibility in pricing), but not necessary lower prices.
- To formulate effective competition policies to ensure that the benefits of liberalization or deregulation and market-based reforms flow through to both industries and consumers.
- The industry trend demonstrates faster and more growth of data (e.g., Internet) and mobile services, both areas which have tended to be more open up to competition, than that of basic fixed voice services.

1.2 The Need of Regulation

The telecom sector has witnessed many changes related to technology and market conditions of telecom sector, and the role of government as regulator has really played a dominant role in protection of both sides of demand (consumers/users of services) and supply (companies and its related players who create telecom infrastructure/software/hardware and content developers) of telecom sector. The telecom sector is typically depicted in terms of technology/market/regulation.

The need of regulation of the telecommunications industry sector is very much required as this sector touches the life of individual, business, and government in similar fashion, and it is now omnipresent in all walks of life, and telecom services are extending almost towards becoming an essential service in the life of people, and hence in order to protect the interest of all, some regulation is inevitable.

Regulatory intervention is required for a variety of reasons. Typically, regulators must authorize or license new operators. They must often remove barriers to market entry by new operators by providing them the level playing field. They must observe interconnection of new entrants with incumbent operators. Regulatory intervention should be in sync with high-cost areas or low-income subscribers of telecom services.

The objectives of telecommunications regulation vary from country to country and governments in most countries continue to see telecommunications as an essential public service. Even after telecommunications networks are no longer run by them, governments normally retain a regulatory role to ensure that telecommunications services are supplied keeping the public interest of their citizens and business interest of the operators.

1.3 Convergence

Convergence has raised new challenges for competition authorities since it is expected to generate pressures for consolidation. We have already witnessed numerous mergers and acquisitions among players in the new market space. In some instances, acquirers have emerged from nontraditional sectors. The following categories of convergence became apparent:

- **Convergence of operators** – Mergers, acquisition, joint ventures, or investment among telecommunications operators or manufacturers used as a strategy for entering new markets or maintaining market share within an existing market, e.g., in Japan, Softbank acquired Vodafone Japan gaining access to the mobile telephony market
- **Convergence of services –** The development of business strategies that either involve the incorporation of one service within another or the simple offering of one service with another, e.g., mobile Internet included with mobile telephony or triple play (package offering cable TV, Internet, and fixed-line telephony for a single price)
- **Convergence of technology –** The incorporation of one technology into another, e.g., incorporating broadcasting technology into mobile phones to allow for mobile TV
- **Convergence of markets –** Services that were once noncompeting become competing or when operators who were once noncompeting become competitors due to substitutability of the service, e.g., broadcasters in the telecommunications market and telecommunications operators in the broadcast market
- **Convergence of regulation –** The alteration of regulatory schemes or regulatory bodies such that they have power over areas of technology which were previously dealt with individually (typically a reaction to one of the other forms of convergence), e.g., the proposed merger of OFTA and the Broadcasting Division of the Television and Entertainment Licensing Authority to create the Office of the Communications Authority (OFCA)

Each of these categories of convergence does not appear in isolation. They are often found together and the appearance of one can cause the appearance of another. For example, the convergence of technology is often the catalyst for the convergence of markets. In the case of mobile TV, 3G mobile technology allows for the provision of video to a mobile handset. The response of mobile telephony providers has been to create content or to license content from content providers, essentially putting these telephony providers in the broadcast market. Table 5.2 provides change of attitudes towards convergence in the Asia Pacific region – country wise.

Convergence brings with it many advantages for consumers and providers, but it also brings with it difficulties, particularly in market regulation. For example, convergence of operators includes the convergence of manufacturers. A possible result of this is vertical and horizontal integration within the market and the concentration of market power. This could cause major antitrust concerns as horizontal and

Table 5.2 Change of attitudes towards convergence in the Asia Pacific region (country wise and government, operator, and consumer perspective)

	Government strategy	Operator strategy	Consumer demand
Hong Kong	Maximization of open competition	Exclusivity of content (the walled-garden approach) to attract customers and differentiate operators	Highly sophisticated consumers
	All markets fully liberalized	Value-added services	Willing to adopt new technologies
	No barriers to convergence	Bundling	
South Korea	Broadband converged network (BCN), executed in three phases, to be completed in 2010	Operators positioned to provide more than voice services as total solutions providers	Very technology savvy
	First mover in the creation of infrastructure	Pilot project for IPTV allowed by KBC and MIC	Willing to adopt new technologies
Japan	The u-Japan program which is moved towards the convergence of communication broadcasting and consumer electronics into a single network	Expand market power or move into new markets by merging with or acquiring another operator(s)	Technology savvy Willing to adopt new technologies
Australia	Slow regulatory reaction	Access to Telstra's fixed network is key	Willing to adopt new technologies if they are cost-effective
	Attempting to apply existing regulatory framework and only making changes as deemed necessary	Value-added services	
	Emphasis on industry self-regulation		
China	State-controlled competition	Competition based on service, no exclusivity of content	High demand for cost-effective services
	Government is fighting the push towards convergence in broadcast and telecommunications	Partnerships are forming to allow telecommunications operators in broadcast and broadcast operators in telecommunications	Huge market potential
	Convergence between telecommunications and broadcast is banned		Willingness to leapfrog technologies indicates a high interest in converged services

Source: (ITU 2007)

vertical monopolies may result. This will also raise the question of whether a natural monopoly will and should exist in the new market of converged services. Antitrust issues are only one of the challenging regulatory issues convergence has raised as regulators attempt to maintain quality and affordability as well as meet community standards for responsibility and accountability while nurturing the markets for these new services.

2 Literature Review

The high growth of telecommunications sector has been mainly because of the well-established notion that there is positive high degree of correlation between telecommunications and national development and secondly the felt need of telecommunications technology for holistic growth of the humanity. Beginning in 1960s, published papers of economists categorically cited a relationship between telephone density and GDP (Mowlana and Wilson 1990). Three important studies have been most influential in this regard. The International Telecommunication Union (ITU) in collaboration with the Organization of Economic Co-operation and Development (OECD) produced the first set of studies in the late 1970s. The result of the studies, later summarized in *Telecommunications for Development,* focused on the role of telecommunications in the process of development and especially in the development of the rural areas of the world's poor countries (Jipp 1963). The literature on flexibility, competitiveness and regulation is reviewed in the coming sub-section.

2.1 Flexibility

In Webster's Dictionary, "flexibility" is defined as "a ready capability to adapt to new, different or changing requirements." Because of the multitude of choices available to customers, today, flexibility is a key factor in business success. Not surprisingly then, it is suggested that the organizations should offer solutions for isolating, extending, and modifying the business rules that drive the processes within digital value chain (D'souza and Williams 2000; Porter 2001). Consequently, much research has demonstrated the importance of flexibility for firms to prosper in turbulent environments (Dreyer and Gronhaug 2004). Flexibility within a business context is a rather complex concept to define as it incorporates several dimensions (Shi and Daniels 2003). Traditionally, flexibility tended to focus on the ability of firms to adjust their manufacturing volumes to varying market demand. However, more recently, the concept of flexibility has been extended to incorporate the ability of firms to develop new products and enter new markets and industries (Dreyer and Gronhaug 2004). According to (Volberda 1996): "Flexibility is the degree to which an organization has a variety of managerial capabilities and the speed at which they can be activated, to increase the control capacity of management and improve the controllability of the organization." The concept of systemic flexibility has been deliberated by Sushil (1997, 1999, 2000).

All organizations face internal and external environment so the flexibility associated with them are also there, i.e., external and internal flexibility. *Ansoff* was one of the first authors to probe more deeply into the concept of flexibility. He suggested that firms need internal and external flexibility to cope with unforeseeable contingencies. According to him, "external flexibility is best described by the maxim of not putting all of one's eggs in a single basket" (Ansoff 1965). This type of flexibility can be achieved *defensively* through a product-market posture which is sufficiently diversified to minimize the effect of a catastrophe and/or *offensively* by putting the firm into areas in which it can benefit from likely breakthroughs. Offensive external flexibility is more elusive and harder to implement than defensive external flexibility, but it maximizes the chance of participating in breakthroughs.

2.1.1 Organizational Flexibility

The organization chart of a traditional enterprise had long been defined as a shrinking pyramid with the CEO at the top. The twenty-first century organisations have started looking like the Web – a horizontal mesh that connects partners, employees, external contractors, suppliers, and customers in various forms of collaborations. The players are likely to grow more and more independent. Tomorrow's corporations are likely to be highly virtual, defined not by their location; cooperation grows in the future due to three broad reasons: regulatory factors, changes in the business, and approach (Volberda 1998).

Organizational flexibility is imperative necessity for its own survival. To be a flexible organization, it, inter alia, should create/observe the following dimensions: First, creating a responsive internal environment that can quickly react to any change in the marketplace, planned or unforeseen, a threat or an opportunity. Second, an organization should have variable cost-dominated structure to manage costs in situation of growth of the organization or recession in industry or change in demand. Third, an organization needs to be focused on profitable and core activities to the enterprise's success. Finally, the organization needs to have a resilient infrastructure that is available around the world and round the clock (Phan 2001).

It is the dynamic environment that these systems routinely perform and create this demand. As a result, there is a reciprocating impact on customer needs that are continuously changing, which results in an exponential increase in complexity.

In order to remain competitive, these systems and the organizations that realize them have to have more options, which is a direct influence on flexibility. These options also create a strain on the resources of any system, both intellectual and physical. To address these constraints while maintaining a requirement for flexibility, the organizations that design these systems have to maintain a competitive advantage and by so doing rely heavily on the outsourcing of capabilities and resources. Outsourcing can enable an organization to be more competitive and offer the customers more value. However, outsourcing and the flexibility potentially propagates and introduces a new set of risks.

Flexible Workforce: The organization chart of a traditional enterprise had long been defined as a shrinking pyramid with the CEO at the top. To keep ahead of the steep new-product curve, it will be crucial for organizations to attract and retain the best thinkers. Companies will need to build a deep reservoir of talent – employees and free agents – to succeed in this new era (Amor 1999; Aalst 2000). Companies should be flexible enough to employ customer-focused people at every level of the organization and build processes that are simple to execute and flexible enough to change with changing times.

Organization Flexibility: The need for organization flexibility to accommodate a changing world is well understood. Today's high-velocity and competitive markets apply added pressure to adapt rapidly and perform at high levels. Organization is essentially a systemized whole consisting of interdependent and coordinated parts. Flexibility, however, centers on modification or adaptation. The more systemized and interdependent a group of humans is, the more difficult the change process. Thus, flexible organizations typically have been thought of as having less top-down control and more than an individual empowerment. Finally, many present-day theorists speak of the importance of possessing the dynamic resources and abilities necessary for rapid and effective action in business activities and decision-making. These action-oriented or kinetic capabilities are presented as essential complements to positional competitive advantages, a view that puts even further demands on the organization. Thus, organizational approaches are cornerstones or kinetic capabilities and are likely to be of primary importance for certain positional advantages, such as relationships with stakeholders. The flexibility in collaboration also refers to organizational flexibility as strategic alliances are more likely to involve competitors (Duysters et al. 2000). Contractor and Lorange (2002) suggest that the role of inter-organizational cooperation grows in the future due to three broad reasons: regulatory factors, changes in the business and economic environment, and changes in industry practice and strategy. Companies must have flexibility in their alliance strategies to allow them to form quickly and effectively virtual supply chains that may transcend industry and national boundaries overcoming regulatory hurdles. Also, intermediaries need to renew organizational skills, resources, and functional competencies to sustain the advantages that they build (Teece et al. 1997).

Flexibility in forming strategic alliances must address issues such as the following:

- The nature of collaboration – as the nature of competition becomes increasingly based on rapidly reconfigurable value chains (Rayport and Jaworski 2001).
- Mechanisms of quality assurance – Digital intermediaries, which assure quality for the company's products and services, should be considered strategic partners

because they can play a critical role in building brand image and enhancing customer satisfaction and loyalty.

The capacity of forming collaboration and alliances maintaining a strong brand image is possible only when companies can afford to be flexible in strategies related to the above issues. Flexible organizations mandate that business processes are integrated end to end, enabling it to respond with flexibility and speed to any customer demand, market opportunity, or external threat (Sethi and Sethi 1990; Shi and Daniels 2003). As organizations use real-time information to accelerate an increasing number of business processes, flexibility and adaptability become fundamental requirements for supporting today's – and tomorrow's – business imperatives (Davidson 1999).

2.1.2 Technical Flexibility

Technical flexibility refers to freedom of choice an organization possesses in terms of technology platforms available. Once the enabling technologies are flexible enough to quickly adapt to a changing market environment, it is important to create flexibility in core processes of technology-related business processes. Many studies in the past have shown that organizations can use technology as a resource to gain competitive advantage (Clemons and Row 1991; Parsons 1983). Technology, which is the primary force behind the emergence of the new economy, has become not only a means of production but also a main component of service, relationship building, collaboration, and coexistence. In this context, the importance of flexibility in technology cannot be overemphasized. Byrd and Turner (2001) identify several dimensions of technological flexibility such as data transparency, compatibility, application functionality, connectivity, technical skills, boundary skills, functional skills, and technology management. They also observe that flexibility in technology as measured by integration, modularity, and IT personnel flexibility is positively correlated to an organization's innovativeness, mass customization, market position, and difficulty to duplicate. Malhotra (2001) identifies technology flexibility as the ability to cope with the integration of new e-business applications with the existing brick-and-mortar infrastructures. Such integration entails flawless fusion of enterprise resource planning, supply chain management, and customer relationship management, which is not possible without having integration standards, network capacity, data storage capacity, and processing power. Gronhaug (1999) links technological flexibility with product and services flexibility by using the open-system metaphor (Katz and Kahn 1966) in which organizations are viewed as input-throughput-output systems. Flexibility in formulating and executing a technology strategy, which is critical to achieving a sustained competitive advantage for firms in the new market environment, must address such issues as impact of technological change within the organization and impact of technological change on the market; technological changes can exert a huge impact on the market by directly affecting the size and nature of customers, partners/suppliers competitors, and products. In order to provide the flexibility, scalability, and reliability required of mobile telephony, service companies need to create a flexible e-business infrastructure. This infrastructure should consist of open interfaces that allow new applications and services to easily connect. The flexible e-business infrastructure should include universal connectivity through the use of open standards and integration with internal and external services. Universal connectivity through the use of open standards implies that companies must allow customers, business partners, suppliers, and influencers to have access to systems and applications with a variety of access devices available. Having interoperability to allow sharing or communicating with mixed technologies across and beyond the enterprise is an important success factor and technology infrastructure should have capability to integrate internal and external services seamlessly. By integrating business applications and data among customers, suppliers, partners, and employees, companies can achieve a more effective and efficient e-business model. Enabling integration is accomplished by using open standards-based infrastructure elements in conjunction with an integration, which allows existing application functionality to be integrated with the new application logic (Shi and Daniels 2003). Byrd and Turner (2001) identify several dimensions of technological flexibility such as data transparency, compatibility, application functionality, connectivity, technical skills, boundary skills, functional skills, and technology management. They also observe that flexibility in technology (measured by integration, modularity, and IT personnel flexibility) is positively correlated to an organization's innovativeness, mass customization, market position, and difficulty to duplicate. Malhotra (2001) identifies technology flexibility as the ability to cope with the integration of new e-business applications with the existing brick-and-mortar infrastructures. Such integration entails flawless fusion of enterprise resource planning and supply chain management.

2.1.3 Operations Flexibility

For consistent customer service and applications, customer data must be integrated with different databases and applications (Oliver 2001). The integration of applications, processes, and data creates a single view of the customer, prevents discrepancies in customer data, and ensures consistent service of the customer, no matter the channel. In addition, any employee who interacts with customers, no matter where they are in the organization, can access any customer information necessary in order to provide superior service (Papazoglou et al. 2000).

Operational flexibility of organizations encompasses people, process, and structure, where operations of an organization is planned, processed, and executed. Volberda (1998) explained that operational flexibility required for changes which are familiar and often led to a temporary change in the activity of level of organization. In the case of operational flexibility, there is no substantial shift in the relationship between an organization and its environment. For consistent customer service applications, customer data must be integrated with different databases and applications (Oliver 2001).

2.1.4 Strategic Flexibility

Strategic flexibility has been considered by previous research in strategic management, economics, organization theory, and marketing. Strategic flexibility (or nonroutine steering capacity) refers to capabilities related to the goals of the organization. This most radical type of flexibility is more qualitative and involves changes in the nature of organizational activities. Such flexibility is necessary when the organization faces unfamiliar change that has far-reaching consequences and needs to be responded quickly. Eppink (1978) explained that strategic flexibility is necessary to compensate for strategic changes which originate in the indirect environment of the organization and reach it via the components of its direct environment. They require immediate attention to prevent the organization from being seriously affected. Eppink (1978) concludes that strategic flexibility is a new area but that organizations are increasingly confronted with strategic change.

Strategic flexibility (high variety, high speed) consists of managerial capabilities related to the goals of the organization or the environment (Aaker and Mascarenhas 1984). The issues and difficulties relating to strategic flexibility are by definition unstructured and nonroutine. The signals and feedback received from the environment tend to be indirect and open to multiple interpretations, "soft" and "fuzzy." Because the organization usually has no specific experience and no routine answer for coping with the changes, management may have to change its game plans, dismantle its current strategies (Harrigan 1985), apply new technologies, or fundamentally renew its products. Its response may also be external, e.g., influencing consumers through advertising and promotions creating new product-market combinations using market power to deter entry and control competitors (Porter 1980) or engaging in political activities management. Strategic flexibility is used by Sushil (2012) as a fountain head of the framework of flowing stream strategy.

2.1.5 Marketing Flexibility

Market is a place where buyers and sellers meet to transfer their products and services for some considerations. Therefore, marketplace has many actors interrelated to each other through different processes to achieve their desired objectives. Companies – an actor in marketplace – are required to be flexible in their product offerings as one variety (or even a few) is (are) not likely to be adequate to cater to the varying needs, tastes, and expectations of an increasingly segmented and global customer base. Flexibility, in this context, refers to the ability of a company to meet this challenge within the overall framework of its business strategy. The capacity and speed of product innovation is an attribute of such flexibility.

2.1.6 Financial Flexibility

The concept of flexibility has basically developed in the context of manufacturing systems and organizational systems. As regards financial management systems, the need and raison d'etre of flexibility has drawn increased attention of professionals only in the recent years. New concept in this area real options and their interaction with the financial flexibility of the firm have been reviewed by Trigeorgis (1993). In the concept of financial management, Gupta (1983) has aptly underlined the significance of flexibility. The balance sheet can be used primarily for assessing the vulnerability of an enterprise in terms of the strength and flexibility of its financial frame which can be best thought as a kind of constraint ring surrounding the enterprise.

Flexibility in financial management refers to liberation of the financial management from the clutches of the strict normative framework for providing freedom of choice to financial managers. Financial flexibility can be defined as "exercise of the freedom of choice within the framework of government's monetary and fiscal policies, capital market regulation, investor's risk returns preferences and corporate strategy, evolving financial processes with versatility, adaptiveness and transparency for better resonance with business environment" (Jain and Sushil 2000).

The investment decisions will be governed by the growth strategy adopted by the organization and matching of the project with corporate strategies and core competencies. This is further compounded by the interplay of "financial flexibility" in terms of capital availability, sources of finances, and the cost of capital.

Flexibility in capital structure process is concerned with exercise of the freedom of choice to dynamically interplay among the various sources of financial providers of fund (individual and institutional investors from the country and abroad) and various financial instruments, keeping in the view the conditions prevalent in financial markets, government regulations in vogue, and firm's own financial profile.

Flexibility in dividend decisions, being open to various policy options as well as different modes of implementation, provides leverage to the decision-maker in terms of speed of adjustment, taking care of extreme financial position of the firm and the liquidity crisis. This will prove to be more "investor friendly" and thereby contribute towards price enhancement of the share, eventually furthering the value of the firm.

2.2 Competitiveness

Firms operating in today's economy are experiencing increased pressures due to several factors including a rapidly changing business environment, shorter product life cycles, increasing demanding and less loyal customers with rapidly evolving preferences, and fiercer competition (Dreyer and Gronhaug 2004). These trends are motivated by an increasingly global economy, deregulation in many industries, and fast developments in information technologies that enable new business models and novel forms of collaboration and competition. This is especially the case for firms that operate within an online environment (such as mobile telephony) which is characterized by lower switching costs, lower barriers to entry, more substitution threats, quickly changing regulations, and increased competition due to lower differentiation and increased geographic reach (Porter 2001).

"Competitiveness" originated from the Latin world, *competer*, which means involvement in a business rivalry for markets. Competitiveness is a complex, multi-dimensional, and relative concept. It is linked to a large number of interdependent variables, thus, making it difficult to sense and define it. Defining and measuring competitiveness is itself a research challenge. It is being relative concept without bearing any direct relationship with economic performance indicators. Competitiveness has been dealt with by coining two separate but related concepts, viz., comparative advantage and competitive advantage. Competitive advantage corresponds to the notion of firm-specific assets and describes the proprietary elements of the firm that determines what activities it should undertake and what distinguishes it from its competitors. The real difference between these two terms in existing literature seems to lie in their levels of analysis. While the literature on comparative advantage deals with the issue of competitiveness of nations and their industries, writers on competitive advantage are more concerned with firm level.

The competitiveness has been getting importance in the USA towards the latter half of the twentieth century. Declining competitiveness of USA in the early 1980s can be attributed to macroeconomic factors. The firm-level behavior is strongly influenced by macroeconomic factors. For example, short-term profit orientation of US firms in this era resulted into high cost of capital due to low private saving. The rising competitiveness of Japan in international trade was interlinked with macroeconomic factors, such as long-run productivity growth, higher savings and investment rates, governments emphasis on quantity and quality of education, and investment in public infrastructure (Baumol and McLennan 1985). Some authors (Vernon 1966; Krugman 1983, 1986; Porter 1990) have argued that while factor advantages were important in the eighteenth and nineteenth centuries, economies of scale, technological change, comparable factor endowments, cheaper transportation costs, and inflow of foreign capital and other factors have pushed firms towards factor-exploiting advantages of multiple nations, thus leading to the emergence of a large number of multinational firms. Some writers (Borrus 1983; Tyson 1988, 1992) have given prominence to the role of the government. It is noteworthy to see that in NICs (newly industrialized countries), governments have nurtured infant industries and shaped competitiveness of firms in these industries to gradually enter the global market and gain prominence. The market promotion policy of the government has been focused on those industries that have spillover effect over entire economy because of "linkage externality" (Krugman 1987) and on which the future competitive success of various industries depend (Tyson 1988).

Competitiveness is also defined as the accumulation of competitiveness of firms operating in nation's boundary cutting across industries or group of industries (Papadakis 1994). Researchers have conceptualized firm-level competitiveness as competitive position of a firm vis à vis its competitors in international markets. This is determined by three sets of interrelated factors, namely, delivered costs. Porter argues that the role played by comparative factor advantage is there but there exist competitive industries in many countries not endowed with comparative advantage in the relevant factors (Porter 1990). Classic example of this argument is Japan. Some writers (Hays and Wheelright 1983) attribute the competitiveness problem and challenges of USA to micro (firm-level) developments, such as lower emphasis on manufacturing and operations, product and process innovation, short-term orientation of corporate managers, and less emphasis on technology development.

2.3 Regulation

In a few short decades, radical changes in technology, market institutions, and regulatory and competition policy have transformed telecommunications markets. Telecommunications service traditionally meant "voice communication"; however, the term now encompasses audio (voice), data (fax and email), and video (graphics and multimedia). It is common to refer to these forms of electronic communication as the "triple play" when made available from a single provider. With these changes, the phenomenon of "convergence" has emerged as both the principal offspring and driver of the technology-market-policy triad. Convergence is bringing together previously disparate communication services, content, and consumer market segments.

This phenomenon raises questions about the future of communications and, in particular, about that of voice communication particularly (1) what place will voice communication have in the converged world of electronic communication? and (2) how will regulation and competition policy shape the environment in which voice communication services will be provided and consumed?

3 Trends in Regulation and Policy

The trends in regulation and deregulation have been of the trigger to change and adopt various measures. The following is the list of issue related to such trends:

- Protect public interests from anticompetitive behaviors of industries and growing cyber crimes.
- Face convergence of ICTs in not mere technologies and services but also legislation and institutions.
- Undertake sector reform or reengineering through liberalization or privatization.
- Ensure fair competition or competition safeguard.
- Be aware of digital divide in ICT infrastructure and applications not only between countries but also within the country.
- Increasing concerns over private anticompetitive practices led by liberalization or privatization.

- Some 80 countries (inc. 50 developing ones) adopted competition policy including laws and other measures to promote competition in the national economy through dealing with price fixing, cartel arrangements, abuses of a dominant position or monopolization, and mergers that limit competition.
- Developing a multilateral framework on competition and e-commerce policy within the WTO is under the review.

The privacy laws, cyber law, dispute settlement over domain names, and certificate authority began to be introduced in the advent of Internet and e-commerce.

3.1 Regulatory Trends for Spectrum Management

In the current situation, the general approach of spectrum regulators remains one of "command and control," where changing uses of spectrum is a deliberative process involving study and opportunities for public comment. However, we can recognize some trends towards a more flexible approach.

3.2 Legal Trends

- Establish new telecom or ICT legislation.
- Modify the existing telecom laws or regulations.
- Harmonize or improve legal environments and frameworks to reflect convergence and its implications in advent of the Internet, e.g.:

- Data protection/privacy, intellectual property rights
- Security (e.g., authentication, digital signatures)
- Harmful and illegal content (e.g., child pornography)
- Domain names and their standardization
- Jurisdiction and cross-border issues
- Cyber crime (e.g., virus, fraud)

3.3 Global Trends on Legislative Reforms

- Over 150 countries have introduced new telecom legislation or modified existing regulations to introduce competition, establish regulatory authority, and privatize the incumbent and/or accommodate convergence of ICT.
- Further changes are anticipated to fit the new realities of convergence.
- Legislation on interconnection.

Table 5.3 provides recently revised ICT legislation in Asia and Fig. 5.1 gives the global trend of regulatory bodies.

Table 5.3 Revised ICT legislation in Asia

Recently revised ICT legislation in Asia

Countries	Years	Laws
India	1999	Telecommunications Policy
	2000	Information Technology Act
China	1997/8	Regulations
Hong Kong	2000	Telecommunications Ordinance (Rev)
		Broadcasting Ordinance (Rev)
Malaysia	1998	Communications & Multimedia Act
		Communications & Multimedia Commission Act
Singapore	1998	Electronic Transactions Act
	1999	Telecom Act
Thailand	1999	Corporatization Law
	Pending	Frequency Bill

{Source: ITU, *Asia-Pacific Telecommunication Indicators, 2000*}

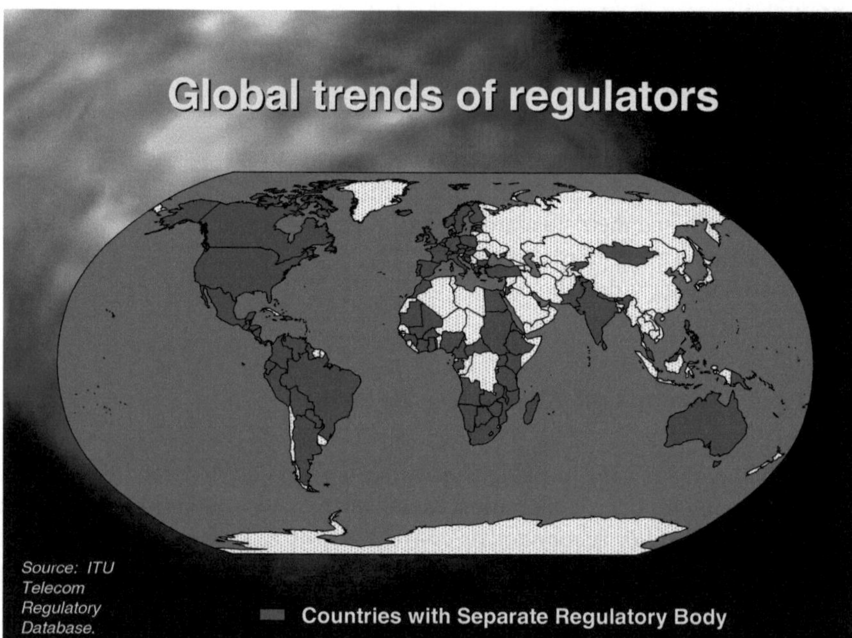

Fig. 5.1 Global trend of regulatory bodies

3.4 Regulatory Trends in India

As mentioned above, India made commitments under the General Agreement on Trade in Services (GATS) to review further opening up of national long-distance service in the year 1999. This commitment was reinforced by the NTP 1999, which declared that the market for domestic long distance (DLD) should be opened up to competition by January 2000. This, however, has yet to occur. The NTP 1999 requested the TRAI to make recommendations to the government in this regard. The TRAI released its discussion paper in September 1999 and announced its recommendations in December 1999. The Telecom Commission has not yet announced the government's definitive policy but this is expected by April 2000. The main elements of the TRAI's recommendations on DLD competition are as follows:

- Creation of a multiplayer environment.
- Competition limited to facilities-based players.
- Entry fee of a one-time Rs.5 billion, with Rs.1 billion in cash and the rest as bank guarantee ensuring rollout.
- Revenue-sharing scheme of 5 %.
- A phased network rollout plan with obligatory coverage of 15–100 % of the total long-distance charging areas in the first 2–7 years.
- Equal access and interconnection to be provided immediately. Thus far, the DoT/DTS has agreed to the separation of accounts proposed by the TRAI in order to set up a distinct long-distance operator. However, it has objected to both the open competition and the recommended level of revenue sharing, set at 5 % of the licensee's revenue, which it considers suboptimal. It is not eager to pay license fees equal to that of private long-distance operators. It argues that India's telecommunications policy does not require the payment of license fees for basic fixed telecommunications.
- Another important regulatory development relates to the government's policy on Internet service providers. The policy stated that ISPs should be allowed to operate their own international gateways and thus be able to lease either satellite transponder or submarine cable capacity for connection to the Internet backbones in other countries. Although the ISP policy was released in 1998, it is only as recently as February 2000 that private ISPs have been given official clearance for setting up international gateways.

3.4.1 Current Status Regulation

The Indian government has also been setting new policy targets, in an effort to modernize the telecommunications sector. The policy also aims to create a modern and efficient telecommunications infrastructure taking account the convergence of electronics, telecom, IT, and media. It commits to a strong and independent regulator and proposes new targets for telecommunications network development. In response to the TRAI's recommendations dated August 29, 2007, DoT announced changes in the telecom policy. The key highlights of the new policy are as follows:

- Removal of cap on the number of access providers in any service area
- Permission to existing UASL operators to provide wireless services using alternate technology
- Implementation of new subscriber norms for allocation of spectrum

3.4.2 Recent Regulations in India

During the year 2011–2012, TRAI issued the following regulations:

(i) The Telecom Commercial Communications Customer Preference (Sixth Amendment) Regulations, 2011 (5 of 2011), dated September 05, 2011
(ii) The Telecom Commercial Communications Customer Preference (Seventh Amendment) Regulations, 2011 (6 of 2011), dated October 25, 2011
(iii) The Telecom Commercial Communications Customer Preference (Eight Amendment) Regulations, 2011 (7 of 2011) dated November 01, 2011
(iv) Telecom Consumers Complaint Redressal Regulations, 2012, dated January 05, 2012
(v) Telecom Consumers Protection Regulations, 2012 (2 of 2012), dated January 06
(vi) Telecom Consumers Complaint Redressal (Amendment) Regulations, 2012 (3 of 2012), dated January 12, 2012
(vii) Telecom Consumers Protection (Amendment) Regulations, 2012 (4 of 2012), dated January 12, 2012 Annual Report 2011–2012
(viii) Telecom Consumers Protection (Second Amendment) Regulations 2012 (5 of 2012) dated February 21, 2012
(ix) Telecom Consumers Protection (Third Amendment) Regulations, 2012 dated March 09, 2012

4 A Case of Indian Telecom Mobile Service Industry

4.1 Industry Overview

The telecom sector continued to register an impressive growth during the year. The number of telephone subscriptions increased from 846.32 million to 951.34 million, registering a growth of 12.41 %. The wireless subscriber base increased by 107.58 million and the wire-line subscriber base recorded a decline of 2.56 million. The wireless segment continued to dominate with a total base of 919.17 million connections. The overall teledensity in the country increased to 78.66 from 70.89. The rural teledensity increased to 39.22 from 33.79.

The growth in subscriber base resulted in an increase in the gross revenue of telecom services from Rs.1,71,719 crore to Rs.1,95,442 crore during the year, a growth of 13.82 %. At the same time, the minutes of usage (MOU) per subscriber per month for GSM and CDMA full mobility service registered a decline from 349 and 263 at the end of March 2011 to 346 and 229 at the end of March 2012, respectively. The average outgo per outgoing minute decreased from Rs.0.51 to Rs.0.49 (a fall of 3.08 %) for GSM full mobility service and the average outgo per outgoing minute remained at Rs.0.47 for CDMA full mobility service during the period. The average revenue per user per month (ARPU) which at the end of March 2011 was Rs.100/- in case of GSM full mobility service decreased to Rs.97/- at the end of March 2012. The monthly ARPU in respect of CDMA full mobility service increased from Rs.66/ to Rs.75/- per month during the same period. Resultantly, the earnings before interest, tax, depreciation, and amortization (EBITDA) for the telecom sector in 2011–2012 was Rs.23,221 crore, as against Rs.23,266 crore in the previous year indicating a decline of 0.19 %. The EBITDA margin declined from 13.95 % in 2010–2011 to 12.91 % in 2011–2012. The capital employed in the sector decreased from Rs.3,37,683 crore in 2010–2011 to Rs.3,21,375 crore in 2011–2012, i.e., a decrease of 4.83 %.

Low Initial Demand for Mobile Services: Mobile telecom services were introduced in India in late 1995 and were marked by low demand and high tariffs, due to large license-fee commitments and capital expenditure requirements of service providers. In March 1998, there were merely 0.88 million mobile subscribers in the country, over half of these being from Delhi and Mumbai.

"NTP 1999" Dialed in Accelerated Growth from 1999 to 2003: The National Telecom Policy, 1999, revolutionized the industry by allowing a shift from a fixed license-fee regime to a revenue-share regime, thereby attracting more players to the market. Consequently, the mobile services industry began to look up and added 0.7 million customers to its base in 1999–2000. The growth accelerated in 2000–2001 with an additional 1.7 million subscribers. In 2001–2002, net additions of the industry increased to 2.9 million and further to 6.7 million in 2002–2003.

In 2002–2003, BSNL launched its services as the third operator across many circles, followed by fourth operators. This, along with the consequent decline in tariffs, accelerated growth, with the total number of mobile subscribers now going up to 13.8 million in March 2003.

The year 2003–2004 witnessed phenomenal growth in the industry with an addition of over 20 million subscribers. This can be attributed to the Calling Party Pays (CPP) regime implemented in May 2003, which made incoming calls free and the launch of services by Reliance Infocomm. While the CPP regime brought more low-usage customers into the mobile telephony fold, Reliance Infocomm lowered entry barriers for mobile services with schemes such as "Monsoon Hungama."

In 2004–2005, the mobile industry witnessed an addition of 21.4 million customers which was lower than the net additions in 2003–2004. This was because Reliance Infocomm disconnected around 1 million subscribers after checks for credit worthiness and customer verification. Moreover, there were no significant growth triggers during this year. However, 2004–2005 turned out to be momentous because by the end of the year, the total mobile subscriber base reached 56.97 million, which outnumbered the total fixed subscriber base. The ratio of fixed to mobile subscribers dropped down from 0.7 times in 2004–2005 to 0.4 times in 2005–2006.

In 2005–2006, the total telecom subscriber base increased by 43.6 million to reach 140.4 million. The mobile subscriber base went up by 43.5 million subscribers whereas fixed services added 0.13 million subscribers during the year. The launch of a 2-year incoming-free scheme by Tata Teleservices and the introduction of lifetime-validity scheme triggered growth, thereby pushing net additions to cross the 4 million mark.

In 2006–2007, the total telecom subscriber base went up by 66.5 million and reached 206.8 million. In June 2006, the government introduced a policy wherein fixed wireless subscribers were included in the mobile segment and fixed wire-line subscribers would alone constitute the fixed telephony segment. As a result, the total wireless segment (mobile plus fixed wireless) went up by 67.2 million subscribers reaching 166.05 million in March 2007 and again soared up by 19.08 million to reach 185.13 million in June 2007. Fixed wire line continued the past year's trend and declined by 0.8 million to reach 40.8 million, as of March 2007. In 2006–2007, the average monthly wireless subscriber net addition was 5.7 million.

Mobile phone subscribers are classified into prepaid and postpaid subscribers. While postpaid subscribers pay for usage of services at the end of the billing period, prepaid subscribers pay a fixed amount in advance for which they get corresponding talk time valid for a certain period.

Between 1999–2000 and 2003–2004, the number of postpaid subscribers as a proportion of total GSM subscriber base witnessed a secular decline. In 2004–2005, the number of postpaid subscribers increased for the first time which is believed to be a result of the aggressive cut in rentals on postpaid services by many operators. This was reflected in the sharp decline in postpaid ARPU in 2004–2005. In 2005–2006, the share of postpaid subscribers went down again to 13 % but picked up in 2006–2007 to reach 16 %.

On the other hand, the share of prepaid subscribers climbed up from 81 % in 2005–2006 to 87 % in 2006–2007. The upward trend of subscribers in the prepaid segment was an outcome of the relaunch of lifetime-validity prepaid scheme by various mobile network operators, available at a minimum charge of Rs.495 as against Rs.999 introduced last year.

Over the last 5 years, while the number of postpaid subscribers expanded at a CAGR of 43 %, the prepaid segment grew at a CAGR of 94 %.

Mobile phone services were initially launched in the metros, which accounted for almost the entire mobile subscriber base and thus the net additions in the first 2 years of operation. Among the metros, Delhi and Mumbai accounted for a substantial portion of the net additions.

However, this scenario changed after the launch of services in nonmetro circles; the share of metros in the total subscriber addition came down from 92 % in 1996–1997 to 42 % in 1997–1998. Category-A circles accounted for 30 % of the net additions, category B for 25 %, and category C for 3 percent in 1997–1998. This trend continued up to 2001–2002. Metros continued to lead the net additions followed by category-A circles. Thus, metros continued to enjoy the largest market share in terms of the total outstanding subscriber base at the end of 2001–2002.

The year 2002–2003 witnessed a change in trend, and category-A and category-B circles surged forward in net additions. Category-A circles led the growth, accounting for around 37.8 % and 38.6 % of the total net additions in 2002–2003 and 2003–2004, respectively. While metros and category-B circles accounted for around 29 % of the total net additions at the end of 2002–2003, category-A circles surpassed the metro circles with a subscriber base of around 4.6 million. Whereas, in 2003–2004, metros continued to grow at 30.1 %, category-B circles experienced a decline in net additions at 27.5 %.

In 2004–2005, category-A circles accounted for the highest proportion of net additions of 34.9 % while the share of metro circles fell quite steeply to 23.3 %. The share of category-C circles, on the other hand, jumped appreciably from around 4 % in the past few years to 7.7 %. In terms of total subscriber base, category A continued to be the highest with a market share of 36.5 %. Category B ranked second with a market share of 29.7 % at 16.4 subscribers. The metros slipped to the third position where its market share stood at 28.5 % accounting for 15.7 million subscribers.

In 2005–2006, category-B circle accounted for the highest proportion of total net additions with 36.1 % of the total net additions, followed by category-A circle at 33.5 %. Category C saw a jump in total net additions, contributing 11.1 % as against 7.7 % in 2004–2005.

In 2006–2007, category-B circles maintained the ace position accounting for net additions of 39.8 %, followed by category A with a share of 35.9 %. However, category-C circle overtook metros in terms of share of net additions, standing at 12.2 %. Metros continued the downward trend and reached 12.1 %.

In 2006–2007, category-A and category-B circles stood at almost the same level of around 35.5 % in terms of total subscriber market share. Metros followed both, placed at 19.5 %. Category-C circle had a market share of 9.6 %.

4.2 *Mobile Penetration by States*

In India, mobile teledensity varies significantly between different circles. Delhi has the highest teledensity, followed by Chennai, while Bihar and West Bengal circles rank the lowest. Broadly, the relative teledensity in different circles corresponds to per capita GDP in a particular circle. States with higher per capita GDP have a higher penetration and vice versa.

4.3 Subscribers by Technology

GSM being the most widespread technology worldwide, mobile services in India were initially provided on GSM and all mobile licensees had to base their services on this technology.

The basic service operators were permitted to provide limited mobility services based on CDMA technology only in 2001. However, limited mobility services were more or less in competition with full-fledged mobile services. This led to disputes between mobile network operators and basic service operators hampering investments and growth of the sector. Subsequently, TRAI introduced Unified Access Service Licence (UASL) in November 2003 wherein a UASL licensee was permitted to provide access services based on any technology. Furthermore, the basic service operator was provided the option of converting to UASL by paying the requisite fees. Pursuant to this, all basic service operators providing limited mobility services converted to UASL and presently provide mobile services based on CDMA technology.

The GSM mobile subscriber base increased significantly at a CAGR of 79.9 % from 3.6 million in March 2001 to around 121.4 million in March 2007, accounting for around 73.1 % of the total mobile subscriber base in India.

Though CDMA operators were late entrants in the mobile services market, the share of CDMA subscribers (including WLL-F subscribers) in the total mobile subscriber base increased from a meager 0.03 % in March 2001 to 26.9 % in March 2007. This was brought about by aggressive schemes launched by Reliance Communications and Tata Teleservices.

4.3.1 Current Scenario of GSM and CDMA Services in India

The GSM subscribers were 808.80 million at the end of September 2012 as against 831.86 million at the quarter ending June 2012, showing a negative growth of 2.77 %. Bharti with 185.92 million subscribers continues to be the largest GSM mobile operator, followed by Vodafone (152.66 million).

The CDMA subscriber base further declined from 102.24 million at the end of Jun-12 to 97.82 million at the end of Sept-12, thereby showing a negative growth rate of 4.32 %. Reliance with 54.49 million subscribers continues to be the largest CDMA mobile operator. However, in terms of net additions during the quarter, only Sistema showed a positive growth, rest of the service providers recorded decline in subscribers.

4.4 All-India ARPU

The All-India blended average revenue per user (ARPU) per month has shown an increase of 3.80 % from Rs.74.91 in QE June 2012 to Rs.77.76 in QE September 2012.

ARPU for prepaid service increased by 1.61 % from Rs.47 in QE June 2012 to Rs.48 in QE September 2012. ARPU for postpaid service has also increased by 1.21 % from Rs.449 in QE June 2012 to Rs.454 in QE September 2012 as per TRAI (2012).

4.5 Industry Structure

Traditionally, services in the telecommunications sector – local as well as national and international long distance – were monopolized by state-owned organizations. Though BSNL and MTNL both provided fixed (basic) services, domestic long-distance services were taken care of by BSNL while VSNL catered to international long-distance services. As the need for developing the telecom sector to promote economic growth was felt and given the government's financial constraints to meet the sector's resource requirements, the central government threw open the doors to private players. Although the mobile services segment had private player participation from the advent itself, other services were opened up subsequently.

4.6 Migration from Fixed License-Fee Regime to Revenue-Sharing Regime (Flexibility to Operators)

In July 1999, private telecommunications operators were offered the option to change the basis of license-fee payment from a fixed amount to a share of revenues. However, these concessions were subject to operators accepting a set of conditions, which included the following:

- The existing cellular operators had to clear all their outstanding dues by January 2000 (effective August 1999).
- The new license agreement would not have the clause relating to exclusiveness of the license. This meant more operators could be provided licenses in future to offer cellular services.

All private telecommunications operators accepted the terms of migration to a revenue-sharing arrangement effective August 01, 1999 and the license fee paid till July 1999 by the existing cellular operators was treated as entry fee. The provisional license fee for all categories of circles was fixed at 15 % of gross revenue, according to the license agreement with the Department of Telecommunication (DoT).

In September 2001, the DoT changed the license-fee payable by the existing or future cellular service providers with retrospective effect from January 26, 2001 to 12 % of AGR (adjusted gross revenue) for metropolitan areas and category-A circles and for categories B and C, it was at 10 % and 8 %, respectively.

4.7 Third and Fourth Cellular Licenses

The government allotted third cellular operator's license for Mumbai and Delhi to MTNL and for the rest of India to BSNL. While MTNL commenced cellular services in Delhi and Mumbai during February 2001, BSNL started operating in Kolkata, Tamil Nadu, and Bihar in July 2002. For the remaining circles, it introduced cellular services in November 2002.

The government issued licenses for cellular services corresponding to the fourth operators' slot in October 2001. Licenses were issued to the Bharti Group in eight circles, Escotel in four, Hutchison Essar in three, and Reliance (through Reliable Internet) and Idea Cellular in one circle each. The entry fee for the fourth cellular license in the four metros and 13 circles aggregated Rs.16.33 billion. The highest quoted fee was Rs.2,060 million for Karnataka. Almost all operators holding the fourth cellular license commenced services during 2002–2003.

4.8 Limited Mobility Services

The technology used by limited mobility service providers is the CDMA-based wireless in local loop (WLL) platform. Limited mobility is a facility offered by basic service operators whereby a fixed-line telephone connection can be used like a cellular service within a short distance calling area (SDCA) with the help of a handset similar to a mobile handset. As compared with full-fledged cellular services, limited mobility has lesser features and does not provide roaming facility which allows subscribers to access the network in other areas.

It was only after a long tussle between basic service operators and cellular service providers that the Telecom Dispute Settlement Appellate Tribunal gave a green signal to the introduction of limited mobility service by basic service companies. The Department of Telecommunication included WLL services in the wireless segment effective June 2006.

4.9 Unified Access Licensing Regime (Flexibility to Operator)

Limited mobility services were in direct competition with full-fledged mobile services, on account of two reasons: first, only a small proportion of the mobile subscribers used roaming services and second, one of the operators used techniques such as call forwarding and multiple registration, which effectively resulted in the subscriber getting roaming facility.

As the license fee paid by the limited mobility providers (the basic service operators) was substantially lower than that of the cellular providers, they could price their services at lower price. This led to litigation between the full-fledged cellular service providers and the basic service providers. The disputes resulted in the operators, particularly the GSM operators, holding back their investment plans and growth of the industry suffered.

The government, however, brought an end to this conflict in November 2003 by introducing the Unified Access Service Licence (UASL) wherein licensees could access services based on any technology. The guidelines of the UASL state that in order to migrate to UASL in any circle, a basic operator would have to pay an amount equivalent to the difference between the entry fees paid by four cellular operators and him. On the other hand, cellular licensees were not required to pay any additional amount to migrate to UASL. Reliance Communications and Tata Teleservices migrated to UASL soon after UASL was implemented by paying the prescribed entry fee of Rs.15.42 billion and Rs.5.45 billion, respectively, to the government and began offering full-fledged mobile services to their subscribers.

4.10 Tariff Structure

As mentioned earlier, the minimum subscription cost is a combination of cost of handsets and the monthly charge paid by subscribers to use the service. The average monthly outflow incurred by a subscriber, i.e., average revenue per user, is a combination of per minute tariff paid and the total minutes used by the subscriber in a month. Over the last few years, the per minute tariff charged by the subscriber has fallen drastically due to economies of scale achieved by operators owing to rising subscriber base, continuously declining cost of capital equipments, and intense competition in the market place.

5 Proposed Conceptual Framework

The proposed framework for the regulation of telecom sector of India based on flexibilities provided to organization by regulators of India enhances competitiveness, i.e., the framework proposes that the resultant flexibility affects the overall competitiveness of the organization manifested in four perspectives of the organization as shown in Fig. 5.2. The important variables in the conceptual framework are as follows.

5.1 External Flexibilities

This relates to external dimension of the strategy that ensures the ability of an organization to grow despite insecurity and turbulence and capitalize on emerging opportunities while maintaining a focus on existing customer, market, and

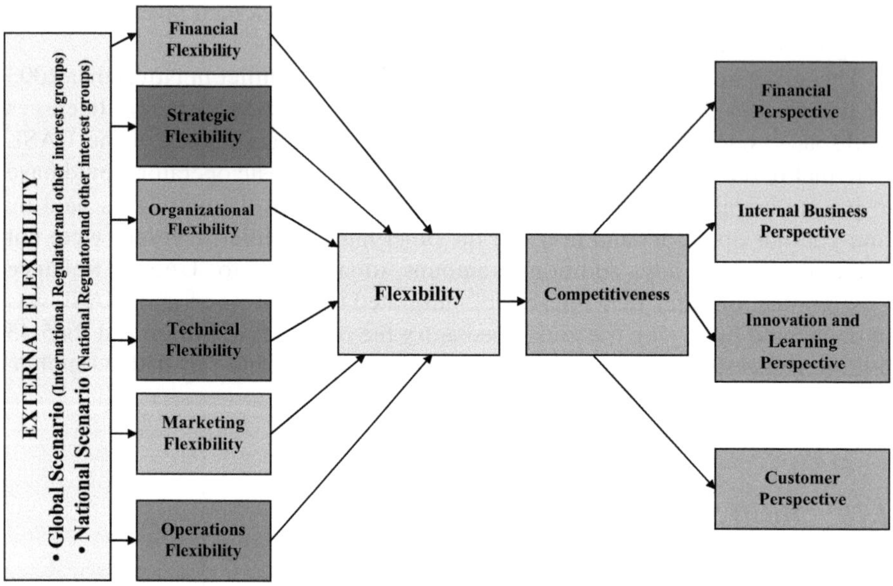

Fig. 5.2 Conceptual framework for flexibility and competitiveness

suppliers. This type of flexibility also originates from regulatory mechanism from the regulators and government departments of the country dealing with the industry segment. This flexibility is also affected by international scenario/global regional scenario/own country scenario in terms of technology available, integration of international regulators, and global service provider in mobile telecommunications sector.

5.2 *Internal Flexibilities*

These flexibilities are related to the internal dimension of the strategy. Internal flexibility of the organizations ensures that the different organizational subunits and linkages continue to work together efficiently even while the organization renews itself for the new operations, market, or customer. The following are the internal flexibilities taken up in the proposed framework:

- Strategic flexibility
- Organizational flexibility
- Technical flexibility
- Marketing flexibility
- Operations flexibility
- Financial flexibility
- Customer perspective

5.3 Competitiveness Perspectives of the Organization

The competitiveness perspectives are based on balanced score card (Kaplan and Norton 1993, 1996a, b) as given below:

- Financial perspective
- Internal business perspective
- Innovation and learning perspective
- Customer perspective

6 Conclusion

The transition from monopoly to competition in telecommunications is well underway in the vast majority of countries and largely completed in many countries. The transition has proved beneficially transformational and has set in motion further dynamic changes that are delivering a vastly expanded set of global opportunities in electronic communications. These opportunities are again positively transformational and are covered in the term convergence. But in order to participate in and maximize the benefits of convergence, a new regulatory framework has to be put into place in India. The new regulatory framework must address the legacy of the earlier transition period while supporting investments in the new period and facilitating new investments in the new market space. Clearly a level playing field would be most advantageous, i.e., an integration of existing regulatory frameworks into a single framework that is coherent across the entire electronic communications market space.

The convergence further call for convergence of regulators and policymakers in India as it happened in Thailand, i.e., (a) the Science and Technology Ministry for information technology; (b) the Transport and Communications Ministry for telephone and other basic telecoms infrastructure; and (c) the Commerce Ministry for e-commerce converged for the purpose of telecommunications. Therefore the convergence whether through technology, business models, or regulation is the future growth road map for India. This type of policy change can be categorized as flexibility in terms of organizational flexibility of Government of India.

Simple offerings of voice services will no longer be able to provide the revenue needed to operate in the emerging competitive environment as revenue and usage of these will continue to decline. However, people will always want some form of voice service, and they will look to those service providers who offer them additional value in the form of value-added services or cost-effective packages. This demand will drive service providers to find and incorporate those additional services or packages that will address the desires of the consumers, but at the same time, the service provider will continually pursue ways to reduce its supply costs and maximize revenue.

Mobile number portability (MNP) is a facility given by operators where a subscriber can move from one service provider to another without changing the number allocated to the subscriber. Thus, under MNP, a subscriber will have the option of retaining the same phone number issued by the old operator even with the new operator.

Telecom regulator TRAI of India has already recommended the implementation of nationwide mobile number portability by June 2009 in a phased manner and has requested DoT to select an operator for providing and operating MNP solutions. This move has pushed operators to provide quality services to retain their subscribers. MNP is expected to lead to shifting of subscribers from one operator to other in large scale and lead to flexibility to subscriber, provided by the regulator, to opt for cost-effective and better quality of telecom service provider. This will lead to competition among service providers to hold their customers.

To achieve the successful implementation of MNP, operators carried out a comprehensive cost-benefit analysis to ascertain whether the implementation of the technology would prove to be profitable for the operator. Cost aspects such as the upgradation of existing networks, software modifications, and assessment of effective call-routing mechanism are some of the areas where operators need to focus their attention. Operators had the option of providing MNP through a centralized or distributed database of ported numbers. Here the role of regulators becomes difficult to manage the balance of interest of customer and telecom service providers.

This framework is a comprehensive framework for telecom industry catering to regulators of telecom service providers where the regulator can create appropriate interventions to manage competition among operators without sacrificing the interest of customers. This framework suggests that by creating appropriate flexibilities, the regulator can enhance competitiveness of service providers in all the four perspectives given in the proposed framework.

The framework is not intended to be prescriptive about how the various processes are carried out, how a regulator of telecom service provider is to be organized, or how the tasks are identified in any single regulator related to mobile telecom service provider.

One of the strengths of this proposed framework is that it can be adopted at enterprise level also by allowing a service provider to enhance their competitive positioning by capturing the opportunities provided by the regulator's flexibility in terms of entry of players or internal business process permitted by their respective regulator.

References

Aaker DA, Mascarenhas B (1984) The need for strategic flexibility. J Bus Strategy 5(2):74–83

Aalst W (2000) Loosely coupled inter-organizational workflows: modeling and analyzing workflows crossing organizational boundaries. Info Manag 37(2):67–75

Amor D (1999) The e-business (R) evolution: living and working in an interconnected world. Prentice Hall, Upper Saddle River

Ansoff I (1965) Corporate strategy. McGraw-Hill, New York
Baumol WJ, McLennan K (1985) US productivity performance and its implications, productivity growth and US competitiveness. Oxford University Press, New York
Borrus M (1983) Trade and development in the semiconductor industry: Japanese challenges and American response, American industry in international competition. Cornell University Press, Ithaca
Byrd TA, Turner DE (2001) An exploratory examination of the relationship between flexible IT infrastructure and competitive advantage. Info Manag 39:41–52
Clemons EK, Row M (1991) Sustaining IT advantage: the role of structural differences. MIS Q 15(3):275–292
Contractor FJ, Lorange P (2002) The growth of alliances in the knowledge-based economy. Int Bus Rev 11:485–502
D'souza DE, Williams FP (2000) Toward a taxonomy of manufacturing flexibility dimensions. J Oper Manag 18(5):577–593
Davidson W (1999) Beyond re-engineering: the three phases of business transformation. IBM Syst J 38(2/3):485–499
Dreyer B, Gronhaug K (2004) Uncertainty, flexibility and sustained competitive advantage. J Bus Res 57:484–494
Duysters G, Kok G, Vaandrager M (2000) Crafting successful strategic technology partnership. R & D Manag 29(4):343–351
Eppink DJ (1978) Planning for strategic flexibility. Long Range Plann 11(4):9–15
Gronhaug K (1999) Technological flexibility and organizational buying strategies. Eur J Purch Supply Manag 5:13–22
Gupta LC (1983) Financial ratios of monitoring corporate sickness: towards a more systematic approach. Oxford University Press, New Delhi
Harrigan KR (1985) Strategic flexibility: the economics of strategic planning. Lexington Books, Lexington
Hays RH, Wheelright SC (1983) Restoring our competitiveness edge: computing through manufacturing. Wiley, New York
International Telecommunication Union (ITU) (1984) The missing link, Report of the Independent (Maitland) Commission for Worldwide Telecommunication Development. International Telecommunication Union, Geneva, pp 1–28
International Telecommunication Union (ITU) (2007) Communications: government and business practices in the Asia Pacific Region, Report. International Telecommunication Union, Geneva
Jain PK, Sushil (2000) Financial flexibility for corporate performance. In: Cornerstones of enterprise flexibility, Global Institute of Flexible Systems Management. Vikas Publishing House, New Delhi
Jipp A (1963) Wealth of nations and telephone density. Telecommunication J 30(1):199–201
Kaplan RS, Norton DP (1993) Putting the balanced scorecard to work. Harv Bus Rev 71:134–147
Kaplan RS, Norton DP (1996a) Using the balanced scorecard as a strategic management systems. Harv Bus Rev 74:75–85
Kaplan RS, Norton DP (1996b) Translating strategy into action: the balanced score card. Harvard Business School Press, Boston
Katz E, Kahn RL (1966) The social psychology of organizations. Wiley, New York
Kim Eun-Ju, ITU (2001) Policy and regulatory overview. Interconnection Workshop, China
Krugman P (1983) New theory of trade and industrial countries. Am Econ Rev 73(2):343–347
Krugman P (1986) Introduction to new thinking about trade policy, strategic trade policy and the new international economies. MIT Press, Cambridge
Krugman P (1987) Strategic sectors and international competition, the US trade policies in changing world economies. MIT Press, Cambridge, MA
Malhotra Y (2001) Enabling next generation e-business architectures: balancing integration and flexibility for managing business transformation. Brint Institute, New York

Mowlana H, Wilson LJ (1990) The passing of modernity: communication and the transformation of the society. Longman, New York, pp 43–75
Oliver RW (2001) Real-time strategy: what is strategy, anyway? J Bus Strategy 22(6):7–10
Papadakis M (1994) Did (or does) the US have a competitiveness Crisis? J Policy Anal Manage 13(1):1–20
Papazoglou MP, Ribbers P, Tsalgatidou A (2000) Integrated values chains and their implications from a business and technology standpoint. Decis Support Syst 29:323–342
Parsons GL (1983) Information technology: a new competitive weapon. Sloan Manage Rev 25:3–14
Phan DD (2001) E-business management strategies: a business-to-business case study. Info Syst Manag 18(4):61–69
Porter ME (1980) Industry structure and competitive strategy: keys to profitability. Financ Anal J 36:30–41
Porter ME (1990) The competitive advantage of nations. Free Press, New York
Porter ME (2001) Strategy and the internet. Harv Bus Rev 79(3):62–78
Rayport JF, Jaworski BJ (2001) Introduction to e-Commerce. McGraw-Hill, New York
Rugman AM (2006) The rise of the regional multinationals. Int J Glob Bus Competitiveness 2(1):9–17
Sethi AK, Sethi SP (1990) Flexibility in manufacturing: a survey. Int J Flex Manuf Syst 2(4):289–328
Shi D, Daniels RL (2003) A survey of manufacturing flexibility: implications for e-business flexibility. IBM Syst J 42(3):414–426
Sushil (1997) Flexible systems management an evolving paradigm. Syst Res Behav Sci 14(4):259–275
Sushil (1999) Flexibility in management, Global Institute of Flexible Systems Management. Vikas Publishing House, New Delhi
Sushil (2000) Systemic flexibility. Glob J Flex Syst Manag 1(1):77–80
Sushil (2012) Flowing stream strategy: leveraging strategic change with continuity. Springer, New York
Sushil and Kak A (1997) Global competitiveness with core competence: a study of HCL. International Conference of Technology (ICMOT) Proceedings, IIT, Delhi, pp 75–84
Teece DJ, Pisano G, Shuen A (1997) Dynamic capabilities and strategic management. Strat Manag J 18(7):509–533
Trigeorgis L (1993) Real options and interactions with financial flexibility. Financ Manag 22:202–223
Tyson LD (1988) Making policies for national competitiveness in a changing world, cooperation and competition in the global economy. Ballinger Publishing Co, Cambridge
Tyson LD (1992) Who's bashing whom? IIE, Washington, DC
Vernon R (1966) International investment and international trade in the product cycle. Q J Econ 80:190–207
Volberda HW (1996) Towards the flexible form: how to remain vital in hypercompetitive environments. Organ Sci 7(4):359–387
Volberda HW (1998) Building the flexible firm: how to remain competitive. Oxford University Press, Oxford

Reports

Annual Report 2011–12 of TRAI, New Delhi, India (11th January, 2013)
The Indian Telecom Services Performance Indicators July - September, 2012, of TRAI, New Delhi, India (11th January, 2013)

Web Sites

www.bhartiteleventures.com
www.coai.com
www.exp.talecomitelailab.com
www.gsmworld.com/news/press_2006/press06_29.shtml
www.itu.int
www.mtnl.net.in
www.russellbeattie.com
www.trai.gov.in
www.oecd.org/document/25/0,2340,en_2649_37441_37571993_1_1_1_37441,00.html

Chapter 6
Theoretical Roots of Flexible Strategy Game-card: An Evolving Strategic Performance Management Framework

Neetu Yadav and Sushil

1 Introduction

The changes in the business environment demand changes in the systems or models being used by enterprises. Globalization, competition, and changing customer demands have made the lives of the enterprises tougher and forced them to look beyond annual reports and financial statements. In the last two decades, there is a notable interest related to research on performance measurement and management (Taticchi et al. 2010). There is plethora of performance management frameworks/ models proposed and discussed by the researchers which deal different issues related to enterprise performance. Some major developments are performance measurement matrix, results and determinants framework, performance pyramid, balanced scorecard, performance prism, EFQM excellence award, Kanji's business scorecard, system dynamics-based scorecard, proactive scorecard, performance management system framework, etc.

Some of these frameworks have been discussed at conceptual level, while some of them are used by practitioners as well. They have some major contributions to the world of knowledge base but at the same time suffer with some of the criticism. Sushil (2010) made an attempt to develop an integrated performance management framework and proposed *flexible strategy Game-card,* which intends to overcome some of the major shortcomings of existing frameworks.

N. Yadav (✉) • Sushil
Department of Management Studies, Indian Institute of Technology Delhi, New Delhi, India
e-mail: neetu.yadav@dms.iitd.ac.in; sushil@dms.iitd.ac.in; profsushil@gmail.com

Sushil and E.A. Stohr (eds.), *The Flexible Enterprise*, Flexible Systems Management,
DOI 10.1007/978-81-322-1560-8_6, © Springer India 2014

The objective of the chapter is to describe about this evolving performance management framework in terms of its theoretical roots, the evolution of the framework, and application of this framework in general context as well.

The chapter is organized as follows: After introduction, next section highlights the emerging issues related to performance management systems. This is followed by, the limitations of existing performance management frameworks are discussed highlighting proposed solutions. Next section describes about the evolving performance management framework, i.e., flexible strategy Game-card. The theoretical roots of this framework are subsequently discussed. It further exhibits the application of Game-card in the context of Indian automobile manufacturing enterprises. The illustration is presented related to application of this framework. The chapter concludes with highlighting the limitations and future scope of the proposed framework.

2 Performance Management Systems: Emerging Issues

Before moving towards the issues in performance management, it is imperative to detail out the term *strategic performance management,* which can be defined as a performance management tool that translates strategy into a set of performance measures of a chosen strategy (Atkinson et al. 1997; Chenhall 2005). According to Dee Waal (2002), "strategic performance management is the process where steering of the organization takes place through the systematic definition of mission, strategy and objectives of the organization, making these measurable through critical success factors and key performance indicators, in order to be able to take corrective actions to keep the organization on track."

Financial figures and annual reports cannot fully present the real picture of the performance of an enterprise, as these have the limitation to look the enterprise from strategic perspective. These are lagging indicators that are results of past decisions, and they are not concerned about the changing market demands and customer expectations (Ghalayini and Noble 1996). In the last two decades, many researchers have made contributions in terms of discussing diverse issues related to enterprise performance. Looking at pre-2000 developments, one of the dominant frameworks is balanced scorecard (BSC), giving due importance to nonfinancial performance parameters. *Harvard Business Review* has listed it as one of the 75th most influential ideas of twentieth century (Bible et al. 2006). Other developments have highlighted the issues as leading and lagging indicators (results and determinants framework), organizational hierarchy view (performance pyramid), increasing wealth of shareholders (shareholder value), bringing dynamics in performance measurement systems (dynamic performance measurement system), etc.

Changing business environment, business dynamics, and turbulent situation lead the practitioners and researchers to consider some other major emerging issues related to performance measurement and management (PMM). Some of the issues are as follows: incorporating all the stakeholders (performance prism), updates in scorecard approach (Kanji's business scorecard, holistic scorecard, total performance scorecard, proactive balanced scorecard, etc.), integration of people development (dynamic multidimensional performance framework), etc. Taticchi et al. (2010) point out clearly that now it is "second generation of PMM research" where researchers are looking for developing effective PMM systems and incorporating methodologies and techniques to transform the information in value-making activities and integrate it with strategic objectives and business plans.

No doubt, these existing performance management frameworks have their own contribution(s) to the world of knowledge base, but there are many shortcomings related to these frameworks which need to be overcome to effectively execute these models/frameworks.

3 Existing Performance Management Frameworks: Limitations and Proposed Solutions

The literature review reveals that there is enormous work done related to PMM and strategic performance management frameworks. The Google Scholar search results related to keyword "strategic performance management frameworks" for the period 1990–2011 are around 16,200. For this study, some of the classical and well-cited works have been reviewed. The papers discussing the critics of these frameworks have also been reviewed. The major shortcomings as a whole related to performance management systems have been culled out that are summarized in Table 6.1.

Considering the above limitations, the literature has proposed some solutions that can help to develop effective performance management system for an enterprise; some of the proposed solutions are listed in Table 6.2.

Table 6.1 Limitations of existing performance management frameworks

Limitations	References
1. The selection of the right performance measures is cumbersome	Neely and Broune (2000)
2. Customer's viewpoint of performance is discussed in a limited manner	Sushil (2009)
3. Frameworks are largely static in nature which does not consider competition and technological developments	Norreklit (2000)
4. The causal linkages and feedback learning are rarely applied and unclear	Akkermans and van Oorschot (2005)
5. The impact of "time delay in cause and effects" is not highlighted	Bianchi and Montemaggiore (2008)
6. These frameworks advocate more closed system approach, which is hard to implement in turbulent, volatile, and competitive environment	Hamel (1998), Keely (1999)
7. 70 % of BSC implementations fail	Neely and Broune (2000)

Table 6.2 Proposed solutions for effective performance management system

Proposed solutions	References
1. To ensure you are measuring the things that matter	Neely and Broune (2000)
2. The use of mapping tools and detailed development and analysis of strategy maps	Barnabe (2011)
3. Development of dynamic strategy maps, incorporating polarities and time delays	Barnabe (2011)
4. Balance among internal and external situations, actors, and processes	Sushil (2009)
5. Performance management system's implementation should be effective	Taticchi et al. (2010)

4 Description of Flexible Strategy Game-card

Sushil (2010) has proposed an enterprise performance management framework intending to overcome above-mentioned limitations and named this framework as Game-card looking ahead of scorecard. The structural overview of this framework is exhibited in Fig. 6.1. Game-card looks the performance dominantly from two perspectives, i.e., enterprise perspective and customer perspective. All the internal and external stakeholders are considered under enterprise perspective, and as customers are the center point for any strategic decision, they are kept as an independent perspective.

Enterprise perspective deals with S-A-P-P framework (Situation-Actor-Process-Performance); here situation deals with external and internal situation factors, which lead to proactive and reactive measures of strategic decisions and actions. Some examples may be globalization, changing customer demands, government policies, etc. Actor-related factors deal with internal and external stakeholders who play a crucial role in strategy formulation as well as execution. Actor-related strategic factors may be customer satisfaction, employee productivity, training activities, etc. Process factors deal with internal and external business processes that are related to strategy execution. Process-related factors may be process innovation, new product development, etc. These three factors are leading factors, which help to drive for better performance results. Performance-related factors can be considered as lagging indicators consisting of both financial and nonfinancial performance. These measures may be market share, ROI (Return on Investment), number of subscribers, growth in revenues, etc.

Customer perspective considers the enterprise performance from the customer's viewpoint. This is linked to value in offerings and value in relationships. Strategic factors related to value in offerings may be quality of services, product features/attributes, etc. Value in relationships may be depicted by factors as after sales services, brand image of enterprise, customer relationship services, etc.

Besides measuring the performance, this framework considers to manage the performance by supporting the full cycle of strategy formulation, execution, measurement, feedback, and corrective actions and thus leading to a dynamic performance management framework. The LAP (Learning-Action-Performance) framework gives

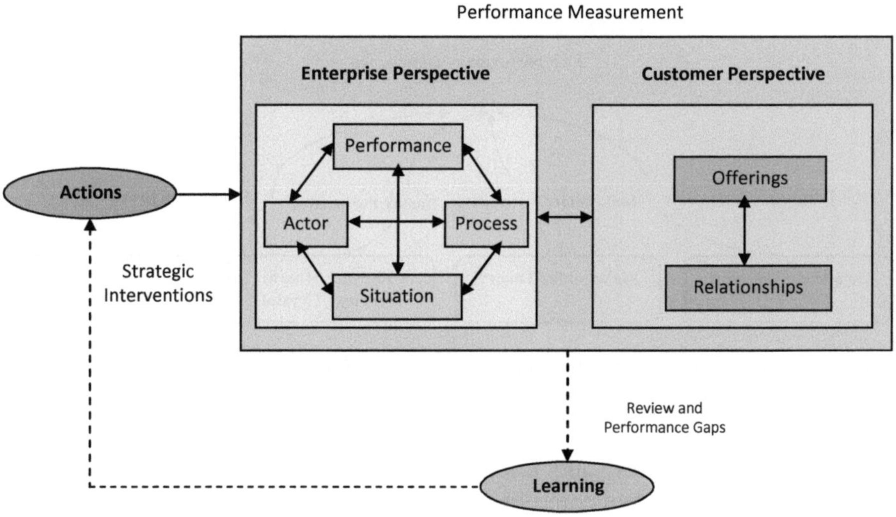

Fig. 6.1 Flexible strategy Game-card (Adapted from Sushil 2010)

it an edge over other performance management frameworks. It helps to make and review strategic interventions as required by getting the learning from performance measurement to get better performance outcome.

Thus, this evolving performance management framework intends to provide a dynamic, integrated, and holistic framework to enterprise and industry. It is imperative to discuss about the evolution of this evolving performance management framework. The evolution highlights the theoretical roots of this framework, which is described in the next section.

5 Theoretical Roots of Flexible Strategy Game-card

This evolving performance management framework has its strong theoretical roots which come from strategic management theories and some popular performance management frameworks. The theoretical roots are portrayed and exhibited in Fig. 6.2.

5.1 Integrative Perspective (Balanced Scorecard)

Balanced scorecard (BSC) (Kaplan and Norton 1992, 1996) is one of the most dominating performance management frameworks, which has brought revolution by integrating financial perspective with nonfinancial performance perspective. The integration of bringing financial and nonfinancial measures, short-term

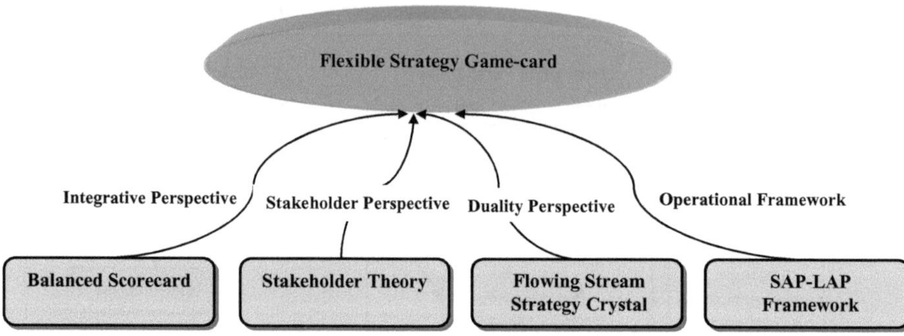

Fig. 6.2 Theoretical roots of flexible strategy Game-card (Source: Yadav et al. 2011)

and long-term measures, and leading and lagging indicators together as an integrated framework has come from BSC. There are some criticisms of BSC highlighted in the literature; this framework makes an attempt to overcome them as highlighted above.

5.2 Stakeholder Perspective (Stakeholder Theory)

Stakeholders are the integral part of any enterprise. Freeman's stakeholder theory (1984) addresses the issue of who and what are the stakeholders of any company and whom or what do the managers pay attention? The definition of a stakeholder given by Freeman says, "Any group or individual who can affect or is affected by the achievement of organization's objectives" (1984, p. 46). The existing performance management frameworks highlighted the issue of inclusion of many stakeholders, but there is limited work incorporating all the stakeholders. This framework intends to cover all the major stakeholders under two perspectives dominantly, i.e., enterprise perspective and customer perspective. As customers are at the center for making any strategic decision, they are taken as independent perspective. Enterprise perspective incorporates all the major internal and external actors related to enterprise. Thus, this framework follows the stakeholder theory and incorporates almost all of the relevant stakeholders.

5.3 Duality Perspective (Flowing Stream Strategy Crystal)

Flowing stream strategy crystal brings the confluence of continuity and change by dealing with these opposite forces effectively (Sushil 2012). The crystal balances the continuity and change forces for an enterprise with balancing the enterprise and

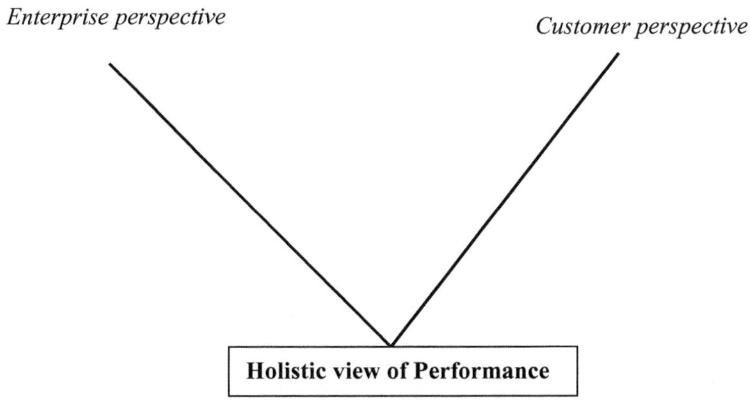

Fig. 6.3 "V" model of strategic performance management

customer strategic factors. For an enterprise, continuity and change forces present current reality, whereas customer and enterprise factors depict the decomposition of strategy. Bhat et al. (2011) had used this framework to analyze the complex dynamic of innovation in Moser Baer Industries Ltd. (MBIL), one of the world's largest manufacturers of optical storage media. Graetz and Smith (2009) and Nasim and Sushil (2011) had also highlighted the importance of managing the balance between continuity and change forces. This evolving performance management framework adapts the dual perspective of performance and proposes a holistic view of performance by "V" model of strategic performance management, which is shown in Fig. 6.3.

5.4 Operational Framework (SAP-LAP Framework)

In the competitive scenario, the enterprise performance management framework should be dynamic, which can be updated as per the changes in the external environment. Situation plays an important part in strategic decision and performance. The operational aspects of flexible strategy Game-card are derived from SAP-LAP (Situation-Actor-Process Learning-Action-Performance) framework, which is a popular framework used for analyzing and synthesizing any case context (Sushil 1997, 2000, 2001).

Situation-Actor-Process parameters are the leading indicators of performance. The performance can be treated as a lagging indicator. These aspects have been taken from SAP-LAP as the interplay of situation, actor, and process helps to analyze the context related to business and better interplay leads to better results which can be measured by performance measures or KRAs (key result areas).

6 Application of Flexible Strategy Game-card: An Illustration

For developing a better understanding of this framework, it is imperative to illustrate the application of this framework in a general context. Here, an illustration has been presented in the context of Indian automobile manufacturing enterprises. Strategic factors related to performance have been identified for two perspectives, i.e., enterprise perspective and customer perspective.

To capture context-specific strategic factors, semi-structured interviews have been conducted with the top management of automobile firms and with the customers as well. The data of these interviews have been analyzed to cull out the factors for four dimensions of enterprise perspective and two dimensions of customer perspective. Strategic factors for enterprise perspective and customer perspective have been showcased in Tables 6.3 and 6.4, respectively.

This illustration showcases that financial performance factors are the lagging indicators of performance, which can be achieved by properly responding and strategizing for leading indicators. One of the unique features of the framework is capturing the customers' viewpoint related to performance of enterprise, which highlights that customers are expecting to get lifetime value for the products and services, and their feedback should be taken care of by the enterprises.

Table 6.3 Strategic factors related to enterprise perspective

Dimensions	Strategic factors
1. Situation	PE1: Technological transformations
	PE2: Changing customer demands
	PE3: Government policies
2. Actor	PE4: Customer satisfaction
	PE5: Dealer's performance
3. Process	PE6: Process innovation
	PE7: New product development
4. Performance	PE8: Profitability
	PE9: Revenues growth
	PE10: Market share

Table 6.4 Strategic factors related to customer perspective

Dimensions	Strategic factors
1. Value in offerings	PC1: Lifetime value
	PC2: Product features
2. Value in relationships	PC3: After sales services
	PC4: Improvement through customer feedback

7 Conclusion

This chapter can be considered as a conceptual one highlighting the conceptualization of flexible strategy Game-card through discussion of its evolution and theoretical roots. Some issues identified in this chapter can be summarized in the following points:

- Strategy Game-card incorporates situation factors as its operational aspect which highlights the dynamism of the framework.
- The framework highlights the importance of stakeholders for any enterprise which have a crucial impact on the performance of the firm. The most important stakeholder, i.e., customer, is represented as most of the performance management frameworks as customer satisfaction index and customer retention. There is a need to relook this aspect in an explicit manner by highlighting customer relationships and customer offerings as a central focus of strategy, and this attempt has been made by strategy Game-card.
- Strategy Game-card highlights the need to think beyond scorecard and attempts to support the whole cycle of strategy formulation and execution, thus helps to bring a Game-card both for playing the strategy game and for scoring the performance in the game.
- Strategy Game-card can work as a powerful tool for developing strategic performance management framework for any enterprise, a sector or the industry as a whole.
- This framework may be helpful to move one step ahead in terms of performance management for the enterprise by not only monitoring and controlling the performance but also formulating, executing, and making corrective actions in the strategies for better performance results.

This chapter contributes to knowledge base by reporting and discussing this recent development and highlights that the evolution is deeply rooted in classical concepts and theories of strategic management combining the dynamism and integration to be effectively utilized in turbulent and dynamic business environment.

The methodology for development of flexible strategy Game-card has been proposed in the literature (Sushil 2011) which can be adopted for development of flexible strategy Game-card for any enterprise of choice. The mechanism highlights that there should be feedback from existing performance results and new strategic interventions or some corrective actions can be taken to get the desired performance outcome. Thus, the dynamics of the framework provides it an edge over existing performance management frameworks/systems. Integration of flexible strategy Game-card with "system dynamics" methodology can help to explore the performance results for the future scenarios, and on the basis of future results, the corrective actions in strategies can be taken to get desired performance results (Yadav et al. 2012). Now, the field of performance measurement and management has not restricted to management control, but widened towards dynamic business performance systems which lead to execute effectively in current business environment.

References

Akkermans HA, van Oorschot KE (2005) Relevance assumed: a case study of balanced scorecard development using system dynamics. J Oper Res Soc 56(8):931–941

Atkinson AA, Waterhouse JH, Wells RB (1997) A stakeholder approach to strategic performance measurement. Sloan Manage Rev 38(3):25–37

Barnabe F (2011) A system dynamics-based balanced scorecard to support strategic decision making. Int J Prod Perform Manag 60(5):446–473

Bhat JSA, Sushil, Jain PK (2011) Innovation by harmonizing continuity and change. J Bus Strateg 32(2):38–49

Bianchi C, Montemaggiore GB (2008) Enhancing strategy design and planning in public utilities through 'dynamic' balanced scorecards: insights from a project in a city water company. Syst Dyn Rev 24(2):175–213

Bible L, Kerr S, Zanini M (2006) The balanced scorecard: here and back. Manag Account Q 7(4):18–23

Chenhall RH (2005) Integrative strategic performance measurement systems, strategic alignment of manufacturing, learning and strategic outcomes: an exploratory study. Account Org Soc 30(5):395–433

de Waal AA (2002) The role of behavioural factors in the successful implementation and use of performance management systems. VrijeUniversiteit, Amsterdam

Freeman RE (1984) Strategic management: a stakeholder approach. Pitman, Boston

Ghalayini AM, Noble JS (1996) The changing basis of performance measurement. Int J Oper Prod Manag 16(8):63–80

Graetz F, Smith ACT (2009) Duality theory and organizing forms in change management. J Change Manag 9(1):9–25

Hamel G (1998) Strategy innovation and quest for value. Sloan Manage Rev 39(2):7–14

Kaplan RS, Norton DP (1992, Jan/Feb) The balanced scorecard – measures that drive performance. Harv Bus Rev 70:71–79

Kaplan RS, Norton DP (1996) Using the balanced scorecard as a strategic management system. Harv Bus Rev 74(1):75–85

Kelly K (1999) New rules for the new economy: 10 radical strategies for a connected world. Viking/Penguin, New York

Nasim S, Sushil (2011) Revisiting organizational change: exploring the paradox of managing continuity and change. J Change Manag 11(2):185–206

Neely A, Bourne M (2000) Why measurement initiatives fail. Meas Bus Excellence 4(4):3–6

Norreklit H (2000) The balance on the balanced scorecard – a critical analysis of some of its assumptions. Manag Account Res 11:65–88

Sushil (1997) Flexible systems management: an evolving paradigm. Syst Res Behav Sci 14(4):259–275

Sushil (2000) SAP-LAP models of inquiry. Manag Decis 38(5):347–353

Sushil (2001) SAP-LAP framework. Glob J Flex Syst Manag 2(1):51–55

Sushil (2009) Is balanced scorecard a balanced strategic system. Drishti- Insight, Publication of ARTDO International, Philippines, 34–40

Sushil (2010) Flexible strategy game-card. Glob J Flex Syst Manag 11(1&2):iii–iv

Sushil (2011) Implementing flexible strategy game-card. Glob J Flex Syst Manag 12(3&4):iii

Sushil (2012) Flowing stream strategy: leveraging strategic change with continuity. Springer, New York

Taticchi P, Tonelli F, Cagnazzo L (2010) Performance measurement and management: a literature review and a research agenda. Meas Bus Excellence 14(1):4–18

Yadav N, Sushil, Sagar M (2011) The evolution of flexible strategy game-card: a framework rooted in dual perspective of performance. In Proceedings of 11th global conference on flexible systems management, IIM, Kozhikode, pp. 29–47

Yadav N, Sushil, Sagar M (2012) Dynamics of strategic initiatives and expected performance: an application of flexible strategy game-card. In Proceedings of 30th international conference of system dynamics society, University of St. Gallen. Available at: http://www.systemdynamics.org/conferences/2012/proceed/index.html, also available at: http://www.systemsmodelbook.org/viewModel.aspx?id=1788b377-de4c-413d-afc6-4110915b9211

[illegible]

Part II
Organizational Flexibility

Chapter 7
Architecting Flexible Organizations

Joseph Morabito, Ira Sack, Edward Stohr, and Anilkumar Bhate

1 Introduction

The twenty-first-century organization is faced with the apparent dilemma of being efficient and innovative, lean and flexible, and hierarchical and flat. The seemingly contradictory characteristics extend into every organizational system, from culture and strategy to process and technology. The flexible organization must embrace and cultivate opposites; indeed, the organization should recognize opposites as opportunities for inventiveness and synthesis and not a dilemma that requires a choice between opposites (Takeuchi and Nonaka 2004). This is in contrast to a more traditional organization that either chooses one principle over its apparent opposite or adopts an engineering perspective that optimizes something between opposites. The knowledge organization, in contrast, synthesizes opposites into something unique and new.

At its source, apparent contradictions arise from the relative tacit and explicit knowledge content of organizational systems. Flexibility, then, arises from the capability of managers to manipulate the interaction and knowledge content within and among systems. For example, Toyota developed its Lexus product by embracing the seemingly contradictory product requirements of fast ride and fuel economy, noise reduction and lightweight, warmth and function, and so on. By implementing both early and late knowledge construction (Morabito et al. 2000), product development followed, in sequence, an intended, emergent, and intended strategy. By understanding the knowledge creation process, Toyota was able to manipulate and combine their systems to produce a best-selling luxury car (Osono 2004).

Classical approaches to design have typically leveraged context-specific knowledge to create a separate structure for each organizational dimension. This has led to a wide assortment of single-threaded architectures with specific purposes but with little integration or synergy. By single threaded, we mean that the architecture processes decisions or performs actions independently of other architectures. Other

J. Morabito (✉) • I. Sack • E. Stohr • A. Bhate
Stevens Institute of Technology, Hoboken, NJ 07030, USA

Sushil and E.A. Stohr (eds.), *The Flexible Enterprise*, Flexible Systems Management,
DOI 10.1007/978-81-322-1560-8_7, © Springer India 2014

approaches attempt to integrate dimensions but in effect create bulky structures that mirror management knowledge of context. As useful as this may appear to be locally, it operates suboptimally at the organizational level. Moreover, each architecture or framework is not inventive within itself.

1.1 Elegant Ideas and Design

In the October 2006 issue of the Harvard Business Review, Stanford management guru James March discussed the importance of the elegance of ideas as opposed to their relevance. He does not mean that relevance is unimportant, only that the "beauty of ideas" (or "modeling as an art form") is the essence of scholarship. Management knowledge of context must be embedded within those elegant ideas. "It is the combination of academic and experiential knowledge, not the substitution of one for the other, that yields improvement" (March 2006).

This chapter discusses several "elegant ideas" in a broader "modeling as an art form" known as *organization modeling* (Morabito et al. 1999). We draw on the work of Herbert Simon and existing research on contracts to create a flexible approach to interrelate and specify the seemingly contradictory dimensions of an organization, using, for example, precise (fully explicit), relational (part explicit, part tacit) to psychological (fully tacit), to design the behavior of organizational dimensions.

2 Dimensions of Organizational Flexibility

Organizational flexibility is a concept that, at its core, refers to the capacity to rearrange or reconstitute a system configuration to adapt to an internal or external imperative. Flexibility extends to all areas of the organization, from its strategy to its technical systems. Moreover, at the organization level, flexibility must encompass all of an organization's systems simultaneously.

Flexibility has taken shape in various forms. For example, systems engineering, service-oriented or enterprise architectures, and adaptive strategies are ideas that, in principle, promote flexibility; otherwise, there is no reason for their being. In fact, every area of the organization, from its lowest-level technical systems to its learning and cultural systems, may be characterized by a corresponding framework or architecture that promotes design and flexibility.

Flexibility also extends to the knowledge characterization of the system itself. For example, a technical system is fully explicit, while culture and learning are primarily tacit. This is significant since explicit and tacit systems are fundamentally different and hence must be characterized and designed differently – yet, they too must be embedded within all of an organization's systems.

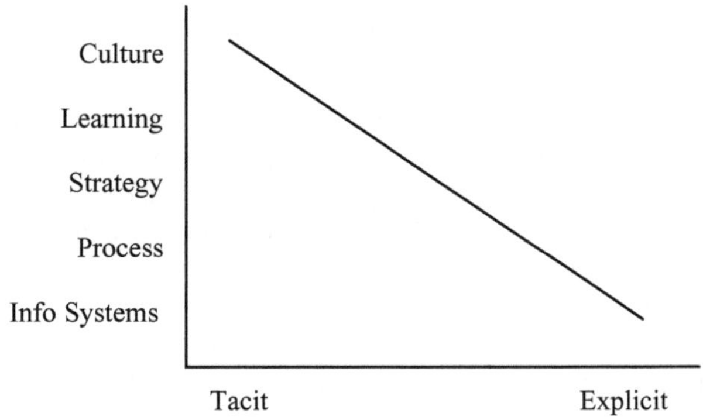

Fig. 7.1 Organizational systems and knowledge

2.1 Systems and Knowledge

In this chapter, we take the view that the organization's systems may be characterized by a hierarchical relationship and their corresponding knowledge content in terms of explicit and tacit knowledge. Thus, the organization may be characterized by both levels of systems and by system knowledge characterization. This is illustrated in Fig. 7.1.

Figure 7.1 states that higher-level organizational systems have a comparatively larger tacit knowledge component than lower-level systems. As we discuss below, higher-level systems have a lower frequency and respond more slowly than lower-level systems (Simon 1973). Similarly, building tacit knowledge is a function of time and experience (Gill 2000); hence, we argue that a comparatively high-level system has a larger tacit knowledge component than a lower-level system in the same organization.

Culture, for example, is a system where tacit knowledge is the dominant constituent. Edgar Schein has described culture as having three constituents: shared tacit assumptions that are the essence of culture, espoused values that expresses what tacit assumptions an organization would like to develop or be seen as representing, and overt behavior which indicates how it explicitly operationalizes the tacit assumptions; yet, it is shared tacit assumptions that shapes the other constituents (Schein 1992). To continue the argument illustrated in Fig. 7.1, learning is largely determined by the organization's culture or subcultures; in fact, the learning associated with transformational change involves changing the basic assumptions of an organization – "basic assumptions about the culture lead to learning values and investments that produce a different learning style from a culture with another pattern of values and investments" (Nevis et al. 1995). Thus, culture and learning are intertwined through their tacit knowledge content; Schein, for example, claims that organizations have difficulty learning because occupational subcultures often have different and incompatible tacit assumptions that resist change and prevent the communication necessary for learning (Schein 1996). Finally, an information system shown at the bottom of Fig. 7.1 is entirely explicit, as all nonhuman, machine-based systems must be.

2.2 Flexibility and Managerial Choice

Flexibility exists within and between systems and may be configured based on the comparative tacit-explicit knowledge content of the systems. For example, where do we place *structure* in Fig. 7.1? In the classical organization, structure is immediately above process; however, in the modern process enterprise, process is above structure (Rummler and Brache 1995). That is to say, the twenty-first-century organization chart (i.e., structure) is constrained by process requirements and not the other way around. This is one example of flexibility and managerial choice: the process organization *chooses* to place process above structure.

2.3 Architecting Systems

What most existing architectures have in common is that they are single threaded and represent experiential, management knowledge of an area such as strategy or process. There are no underlying concepts that span all disciplines or that can be said to represent modeling organizations as such.

Organization modeling is a level of abstraction that spans all the areas of an organization. Its ideas and principles are drawn from a variety of disciplines, including hierarchy theory, organization science, art, law, and software engineering, among others. Through the blending of a rich assortment of ideas, an elegant, inventive framework emerges that lends both rigor and discipline to design while promoting creative insights and design flexibility. Organization modeling, then, is our attempt at the "beauty of modeling" – a set of elegant, interlocking ideas with analytical discipline that encompasses and interrelates all the systems of an organization.

3 Properties of Organizational Systems

Discussed below are selected properties of systems that have a significant impact on organizational flexibility. We draw upon and extend the work of Herbert Simon on **hierarchy theory** to create a distinct perspective of organizational systems and then use elements of organization modeling such as **molecules** and **contracts** to account for these properties within the framework shown in Fig. 7.1.

3.1 Thin and Thick Dimensions of Organizations

All social institutions have both visible and hidden characteristics. We borrow from the field of ethnography and describe these characteristics as *thin* and *thick*, respectively (Geertz 1973). Thin systems are characterized by visible, well-defined attributes and include information systems and routine process workflows. In contrast, thick systems are distinguished by their tacit belief content and include, for example, organizational culture and learning. The characteristics of thin systems come closest to explicit knowledge, while that of thick systems to that of tacit knowledge.

The design of thin and thick systems is fundamentally different. The former requires the detailed structuring of content (lower right of Fig. 7.1) (Drucker 1999), while the latter involves the design of the surrounding context (upper left of Fig. 7.1) (Davenport 2005). Moreover, the systems must complement and reinforce each other. Successful organizations build and interrelate both their thin and thick systems.

As an example, Toyota characterizes itself in terms of explicit and tacit knowledge, known as the "Toyota DNA": one strand for thin and the other for thick. The visible thin strand includes elements of the Toyota Production System (TPS) such as just-in-time, leveled production, one-piece flow, and so on. The softer thick strand includes respect for people, change, and learning. Management practices and policies such as quality circles and continuous improvement represent the cross-links: they connect and build both strands *simultaneously* – improving thin TPS elements through the active participation of employees shapes the thick elements of respect for people and learning (Liker 2004). In contrast, many organizations adopt "lean production" but in fact are borrowing only the thin strand from the Toyota model. The thick dimension is either ignored or subsumed within the thin. It is no surprise, therefore, that no current "lean organization" even comes close to the "Toyota Way" (Liker 2004).

3.2 Hierarchy Theory and System Layering

We draw on hierarchy theory to elucidate the layering of systems illustrated in Fig. 7.1. A **hierarchy** of systems is one where a system at any level corresponds to a *set* of lower-level systems, known as a partial ordering or a tree. This is in contrast to a complete ordering where a system corresponds with only one other system below it. By way of illustration, Herbert Simon uses the metaphor of Chinese boxes: opening one box reveals a *set* of smaller boxes, opening any of which reveals yet another set, and so on (Simon 1973).

System interaction is of two types. The first is symmetrical and characterizes tissues, such as crystalline or lattice structures as found, for example, in rocks. The second is asymmetrical, meaning the behavior across layers is different in each vertical direction. Partial ordering coupled with asymmetry characterizes a

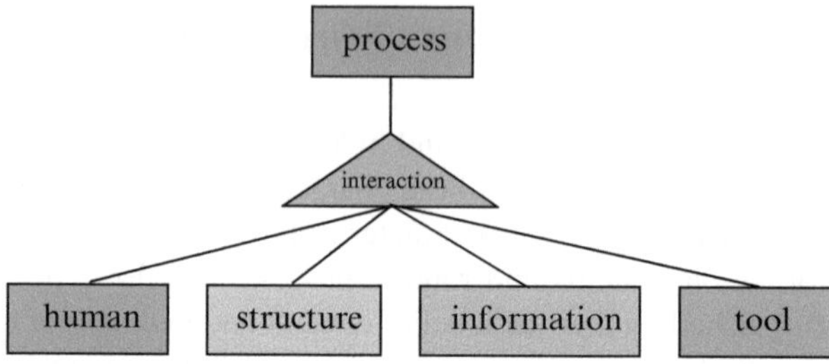

Fig. 7.2 Generic process molecule

molecule (Simon 1973). Both biological and organizational systems may be configured as molecules. An example of a molecule in an organizational system is illustrated in Fig. 7.2 – a process molecule (Morabito et al. 1999).

Observe in Fig. 7.2 that the higher-level {process} is a system whose constituents include {human}, {structure}, {information}, and {tool} at the next lower level. These lower-level systems are subsystems from the standpoint of process design: the subsystems *implement* the higher-level process *specification*. The asymmetry is manifested in the molecule itself and is illustrated by the triangle identifying some type of interaction. Furthermore, the subsystems communicate through messages, that is, the pre- and post-conditions across the subsystems. The interacting subsystems implement and explain the structure and workings of the higher-level process. The systems within the molecule as a whole – the higher-level system specification and the set of lower-level implementation subsystems – are tightly bound. By tightly bound, we mean that the interaction of the defined implementation subsystems delivers the functional requirements of the process specification; that is, tightly bound systems are those with the shortest functional distance (see below) for a specific design defined by the molecule itself.

Note that we do not mean "tightly coupled" systems, which are interdependent and reduce flexibility. Implementation constituents in a molecule are not necessarily interdependent; rather, the molecule subsystems communicate *independently* of their internal structure and provide context to the specification they operationalize and in fact, increase flexibility by interacting through the mechanism of loose horizontal coupling (discussed below). A given {process} specification may be implemented through any number of subsystem {human}, {structure}, {information}, and {tool} combinations, known as a refinement path (discussed below). For example, we have the option of automating a {process} specification by replacing the {human} with sufficiently robust {information} and {tool} constituents. In contrast, Toyota often chooses *not* to automate {process} specifications even when the appropriate implementation constituents are available. The reason is that the {human} constituent in the process molecule is the "most flexible" constituent and removing it would reduce overall process flexibility. Toyota only chooses to automate a {process} when that specification qualifies as both an industry best practice and a Toyota standard (Liker 2004).

Finally, for convenience, we usually replace a picture of a molecule with its corresponding linear notation, as follows for process:

Generic process: interaction (process {human, structure, information, tool})

3.3 Organization Levels and Molecules

The question that naturally arises concerns the relationship between system levels as illustrated in Fig. 7.1 and the idea of molecules illustrated in Fig. 7.2. This requires a more detailed discussion of hierarchy theory.

There are two types of hierarchies – **empirical** and **definitional**. Definitional entities are postulated before measurements are taken, while empirical entities correspond to some observation and measurement and typically arise post hoc to that observation. Definitional entities are indispensable to the development of research questions and their assumptions; they are scale and rate independent and based on observer-generated criteria. Definitional entities guide the process of analysis; experience and observation may lead to the discovery of empirical entities or insights, which in turn yield a further refinement of definitional entities. It follows, then, that definitional entities are ordered into levels of organization, while empirical entities are ordered into levels of observation (Ahl and Allen 1996).

The sample hierarchy shown in Fig. 7.1 is an empirical hierarchy arising from observation, i.e., the higher-level systems have an observable lower frequency and longer response time than lower-level systems. An organization molecule, in contrast, is a definitional hierarchy and is described according to the criteria of design, specifically context-specific specification and corresponding subsystem constituents that are tightly bound (close functional distance) during implementation.

When configuring a molecule for design purposes, we naturally define a context specification with a set of subsystems drawn from the entire pool of organizational materials (i.e., organizational systems). The generic process molecule, for example, was defined from our reading of organizational and management literature as well as management practice.

Let us extend our thinking into the context of strategy: a working model for configuring a strategy molecule (i.e., specification and implementation) may be as follows:

Generic strategy: interaction (strategy {process, structure, information, culture})

In this case, we see that strategy leverages the values associated with culture during its implementation, even while culture constrains that implementation (Sushil 2007, 2012). Since culture is a high-level, low-frequency system, it acts, in effect, as a *constant* during strategy formulation and implementation. Is this true? Toyota, for example, was able to synthesize both intended and emergent strategy because of its culture of learning, change, and continuous improvement; that is, Toyota was able to implement a dynamic and changing communication pattern (i.e., univocal and multivocal dialogue) during its strategy-making process (Osono 2004). Other organizations with a culture of conformity may have difficulty synthesizing the contradictory principles of intended and emergent; in fact, a bureaucratic culture would most likely restrict strategy implementation to intended (Mintzberg 1983). That is to say, the values and assumptions associated with culture are tightly bound to strategy design (at least in the case of Toyota's Lexus product strategy) and thus provide empirical evidence for including {culture} as a subsystem constituent of a strategy molecule.

Design flexibility arises from the definition of a molecule. Academic literature, practitioner experience, and organizational context are factors that a designer may use to configure a given molecule. Thus, there is managerial choice in the design of a molecule, which, of course, may be subsequently refined after implementation in the real world.

3.4 Functional Distance

Systems at all levels communicate with each other on a *sliding scale of influence*: the further away a system is, the less is its direct influence (Simon 1973). For example, a process molecule represents a tightly bound coupling of systems for a given process implementation; however, it is influenced by other systems "further away," including, in decreasing scale of influence, process funding, process support, strategy, and culture. Furthermore, this sliding interaction occurs both vertically and horizontally as shown in Fig. 7.1.

3.5 Loose Vertical and Horizontal Coupling

Systems interact within and between levels. Interaction among systems within a given level is known as loose horizontal coupling. Loose horizontal coupling means that the internal dynamics of participating systems are *hidden* and *isolated* from each other through clearly defined boundaries and thus may be seen as black boxes with respect to each other. The systems, in turn, communicate through inputs and outputs (Simon 1973). As we will see in our discussion of contracts, we can extend horizontal interaction to include invariants that act as constraints on communication. Similarly, systems communicate vertically, and here too communication is constrained by the invariant underlying the layering logic.

Loose vertical coupling permits behavior *independence between levels* and thus permits the assemblage of larger structures, provided subsystem equilibrium properties do not affect the system behavior at higher levels. Similarly, loose horizontal coupling also permits the creation of a larger structure, but here the key interaction considerations are the inputs and outputs between subsystems (Simon 1973). Both loose horizontal and vertical coupling share the properties of allowing system communications and independence, thus promoting flexibility during design.

Formally, a given association between entities in different levels is determined by the invariant governing the layering logic. An invariant is the background of

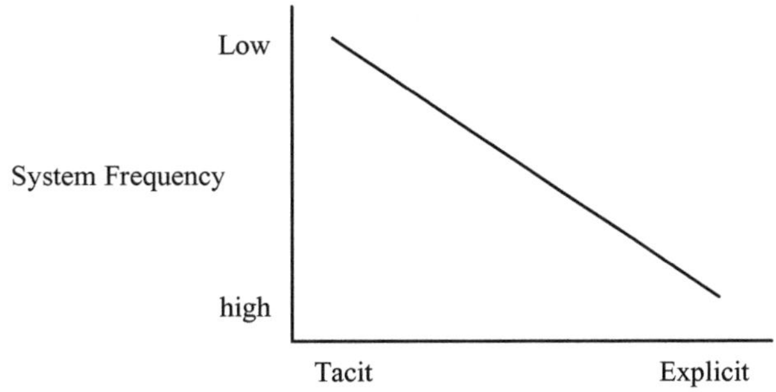

Fig. 7.3 System frequency and knowledge content

procedures, rules, and relationships between entities that never change. The invariant, then, defines the association and the ordering logic. Note too that an invariant is not a state – a state is a function of time – while an invariant is not expected to change with time (Morabito et al. 1999). In contrast, the inputs and outputs of subsystems within the same layer associated with loose horizontal coupling may change the states of participating entities.

3.6 Level Ordering

A level is distinguished by a logical grouping of entities. There may, of course, be a set of subsystems at the same level that correspond to a given logical grouping. For example, {animal} at a high level may be associated with both {carnivore} and {herbivore} at the next lower level. Both {carnivore} and {herbivore} are of the same logical type – they share properties of animals and thus are at the same level – yet they differ by the criterion of diet and are therefore distinct subsystems (Ahl and Allen 1996).

The ordering of levels is based on several criteria. As is illustrated in Fig. 7.3, a high-level entity has a slower frequency than a corresponding lower-level entity and in fact is one criterion that determines level ordering. We may also say that a higher-level entity has less bond strength and integrity, offers context to, constrains, or is a composite of a lower-level entity. Finally, more than one association type often holds for a given hierarchy (Ahl and Allen 1996). For example, the {process} in the process molecule specifies or describes a given process and therefore contains, offers context, and constrains the set of lower-level subsystems, which, in turn, implement and explain the function of the higher level {process}.

3.7 System Frequency (Time-Sensitive Response)

It is a characteristic of system interaction that high-level systems respond slowly to inputs from systems at lower levels. This is a function of the comparatively different frequencies with which each vibrates and is illustrated in Fig. 7.3.

Those behaviors or motions of a system that depend on low-frequency levels (high in the hierarchy of systems) are so slow that they will be difficult to observe and may be replaced by *constants*. In contrast, motions determined by high-frequency modes within a subsystem (low in the hierarchy) will be, of course, isolated from that of other high-frequency subsystems and be so rapid that the corresponding subsystems will appear to be in equilibrium with no internal degrees of freedom. The result is that corresponding subsystems within the same low level will behave, with respect to each other, like *rigid bodies*. After eliminating the very high and low frequencies, then, it is the middle frequency layers that determine, to a good approximation, the observable dynamics of the major systems. Hence, the efficacy of a system model built on the interactions of middle frequency subsystems will be largely determined by the sharpness of the boundaries above and below the middle-frequency layer (Simon 1973). At the end of this chapter, we discuss this in more detail with an example of varying frequencies and organizational structure.

3.8 Near-Decomposability

The notion of asymmetry leads to the idea of near-decomposability. A system is nearly decomposable, meaning, by virtue of its asymmetrical association, it cannot be completely decomposed (Simon 1973). Near-decomposability implies that a level, or a specific thing in a system known as an *entity*, is not merely a collection of the set of entities at the next lower level. For example, a single molecule of water (at a high level) is more than a collection of one oxygen and two hydrogen atoms at the next lower level; rather, combining entities at the lower level produces certain properties in the corresponding higher-level entity. These properties are *system level* – they are displayed in the higher-level entity or level, but depend on the elements at the lower level, and therefore are functions of the entire system. The weight of a water molecule, for example, is a system-level property that, in this case, is a summation function corresponding to the weight of individual atoms at a lower level. In contrast, properties specific to an element, such as the specific weight of individual atoms of hydrogen and oxygen are said to be *deliberate*.

At this point, we need to make a fine modeling distinction often overlooked in the literature. System-level properties (also known as *bulk* or *global* properties) are functions of the system itself – that is, its multiple layers – and are of two types: the first are **resultant properties**, sometimes known as hereditary properties, and the second are **emergent properties** (Bunge 1977). Resultant properties are typically *functions* corresponding to lower-level properties and therefore exist in at least one lower-level subsystem. We believe Simon's reference to "weak emergence" as "the parts of a complex system have mutual relations that do not exist for the parts in isolation" (Simon 1996) comes closest to the terms resultant or hereditary property. Emergent properties do not exist in any of the lower-level subsystems and arise from the layering logic; that is, as a consequence of the *layering invariant*. Typically, emergent properties cannot be predicted on the basis of lower-level properties and thus are not mechanical but "creative" in character.

3.9 The Paradox of Tacit Knowledge and Flexibility

At first glance, it may seem that tacit-oriented, low-frequency systems are resistant to change and hence inflexible. Actually, the reverse is true. If an organization's thick strand of DNA is constructed to embrace change, learning, and respect for people, then, in fact, people as individuals and in groups are an organization's *most* flexible system, not in spite of but because of their tacit knowledge. As mentioned above, Toyota considers people its most flexible process constituent and hence resists automation even when technically possible. The result is "automation with a human touch" (also known as "autonomation"), where automation takes place only as part of a broader human system (Ohno 1978).

In fact, culture and learning systems can be changed, but the mode of change is different from that of explicit systems. Schein has defined the process of culture change as having three stages: unfreezing and creating the motivation to change, learning new concepts and new meanings for old concepts, and refreezing and internalizing new concepts and meanings. Change starts with *disconfirmation*, or some new force which upsets the stability of the high-level systems. Disconfirmation may include, for example, economic threats (e.g., a pharmaceutical firm having a drug removed from the market for safety reasons), technological threats (e.g., the Internet), and mergers and acquisitions. Eventually, it comes down to individuals who must learn and imbibe new concepts. Schein uses the term *cognitive redefinition* to describe this process of individual transformation where, in essence, the individual learns a new way of thinking that depends on several organizational factors, such as training, positive role models, consistent systems, and organizational structures, that support the new way of thinking and working, and so on (Schein 1999). Furthermore, the transformational learning and the ensuing *psychological contract* may be coercive or cooperative. For example, the authors' experience with a large corporate acquisition was that the disconfirmation was largely coercive or, to use Schein's words, the acquiring firm's culture simply "imposed itself on the other" (Schein 1999).

Finally, the knowledge organization is, by definition, flexible in that new threads of knowledge, and therefore organizational possibilities, are being created. Here too, knowledge creation originates with individuals and depends on the organizational context (known as "ba") that should be designed to cultivate tacit knowledge and its amplification throughout the organization (Nonaka and Takeuchi 1995). Several examples of the role of tacit knowledge in knowledge creation and organizational flexibility are described in the remainder of this chapter.

In summary, we argue that tacit-oriented systems have the potential to be the organization's most flexible systems, right down to the individual. The real question is whether the tacit systems encourage creative and engaging flexibility or whether the effect will be restrictive and controlling. This is elaborated below in our discussion of psychological contracts.

3.10 Modular Versus Integral Architectures

Modular architectures characterize thin or explicit systems; that is, systems with clearly defined boundary conditions that communicate through messages within the same level (i.e., loose horizontal coupling). In contrast, thick systems are characterized by unclear boundary conditions where many systems, context-specific subsystems, as well as organization-wide systems (high level, such as culture) all interact. The combination of systems creates a context for thick behaviors such as research and development (R&D).

The source of flexibility is different for thin and thick systems. Designing thin systems involves rigorous analysis and design of content. For example, automating a given process requires a detailed functional specification of {process} if we are to replace the {human} with a {tool} constituent illustrated in Fig. 7.2. Modularity, that is, entities with clearly defined boundaries in combination with both vertical and loose horizontal coupling represent the mechanism underlying thin system flexibility. Modularity makes possible reuse, recombination, and choice.

In contrast, designing thick systems relies on anthropological-like analysis and the design of context. Context design, in turn, involves the design and *interweaving* of both thick systems (e.g., culture and learning) and thin systems (e.g., supporting information and tools) – that is, context is a consequence of systems interaction. For example, if we are to support "socialization" during a knowledge creation process (e.g., R&D), we would need to weave together the physical space to facilitate in-person interaction, organizational intention, respect for the individual, individual and group learning attributes (e.g., motivation), the willingness for people to share without judgment, among other system elements – we would not, in fact could not, design the creative process itself. Hence, flexibility arises from context, the design of which arises from the appropriate interaction of systems, the architecture of which is not modular but integral. With thick systems, flexibility ultimately extends to the tacit content of the individual or group.

As an example, a routine process may be specified independently from the corresponding implementation subsystems. This separation of concerns (e.g., abstraction) makes detailed specification possible, underlies scientific management, and therefore facilitates the design of complex industrial processes. In contrast, when designing knowledge work, the systems that comprise its context are intertwined and cannot be separated. In fact, detailed specification is not possible. The task cannot be separated from the {human} performing the task – the structure and workings of the task are inside the head of the knowledge worker (Drucker 1999).

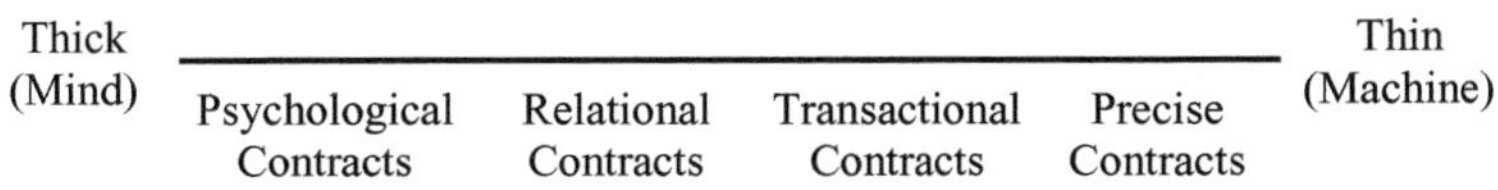

Fig. 7.4 A new contract continuum

4 Contracts

Loose vertical and horizontal coupling describe subsystems that are, at once, isolated and interacting. It follows, then, that a key design decision, in addition to the selection of the levels themselves, is the identification of boundary conditions and the energy or information transfer between them. This holds for both vertical conditions between levels and horizontal conditions between subsystems within a given level.

We propose to address both system specification and interaction, between and within levels, through **behavior** and the notion of a **contract**. The use of behavior as a specifying construct frees us from all implementation concerns, including "objects," "agents," and "roles." Furthermore, though systems are typically recognized by their states (i.e., attribute values), it is behavior that is responsible for state changes. This is true even in social systems such as organizations where behavior is not independent of internal state.

We specify behavior with a contract. A contract is a self-contained construct that specifies or describes a given behavior – each distinct behavior and its boundary conditions may be specified with a corresponding contract. Furthermore, complex behavior may be specified with a *hierarchy of contracts* (Morabito and Singh 1993).

Where the behavior being specified is *mechanical* in nature (e.g., software), we say the contract is fully explicit and **precise**; however, as we move along the knowledge continuum shown in Fig. 7.1 toward the tacit pole, a more *thoughtful* analysis arises, and we necessarily accommodate people – observer and participant – and the contract becomes **relational** or even **psychological** in nature. Each of these ideas has been described in the literature, in everything from software engineering to economics and law. The legal system considers a contract continuum as having a transactional and relational pole (MacNeil and Gudel 2001). In organization modeling, we have extended this model in each direction – fully explicit at one end and fully tacit at the other – to accommodate organizational systems. This new contract continuum is illustrated in Fig. 7.4 and represents a range of possible specifications based on explicit and tacit knowledge content.

Industrial-era organizations are characterized by contracts that are, for the most part, mechanical-like descriptions of work. In fact, such specifications lead to the routinization of work. These contracts are *precise* or *transactional* and have a certain exactness and clarity that leads to engineering-like design.

In contrast, the knowledge era has brought a new requirement: the specification of non-routine work and the application or creation of knowledge. In this case, mechanical descriptions are not sufficient; rather, values and expectations are often the primary parameters in the contract. Generally, as we move toward the thick pole in the new contract continuum, the contracts become more open and dynamic and subject to late knowledge construction (Morabito et al. 1999).

In a modern organization, we must be able to specify both forms – everything from routine workflows to cultural processes – and thus accommodate both precise and rather implicit intentions.

The contract is distinguished by a certain intent, which may be communicated directly with explicit assertions, indirectly through a process of assimilation, or, of course, some combination. Thus, the concept of a contract embodies a range of communication modes, from explicit assertions such as "business rules" to implicit intentions in the form of strategic intent, cultural assumptions, or personal intentionality.

Contract Type 1. Precise Contracts for Specifying Behavior in Software and Other Fully Explicit Systems

The essential property of a precise contract is that it explicitly defines some behavior or operation in a system. The semantics of the behavior specified must be precisely and fully defined – there can be no room for ambiguity or interpretation. This requires the use of fully explicit *assertions* – logical statements or functions that define the parameters of the contract (Kilov and Ross 1994). Precise contracts are ideal constructs for specifying the behavior of systems with clearly defined inputs and outputs, such as information systems, most workflows, and corresponding workflow management systems. The formal use of assertions and contracts, in fact, is increasingly common in the development of high quality, complex software (Meyer 1992).

There are four categories of assertions: *invariant*, *precondition*, *post-condition*, and *trigger* (Kilov 2002). An invariant is a logical assertion given in the form of rules that the behavior described in the contract may not violate. A precondition lists the inputs and system states that are required to exist before the contract can be satisfied. The third component of a contract is the post-condition that lists the outputs and system states that are expected after the contract is executed. The last component is a trigger, which lists the events and states that initiate execution of a contract. Triggers, pre-, and post-conditions are functions of time. In contrast, an invariant is the background of procedures, rules, and relationships that never should change (and hence, an invariant is not a function of time). Collectively, these four constructs constitute a mechanism for the *precise specification of behavior* – and hence are most suitable for explicit contracts. Note too that we have enriched the concept of loose horizontal coupling to include triggers and invariants in addition to pre- and post-conditions.

The participants to a precise contract are the entities (i.e., software systems or objects within a system) participating in the contract. When describing the behavior of information systems (e.g., human resources (HR)), the contract describes the protocol of data exchange between them, where, for example, one system may be thought of as a producer and, another, a consumer. When describing the behavior of objects within a system, the contract describes operations on its objects. For example, a *performance history* "depends on" a corresponding *employee*. The "depends on" is a dependency association; the invariant states that the existence of a dependent (*performance history*) implies the existence of a corresponding parent (*employee*). This means that a contract that deletes an *employee* instance from an HR database must also delete all corresponding *performance history* instances (Kilov and Ross 1994).

Precise contracts typically exhibit an all-or-nothing pattern of operation: each and every assertion must be logically true if the behavior described by the entire contract is to exist. The all-or-nothing precise contract is typically the type that is used in software. A precise contract may also be used to describe behaviors with a parameterized range of possible pre- and post-conditions. Such *relativized* contracts may be used to describe decision-making processes. The business rules of relativized contracts, stated with assertions, are sometimes called *decision rules*. Both all-or-nothing and relativized contracts are explicit in that the assertions may be described with clearly defined statements, algorithms, or functions. Furthermore, relativized contracts may be dynamic in that the assertion parameters may be dependent on a feedback loop, thus promoting a certain amount of learning with each instance or occurrence of the process. Both all-or-nothing and relativized contracts lend themselves to quantitative analysis.

The *signature* of a precise contract is typically a set of parameters that serve as input into the contract and another set of parameters that serve as the expected outcome. In both cases, the signature of the contract is defined by both its parameters and their specific sequence. The signature serves as the communication vehicle between objects; a user needs not know the internal workings of a contract, only its signature (i.e., interface). This is an example of encapsulation or information hiding.[1] Both the specification of a contract and its signature collectively represent the design rules underlying the contract and are necessary to support modular design and architecture.

Contract Type 2. People and Exchange: Transactional and Relational Contracts

Outside of formal systems analysis, contracts, as are commonly used, involve people and some sort of an exchange, or an expectation of an exchange. Such contracts concern human behavior and are simultaneously individual and social in nature (MacNeil and Gudel 2001). Any discussion of contracts must include the individual, his or her social relationships, and context. Certainly, contracts can be studied in isolation, and for certain analyses, this may be useful, but we must always recognize that most such analyses are necessarily incomplete (MacNeil and Gudel 2001).

[1] In strict modeling terms, there is a difference between *encapsulation* and *information hiding*. The former represents the case where the contract is like a "glass box" – the inner workings are visible to a user – while the latter, the inner workings are not visible and may be thought of as a "black box." In either case, the user can change neither the inner workings of the contract nor its signature – both (inner workings and signature) collectively represent the design rules necessary for the contract's modularity.

For example, in our discussion of relativized contracts and decision making above, the feedback loop by which most managers operate may be structured in a precise way, but the latitude and interpretation of the manager is largely a function of his or her context, organization, and relationships within that organization. *All contracts involving human beings, even transactional contracts, have a relational and even psychological component.* A key design issue, then, is to know when we can isolate a transactional contract from its relational context in order to solve some restricted analysis or when we have to recognize that we must accommodate an array of contracts to specify our intention.

Both transactional and relational contracts concern exchange and coordination. In fact, there is a continuum of contracts where, at one end, we have the transactional pole and at the other the relational pole. This represents a continuum from discrete exchanges to ongoing relations. Discrete exchanges are relatively short in duration and involve limited personal interaction with no entangling responsibilities beyond what is clearly and precisely specified. The parameters of these transactional contracts are fully defined and, in fact, are not very different from that of precise contracts. In contrast, relational contracts tend to be either long duration or ongoing, involve close "whole person" relations, and the objects of exchange typically include both easily measured quantities and not easily measured outcomes.

The participants to a transactional or relational contract may be individuals, groups, organizations, or any combination. For example, at the end of this chapter, we describe two types of relational contracts coordinating the behavior of organizations participating in inter-organizational knowledge creation.

An example of a contract that is toward the transactional pole is a labor contract where, by design, all relational components are removed from the contract. It is essentially an agreement between a union (on behalf of its members) and an organization where every anticipated contingency is explicitly stated and accommodated. Hence, most labor contracts are quite lengthy with little or no flexibility. A labor contract is negotiated and covers a finite period time; after which, another agreement is required. Its sanctions are primarily legal. In contrast, an employment contract (e.g., an offer letter between an individual and an organization) is toward the relational pole and contains both explicit statements and tacit assumptions. Hence, it is fairly small, often no more than one or two pages, and quite flexible. Moreover, it is reinforced or undermined during execution of the contract – the primary means of control are the expectations and interests of the parties to the contract (Kay 1995).

Contract Type 3. Psychological Contracts

While transactional and relational contracts have some level of formalism, psychological contracts describe the relationship between an individual and an organization in entirely unstated expectations. These expectations, in turn, guide and characterize the behavior of both the individual and the organization (Handy 1993).

Schein has described three categories of psychological contracts representing increasing levels of involvement: coercive, calculative, and cooperative (Schein 1980). While each exists in an organization, one will predominate and thus characterize the organization's prevalent mindset. This comes closest to our notion of an essential architecture where the predominant level of involvement in an organization will govern the motivation, cooperation, and inventiveness of its employees and, ultimately, the organization itself. The essential or cognitive architecture of an organization – its set of psychological contracts – is simultaneously individual and organizational in nature.

Coercive, calculative, and cooperative contracts represent a range of attachments and commitments, from involuntary compliance to transactional behavior, to fully engaged dedication. In practice, calculative contracts are associated with the transactional pole of the contract continuum, while cooperative contracts are associated with the relational. (The coercive contract does not appear on the legal continuum of type 2 contracts since there is no "agreement" among participants in a coercive contract, such as a prisoner and a prison inmate.) While the calculative contract appears to predominate in most organizations, cooperative contracts are increasingly necessary if the organization is to flourish in the knowledge society.

The participants to a psychological contract are an individual and an organization. This is because, as defined by Schein, a psychological contract is a measure of engagement between an individual and an organization. This is particularly important to the knowledge organization and its knowledge workers where an individual's motivation and discretionary effort are critical to knowledge work. Furthermore, the factors that impact this level of engagement may be found in an organization's DNA – both in the strands and in the cross-linkages – the specific elements of which constitute an organization's cultural and learning systems.

4.1 The Contract Continuum

In the contract continuum illustrated in Fig. 7.4, contracts range in character from formal, and sometimes legal, specifications to partially formulated (and formed) relationships, to entirely tacit psychological mindsets. As requirements increase in richness, the contract shifts in character from thin to thick, from a "specification" in an engineered to a "relationship" in a framed context. In practice, this means that the assertions of an explicit contract – invariant, precondition, post-condition, trigger – become less precise. The explicit contract is an engineering or legal mechanism for specifying behavior and is not suitable for rich contexts. This is where both relational and psychological frameworks come into play. Specifying non-routine work, particularly knowledge work, requires developing and reinforcing expectations and the prospect of a long-term relationship. This cannot be done in a formal sense but depends on cultivating trust and social relationships.

The central motivation or requirement of thin design is to satisfy the corresponding (thin) contract specification by reducing organizational uncertainty. Thin contracts completely specify both discrete functions and their interfaces and easily lend themselves to thin forms of abstractions (e.g., encapsulation). In contrast, the motivation underlying thick design is to arrive at an acceptable agreement among participants to the corresponding design contract. Thick design is ideal for ambiguous situations where a specification is satisfied through the attitudes and expectations that embody the human constituent of the design – thick contracts that focus on relationships, psychological orientations, and context of the design itself. The people or groups participating in thick contracts determine the design's structure, workings, and output.

4.2 Refinement Path

As discussed above, one source of design flexibility is the definition of a given molecule. A second source concerns the development of the molecule itself. For example, let us consider the process molecule and center our attention on the {tool} constituent. One of the design choices that needs to be made concerns the type of database. There are several possibilities, all existing at the same level immediately below {tool}: a relational database management system (RDBMS), an object-oriented DBMS, etc. After a given selection, say an {RDBMS}, there are several possible vendor products below {RDBMS}, such as IBM, Oracle, and Sybase. Moreover, the entire pathway down the hierarchy is almost always a function of the {process} specification itself – transaction vs. decision process processes, for example. Furthermore, the entire downward pathway, sometimes known as a *refinement path,* is often *preselected* by an organization. This is particularly true with information technology tools, such as databases, networks, servers, and desktop computers. When a fully instantiated refinement path is preselected, organizations call the pathway a **standard** or **architecture**.

5 An Example from Organization Theory

As with any hierarchical system, organizational elements exist and interact within a wide range of frequency behavior. For example, the CEO, at the top of the hierarchy in the organization chart, is functionally a constant, while the lowest-level employees are rigid bodies with respect to each other. That leaves it to middle management to determine the dynamics of structure. In fact, it *is* middle management that largely determines structural behavior and has occupied the attention of organizational scientists. One perspective, for example, is that the *middle line* (i.e., the middle-frequency layer in an organization's formal structure) is essentially an *information relay* in a firm operating as an information processing mechanism (Nonaka and Takeuchi 1995). This perspective is largely responsible for middle-level downsizing so apparent in American firms over the years. In contrast, a more modern perspective, one reflecting the emerging knowledge era, is that the firm is a knowledge-creating entity, and therefore, the middle line consists of *knowledge engineers* (Nonaka and Takeuchi 1995). In either case, it is the middle line – the middle-frequency layer – that rightly occupies so much academic and management attention.

The notion of high-, middle-, and low-frequency motion is critical in organization design, and attention is not exclusively confined to the middle-frequency layer. For example, *organizational culture* sits at the very top of the organization, and hence, its motion is so slow that it may be taken as a constant. This is one reason management is attracted to "culture change" initiatives – changing an organization-wide constant should have a dramatic effect on the organizational system as a whole. Similarly, *organizational learning* – another low-frequency subsystem closely associated with culture – has attracted management effort in an attempt to create the "learning organization." Edgar Schein argues that such efforts often meet with failure: occupational subcultures (i.e., cultures based on education and work roles) – each with different and contradictory constants known as *tacit assumptions* – work against the communication necessary for learning (Schein 1996).

Attempts to change very low-frequency subsystems – culture or learning, for example – often meet with difficulty. As we have seen in hierarchy theory, the low-, middle-, and high-frequency layers are isolated and therefore not easily affected by each other. Low-frequency layers such as culture and learning are largely created through organizational evolution and are resistant to the effects of changes in high-frequency subsystems. This is in contrast to changes in subsystems within the same layer – information technology subsystems within a given level, for example, are directly changed and integrated.

6 An Example of Inter-organizational Knowledge Creation Networks

In this example, we discuss two types of relational contracts, differing in the factors associated with the context each creates. Knowledge-creating context is known as a *ba* or "place" where knowledge creation occurs. Organizations that want to build an inter-organizational knowledge network must find a way to build a *shared ba* in which all participating firms may participate (Ahmadjian 2004). The system elements associated with this shared ba include culture, language, and an atmosphere of trust and care. The factors that impact these elements include the number of participating firms, the ties (e.g., closeness, ownership stakes, trust) by which the firms are linked, and the temporal duration (i.e., short or long) of these relationships (Ahmadjian 2004). The first approach is known as the Toyota model and is characterized by an integral architecture. In contrast, the second approach is known as the Silicon Valley model and is modular in nature.

The Toyota model includes a primary organization (e.g., Toyota) with a set of comparatively few associated organizations with deep, long-term, and stable relationships. The participating organizations often share ownership ties. The ba is formed by the primary organization and spreads outward. The arrangement is one of a tightly linked set of firms that engage in activities that operationalize the SECI model of knowledge creation (Nonaka and Takeuchi 1995). For example, the participating organizations rotate employees and participate in activities (e.g., problem-solving groups, plant tours) that promote the creation of tacit knowledge and other activities (e.g., seminars, lectures, manuals) that subsequently promote externalization to make this knowledge explicit. One striking characteristic of this ba is the shared sense of identity between Toyota and its suppliers which has led to a strong, shared commitment to the Toyota Way (i.e., the Toyota DNA discussed above) (Ahmadjian 2004). The Toyota model is common within the Japanese automobile manufacturing industry and within the Japanese economy generally. *Flexibility arises from the integral nature of tacit knowledge and a ba designed to maximize the sharing of experiences and ideas through interpersonal and group communication* – that is, *socialization*.

The second approach is known as the Silicon Valley model. The ba is defined by an industry or geographic region (e.g., Silicon Valley) and includes dynamic links among many organizations (i.e., firms, universities, and research institutes). Inter-organizational relationships are many, thin, fluid and depend on the need of any one firm. This type of ba is particularly effective at sharing and *recombining* existing, explicit knowledge. The Silicon Valley ba is appropriate where there exists a highly mobile workforce of knowledge workers. Learning occurs through recombination of existing knowledge across firms where only recombinations with market potential will be selected. A dynamic workforce maximizes the possible number of recombinations, thus providing a greater likelihood of market success than otherwise. *Flexibility arises from the modular nature of explicit knowledge and a ba designed to maximize the number of shared threads of explicit knowledge and possible recombinations.*

The Toyota model creates a ba that facilitates socialization (i.e., tacit knowledge) and focuses on process innovation. In contrast, the Silicon Valley model creates a ba that is effective at knowledge recombination (i.e., explicit knowledge) and focuses on product or technology innovation. Each model illustrates the importance of context in knowledge creation and how differing styles of relationships (i.e., relational contracts) may be used to create that context. This also illustrates the workings of architecture: the ba that each model creates shares characteristics (tacit vs. explicit knowledge) with, and cannot be separated from the, wider context or ba (societal culture) within which each operates. This should not be surprising: Nonaka has stated that Japanese society is primarily tacit and the organizations that exist within that culture would create a ba that emphasizes *socialization*. In contrast, US firms operate within an explicit societal culture, and, hence, their respective inter-organizational ba emphasizes *combination* (Nonaka and Takeuchi 1995). The wider lesson, of course, illustrated by the SECI model, is that optimum knowledge creation should emphasize all phases of socialization, externalization, combination, and internalization.

7 An Example from Process Integration and Service-Oriented Architecture

Figure 7.2 is a representation of the process molecule – a process architecture that supports specification of {process} as well as its corresponding implementation subsystems {human}, {structure}, {information}, and {tool}. Figure 7.2 also shows the system and subsystem systems as separate and interacting entities. If the specifications of all participating systems are sufficiently rigorous – i.e., clear boundaries with system separation and communication (loose vertical and horizontal coupling), we would have a fully modular system. In such a case, flexibility arises from the options we have as designers: we may interconnect {process} task specifications (horizontally) in any appropriate configuration (i.e., a process map) to satisfy a particular business requirement (itself a high-level contract specification); we may also select any number of implementation options (vertically downward). Furthermore, the precise contract shares properties with "object-oriented" objects that include, for instance, reuse, composition of contracts, and contract sub-typing and dependencies. Thus, the approach we have been discussing in this chapter is an abstract representation of the underlying logic of service-oriented architectures.

8 Conclusion

In this chapter, we have presented a framework that extends Herbert Simon's work on hierarchy theory. Our framework associates levels of systems and their comparative knowledge content in terms of tacit and explicit knowledge. Systems are ordered based on several empirical criteria, such as frequency. A higher-level system typically has a lower frequency and therefore responds more slowly to input than a lower-level system. Also, a higher-level system has a comparatively larger tacit knowledge content than a lower-level system. This is a partial explanation of the behavior of systems – tacit systems are experiential and change more slowly than explicit systems.

We have also described an organization molecule as a special type of definitional hierarchy configured to specify and implement an organizational context, such as process or strategy. Both context and the subsystems associated with its implementation are the "organizational materials" with which we design organizations.

We have also described contracts as a mechanism to specify both contexts and their corresponding subsystems. Contracts exist in various forms, based on their knowledge content, from fully explicit, to some mix of explicit and tacit, to fully tacit. Thus, there is a "new contract continuum" that may be used to describe organizational systems in terms of their comparative tacit and knowledge composition.

An empirical hierarchy of organizational systems, definitional organization molecules for context design, and contracts for specification all intersect and produce a rich framework – organization modeling or "modeling as an art form" – that may be used to design, reconstitute, and align virtually every context in the organization. Flexibility largely depends on how we use these three pillars of organization modeling to reflect our design intention.

For example, we may manipulate system ordering to reshape our organization's work practices, from a traditional organization where process follows structure to a process enterprise where the reverse is true. Similarly, we may define an organization molecule to reflect a particular perspective where, for example, we may include culture as a subsystem in strategy design. To continue, we may also follow a particular refinement path during detailed design of a molecule to adopt, for example, a specific technology implementation; or, alternatively, we may preselect a refinement path and thus establish an organization-wide standard. Finally, we may use contracts to precisely specify our technical systems and relational and psychological contracts to design an organization's "space" to cultivate its tacit knowledge systems.

Finally, we have seen that the twenty-first-century organization must transcend the limitation of omitting or dealing separately with its mechanical and human systems. Rather, it has the option of designing its DNA molecule to define and interrelate virtually all the elements that constitute the organization itself. Thus, the organization may be designed as an organic configuration of systems and structures where "flexibility" is part of organizational life.

References

Ahl V, Allen TFH (1996) Hierarchy theory: a vision, vocabulary, and epistemology. Columbia University Press, New York

Ahmadjian CL (2004) Inter-organization knowledge creation: knowledge and networks. In: Takeuchi H, Nonaka I (eds) Hitotsubashi on knowledge management. Wiley, Singapore

Bunge M (1977) Emergence and the mind. In: Mahner M (ed) Scientific realism. Prometheus Books, Amherst, 2001

Davenport TH (2005) Thinking for a living. Harvard Business School Press, Boston

Drucker PF (1999) Management challenges for the 21st century. Harper Business, New York

Geertz C (1973) The interpretation of cultures. Basic Books, New York

Gill JH (2000) The tacit mode: Michael Polanyi's postmodern philosophy. State University of New York Press, Albany

Handy C (1993) Understanding organizations. Oxford University Press, New York

Kay J (1995) Why firms succeed. Oxford University Press, New York

Kilov H (2002) Business models: a guide for business and IT. Prentice-Hall, Upper Saddle River

Kilov H, Ross J (1994) Information modeling: an object-oriented approach. Prentice-Hall, Englewood Cliffs

Liker JK (2004) The Toyota Way. McGraw-Hill, New York

MacNeil IR, Gudel PJ (2001) Contracts: exchange contracts and relations, 3rd edn. Foundation Press, New York

March JG (Interview by Coutu D) (2006) Ideas as art. Harv Bus Rev 84(10): 82–89, 148

Meyer B (1992) Applying 'design by contract'. Comput IEEE 25(10):40–51, October
Mintzberg H (1983) Structure in fives: designing effective organizations. Prentice Hall, Englewood Cliffs
Morabito J, Singh M (1993) A new approach to object-oriented analysis and design. In: *Tools USA 93* (Proceedings of the 11th international conference of object-oriented languages and systems, Santa Barbara) Prentice Hall, pp 45–55, Subsequently accepted as a position paper on object-oriented enterprise modeling by ISO/IEC/JTC1/SC21, Working Group – *Conceptual Schema and Data Modeling Facilities*. Yokohama
Morabito J, Sack I, Bhate A (1999) A organization modeling: innovative architectures for the 21st century. Prentice Hall, Upper Saddle River
Morabito J, Sack I, Bhate A (2000) Dimensions of organizational design: the architectural continuum and knowledge binding. Stevens Alliance Technol Manag (SATM), 4(2)
Nevis EC, DiBella AJ, Gould JM (1995) Understanding organizations as learning systems. Sloan Manag Rev 36(2):73–85
Nonaka I, Takeuchi H (1995) The knowledge-creating company. Oxford University Press, New York
Ohno T (1978) Toyota seisan hoshiki. Diamond Inc., Tokyo (Original Japanese Edition), English translation: (1988) Toyota production system: beyond large-scale production, Productivity Press
Osono E (2004) The strategy-making process as dialogue. In: Takeuchi H, Nonaka I (eds) Hitotsubashi on knowledge management. Wiley, Singapore
Rummler GA, Brache AP (1995) Improving performance, 2nd edn. Jossey-Bass, San Francisco
Schein EH (1980) Organizational psychology. Prentice-Hall, Englewood Cliffs
Schein EH (1992) Organizational culture and leadership, 2nd edn. Jossey Bass, San Francisco
Schein EH (1996) Three cultures of management: the key to organizational learning. Sloan Manage Rev 38:9, Fall 1996
Schein EH (1999) The corporate culture survival guide. Jossey-Bass, San Francisco
Simon HA (1973) The organization of complex systems. In: Pattee HH (ed) Hierarchy theory: the challenge of complex systems. George Braziller, New York
Simon HA (1996) The science of the artificial, 3rd edn. The MIT Press, Cambridge
Sushil (2007) Flowing stream strategy and blue ocean strategy: strategic flexibility to manage continuity and change. Lecture given at the Howe School of Technology Management, Stevens Institute of Technology
Sushil (2012) Flowing stream strategy: managing confluence of continuity and change. J Enterp Transform 2(1):26–49
Takeuchi H, Nonaka I (2004) Knowledge creation and dialectics. In: Takeuchi H, Nonaka I (eds) Hitotsubashi on knowledge management. Wiley, Singapore

Chapter 8
Towards Understanding the Effects of Outsourcing on the Flexibility Dynamic of System of Systems

S. Jimmy Gandhi, Alex Gorod, and Brian Sauser

1 Introduction

Systems are an integrative part of the global business scenario, and organizational flexibility is becoming a requirement in order to remain competitive and keep pace with the changing operating environment and increasing complexity of systems. In recent years, the term System of Systems (SoS) has been increasingly discussed in both industry and academia as an emerging systems solution to complex problems. These complex problems with emergent and adaptive behaviors have also created a demand for flexibility in these systems. It is the dynamic environment that these systems routinely perform in that has begun to create this demand. As a result, there is a reciprocating impact on customer needs that are continuously changing, which results in an exponential increase in complexity. In order to remain competitive, these systems and the organizations that realize them have to have more options, which is a direct influence on flexibility. These options create a strain on the resources of any system, both intellectual and physical. To address these constraints while maintaining a requirement for flexibility, the organizations that design these systems have to maintain a competitive advantage and by so doing rely heavily on the outsourcing of its constituents. Outsourcing can enable an organization to be more competitive and offer the customers more value. However, outsourcing and the flexibility it potentially propagates or hinders introduce a new set of risks. In this

S.J. Gandhi (✉)
California State University, Northridge, USA
e-mail: sj.gandhi@csun.edu

A. Gorod
University of Adelaide, Adelaide, Australia
e-mail: Alex.gorod@adelaide.edu.au

B. Sauser
University of North Texas, Denton, USA
e-mail: bsauser@unt.edu

Sushil and E.A. Stohr (eds.), *The Flexible Enterprise*, Flexible Systems Management, DOI 10.1007/978-81-322-1560-8_8, © Springer India 2014

chapter, we will describe these emerging systems called System of Systems, discuss a set of challenges to outsourcing, and conclude with a discussion of the implications these outsourcing challenges have on an SoS and their flexibility dynamic. To exemplify this we will use a case study of the Yellow Cab SoS (Gorod et al. 2008). We will then describe the effects of outsourcing on the Yellow Cab SoS with respect to the flexibility dynamic as this becomes a delicate balance between insufficient and excessive outsourcing of its constituents.

2 SoS and the Flexibility Dynamic

During World War II and the post-World War II period, the level of complexities in programs rose significantly due to the introduction of new engineering techniques, which focused on a single complex system rather than separate individual components. This caused a paradigm shift with regard to how to deal with these complexities, and the new methods considered constituted the discipline of systems engineering (SE). The objective of this paradigm shift was to address "…shortcomings in the ability to deal with difficulties generated by increasingly complex and interrelated system of systems" (Keating et al. 2003). There was a need for a discipline that focused on engineering of multiple integrated complex systems (Keating et al. 2003).

Today, these systems are defined as System of Systems, and the discipline for developing their realization is known as System of Systems Engineering (SoSE). Some of the examples of SoS are the Internet (Maier 1996), the Transportation System (DeLaurentis 2005), the Integrated Deepwater Systems (IDS) program (O'Rourke 2007), the Future Combat System (FCS) (Lane and Valerdi 2005), and the Yellow Cab System (Gorod and Sauser 2007).

Due to SoS being a relatively new concept, there have been numerous attempts to define it. For example, Kotov (1997) defined them as "large scale concurrent and distributed systems that are comprised of complex systems"; Manthorpe's (1996) military-specific definition states, "system of systems is concerned with interoperability and synergism of Command, Control, Computers, Communications, and Information (C4I) and Intelligence, Surveillance, and Reconnaissance (ISR) Systems," and Luskasik's (1998) education-specific definition states, "SoSE involves the integration of systems of systems that ultimately contribute to evolution of the social infrastructure."

Alternatively, some scientists took a different approach by focusing on distinguishing characteristics rather than providing an abstract definition. According to Boardman and Sauser (2006), there are five "…distinguishing characteristics (i.e. autonomy, belonging, connectivity, diversity, and emergence), that can help us to recognize or to realize a System of Systems (SoS)." Boardman and Sauser also proposed that there are opposing forces or paradoxes within each characteristic "that are influenced by fluxes in realizing or recognizing a system" (Boardman and Sauser 2006).

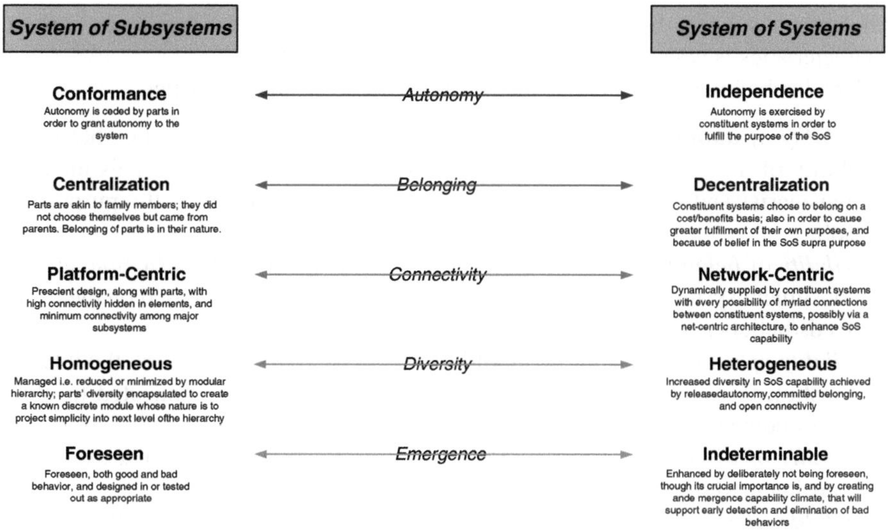

Fig. 8.1 System characteristics and their paradoxes (Adopted from Sauser et al. 2008)

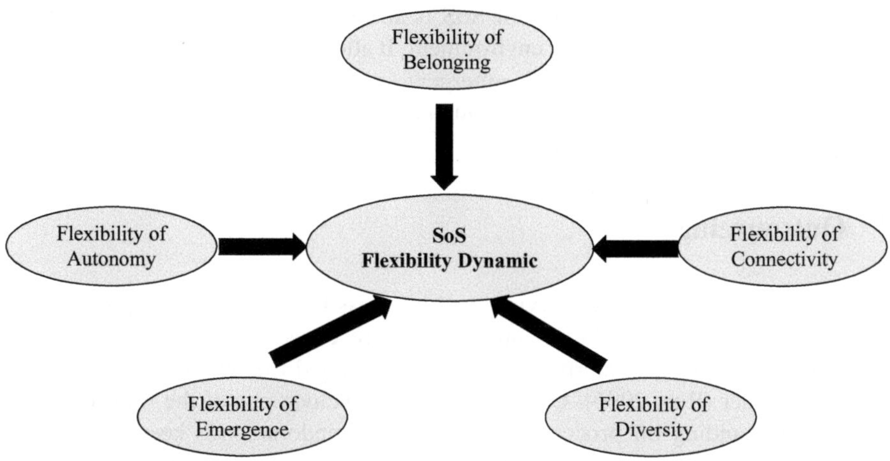

Fig. 8.2 SoS flexibility dynamic (Adopted from Gorod et al. 2008)

The characterization approach for explaining SoS is better than defining it, because definitions tend to be industry specific and also lack the general flexibility necessary in successful dynamic transdisciplinary engineering processes. This view is supported by Boardman and Sauser (2006), who state that the use of characteristics enables us to better identify the dynamics within an SoS. Figure 8.1 depicts these five distinguishing characteristics and their paradoxes.

Gorod et al. (2008) suggested to further extend this theory and combine the ideas of the distinguishing characteristics with the concept of flexibility (see Fig. 8.2).

The authors suggest that an SoS's ability to balance between the paradoxes of these characteristics is what defines its flexibility.

The list below further defines the flexibility of these characteristics:

Flexibility of autonomy – The flexibility of autonomy shows how flexible is the ability of a system as part of SoS to make independent choices. This includes managerial and operational independence while accomplishing the purpose of SoS.

Flexibility of belonging – The flexibility of belonging shows how flexible are the constituent systems to choose to belong to SoS. This choice is based on their own needs/beliefs and/or fulfillment.

Flexibility of connectivity – The flexibility of connectivity shows how flexible the constituent systems are with regard to their ability to stay connected to other constituent systems.

Flexibility of diversity – The flexibility of diversity shows up to what extent the constituent systems can be diversified.

Flexibility of emergence – The flexibility of emergence shows how flexible the constituent systems are in order to result in emergent properties of the SoS as a whole.

We contend that this flexibility of SoS is an important phenomenon in today's ever-changing complex dynamic environment. It allows us to engineer complex systems, which can be simultaneously, emergent enough in order to keep up and cope with the changing operating environment and yet be effectively governable.

3 Outsourcing

The term outsourcing defines services and business functions that are provided by an external organization. The organization that receives the services is called the client or buyer, and the external organization is called the outsourcer, vendor, or service provider (Rost 2006). Outsourcing could include one of the following two options: (1) handing off processes to third-party vendors or (2) keeping the processes in-house but sending them to internal lower-cost locations within the organization (Robinson et al. 2005). Outsourcing can encompass, for example, manufacturing, IT, and back-office services. Alternatively, international outsourcing can be defined as international fragmentation of the value-added chain (Egger and Egger 2006). For this chapter, we scope the term outsourcing in relation to modern outsourcing or partnerships (Grover et al. 1996; Marguilius 2005).

The global workforce has long sought to economize the production of goods and services through outsourcing. Thus, globalization of the economy has acted upon us and no product can be designed, developed, and manufactured in a vacuum. Henry Ford's vision of the "specialization and division of labor" is no longer economically feasible under a connected global economy. Parts and people must be outsourced in order to provide an economically, as well as technically, competitive product. In contrast, to "in-house" (where variables such as parts, material, and labor are fused together at one location), outsourcing requires explicit coordination and cooperation. However, to some degree, this relinquishes control of the product during the development and production phases.

Outsourcing is a strategically important activity that has both positive and negative influences that can be both acute and chronic (Wu et al. 2005). In order for outsourcing of SoS to work effectively, supply chain management must work in a timely, as well as effective manner to provide products/services to the consumer. This does not come without risk, which has to be identified, and the effects of this risk on the SoS have to be analyzed.

While there are advantages, there are equally disadvantages that are thought of as consequences of outsourcing. We define these advantages and disadvantages as challenges that can be mitigated or embraced with proper risk management. These challenges which we contend have a dynamic influence on SoS when its constituent systems outsourced are as follows:

(i) ***Schedule*** – The ability of a project to deliver the end product within a specified period of time (Browning 1998). When constituent systems are outsourced, control of the decision-making process that influences the efficiency of task execution does not necessarily rest with the outsourcer (Gandhi and Eschbacher 2007).

(ii) ***Technical*** – The capability of the technology to provide the expected performance benefits (Browning 1998). Two subcategories of technical challenges applicable to outsourcing of SoS are interoperability and supportability and testing and verification risks (Gandhi and Eschbacher 2007).

  a. *Interoperability risk:* When two or more constituent systems are integrated and need to interact with each other to perform a certain task, the capability to operate as desired is called interoperability of SoS, which is considered an essential aspect of correctness of integrated systems (Hao et al. 2004). However, constituent systems of SoS from different vendors have a much higher probability of not interoperating properly which is called interoperability risk.

  b. *Supportability and testing risk:* Supportability is defined as the fielding and maintaining of systems which are currently being developed and deployed (FAA 2005). If the constituent systems that are being used are provided by outside vendors, the challenges associated with supportability increase as the support staff of the organization would not know as much about the constituent system which would be acting as a black box. This would also be the reason for an increase in the testing associated with complex system.

(iii) ***Cost*** – Not being able to complete the project within a given budget and the consequences thereof (Browning 1998). Most outsourced constituent systems of SoS only result in about 50 % of the expected cost savings in the first few months and only become fully effective after a year (Kelly 2007).

(iv) ***Intellectual property (IP)*** – The organization's internal intellectual property being used by the supplier to develop a competing product (Sullivan 2004). The likelihood of this occurring will increase considerably when constituent systems of SoS are outsourced, particularly to countries where IP laws are not implemented as strictly as they are in the USA.

(v) ***Quality assurance*** – Whether adequate quality assurance processes will be in place (Gandhi and Eschbacher 2007). Even the best development teams create code that have "bugs," which is why quality assurance, especially when done offshore, is extremely important.

(vi) ***Communication barriers*** – Almost every significant study of outsourcing risks in the past decade has brought up the issue of communication. Communication barriers arise when outsourcing because even though English is a common language, differences in expressions and dialects causes huge communication barriers.

(vii) ***Scope creep*** – There is a gradual introduction of requirements that were not part of the project's initial planning. This can be a result of the communication barriers previously defined, which results in costly delays to the outsourced project (Lorber 2007).

(viii) ***Flexibility*** – Nilchiani and Hastings (2007) defined flexibility in the systems engineering field as the ability of a system to respond to potential internal or external changes, affecting its value delivery, in a timely and cost-effective manner. The existence of flexibility can help the system adapt itself to the new conditions that arise because of changes in the environment.

4 Effects of Outsourcing on the Flexibility Dynamic of SoS

With the occurrence of outsourcing, the amount of flexibility associated with an SoS could either increase or decrease, depending on the situation under consideration. Gorod et al. (2008) suggested that there are opposing forces in the flexibility spectrum where one side points us towards a rigid form of SoS and the other leads towards a chaotic SoS. If the SoS under consideration is either extremely rigid or chaotic, the flexibility would become a significant challenge and even catastrophic; thus, outsourcing has no beneficial influence. Conversely, if the SoS being considered is in the "optimization area," that is, neither too rigid nor chaotic, then the impediments to flexibility are likely to decrease. This would thus make outsourcing beneficial to SoS. That is, the effectiveness of outsourcing on an SoS is partially contingent upon the SoS balancing in the "optimization area." Conversely, outsourcing has an effect on the flexibility dynamic as defined earlier by the flexibility of SoS (i.e., autonomy, belonging, connectivity, diversity, and emergence; see Fig. 8.1). For example:

(i) ***Autonomy***: When an SoS is outsourced, the tendency would be to shift towards conformance as there would be a significant reduction in independence. This is because of the reliance on vendors who could make up the critical path due to which the overall risk of the project increases significantly.

(ii) ***Belonging***: Outsourcing would also have an effect on the belonging of an SoS. Outsourcing to a very high degree could lead towards decentralization. Conversely, insufficient outsourcing could lead to centralization.

(iii) ***Connectivity***: When considering connectivity, outsourcing could result in a network-centric SoS. This helps to enhance the SoS capability, which can be seen as a benefit by outsourcing SoS.

(iv) ***Diversity***: When the diversity aspect is taken into consideration, outsourcing could result in heterogeneous SoS. This could be possible because outsourcing could increase the diversity of the SoS due to different vendors supplying parts from different parts of the country or even world.

(v) ***Emergence***: When an SoS is outsourced, more than likely it could result in a highly emergent behavior pattern, which would result in a high level of indeterminability. The spike in the level of indeterminability is because of the lack of control that occurs as a result of outsourcing and also because of the heightened risks that are associated with outsourcing of SoS, which have been discussed in the earlier section of this chapter.

These influences of the flexibility dynamic and the effects of outsourcing are further depicted in Fig. 8.3, which represents the continual balancing that SoS attempts to sustain to subsist within the "optimization area." This illustrates to practitioners that selective outsourcing is important to the successful functioning of the SoS (Lacity et al. 1996).

From Fig. 8.3, we can see that insufficient outsourcing of the constituents of the SoS would lead towards conformance of the SoS, but excessive outsourcing would influence an excessive independence of the constituents, neither of which are beneficial for an SoS to operate. This is because too much conformance would result in the SoS not being flexible enough to react appropriately with changes in the environment, whereas excessive independence would result in chaos as there would be no common ground or platform based on which the constituents could relate to each other as part of the overall SoS.

Similarly, when considering the belonging of an SoS, insufficient outsourcing would result in potential centralization, whereas excessive outsourcing would influence decentralization.

When thinking about the connectivity associated with an SoS, limited outsourcing of its constituents would result in a platform-centric/hierarchical structure, whereas excessive outsourcing would cause a predominately network-centric structure to be formed, with no clearly defined boundaries.

The two ends of the spectrum represented in this balance when considering the effects of outsourcing on diversity would be homogeneity and heterogeneity. Too much homogeneity would not be beneficial for an SoS because there would be no variation among its constituents resulting in not sufficient flexibility of the SoS. On the other extreme, too much heterogeneity would result in so much variation that it would lead to chaos and affect the functioning of the SoS negatively.

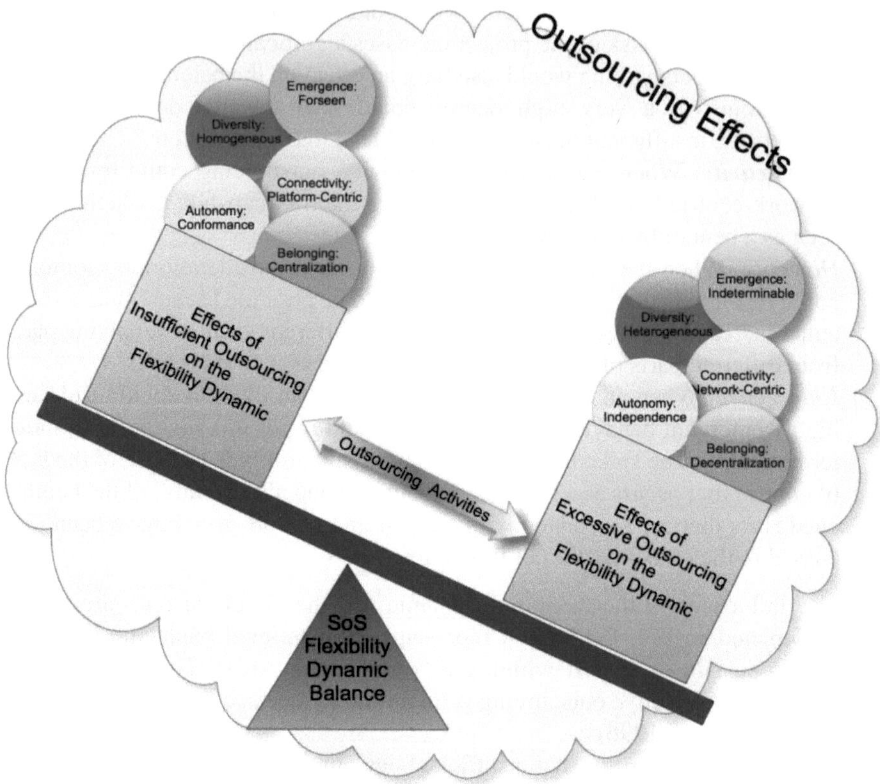

Fig. 8.3 Outsourcing effects on flexibility dynamic of SoS

Lastly, when examining the effects of outsourcing on emergence, we found that insufficient outsourcing would result in foreseen outcomes, which would affect the adaptability of the SoS negatively. Excessive outsourcing with reference to emergence of the SoS would result in indeterminable outcomes, which also would affect the adaptability of the SoS because the constituents would not know how to deal with the situation which has arisen.

In order to explain these results better, in the next section we have discussed an example of an SoS and how its characteristics get affected by outsourcing the SoS' constituents.

5 A Case Study with the Yellow Cab SoS

The New York City (NYC) yellow cab case was introduced as an SoS by Gorod et al. (2008) and Sauser et al. (2008). The NYC Yellow Cab SoS is an essential part of the NYC transportation network. It consists of over 13,000 licensed medallion taxicabs

Effects of Outsourcing
(Yellow Cab Case)

Flexibility Dynamic	Insufficient	Excessive
Autonomy	Complete control by TLC on the dynamics of the Yellow Cab SoS	Complete independence of medallion operators without any governance by TLC, causing chaos
Belonging	Will result in centralized structure, with the TLC having full control.	Will result in a decentralized structure in which the TLC will have no governing role causing chaos
Connectivity	Will result in a purely hierarchical structure, with no network	Will result in a high Net centricity with unclear boundaries, causing chaos
Diversity	Will result in the TLC being a completely homogenous organization with no variations in the individual taxi cabs	Will result in a completely heterogeneous organization in which there will be no standards to abide by, which will cause chaos.
Emergence	Will result in highly foreseen outcomes due to which the TLC will static and be unable to cope with changes in the dynamic environment	Will result in highly indeterminable outcomes for which the TLC will not be prepared and hence unable to cope with change in a highly dynamic environment, causing chaos

Fig. 8.4 Effects of outsourcing on flexibility dynamic of the Yellow Cab SoS

(Commission 2007) and serves about 240 million passengers every year, which creates a 1.2 billion dollar industry (Schaller Consulting 2006). NYC yellow cabs bring in around 30% of all fares paid by passengers for all trips in NYC and approximately 45 % of fares paid for trips within Manhattan (Schaller Consulting 2006). The taxicabs are privately operated by independent companies or individuals. At the same time, they are regulated by the NYC taxi and limousine commission (TLC).

Since these taxicabs are operated by independent companies or individuals, the TLC is effectively outsourcing the operation of each cab. The Yellow Cab SoS can be considered to be an example of outsourcing constituents of an SoS on a large scale. In Fig. 8.4, we have mapped the effects of outsourcing on the Yellow Cab SoS, in the case of both insufficient outsourcing and excessive outsourcing. This example shows the effects of outsourcing on the Yellow Cab SoS and thus helps us theorize that an SoS could have difficulties functioning properly if the outsourcing of the operations of taxicabs is not done selectively and in the right proportion.

From Fig. 8.4, we can see that the key to outsource without having heightened risks for the SoS is to effectively ensure that there is the appropriate amount of outsourcing in regard to the yellow cab operations so that all the characteristics of the SoS remain within the "optimization space" (Gorod et al. 2008).

6 Conclusion

While engineering an SoS, we have important choices to make regarding outsourcing constituent systems of the SoS or have them engineered in-house. If we were to outsource certain constituent systems of the SoS, we need to keep in mind that there could be dual effects on the flexibility of the SoS, that is, it could be beneficial for the flexibility of the SoS or could lead to a reduction in the flexibility. Organizations should also keep in mind to outsource constituents of the SoS selectively to try and maximize the benefits of outsourcing. With respect to this research project, when we discuss maximizing the benefits of outsourcing, we are referring to outsourcing the constituents of the SoS without having heightened risk.

This gives the organizations that operate as an SoS an opportunity to better manage their realization. By this we mean that outsourcing adequately can create more choices for the organization, which would result in increased flexibility of the SoS. Conversely, either excessive or a significant lack of outsourcing could lead to excessive choices and thus lack of governance of the SoS, or alternatively it could result to few choices which would translate into increased risk which would affect flexibility negatively. Thus, it is important that a thorough assessment be done to see how flexibility of each of the characteristics is affected by outsourcing, and only then a decision should be taken about whether to undertake it and to what extent.

References

Boardman J, Sauser B (2006) System of systems – the meaning of of. IEEE international system of systems conference. Los Angeles, CA

Browning T (1998) Sources of schedule risk in complex system development. Eighth annual international symposium of INCOSE. Vancouver, Canada

Commission N. Y. T. C. T. L. (2007) Current medallions – sorted by TLC medallion number, current_medallions.xls, TLC

DeLaurentis D (2005) Understanding transportation as a system of systems design problem, 43rd AIAA Aerospace Sciences Meeting. Reno, NV

Egger H, Egger P (2006) International outsourcing and the productivity of low skilled labor in the EU. Econ Inq 44(1):98–108

FAA (2005) National Airspace system documentation – acquisition and program risk management guide. FAA

Gandhi J, Eschbacher G (2007) Risk of outsourcing complex systems – a growing phenomenon, American Society of Engineering Management (ASEM) annual conference Chattanooga, TN

Gorod A, Sauser B (2007) An application of Prim's Algorithm in defining a SoS operational boundary. 5th conference on systems engineering research. Hoboken

Gorod A, Gandhi SJ et al (2008) Flexibility of system of systems. Glob J Flex Syst Manage 9(4):1–12
Grover V, Joong M et al (1996) The effect of service quality and partnership on the outsourcing of information systems functions. J Manage Inform Syst 12(4):89–116
Hao R, Lee D et al (2004) Integrated system interoperability testing with applications to VoIP. IEEE/ACM Transactions on Networking 12(5):823–836
Keating C, Rogers R et al (2003) Systems of systems engineering. Eng Manage J 15(3):36–45
Kelly W (2007) The risk manager's survival guide. Risk Management Magazine, pp 22–28
Kotov V (1997) Systems of systems as communicating structures, Hewlett Packard, HPL-97-124
Lacity M, Willcocks L et al (1996) The value of selective IT sourcing. Sloan Manage Rev 37(3):13–25
Lane JA, Valerdi R (2005) Synthesizing SoS concepts for use in cost estimation. IEEE conference on systems, man, and cybernetics at Waikoloa, HI
Lorber L (2007) An expert's do's and don'ts for outsourcing technology. The Wall Street Journal, New York B8
Luskasik SJ (1998) System, systems of systems, and the education of engineers. Artif Intell Eng Des Anal Manuf 12(1):55–60
Maier M (1996) Architecting principles of systems-of-systems. 6th annual international symposium of the international council on systems engineering. Boston
Manthorpe WH (1996) The emerging joint system of system: a systems engineering challenge and opportunity for APL. J Hopkins APL Tech D 17(3):305–310
Marguilius D (2005) The new business process partnership. InfoWorld 27:33–37
Nilchiani R, Hastings D (2007) Measuring the value of space systems flexibility: a six element framework. Syst Eng 10(1):26–44
O'Rourke R (2007) Coast guard deepwater program: background, oversight issues, and options for congress, CRS Report for Congress, C. R. Service
Robinson M, Kalakota R et al (2005) Global outsourcing: executing an onshore, nearshore or offshore strategy. Mivar Press, Inc, Alpharetta, GA: Mivar Press
Rost J (2006) The insider's guide to outsourcing risks and rewards. Auerbach Publications, Boca Raton, FL: Auerbach Publications
Sauser B, Boardman J et al (2008) SoS management. In: Jamshidi M (ed) System of systems – innovations for the 21st century. Wiley, Hoboken
Schaller Consulting (2006) NYC Taxicab Fact Book New York, TLC
Sullivan L (2004) The O word: outsourcing overseas. Risk Manage 51:24–30
Wu F, Li HZ et al (2005) An outsourcing decision model for sustaining long-term performance. Int J Prod Res 43(12):2513–2535

Chapter 9
Creating Order Out of Disorder Through Intuitive Flexibility

Brig. R.C. Pathak and H.D. Patil

1 Introduction

The fast-changing world is in turbulence and is generating an inhospitable environment for ad hoc and informal ways of creating and selling products. Due to breakthrough technological changes, the business competition is becoming more complex. In this scenario, one has to find certainty out of uncertainty, linearity out of nonlinearity, order from disorder, and harmony from chaos for sailing through the business turbulent water. It should be our endeavor to find stability out of instability.

Chaos is a form of instability where the specific long-term future is unknowable. Stacey (1993) has defined chaos as "an irregular pattern of behavior generated by well-defined non-linear feedback rules, commonly found in the nature and human society." Also, chaos means disorder and randomness in the behavior of a system at the specific level; it also means that there is a qualitative pattern at a general, overall level. The future unfolds unpredictably but it always does so according to recognizable family-like resemblances. History repeats itself, but never in the same way. Chaos theory expert Edward Lorenz (1961) asks: "does the flap of butterfly wings in Brazil set off tornado in Texas." Every problem is intertwining of order and disorder and is a function of some recognizable variables from where a predictive model should be found out of the complex problems. This is generally done by finding localizing temporary regions of stability out of instability.

Communication chaos is the worst disorder/uncertainty found today due to IT-enabled services and IT boom taking place in technological/managerial issues. Due to the presence of many means of communication like Internet, mobiles, telephones, and e-services, dependency has increased on these without efficiently getting feedback communications. The "process" and analytical techniques including fuzzylogy or

B.R.C. Pathak (✉) • H.D. Patil
Imperial College of Engineering and Research, 412 207 Wagholi, Pune, India
e-mail: rcpathakindia@yahoo.com; patil_hrishikesh@rediffmail.com

Sushil and E.A. Stohr (eds.), *The Flexible Enterprise*, Flexible Systems Management, DOI 10.1007/978-81-322-1560-8_9, © Springer India 2014

fuzzy set theories do something to solve and address the chaotic disorders, but intuition as well as experiential learning comes more handy, most of the times. Herein, intuition may be defined as "the way we translate our experience into action" or in other words: "ability to sense or know immediately without reasoning" (Klein 2004). As most of us know that even the predictive models like decision making fail, the intuition takes over as fail-safe method, since these dimensions come out from depth of "experiential learning." Once intuition combined with flexibility, it becomes a powerful tool to cope with complex problems. Flexibility is holistic approach – synthesis and not simply analytical – which can be defined as ability to change or react with little penalty in time, effort, cost, or performance. Flexibility is a multidimensional concept, which demands agility and versatility for coping complex situations (Sushil 2008).

Intuition sometime is also interpreted as "sixth sense." "Intuitive flexibility," thus, can be defined as "translating learning experience into a versatile potential activity to facilitate solving a problem." There are definitely some regular patterns found in irregular or chaotic categories, and with analysis and processing technique, new order can be found out from chaos. The process may be defined as "an organized group of related activities that together create a result of value to customers" (Hammer 2001). Any process is better than no process. There are many sources of chaos and uncertainty. There should be strategy and tactics to deal with uncertainty and disorder.

In this chapter, few live case studies have been discussed. These are as follows:

(a) Toyota Motors of Japan – manufacturing uncertainty
(b) Labor union case study of a DRDO organization
(c) Intuitive forecasting of snow avalanches

Any organization must remove the existing instability of chaos or uncertainty for effective performance and efficiency. The systematic structured work culture, process-based analysis, logical thinking, and eventually creative and intuitive flexibility are the answer to most of the chaos and disorder obtaining in the business world (Pathak 2005).

2 Cause and Effect to Chaos Theory

In true sense, "chaos theory" was first discovered by a meteorologist, Edward Lorenz (1961/1972), in the American Association of Advancement of Science in Washington D.C. In mathematics and physics, "chaos theory" describes the behavior of certain nonlinear dynamical systems that under certain conditions exhibits dynamics that are sensitive to initial conditions. Simply, "chaos theory" comes from the fact that the systems that the theory describes are apparently disordered, but theory is really about finding the underlying order in apparently random data (Edward 2002; Gollub and Baker 1996). According to Stacey (1993), chaos unfolds unpredictably, but always it does so according to recognizable family-like resemblances.

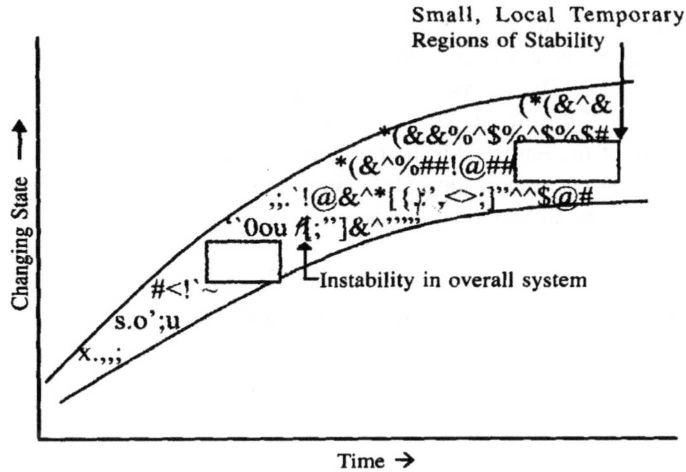

Fig. 9.1 Chaos theory: chaos and complexity

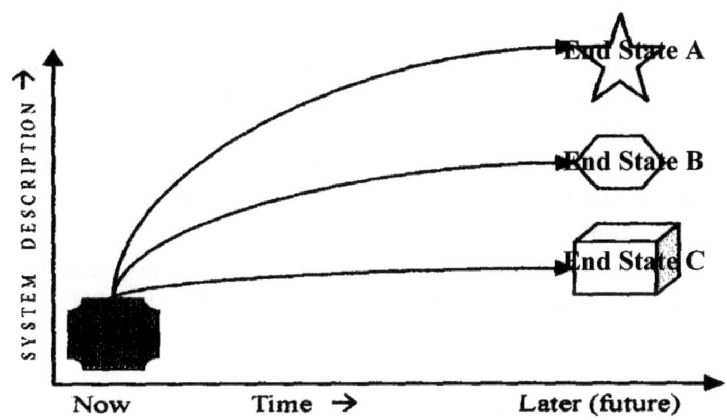

Fig. 9.2 Future emerging scenarios

Chaos is the result and repercussions of the cause and effect. Chaos has number of potential variables and there can be infinite number of outcomes-solutions. As can be observed in Fig. 9.1, there are few patterns of stability amidst instability chaos. In the nature, cases of snow precipitation – pattern of snow flakes, from dendritic to round stable grains and examining the pattern of waves of ocean from beach level and observed from a higher cliff gives distinct pattern of the waves in their ebb and flow exhibit such patterns (Patel 2005). Both the patterns may lead to immediately a conclusion – a viable variable outcome. The various emerging outcomes- solutions can be noticed from Fig. 9.2, which gives concept of emerging scenario in the form of End State A, End State B, and End State C (Allio 2002).

Observing the chaos and disorders from a worker's level and at CEO level makes a difference. The universe works with clockwise precision, in spite of many local disorders and chaos. The cosmos solar system and the study of our planet reveal many patterns of the flow of forces between and on planets. We should not go beyond the law of the nature. All the outcomes of infinite variables are the consequences of the intersection of tangible/intangible snapshots and have interconnectedness which is to be understood clearly.

2.1 Some Steps to Create Order Out of Chaos

Managers and the top leaders (CEO) should exercise the following steps (de Wit and Meyer 2004):

(a) Encourage self-organizing groups: Top managers encourage to create this type of conducive environment.
(b) Provoke multiple cultures: The people should be rotated between functions and business units.
(c) Design of the use of power: The application of power in particular forms has fairly predictable consequences of group dynamics.
(d) Expose the business to challenging situations: Most imaginative and competent competitions will be a unified effort for all to build sustainable competitive advantage on global scale.
(e) Devote explicit attention for improving group learning skills: This eradicates the existing mental blocks and inculcates absorbing and harmonious work culture and interconnectedness.
(f) Creating resource slack: At least people will not be negative minded for generally complaining about lack of resources (Simchi-Levi et al. 2004).

3 Process as a Problem-Solving Technique

Systematic process and its analytical approach to the problem solves many disorders. Process is a technical form and is defined as "an organized group of related activities that together create a result of value to customers" (Hammer 2001). Process has four main ingredients which are to be correctly understood:

(a) Group of activities
(b) Related and organized
(c) Together
(d) Result

Process is decidedly distinct clarity. The absence of process is not freedom – it is anarchy (chaos). With a disciplined process, rework, repair, and redesign are reduced, which reduces last-minute fire drills and results into both greater customer satisfaction and reduced costs. With power of process, the order can be created where chaos reigns. Some broad steps have been cited as follows:

(a) Identify signs of dysfunction.
(b) Leverage people's creativity with the power of process.
(c) Make innovation repeatable through detailed process design.
(d) Don't let people tell you that creativity conflicts with process.
(e) Create a process-friendly company by aligning facilities, compensation, and structure around processes.
(f) Ensure everyone understands process.
(g) Be resolutely committed to discipline, teamwork, and shared responsibility.
(h) Accept the fact that not everyone will get it.

4 Information Uncertainty: A Major Communication Threat

There are five uncertainties of information: missing information, unreliable information, conflicting information, noisy information, and confusing information. We can be uncertain because we are not able to trust the information. Similarly, today having most of the technological devices, communication can be confusing, as there are too many media of usage and feedback communications are used sparingly. The voice mails, e-mails, SMS or fax, telephones, video, sound clips, pictures, schedules, calendars, workflows along with web browsing, e-commerce, IT-enabled services, etc., complications have increased.

Microsoft Head, Bill Gates suggests "unified communications to enable close the gap between the devices we use to contact people about business information" (Indian Express, Pune, 28 Jan 08). We should also understand the difference between information and communication. The former is one way traffic whereas communication is a two-way activity and "feedback communication" is a significant tool and dominant factor which makes all the difference.

There are following tactics for managing uncertainty:

(a) Delaying: Many cases of yesterday's chaos/problem turn out to be solved today – with the lapse of time. Intuitive delay brings calm in real crisis.
(b) Increasing attention: Monitoring and paying more attention to the situation is one way out.
(c) Simplifying the plan: This is one of the easiest way to reduce uncertainty by reducing complexity of the plan we are formulating.
(d) Shaking the tree: Sometimes the best way to handle uncertainty is to conduct a preemptive strike against it, to actively shape the environment.
(e) Intuitive decision making: The process of sense-making intuitively brings in desired solution.
(f) Filling the gap with assumptions: Instead of gathering more data, we can reduce uncertainty by making assumptions about missing data (what are they like).

(g) Using incremental decisions: One of the most common tactics for handling uncertainty is to take an incremental approach. Instead of deciding all the issues at once, we can make a small investment and see if it works. We don't always have to commit to a new product.
(h) Embracing the uncertainty: When the organization is more adaptive than the competitors, then uncertainty works better. We can embrace uncertainty, when we treat our plans as platform for change. Also, sometime "tolerance for ambiguity" works as a smoke screen that preserves harmony while an organization works its problems out.

5 Opening the Door of Intuitive Flexibility

We have seen a few definitions about "intuition" earlier. In this section, we will arrive at fulsome definition of intuition and "intuitive flexibility." Researchers and psychologists have difficulty in agreeing on a clear definition of intuition. However, some consensus is reached that intuition:

- Is a nonconscious process
- Filters information nonsequentially
- Relies on emotional cues (www.icaa.org.au/charter, 2008)

"Intuition is the way we translate our experience into action." Or, intuition may be "the ability to sense or know immediately without reasoning" (Klein 2004). Or "intuition is apparent ability to acquire knowledge without a clear inference or reasoning process" (www.wikipedia.com, 2008). Or, "intuition is knowledge gained of something without the use of reasoning or the five basic senses" (www.blogs.ibobo.com/mehndi, 2008).

But "intuitive flexibility" takes us further, which may prepare us for the future (whether immediate or farther) with vision, solve problems with insight, and use a sharing (people-oriented) approach to work. The earlier definition of "*intuitive flexibility*" in this chapter can be fine-tuned to "Learning non-consciously to recognize patterns and translating experiential reflections to facilitate evolving competitive decisions for solving problems (Sushil 2008)."

Herein it is observed that "intuitive preference" is somewhat different than "rational preference," which is solving problems with insight, rather than analysis.

In this chapter, few case studies have been discussed wherein "intuitive flexibility" has been applied for better performance and throughput of the product. The lessons learnt from these cases have been highlighted.

6 Combating Technology-Based Uncertainties

High technology is full of challenges due to its inherent uncertainty and the associated risk and complexity. The projects are multiuser, multi-project environment, and complex. This calls for the integration of technology development into product

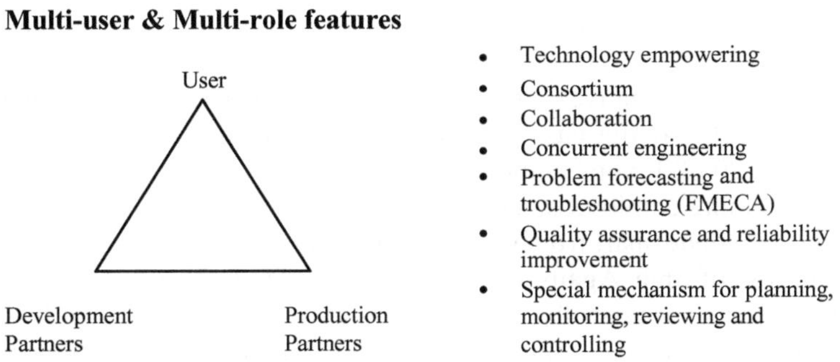

Fig. 9.3 Combating the uncertainty

development projects. The various approaches required to combat the uncertainty are as follows:

(a) Specific focus is required on problem forecasting, troubleshooting, and contingency planning.
(b) Technology empowering.
(c) Consortium approach.
(d) Collaboration.
(e) Concurrent engineering.
(f) Quality assurance and reliability improvement.
(g) Problem forecasting, modeling, and simulation.
(h) Special monitoring mechanism for planning, reviewing, and controlling.

The technology also has to be contemporary and product development should take into account multiuser and multi-role features. Some of the remedial measures taken for high technological uncertainties are depicted in Fig. 9.3 briefly.

Ramanan and Sushil (2001) have also discussed complexity and science of chaos theory – has been discussed for an IT-service company. It brings out statistically important features and variables for a problem-solving technique.

7 Toyota Motors: The Power of Intuitive Flexibility

On Monday, 3 Feb 1997, Japan's largest motor manufacturer, Toyota Motor Company, announced that all the assembly lines had come to grinding halt due to a devastating fire which took place at the premises of one of its affiliated suppliers – Aisin Seiki. The company was producing brake master cylinder for several of Toyota's models and was the only supplier of brake fluid proportioning valves. Though, Toyota works on JIT (just-in-time) and manufacturing flexibility principles, Toyota founder Shoichiro Toyoda was among the first to admit that his company's brand of JIT is still not perfect but remains convinced that this system is still the best in longer term. The system still allows the cost reduction through suppliers' economies of scale and engenders a spirit of commitment among the affiliates.

There were no alternatives left for harnessing the particular component parts from anywhere else. In this case of the unfortunate incident, the Toyota's founder rallied around 20 of Toyota's other affiliated suppliers to immediately set about retooling, retaining employees, and setting up new production lines in an "intuitive flexibility" mode apart from showing his organizational coordinated flexibility without loss of time. Again by 7 Feb 1997, Toyota had started assembly line at all of its plants successfully restoring output to 90 % of its usual level. Full production was resumed by following Monday. Resuming production and harnessing assembly lines by rallying around 20 of Toyota's affiliated suppliers after the catastrophe probably is the highest degree of intuitive flexibility within only four days time (Christopher 2001; Chopra and Meindel 2003).

Lessons learnt from the above case study are as follows:

(a) The founder of Toyota Motors, through his intuitive flexibility, showed exemplary organizational capability in rallying around 20 of the suppliers/vendors and harnessing the resources immediately after the catastrophe.
(b) The founder of Toyota, Shoichiro Toyoda, with his indelible experiential reflections recognized the impending chaos of production of the components and took the intuitively competitive decision within an unimaginable short period of time, whereby resuming the full production.

8 Labor Union Case Study of a DRDO Establishment

This is another live case study of a union labor chaos during 1999 – a case of Defense R&D Organization (DRDO) at Pune. For secrecy's sake, the organization is named as "*XYZ DRDO Lab or Unit*." During a span of hardly 6–7 years, three directors were changed due to superannuation. Call them Directors A, B, and C. Directors A and B have retired since and Director C is serving still. Both Directors A and B were from XYZ DRDO unit only, and they had started their career from this laboratory and risen to director level.

Director A towards his retirement time during 1999 had conveyed the employees for considering the cases of their children wards for providing more job opportunities. Style of Director A was rational and was based on "balanced scorecard" as well as under the rules only. Work was being done in a regular way under packaged-time-bound program, and workshop productivity was more resorted to on OT (overtime) based incentive. Productivity and growth of this establishment was quite good in the Director "A" period. Many new projects and new programs had been arranged in this period apart from infrastructural developments. People and workers had faith in Director "A." After taking over by Director B from Director A during the year 1999, the new incumbent became more strict/stringent as well as rigid on many fronts. Some of the broad issues considered were as follows:

(a) Jobs for employee relations strictly on high-merit basis and after passing some strict tests.
(b) Attendance of staff/officers, almost four times a day.
(c) OT (overtime) doing the job in the workshop should be stopped/curbed.
(d) Contractual/tendering not from the relations of serving/non-serving (retired) personnel.
(e) Temporary duties (TD) and TA/DA became more stringent.
(f) Natural growth of the establishment due to new projects/programs including infrastructural facilities.

Some routine facilities were also put on restrictions like parking the visitor vehicles outside the main gate (also implied for employees of the unit). Some facilities like unit CSD (Canteen Store Department) and taking petrol/diesel, pollution checks (PUC), etc., were also denied. Also closing the main gate of DRDO colony was done which later yielded to the pressure of workers and only a wicket gate was provided. Just after taking over the command/control of XYZ DRDO unit by the Director "B," the very first point of employment of wards/relations of the employees caught fire and employees started agitating. Intuitively sensing the result of union, CCR&D (Admin) – Chief Controller R&D from DRDO HQ, New Delhi – came to Pune and intervened the whole affair. The CCR&D devised a moderate plan of employment before the Pune Unit Union Leader could approach the National Union Leader and JCM (Joint Consultative Machinery) in this regard and could appraise of the unrest. This timely intervention from CCR&D averted the major crisis from breaking down the organizational machinery.

Later on during early 2006, the new Director C (outsider – from other establishment) took over the command from Director B and, within a span of 6 months, intuitively liberalized the above-cited essential facilities without hampering the discipline and performance of the unit. The much talked about main gate was also opened as desired – the people sighed in relief. In the present scenario, there is no problem to the people of the organization and deliverables to the customers. Both the interventions of higher command (CCR&D) and Director C have given examples of "intuitive flexibility" and averted the major crisis on the face value or also have taken care for future eventualities as well.

The present case of possible labor union chaos cites the following significant points:

(a) Director C, sensing the state of uneasiness, within a short span of time, liberalized the essential facilities without hampering organizational efficiency.
(b) Opening of the main gate also eased out the tension of employees.
(c) Both the interventions of higher command (CCR&D) as well as Director C have shown higher degree of intuitive flexibility in averting the major impending crisis.

9 Intuitive Forecasting of Avalanches

Snow avalanche occurrence takes place in hilly terrains, which are snow bound either seasonal or perennial pattern. In India especially the snow-bound regions of Himalaya pose this threat. It becomes more aggravating where the defense personnel and the villagers in those remote areas live round the year. One of the defense establishments, Snow and Avalanche Study Establishment (SASE) located at Manali (HP) and Chandigarh, looks after the prediction of snow avalanche for the safety/ security of the line of communications (L of C) and people living in those regions (Perla and Martinelli 1975).

In this chapter, a case study of avalanche forecasting of Sonamarg (J&K) area near to Baltal area has been taken. A road passes from Srinagar, Z-Mode, *Sonamarg,* Drass, and Kargil to Leh. The predictions of avalanches are mainly based on the following parameters (Pathak 2008):

(a) Terrain configuration of the avalanche gulley – its slope, vegetation, geometry, etc.
(b) Roughness of the base of gulley, boulders, vegetative cover, and cross-sections of avalanche formation zone, avalanche path, and debris zone
(c) High intensity of snow pattern (precipitation)
(d) Weakening of snow cover by snow metamorphism
(e) Diurnal thermal regime
(f) Moisture conditions of snow cover
(g) Meteorological and environmental parameters
(h) Sun orientation (SE or NE facing) of the gulley and slope exposition
(i) Fragility of the mountainous track/terrain

In the Sonamarg area, there are five avalanche sites: A1, A2, A3, A4, and A5. Every year either of them should occur. The first author is associated with over three decades with SASE and its geocryological activities. The "intuitive reflections" of forecasters and the experiential prediction of the locals are also one of the important factors. Right from 1978 to 1979 winters till recently, it has been observed that "intuitive flexibility"-based prediction of avalanches occurs to the accuracy of 75 %. A5 avalanche site has especially responded to this monitoring study. Even in other countries like Switzerland (Davos area), Austria, and White Mountains of New Hampshire (USA), these types of studies are resorted to.

10 Conclusion

The fast-changing business world is becoming turbulent and generating an inhospitable environment for ad hoc and informal ways of making the products and services. The competition is becoming more complex and chaotic. The uncertainty of information and communications in the era of IT-enabled services is creating more disorder. In any amount of chaos, disorder, and instability, some pockets of stability do exist, and from that, by application of "intuitive flexibility," some competitive decisions can be evolved, which ultimately solve the problem.

"Chaos theory" has been defined and analyzed for combating organizational and technological uncertainties. Chaos unfolds predictability, but always it does so according to recognizable family-like resemblances. Few case studies like Toyota Motors of Japan, DRDO labor union crisis, and avalanche forecasting based on "intuitive flexibility" process have been suitably presented. "Intuitive flexibility" of the top management has solved the major critical issues of both Toyota Motors and DRDO labor union cases.

This chapter deals with various cause and effects of chaos, disorder, information, and communication uncertainties. The few case studies discussed herein may open up new vistas for coping with chaos and disorder in the organizations, thereby transforming them to achieve organizational excellence.

References

Allio RJ (2002) Leadership-myths and realities. Tata McGraw Hill, New Delhi

Chopra S, Meindel P (2003) Supply chain management. M/s. Pearson Education, Indian Branch, New Delhi

Christopher M (2001) Logistics and supply chain management, 2nd edn. Financial Times, Pitman, London

de Wit B, Meyer R (2004) Strategy- process, content and context, 3rd edn. Thomas Learning, London

Edward O (2002) Chaos in dynamical systems. Cambridge University Press, New York

Gollub JP, Baker GL (1996) Chaotic dynamics. Cambridge University Press, New York

Hammer M (2001) The agenda. Random House Business Book, Britain

Indian Express Pune (2008) Career education forum. 28 Jan 2008, Pune

Klein G (2004) The power of intuition. M/s. Dumbleday, Random House, Inc, New York

Lorenz, E (1961/1972) Chaos theory.Wikipedia

Patel KJ (2005) The master strategist. Hutchinson, London House Group, London

Pathak RC (2005) Flexibility-thinking shift for organizational excellence. Glob J FSM 6(3&4):59–69

Pathak R (2008) Communication with Rajesh, a PRTM Management Consultant, based at Dundee, Scotland

Perla RI, Martinelli M Jr (1975) Avalanche handbook. US Department of Agriculture Handbook

Ramanan SV, Sushil (2001) Strategic management: a complexity and chaos perspective. In: Sushil, Momaya K (eds) Globalization, flexibility and competitiveness. Vikas Publishing House, New Delhi, pp 440–453

Simchi-Levi D, Kaminsky P, Simchi-Levi E (2004) Designing and managing the supply chain. Tata McGraw Hill, New Delhi

Stacey R (1993) Strategy as order emerging from chaos. Long Range Plann 26(1):10–17, Elsevier

Sushil (2008) Personal communication on *'Intuitive Flexibility' Dimensions*, DMS, IITD, New Delhi – 110016, India

www.blogs.ibobo.com/mehndi (2008)

www.icaa.org.au/charter (2008)

www.wikipedia.com (2008)

Chapter 10
Framework for Utilization of Global Resources for Knowledge Creation and Application Through Flexible Organizations

Babu Lal

1 Introduction

When billions of single logic units are integrated and controlled, what we get is unimaginable computing power of modern day microprocessors. The power of computing comes by controlled interconnections. Similarly, every human being is a potential knowledge processor, who has capability to create and apply knowledge. If we can design systems and processes which can interconnect these human knowledge processors in a meaningful manner, then enormous capacity and capability could be created to create new knowledge and apply existing knowledge. This can change the entire spectrum of our civilization by way of providing technologies, products, and processes that will be capable of dealing with miseries like hunger, malnutrition, disease, and suffering. The concept is like fusion reaction, where in light atoms of hydrogen are fused together to release enormous energy. In a similar manner, if systems and processes could be devised to bring isolated brain power distributed across the globe, then the society tend to have a mega mind capable of churning out new knowledge at a speed beyond imagination.

I am extremely thankful to the management of my company (BHEL, India) for providing an open and conducive environment for pursuing my intellectual journey and allowing me to publish this chapter. I am very grateful to Prof. Prem Vrat and Prof. Sushil, who have been very inspiring and encouraging all throughout my Ph.D. program and helped me think holistically at a global scale. The credit for any intellectual pursuit from my end goes to them as they have sown the seed of knowledge in me. I bow my head in full sincerity to them.
(Views expressed in this chapter are those of the author and not of the organization with which author is associated.)

B. Lal (✉)
Bharat Heavy Electricals Limited (BHEL), New Delhi, India
e-mail: monbl@bhel.in

Sushil and E.A. Stohr (eds.), *The Flexible Enterprise*, Flexible Systems Management,
DOI 10.1007/978-81-322-1560-8_10, © Springer India 2014

2 Knowledge Economy

Products are By-Product of Application of Knowledge: Products, services, and processes of knowledge economy are the outcome of integration of diverse knowledge elements. Every time a new knowledge gets developed somewhere in some corner of the world, a product and process becomes potent for new features which are superior to the existing levels.

Power of Collaboration and Connectedness: Knowledge resides in individuals and nurtured in communities through collaboration. Communities are forums of connected people with shared vision. There is rich to-and-fro flow of knowledge among members.

Knowledge Networking: It is the process of harnessing the knowledge at global level. The prime objective of knowledge networking is to spot potential knowledge creators at a global scale to nurture them, help them to complement, and collaborate with peers around the globe in the process of knowledge creation. Without support of effective communication and collaboration, knowledge remains fragmented in small pieces in the heads of people. In the universal population set, there are enormous potential knowledge creators spread across the globe in different national boundaries. If these talented people are spotted in their early life and carefully nurtured to their full capacities and capabilities through effective knowledge networking, they will create new knowledge. This knowledge when applied will generate new technologies, products, processes, and systems that are superior to the existing ones and will have far-reaching impacts in better utility to the society at large.

Design of Flexible Institutions for Knowledge Creation: The primary objective of organization design is to devise social institutions that mobilize human knowledge, capabilities, and resources around the globe for productive purposes with a view to improve the well-being of the society and the constituent members. The new information and communication technologies and new ideas in organizational design are providing a large number of choices for new variants of organizational forms with a lot of built-in flexibility to harness knowledge resources at global canvas. Wikipedia defines flexibility as the popular term for the ability to adapt to different circumstances. In systems theory, the flexibility of a system is related to its adaptation to a new environment or its resilience in recovering from a shock or disturbance. The flexibility in system comes when a large number of options are made available at the design stage itself.

Flexibility provides knowledge systems with possibility of increased participation and collaboration and offers higher degree of freedom of choice. The more are the options available, the more are the feasibility space and chances for more scope of innovation. The diverse supply networks involving customer-driven product development require integration of diverse knowledge in a flexible domain to enhance the speed of innovation and product launch. The ability to satisfy customer demands while responding to relentless competitive pressure requires creative and often complex approaches to manage a firm's knowledge effectively. Perhaps more

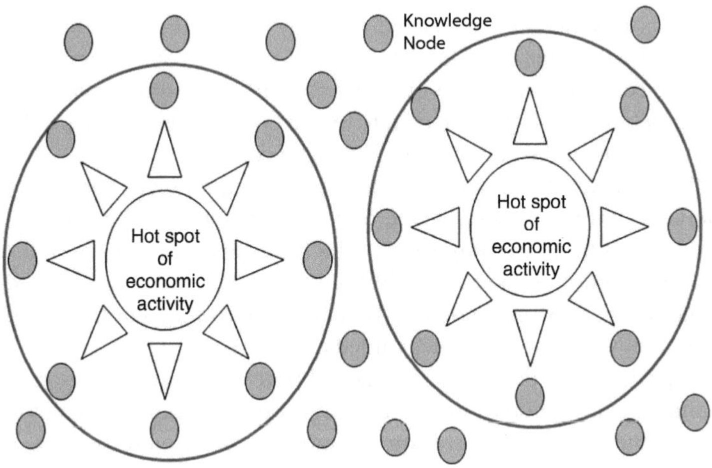

Fig. 10.1 Disconnected knowledge systems

than any other area, now there is increasing belief that a concept called globalization offers enormous opportunities to achieve major performance gains. Companies have begun to capture the benefits of globalization through global sourcing, which involves the worldwide integration of knowledge in R&D, engineering, operations, and procurement centers of a company.

The focus so far has been on disconnected knowledge systems, where different knowledge producers and users are restricted in connectivity as depicted in Fig. 10.1. In such systems, knowledge dissipation rate is very slow.

Unfortunately, capturing the benefits potentially offered by globalization is often limited by a lack of understanding concerning how to pursue this important area. To mitigate this limitation multilevel continua for the factors that are the most critical to global success are discussed to arrive at a broad framework which could set the future directions for knowledge management at global scale:

- Knowledge is a global resource which is meant for the betterment of entire universe.
- Enough opportunities exist for everyone to create new and diverse knowledge which could be converted to utility through products and processes resulting in prosperity and well-being of people who are creating it.
- World is going to face talent crunch in the pursuit of knowledge creation. The civilization is at the beginning of knowledge economy. With the creation of every new knowledge in any corner of the globe in any field opens many new fields through analysis, combination, and synthesis of existing and the newly created knowledge. The accelerated pace of knowledge creation will put the talent in short supply.
- Basic raw material (i.e., human beings) for knowledge processes is spread across the globe. It is high time now that all out efforts are put in place at global scale to

process this raw material in usable form by enhancing their basic skill sets. People located in far-flung isolated places need to be integrated with the knowledge economy. To start with, concerted efforts could be made to integrate large population with high literacy rate located in tier 2 and 3 cities to knowledge creation systems of the emerging knowledge economy.
- Principles of coexistence are the fundamental requirement for the knowledge economy. It is through coexistence and cooperation that the human race will enjoy the fruits of an exciting future which has just begun to unfold. The new future is being built on the rock solid foundations of emerging knowledge economy. The divisive forces guided by fundamentalists may put the world on war-like situation, which needs to be avoided at any cost.
- Knowledge economy puts greater responsibilities on knowledge-rich economies for equitable distribution of the fruits to the entire population. They will have to learn from the fruit-bearing trees to be more humble, more serving, and more responsible. The excessive divide between haves and have-nots will always create a threat to the peace and prosperity of the world.
- World leaders will have to work for a boundaryless world for frictionless movement of knowledge in explicit and tacit form along with physical goods. World is moving towards global integration and hence more democratization is required to listen the aspirations of different stakeholders on this mother earth.
- Open, adaptive, tolerant, and flexible mindset for co-creation with multicultural work force and different stakeholders needs to be built.
- The world over governments will have to develop processes and systems for ensuring dignity, freedom, and economic well-being of individuals.
- Global highways for frictionless movement of goods and knowledge across the globe are becoming the basic requirement to harness the fruits of knowledge economy.
- Knowledge has many dimensions like explicit and tacit and each one has to be tackled differently. Just like heat energy moves from once place to another through processes like radiation, conduction, and convection.
- Human race is facing many challenges like global warming, environmental concerns, melting of glaciers, poverty, epidemics, and fundamentalism to name a few. To tackle these problems the entire world resources (both intellectual and physical) need to be put to use. For this to happen, great minds and world leadership have to come together by forgetting petty considerations of regionalism and individual gains. This is necessary for the long-term safety, security, and prosperity of the human race.

The proposed framework as depicted in Fig. 10.2 heavily banks on high degree of collaboration and freedom of choice in terms of collaboration. It suggests a networked architecture and managerial, legal, and technology framework in place to support the same.

The broad framework mentioned above and depicted in Fig. 10.2 has been further amplified in four dimensions of people, process, technology, and performance or results and rests on the basic building blocks shown in Exhibit 10.1.

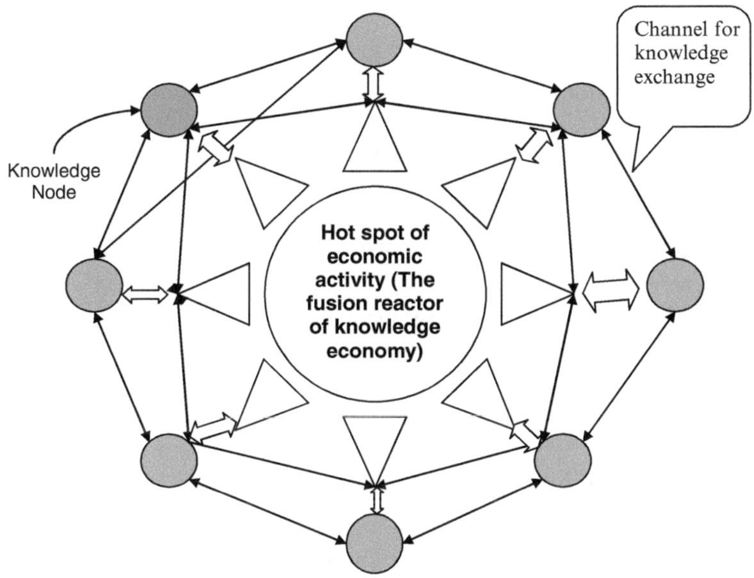

Fig. 10.2 Networked knowledge system

Exhibit 10.1 Basic Building Blocks of the Framework

- Mother Earth belongs to all of us; therefore, we all have to coexist in harmony.
- We are the trustees for future generations hence need to focus on Sustainability
- Globalization is mutual dependability for mutual good.
- The notion of boundary is in the human mind, i.e., self, family, town, state, nation, and globe.
- Boundaries are man-made so they could be altered and hence offer a freedom of choice.
- Cast, creed, and religion are invented by man for a specific purpose relevant for a specific period.
- Knowledge and skills are people centric.
- Our thought is the limiting factor of our growth.
- Raw talent is scattered around the globe in abundance. They are like stem cells to knowledge systems.
- Knowledge is nurtured through analysis, synthesis, and cross-pollination and requires deeper engagement.
- Knowledge creation and application is more of a social phenomenon.
- Products are by-product of application of knowledge.

(continued)

(continued)

- Knowledge resides in individuals and nurtured in communities through collaboration.
- Communities are forums of connected people with shared vision.
- Knowledge networking is the process of harnessing the knowledge at global level.
- Knowledge is a global resource which is meant for the betterment of entire universe.
- Fruits of collective efforts are for inclusive growth and development of the society as well as individual freedom, liberty and prosperity.

3 People Dimension of Knowledge

Getting Rid of Rigidity: The biggest challenge in knowledge management is not of technology but of mental blocks and rigidity at thought and vision level. Breaking the silos at thought and vision level is the most challenging one. The world is rigidly divided on issues like cast, creed, religion, and geographic locations. Cultural rigidities also act as a barrier in smooth flow of knowledge across the globe. The past mindset of working in isolation has to give way to collaborative working at a global scale. An infrastructure of soft issues enabling linking of minds across the globe has to be made available so that flexible teams of different age, different culture, and diverse fields can work at ease for smooth transfer of explicit and tacit knowledge. Minimum universal education to world population has to be the agenda. Figure 10.3 depicts some of the people dimensions on two extreme ends of continua.

4 Technology Dimension of Knowledge

The Challenge of Leveraging Flexibility and Connectedness: The development in the field of information and communication technology has opened vast opportunities in the field of knowledge transfer across the globe at a faster rate. The diverse fields of information and communication are converging, and time is not far off when there will be a universal device available with capabilities of phone, computer, and TV at affordable price to masses. The capabilities of this device will further improve by high-speed Internet and three-dimensional high-definition TV technologies, application of artificial intelligence tools, and connectivity through high-bandwidth networks from anywhere to anywhere. Figure 10.4 depicts some of the technology dimensions on two extreme ends of continua.

Flexible knowledge transfer networks for sharing proprietary knowledge through partnerships have to be developed. Sharing of laboratories and contract research and

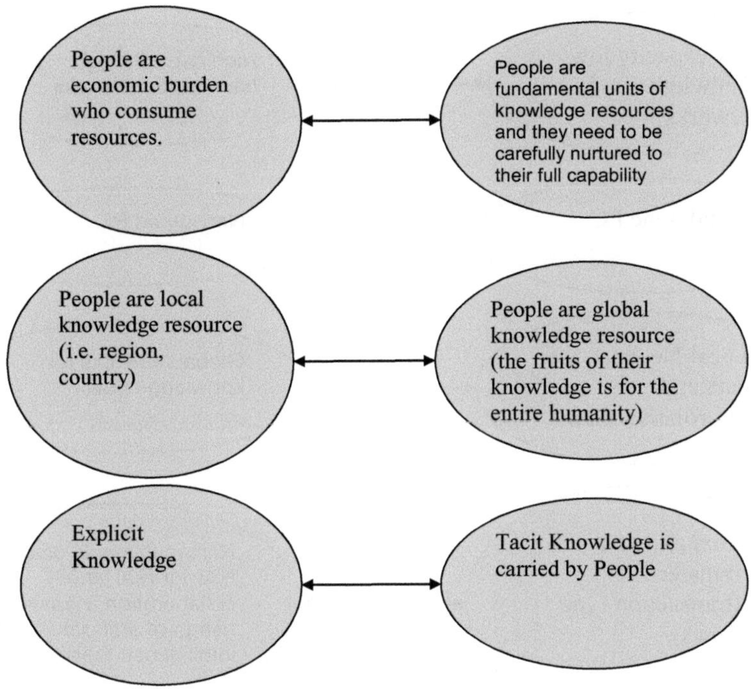

Fig. 10.3 People dimension of knowledge

development beyond national boundaries is one of the emerging area for knowledge creation and transfer. Large-scale funding from different industries and nations on consortia basis for future promising technologies is another area of focus. Large-scale participation of public and private institutions and cooperation between industry and educational and research institutes in knowledge creation also offer a big potential in knowledge creation.

5 Process Dimension of Knowledge

Flexible Networks for Knowledge Transfer: These networks allow easy entry and exit routes for knowledge creators and users. They should be plug and play type arrangements so that these networks can easily become part of a larger network. Transnational consortia for knowledge creation need to be worked out in different emerging technologies with a specific focus on free flow of man, material, and information.

Managing the Paradox of Global and Local: The biggest challenge in designing the processes in the area of knowledge management is resolving the paradox of local and global, competition and collaboration, public versus private, and

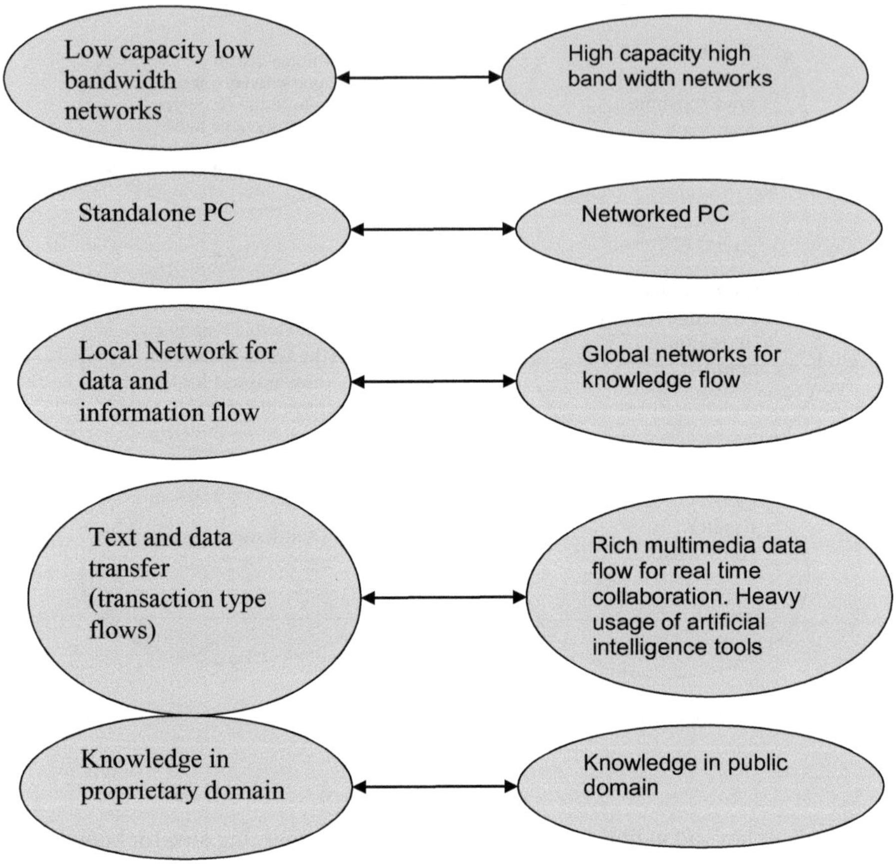

Fig. 10.4 Technology dimension of knowledge

limitations of geographic boundaries to name a few. Figure 10.5 depicts some of the process dimensions on two extreme ends of continua.

Organize Knowledge Fairs, Exhibitions, and Conferences: These arrangements provide opportunities for research, policy, and development institutes to broadcast their achievements, exhibit their research products, and market new research programs to donors, policy makers, other institutes, and potential partners. These also facilitate networking with pears and also different stakeholders. This will help in setting common research agendas, help think tanks benefit from each other's experiences, and stimulate interest in future research collaboration and the development of new programs. These will also provide a forum to share tacit knowledge through face-to-face interaction, which is otherwise difficult to transfer. For knowledge processes to be effective, two-pronged strategy for convergence of technology and convergence of mind is required.

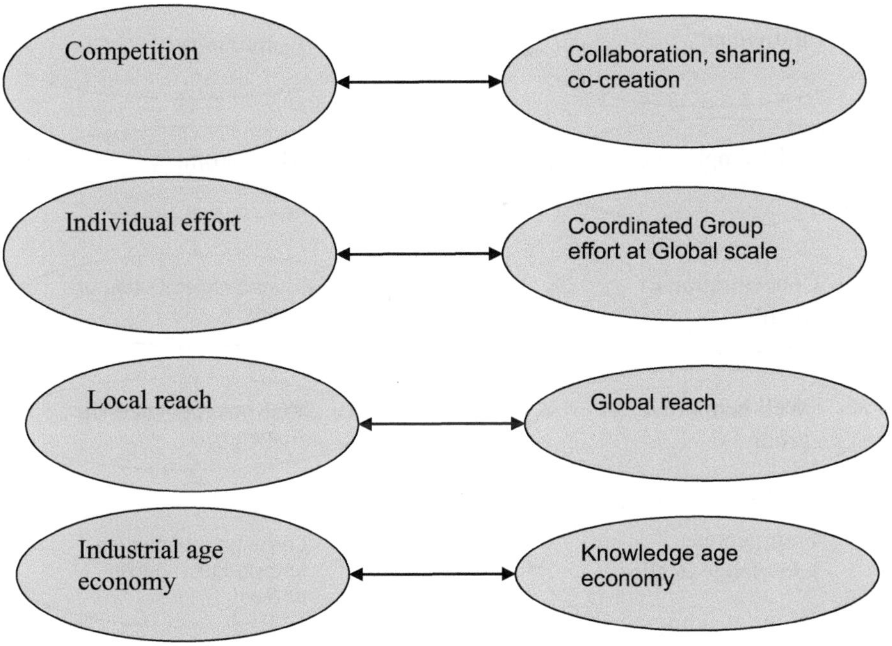

Fig. 10.5 Process dimension of knowledge

6 Performance Dimension of Knowledge

The most important issues are the sharing the benefits of global knowledge resource utilization in a just and equitable manner. It should not lead to exploitation and imbalances in the society. It is a delicate issue and requires well-thought-out consideration by different stakeholders. The outcome of the interplay of three enablers of knowledge creation will decide whether the fruits of knowledge processes are directed towards a select group or a larger community or for the entire world population. For a peaceful, progressive, and stable world, we should talk of inclusive growth. Figure 10.6 exhibits the performance dimension of knowledge.

7 Some Inspiring Success Stories

7.1 IITs in India

Indian Institutes of Technology were set up in India with state-of-the-art facilities and practices followed in best institutes abroad. These institutes attracted best talent in India through rigorous selection process and provided leading edge inputs to

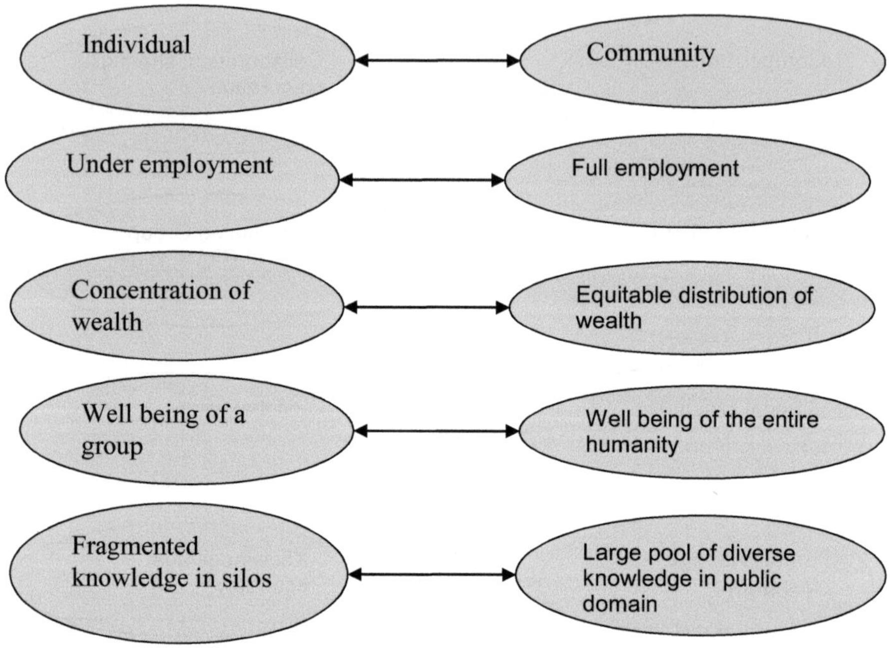

Fig. 10.6 Performance dimension of knowledge

these students with the help of faculty members having exposure to contemporary knowledge through different collaborative processes with leading technical institutes all over the world. The talent pool generated by IITs is in heavy demand world over and has become a global knowledge resource. The graduate students from IITs are recruited by companies working on cutting-edge technologies in the USA and other advanced countries. Dr. Subra Suresh an alumnus of IIT Madras has been appointed as the 13th director of the prestigious National Science Foundation (NSF) of US administration, which is a rare achievement for a person of Indian origin. Based on the success of the existing IITs, Government of India has announced to set up more such institutes in different parts of India. This initiative of government will go a long way in creating a diversified pool of knowledge. This knowledge pool will be the primary fuel for the emerging knowledge economy and will be available for the world as a whole.

7.2 The International Space Station (ISS)

It was proposed under the name of Space Station Freedom by President Reagan in 1983, 4 years after Skylab burnt up. As the cost and complexity of the station grew, NASA invited other space agencies to join it, gaining support from Russia, Japan,

Europe, Canada, and Brazil. Since 1998, when the first modules were launched, more modules and a rotating crew of astronauts and cosmonauts have ascended to low Earth orbit to live and work in outer space work with scientists on fundamental science for the benefit of humanity. China and India are likely to join this club.

7.3 *Space Shuttle Columbia*

Kalpana Chawla of Indian origin graduated from Tagore School, Karnal, in 1976, bachelor of science degree in aeronautical engineering from Punjab Engineering College in 1982, master of science degree in aerospace engineering from University of Texas in 1984, doctorate of philosophy in aerospace engineering from University of Colorado in 1988 was a member of crew in Space Shuttle Columbia in 2003. This again is a live example of using global talent for a global mission.

7.4 *European Organization for Nuclear Research (CERN)*

This is an example of scientific collaboration at global scale where government representatives of 20 European States meet regularly in the CERN Council to address research in elementary particle physics and related subjects in accordance with an international treaty. The convention bestows upon the organization's two missions, namely, the operation of laboratories and the organization and sponsoring of international cooperation in the field. CERN has the world's largest elementary particle physics laboratory and provides research infrastructure for around 8,000 scientific users from the Member States and other regions in the world including the USA, Russia, Japan, and France. High-energy physicists from India, from institutes like Tata Institute of Fundamental Research (TIFR), have been participating in experiments at CERN.

8 Broad-Based Framework

According to Hindu mythology, demons and demigods collectively worked together to churn the ocean using all their strengths and resources to get valuable outcomes like divine nectar. The moral of the story here is to identify, nurture, and use all the talent and resource spread across the world for a greater cause requiring huge resources as outlined in Fig. 10.7, which has been prepared from a picture taken from Wikipedia (http://en.wikipedia.org/wiki/File:Sagar_Manthan.jpg). The underlying principle is that collective will of collaboration and cooperation will bear the fruits of collective gains to be shared equitably among all the stakeholders. Lou Friedman, PhD from MIT, a longtime Executive Director and Cofounder of The Planetary

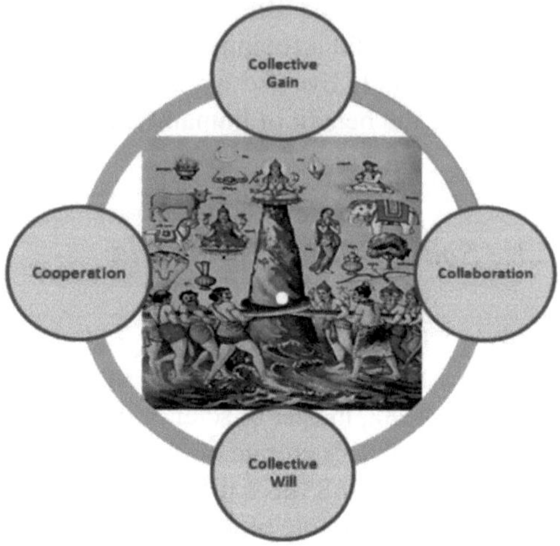

Fig. 10.7 Broad-based framework

Society, along with Carl Sagan and Bruce Murray shares the similar opinion that the world needs a positive, inspiring, outward-looking venture that can engage skilled personnel around the world in developing new technology. Let's back off from the national-only planning and start planning internationally.

9 Conclusion

Knowledge processes have large number of micro level dimensions under broad three heads, which can interact on many planes to provide knowledge for a select group or for the well-being of the world. The outcome of a myopic vision cannot be expected to be grand. The framework discussed above offers recipe for diverse outcomes. If full potential of potent knowledge workers across the globe is made use of, for the good of the entire world population, then outcome will be such knowledge systems, which are broad-based, long-lasting, and generating fruits for the total population of the world. The broad-based framework will reduce disguised unemployment for those who are engaged in work which is far below their intellectual capabilities. This will provide an opportunity to individuals in rural and remote areas to be part of the mainstream of knowledge creation and promote technical skills in rural communities which in turn empower them to make efficient use of local resources. The slogan for the twenty-first century should be knowledge of the people to be applied by the people for the well-being of the people following principle of one world one family with opportunities for all. One of the important tasks of governments will be to raise the intellectual capabilities of its population on a continuous basis.

Chapter 11
Flexibility, Controllability and Risk Measurement Metrics in Changing Pattern of Business Environment

Arnab Mitra

1 Introduction

Today's competitive market companies are under pressure as customers want new and more innovative products that are tailored to their specific needs. They also want cost-effective, timely service and responsive support which meets their requirements. As always, reducing cost and improving quality requires ongoing initiatives within every enterprise. Delivering higher value, whether within the supply/value chain to partners and OEMs or to the end user, has become more and more important.

All businesses today operate in a marketplace characterized by change. The challenge is to become flexible in order to ensure an agile response to changing market conditions. Managing planned change, for example, through business process reengineering (BPR), is difficult in itself. However, managing unplanned change demands the ability to react faster and use new technology to match market conditions and customer demands in a way that maintains or creates competitive advantage.

As business strategies have evolved, the focus has shifted away from being big and stable with complete control to being small, nimble, and more responsive to the market. This evolution reflects the introduction of new technology, new trends, and, in particular, new customer behavior. New markets are up for grabs because being big and stable is no longer a competitive formula. Flexibility creates the chance to seize the market by responding faster to customer demands. Today's world leaders are characterized by their ability to deliver the products that customers want with minimum time-to-market and maximum capability to revamp products to meet market expectations.

This chapter is an attempt to identify, select, and establish Flexibility, Controllability and Risk Parameters that support effective way of doing business. The objective is

A. Mitra (✉)
KPMG, Gurgaon, India
e-mail: arnabmitra.iitd@gmail.com

Sushil and E.A. Stohr (eds.), *The Flexible Enterprise*, Flexible Systems Management,
DOI 10.1007/978-81-322-1560-8_11,

to focus on how a business house can fit into addressing the new paradoxical pattern in modern environment.

To become flexible, a company must recognize change in the marketplace and then manage and master that change.

Finally, flexible enterprises change the way that they interact with their business partners so that they can compete more effectively through cooperation. Today's successful enterprise knows that it does not dictate market demands – it listens to its customers. It finds its core competence and makes partnerships when it is necessary to provide the customer with a solution. Supply chain cooperation is only one aspect of becoming more cooperative – knowledge sharing is another. A competitive company is a company looking for partners to benefit its own products and services.

> The system age, is a synthesis of the Machine Age and its antithesis. The antithesis gives focus on synthesis rather than analysis, and is governed by the doctrine of expansionism. It is looking the reality to be much more integrated and unified, as the organic systems once disassembled could not be fully reassembled. Thus, it looks at the system under consideration to be part of a larger whole called as 'suprasystem'. The containing whole is to be first identified and its properties are to be explained. Then the role or function of the system within the containing whole needs to be explained (Sushil 2000).

The study tries to identify factors concerning flexibility, controllability, and risk and tries to identify a confluence among them.

2 Objective

The research objective is to establish list of flexibility, controllability, and risk measurement metrics in changing pattern of business environment.

This is an attempt to substantiate "No Tyranny of the OR" and "embrace the Genius of the AND." Instead of being oppressed by the "Tyranny of the OR," highly visionary companies liberate themselves with the "Genius of the AND" – the ability to embrace both extremes of a number of dimensions at the same time.

3 Research Approach

Figure 11.1 illustrates the approach to achieve the above research objective.

3.1 Review of the Literature

Literature survey is a background work that is made personally. It is based on books and academic publications. The topics of literature survey are selected so that they support the study. The main goal of a literature survey is to gather a basis for the

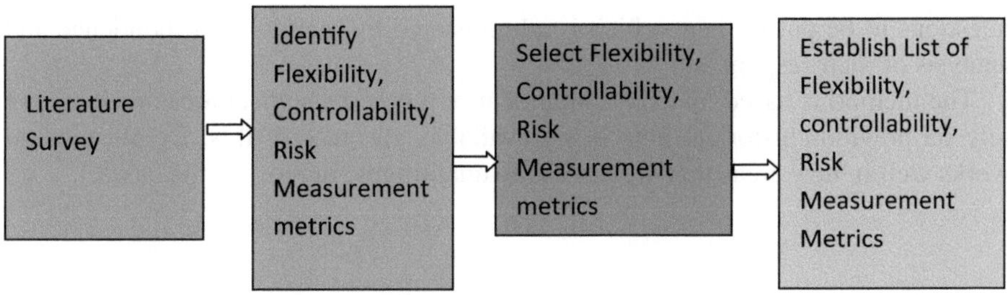

Fig. 11.1 Diagrammatic representation of research approach

practical work and to get familiarized with existing literature and research on the topic. The objective is not to reinvent the wheel and take a stock of work that has already been done in the area of the study.

3.2 Grounded Theory: Identify Flexibility, Controllability, and Risk Measurement Metrics

Grounded theory (GT) is a systematic methodology in the social sciences involving the generation of theory from data. It is mainly used in qualitative research but is also applicable to quantitative data. Grounded theory is a research method, which operates almost in a reverse fashion from traditional research and at first sight may appear to be in contradiction to the scientific method. Rather than beginning with a hypothesis, the first step is data collection, through a variety of methods. From the data collected, the key points are marked with a series of codes, which are extracted from the text. The codes are grouped into similar concepts in order to make them more workable. From these concepts, categories are formed, which are the basis for the creation of a theory or a reverse engineered hypothesis. This contradicts the traditional model of research, where the researcher chooses a theoretical framework, and only then applies this model to the phenomenon to be studied. Grounded theory was developed by two sociologists, Barney Glaser and Anselm Strauss. Their collaboration in research on dying hospital patients led them to write the book *Awareness of Dying*. In this research, they developed the constant comparative method, later known as grounded theory.

3.3 Delphi: Select Flexibility, Controllability, and Risk Factors/Parameters

The concept of Delphi was originally developed from a US Air force project named "Delphi" of the early 1950s, which was related to the use of expert opinions. The Delphi method involves selection of suitable experts, development of appropriate questions to be put to them which is administered by remote correspondence and analysis of their responses.

The method is based on expert judgment of a specific subject area and does not rely on previous historical data being available. Because of this, Delphi method works well in new areas that are not easily quantifiable in most of the cases.

3.4 Statistical Test (t-Test): Establish Flexibility, Controllability, and Risk Factors/Parameters

A t-test is any statistical hypothesis test in which the test statistic follows a Student's t distribution if the null hypothesis is supported. The t-statistic was introduced in 1908 by William Sealy Gosset, a chemist working for the Guinness brewery in Dublin, Ireland. T-test was devised by Gosset to monitor the quality of stout. T-Test can be defined as a statistical examination of two population means. A two-sample t-test examines whether two samples are different and is commonly used when the variances of two normal distributions are unknown and when an experiment uses a small sample size. The test statistic in the t-test is known as the t-statistic. The t-test looks at the t-statistic, t-distribution and degrees of freedom to determine a p value (probability) that can be used to determine whether the population means differ.

4 Literature Survey on Flexibility, Controllability, and Enterprise Risk Management

4.1 Flexibility

The interest on organizational flexibility has been growing in the last decades, and different approaches have emerged with focus on dimensions of organizational flexibility (e.g., Eppink (1978), Volberda (1996), Sanchez (2004), Verdu Jover et al. (2005), Andrew and Hatum (2006)), on the interaction between firm size and organizational flexibility (e.g., Kraatz and Zajac (2001), Ebben and Johnson (2005)), and on context specificity of flexible capabilities (e.g., Eppink (1978), Volberda (1996), Verdu Jover et al. (2005), Nadkarni and Narayanan (2007)).

External Flexibility is best described by the maxim of not putting all of one's eggs in a single basket (Ansoff 1965). Flexibility can be defined as "the ability to change or react with little penalty in time, effort, cost or performance" (Sushil 2000, 2000a). Flexibility is a multifaceted concept with different connotations, paradigms, foundations, and dimensions. Strategic, Organizational, Financial, Information Systems, and Manufacturing Flexibilities have been identified as cornerstones of Enterprise Flexibility (Sushil 2000). Flexibility is not shifting to extremes, but to dynamically balance them. There are many connotations of flexibility like agility, adaptiveness, responsiveness, and versatility. One popular view of flexibility can emerge by mapping it on to functional structure (Sushil et al. 2000) – Strategic Flexibility, Manufacturing Flexibility, Human Resources Flexibility, Financial Flexibility, Technology Management Flexibility, Marketing Flexibility, Organizational Flexibility, and IT/IS Flexibility.

It is widely accepted that organizations today are facing the issue of responding continually to an environment, which is increasingly dynamic, complex, and uncertain as a consequence of demographic changes, a more global economy, the "hypercompetition," or knowledge-based competition (Daft and Lewin 1993).

A company's competitiveness will depend not only on being efficient in their organizational routines but also on their innovative ability at the same time (Abernathy and Utterback 1978; Hayes and Abernathy 1980) which represents the notion of balance between exploration (be innovative – radical change) and exploitation (be efficient in organizational routines – incremental change).

This is a common topic in literature related to organizational adaptation (Benner and Tushman 2002). Such balance allows the firm to obtain and sustain its competitive advantage which, according to Sommer has to be redefined in terms of organizational speed and flexibility (Sommer 2003). This characteristic is related to develop new dynamic processes that enable, for instance, a fast reconfiguration of the resource base (Teece et al. 1997; Eisenhardt and Martin 2000; Helfat et al. 2007), changing the nature of activities (Aaker and Mascarenhas 1984), or dismantling of current strategies (Harrigan 1985).

The interest on organizational flexibility has been growing in the last decades, and different approaches have emerged with focus on dimensions of organizational flexibility. Literature in organizational flexibility is still lacking of comprehensive modeling which explains the relationships between its key variables and consequent side effects of such iterations. Exploring these interactions and the dynamic adaptation processes towards the desired adjustment is the main motivation of the present research.

We decided to start our analysis with Volberda's model on organizational flexibility which addresses how the companies should manage their dynamic capabilities and organizational design, in order to achieve the desired fit by being flexible. He studied how the organizations deal with the paradox of flexibility over time, that means, how they continuously adapt to the changes in the environment and balance corporate discipline with entrepreneurial creativity. Exploring the paradoxical nature of flexibility, Volberda (1998) develops a strategic flexibility framework to configure the resources of the firm for effective responses to organizational change providing a comprehensive set of variables and their linear relationships. In addition to this argument, we found that Volberda anticipated the possibility of modeling the adaptation process from a dynamic point of view – "Flexibility is not a static condition, but it is a dynamic process. Time is a very essential factor of organizational flexibility" (Volberda 1998). However, he didn't focus on such adaptation process as a sequence of stages allowing to understanding key factors of organizational flexibility.

A lot of work has been done to examine Volberda's theory in detail in order to analyze its consistency and effectiveness, especially in terms of its causal explanation of organizational adaptation to changing environments. The causal argument Volberda presents is very detailed and relatively explicit. Therefore, lots of research use Volberda's theory as foundation for its systematic exploration.

4.2 Controllability

Management is the "the process of using organization resources to achieve organizational objectives through the functions of planning, organizing and staffing, leading, and controlling" (DuBrin 2000, p. 3). Each of these functions of management needs careful and detailed managerial attention (Sather 2004). As the purpose of the current chapter is the development of a framework for managerial control, a detailed review of management control literature is essential.

Control is considered a very important function of managers. Control is defined as "keeping things on track" (Merchant 1985, p. 1), and it has been identified as "the final function in the management process" (Merchant 1985, p. 2). Anthony et al. (1989, p. 5) provided a definition of control that emphasized command and control – control is the process of guiding a set of variables to attain a preconceived goal or objective. It is a broad concept applicable to people, things, situations, and organizations. In organizations, it includes various planning and controlling processes.

According to Simons (1995, p. 29), "control implies managing the inherent tension between creative innovation, on the one hand, and predictable goal achievement, on the other, so that both are transformed into profitable growth." This view is more practicable for an organization in which features such as increasing competition, rapidly changing markets, new forms of organizations, and customer orientation are more visible than in other organizations. Simons's (1995) definition is based on the notion that organizations are multifaceted. They are also social systems, collections of individuals bound together to meet personal and social needs. Group norms and patterns of power and influence affect internal decision processes. Organizations are also sets of relationships among self-interested participants, each of whom is balancing personal well-being and organizational needs (p. 13).

Control in organizations is achieved in many ways, ranging from direct surveillance to feedback systems to social and cultural control (Simons 1995, p. 5). Similarly, in the management literature, many definitions of control with differing theoretical perspectives can be found. Many researchers accepted that control means different things to different people. Chua et al. (1989, p. 4), for example, articulated three distinct meanings of control as follows:

1. As a means of steering or regulation, which is the classical cybernetic meaning
2. As a means of domination of one or more people or groups of people by other people or groups, which has more sociological and political overtones
3. As a process of the management control and power

Thus, control can be viewed from many different perspectives. As Otley et al. (1996, p. 6) explained, "'control' is itself a highly ambiguous term as evidenced by the difficulty of translating it into many European languages." In this chapter, the terms control and control systems are used to mean management control and management control systems.

In the literature of management, the term "control" is often used in a comparative sense. Control means a comparison between the planned and actual performance together with identifying possible corrective actions. For example, according to Stoner and Wankei (1986, p. 17), the control process of control consists of defining desired results, .establishing predictors of results, establishing standards for predictors and results, establishing information and feedback network, and evaluating information and taking corrective action.

Such a control process requires the listing of steps consisting of very specific goals and objectives and the measure of how well those goals and objectives are achieved. Many academics and researchers have argued in favor of such a control process. According to Merchant (1982, p. 43), "after strategies are set and plans are made, management's primary task is to take steps to ensure that these plans are carried out, or, if conditions warrant, that the plans are modified." Thus, the function of control is to take measures to increase goal congruence or prevent organizational participants from behaving in ways where goal incongruence exists.

Control is also discussed in the literature as part of the strategic implementation process. The argument for this is that without control, proper execution of strategy may be impossible. Anthony (1988, p. 10), for example, defined management control as "the process by which managers influence other members of the organization to implement the organization's strategies." However, this work "emphasizes the behavioral aspects of control more strongly, still takes strategy as given" (Berry et al. 1998, p. xvi). Anthony (1988, pp. 30–34) further defined strategic planning as a means of formulating strategies. Merchant (1985, p. 3) held the view that "strategy is seen as related to, but usually separable from, control".

Literature reveals that control is considered a principle of management too; the others include planning, organizing, staffing, directing, and coordination. It is assumed that a certain degree of control is necessary to keep things on track in any organization. Control is used as a means of ensuring that participants will do what the organization wants to do and they will not do something that the organization does not want to do. In the words of Merchant (1985, p. 4), control, as the word applies to a function of management, involves influencing human behavior, because it is people who make things happen in an organization. In other words, control involves managers taking steps to help ensure that human beings do what is best for the organization (original emphasis).

Otley (1989, p. 32) pointed out that ". . . a great amount of management activity seems to be concerned with influencing the behavior of others with the object of producing desired outcomes." Organizational participants sometimes fail to act in the organization's best interest so that a set of controls has to be implemented to protect their behavior from undesirable behavior and ensure desirable actions. To establish control over organizational participants' behavior, adequate measures for both expected and actual behavior should be taken into account. Merchant (1985) held the view that "Control is seen as having one basic function" to help ensure the proper behaviors of the people in the organization. These behaviors should be consistent with the organization's strategy, if one exists, which, in turn, should have been selected as the best path to take towards achievement of the organization's objectives.

The absence of adequate control can have many harmful organizational consequences. Problems such as defective products, unsatisfied customers and workers, inability to compete successfully in the marketplace, and weak coordination within the hierarchy levels of the organization might be the results of poor control. On the contrary, too much control can also be harmful for effective and efficient organizational performance. On one hand, tight control may reduce the organization's flexibility and innovation. On the other hand, it may increase the operational cost and employee pressure. Control being a supportive activity will not directly contribute to the value added. Accordingly, too much control may create unwanted financial as well as behavioral consequences. Therefore, maintaining an optimal balance between stability and flexibility through control is very important and has always been a major challenge for organizations. With the changes in the way organizations observe measure and evaluate them, however, an obvious change in both control mechanisms can be seen. The following sections are devoted to a brief discussion of control systems.

The literature holds a large number of definitions of management control. The modern views of management control originated with the influential work of Robert Anthony who drew boundaries between management control, strategic planning, and operational control. Anthony (1965, p. 17) defined management control as "the processes by which managers assure that resources are obtained and used effectively and efficiently in the accomplishment of the organization's objectives." Anthony declared that functions of managers of an organization consisted of planning and control systems and management control was supposed to be a linking process between strategic planning and operational control. Anthony and Govindarajan (2004) defined control as, "The process by which managers influence other members of the organization to implement the organization's strategies" (p. 7). Garrison and Noreen (2000) suggested a different definition of management control as follows: "those steps taken by management that attempt to increase the likelihood that the objectives set down at the planning stage are attained and to ensure that all parts of the organization function in a manner consistent with organizational policies" (p. 378).

4.3 *Enterprise Risk Management (ERM)*

ERM is a data-intensive process that measures all of a company's risks. This includes providing managers with an understanding of the full array of a company's risks including financial risks, investment-oriented risks, operations-based risks, and market risks, as well as legal and regulatory risks for all of the locations in which a company operates or invests (Peterson 2006). Risk can also be a result of political or social conditions in locations where a company has operations, suppliers, or customers (Egelkraut et al. 2005). Risk to a company's reputation is also an important aspect and element of ERM (Ruquet 2007).

In each of the risk areas, there are two primary types of risks that companies face:

- External risk
- Manufactured risk

External risk is the risk of events that may strike organizations or individuals unexpectedly (from the outside) but that happen regularly enough and often enough to be generally predictable.

Manufactured risk is a result of the use of technologies or even business practices that an organization chooses to adopt. A technological risk is caused or created by technologies that can include trains wrecking, bridges falling, and planes crashing (Giddens 1999). Business practice risk is caused or created by actions which the company takes which could include investing, purchasing, sales, or financing customer purchases.

ERM analytical models should encompass both external and manufactured risks which can be identified through historical analysis as well as reviews of current operations and exposures ("Expect the Unexpected," 2009). Once identified, risks can be validated through discussions with corporate executives, operations managers, production managers, and business unit executives. In addition to gaining a better understanding of risks the overall health of a company should be assessed (Coccia 2006; Panning 2006).

Investment advisors, institutional investors, and credit rating agencies are adding to the pressure for companies to develop ERM systems and disclose their risks (Karlin 2007). ERM enables top managers of a company to aggregate, prioritize, and effectively manage risks while enabling business unit managers to improve decision making in operations and product management (Kocourek et al. 2005). In managing risks there are several options that corporate executives can take including accepting, preventing, mitigating, transferring, sharing, or avoiding the risks (Egelkraut et al. 2005).

The ERM process can also support strategic planning activities as well as provide insight into alternative business practices and goals (Millage 2005). One of the biggest challenges in implementing ERM strategies is to make sure that selected analytical methods are appropriate for the type and size of organization to which they are being applied (Milligan 2009). ERM strategies and models as well as the utilization of ERM analyzes will vary with corporate culture, business goals, and risk management objectives. This means that a one-size-fits-all approach towards ERM is not likely to be successful (Lenckus 2006).

Risk and uncertainty are an inescapable part of investing. Fredman and Wiles (1998) called risk "the possibility of loss, damage, or harm" where risk depends on the individual and the individual's appetite or tolerance for risk. Managing risk is very important for successful long-term investing. Investors can use various strategies such as diversification and asset allocation to reduce risk. Ultimately, the investor must compare financial objectives to the risk and return rates of investments.

5 Primary Data Analysis

While structuring the research, the grounded theory approach was chosen to identify the Enterprise Flexibility, Enterprise Controllability, and Enterprise Risk Parameters. Thirty-two industry experts were selected and interviewed to identify the pattern. Once the pattern is identified, the parameters were segregated. Delphi methodology was applied followed by statistical t-test analysis to select and establish the factors.

The study was conducted over a period of 1 month interviewing experts across various industries covering several sectors. Consent was obtained and a copy of the signed consent form was given to each participant. Two face-to-face interviews were conducted with each of the 32 study participants. Interviews lasted 60–90 min and were conducted at intervals convenient to the participant (i.e., usually 20–40 min).

The first interview with each participant was exploratory in nature and involved open-ended questions. At the start of the study, participants were asked general open-ended questions, in order to abide by the grounded theory methodology stance of limiting the influence on participants of previous theoretical constructs of caring (Strauss and Corbin 1990a, b). Furthermore, in grounded theory methodology, it is the incoming information from participants that sharpens the focus of the research question and related general questions (Strauss and Corbin 1997).

One reason for this practice is that in grounded theory methodology, the incoming information from participants determines the information sought. This is referred to as theoretical sampling (Strauss and Corbin 1990a, b). In the study, theoretical saturation of data was achieved with 32 participants (Full list of parameters identified is shown in Appendix 3).

A tentative preliminary model emerged from the first round of interviews with each of the participants. The second interview was used as an opportunity to affirm, modify, add, clarify, and elaborate on what was said in the first interview. The questions were based on the information introduced by participants during the first round of interviews and were effective in checking the content areas introduced and for verifying the emerging output.

5.1 Profile of the Sample

Thirty-two industry experts were identified. Out of 32 experts, 7 belong to countries outside India. Most of the respondents belong to the top management level (CXOs).

Information provided by participants earned its way into the theory when constant comparisons of data revealed the repeated presence of specific content areas in actual participant data. In grounded theory methodology, this is referred to as the constant comparison method of data analysis (Strauss and Corbin 1990a, b, 1998).

In our study, the constant comparison method of data analysis was accomplished by constantly comparing new information with previously identified information (Rinaldi 1995). This was to identify information that was repeatedly present and relevant to participants. These questions were asked to identify (1) categories, (2) relationships between and within categories, and (3) a central phenomenon or core category around which all the other categories revolved.

Through the constant comparison of data, categories that needed further refinement and development were identified and developed. Each happening, incident, idea, and event were given a name or conceptual label that represented what was happening in the data (Strauss 1987). Interviews were transcribed on the left-hand side of the transcript page. Then the categories identified were transcribed on the right-hand side of the transcript. A file folder, labeled according to the category identified, was established and copies of the corresponding section of interview transcript were placed in the folder. As new data were compared with previous data, different levels of codes or labels, corresponding to different levels of the theory (i.e., concepts, categories, subcategories, and basic social processes), were developed. Consequently, as conditions change, it is expected that the theoretical formulation presented will also change in order to reflect new conditions, different settings, and diverse samples (Fig. 11.2). Therefore, one of the limitations of the study is what cannot be found in the actual data at the time of the study (Strauss and Corbin 1997).

6 Delphi Method: Selecting Enterprise Flexibility, Enterprise Controllability, and Enterprise Risk Parameters

The original Delphi method was developed by Norman Dalkey of the RAND Corporation in the 1950s for a US-sponsored military project. Dalkey states that the goal of the project was "to solicit expert opinion to the selection, from the point of view of a Soviet strategic planner, of an optimal U.S. industrial target system and to the estimation of the number of A-bombs required to reduce the munitions output by a prescribed amount" (Dalkey and Helmer 1963, p. 458). Rowe and Wright (1999) characterize the classical Delphi method by four key features:

- Anonymity;
- Iteration;
- Controlled feedback; and
- Statistical aggregation of group response

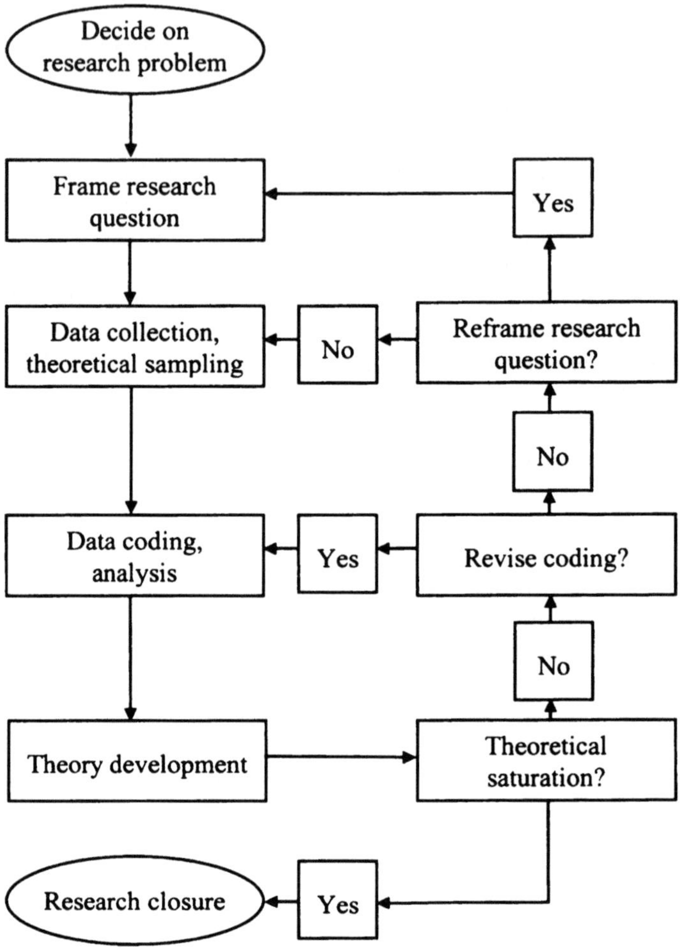

Fig. 11.2 Flow diagram of grounded theory method

Some (Rowe and Wright 1999) suggest that only those studies true to their origins that have the four characteristics should be classified as Delphi studies, while others (Adler and Ziglio 1996; Delbecq et al. 1975; Linstone and Turloff 1975) show that the technique can be effectively modified to meet the needs of the given study. Perhaps a distinction might be made by using the term Classical Delphi to describe a type of method that adheres to the characteristics of the original Delphi as summarized by Rowe and Wright (1999).

The Delphi process has been comprehensively reviewed elsewhere (Adler and Ziglio 1996; Delbecq et al. 1975; Linstone and Turloff 1975), and so I present only a brief overview of how I have used the Delphi in this study (Fig. 11.3).

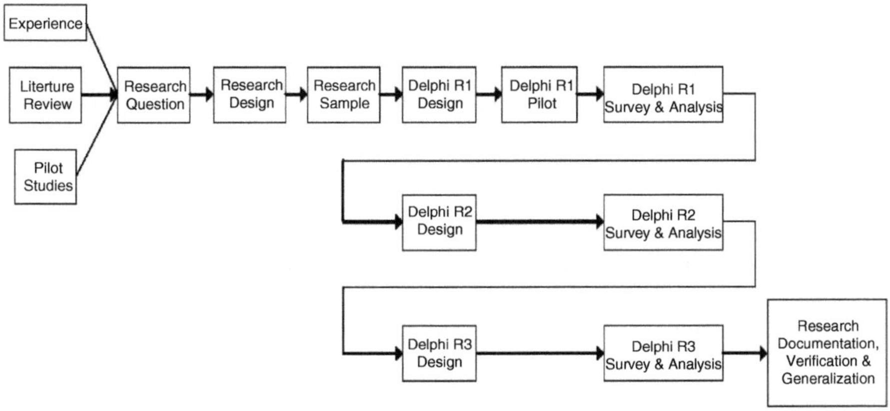

Fig. 11.3 Three-round Delphi process

(i) *Develop the Research Question* – The research question is derived by a number of ways. For example, it might be codeveloped by the student with the help of the supervisor, or the researcher's own industry experience often contributes to his interest in the research area. A review of the literature is also conducted, among other things, to determine if a theoretical gap exists. Often pilot studies are undertaken for numerous reasons: (i) identify the problem, (ii) conceptualize the study, (iii) design the study, (iv) develop the sample, (v) refine the research instrument, and (vi) develop and test data analysis techniques (Prescott and Soeken 1989). Completing a pilot study can also help ascertain the relevance the research question has to industry; some supervisors strongly favor applied rather theoretical research.

(ii) *Design the Research* – After developing a feasible research question, we begin designing the research from a macro to a micro perspective. Typically we review different research methods (both qualitative and quantitative) and after considering the pros and cons of each, we select the most promising method(s) to help answer our research question. The researcher would select the Delphi method when he/she wants to collect the judgments of experts in a group decision-making setting. Both qualitative and quantitative methods can be used in the Delphi process. The Delphi method may be only one component of the research project; for example, the Delphi outputs may be verified and generalized with a survey.

(iii) *Research Sample* – Selecting research participants is a critical component of Delphi research since it is their expert opinions upon which the output of the Delphi is based (Ashton 1986; Bolger and Wright 1994; Parenté et al. (1984). There are four requirements for "expertise": (i) knowledge and experience with the issues under investigation, (ii) capacity and willingness to participate, (iii) sufficient time to participate in the Delphi, and (iv) effective communication skills (Adler and Ziglio 1996). Since expert opinion is sought, a purposive sample is necessary where people are selected not to represent the general population, rather their expert ability to answer the research questions (Fink and Kosecoff 1985). The student may need some help from the supervisor to identify the initial group of experts but may use the "snowball" sampling technique to generate subsequent participants (Hartman and Baldwin 1995; Mason 1996).

(iv) *Develop Delphi Round One Questionnaire* – Care and attention needs to be devoted to developing the initial broad question which is the focus of the Delphi because if respondents do not understand the question, they may provide inappropriate answers and/or become frustrated (Delbecq et al. 1975). Sometimes, the purpose of the first round Delphi is to brainstorm (Schmidt 1997).

(v) *Delphi Pilot Study* – A pilot study is sometimes conducted with the goals of testing and adjusting the Delphi questionnaire to improve comprehension and to work out any procedural problems. The researcher may also pretest each subsequent questionnaire. The Delphi pilot is especially important for inexperienced researchers who may be overly ambitious regarding the scope of their research or underestimate the time it will take a Delphi research participant to fully respond to the Delphi survey.

(vi) *Release and Analyze Round One Questionnaire* – The questionnaires are distributed to the Delphi participants, who complete and return them to the researcher. The results of Round One are then analyzed according to the research paradigm (e.g., qualitative coding or statistical summarizing into medians plus upper and lower quartiles). Reality Maps can also be developed and shared with the Delphi participants. Reality Maps are graphical representations of the key constructs under investigation. They depict reality from the participant's perspective and often illustrate interactions, causes and effects, process flow, and other aspects of their reality. Reality Maps can greatly improve understanding and facilitate the emergence of collective intelligence in subsequent rounds about the topic under investigation (Lindstone and Turloff 1975).

(vii) *Develop Round Two Questionnaire* – The Round One responses are the basis with which to develop the questions in the Round Two Questionnaire. Depending upon the research goals, the researcher may direct the focus of the research or be directed by the opinions of the participants. If the purpose of Round One was to generate a list, then it is common to pare down that list in Round Two (Schmidt 1997).

(viii) *Release and Analyze Round Two Questionnaire* – The Round Two Questionnaire is released to the research participants and, when completed, returned for analysis. However, the participants are first given the opportunity to verify that the Round One responses did indeed reflect their opinions and are given the opportunity to change or expand their Round One responses now that the other research participant's answers are shared with them. Ranking and rating the output of the first round is common (Schmidt 1997).

Continuous verification throughout the Delphi process is critical to improve the reliability of the results (Adler and Ziglio 1996; Delbecq et al. 1975; Linstone and Turloff 1975) and should be factored into the research design. Again, a similar process of analysis is often used in Round Two.

(ix) *Develop Round Three Questionnaire* – The Round Two responses are used to develop the Round Three Questionnaire with additional questions to verify the results, to understand the boundaries of the research, and to understand where these results can be extended. Typically, the questions become more focused on the specifics of the research at each round.

(x) *Release and Analyze Round Three Questionnaire* – The final round of analysis is conducted following a similar process used to analyze the data in Rounds One and Two; use the appropriate technique for the question type (e.g., coding for open-ended, qualitative questions). Again, the research participants are given the opportunity to change their answers and to comment on the emerging and collective perspective of the research participants. The process stops if the research question is answered – for example, consensus is reached, theoretical saturation is achieved, or sufficient information has been exchanged.

(xi) *Verify, Generalize, and Document Research Results* – The Delphi results are verified (usually continuously through the Delphi) and the extent the results can be generalized are also investigated.

The Delphi was conducted over 32 samples (experts) and please find below the parameters selected after two rounds of Delphi.

6.1 General Pattern

1. Flexibility can be measured in three areas – Options, Change Mechanisms, and Freedom of Choice.
2. All risks can be categorized into two major types of risks – risk of not having flexibility and risk of having flexibility.
3. Controllability parameters can be classified into two groups: (1) internal in the system (known as the self-governance) and (2) external (this is controlled from outside the system) (Fig. 11.4).

6.2 Flexibility Parameters

The following flexibility parameters were selected through the Delphi study

(i) Productivity
(ii) Dynamism

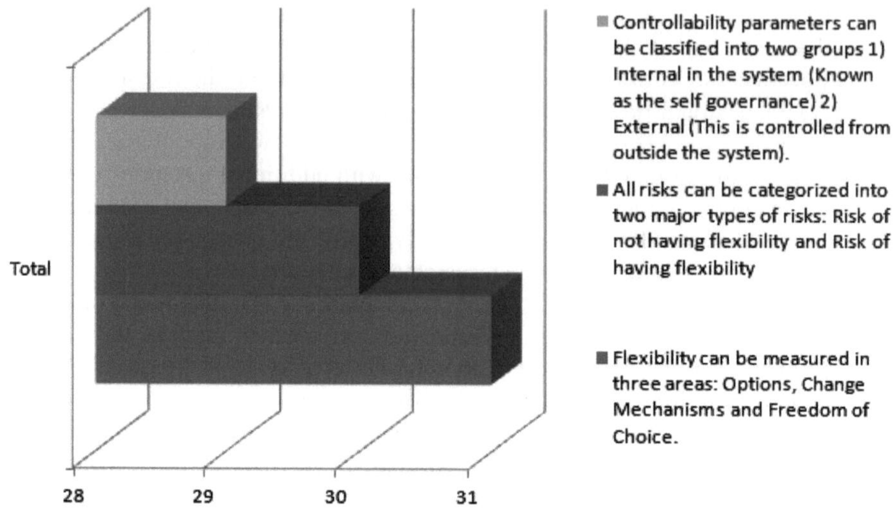

Fig. 11.4 Flexibility, controllability risk confluence pattern bar diagram

(iii) Flexi-Structure
(iv) Adaptability to change
(v) Change Management Procedure
(vi) Manufacturing Process flexibility
(vii) Sales Flexibility measured by time to respond to a change in the market
(viii) Market-side flexibility
(ix) Supply side of people – the variability is in the general economic conditions.
(x) Measure of On-time Delivery
(xi) Sensitivity to the Quality requirement
(xii) Learning Environment measured by the number of initiatives taken to create the Learning Environment
(xiii) Flexibility lies in Business Direction, i.e., allocation of investments across new and old product portfolio, flexibility in Business Direction (e.g., make vs. buy).
(xiv) Flexibility is resilience in customer handling, i.e., openness to customer queries and complaint management across channel (e.g., services handled equally when request placed telephonically, on the web-channel, at the retail store).
(xv) Flexibility in Leadership (in a complex case)
(xvi) Supply Chain Flexibility – demand and supply lines should have sufficient flexible capacity to absorb business demands (Fig. 11.5).

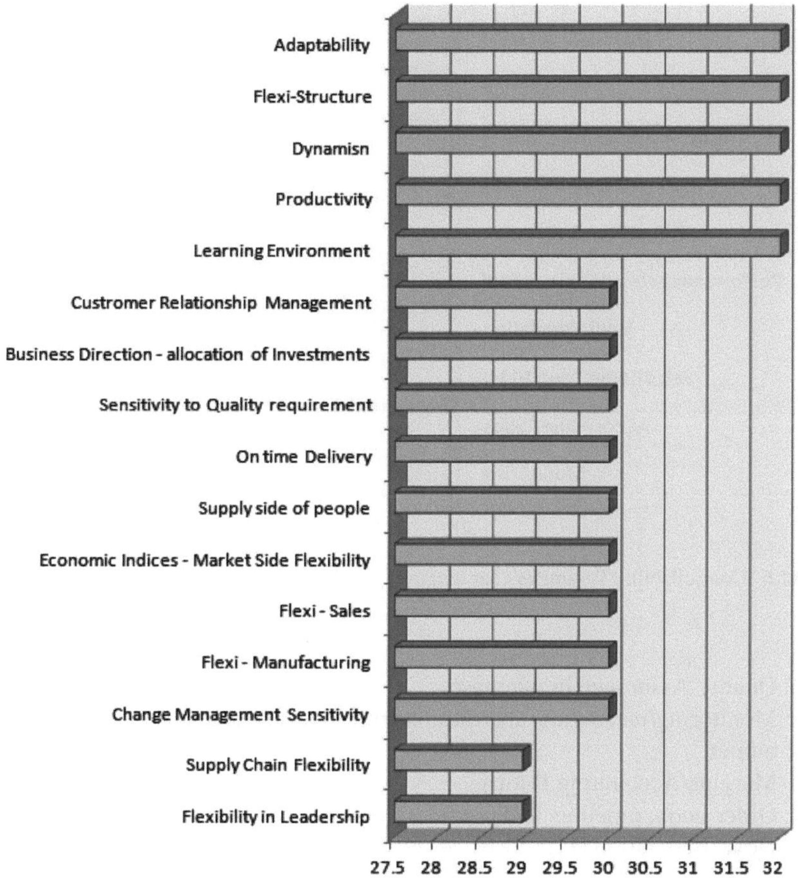

Fig. 11.5 Flexibility Parameters bar diagram

6.3 Controllability Parameters

The following controllability parameters were selected through the Delphi study.

(i) Financial System (Triple Audit System – internal, external, and statutory).
(ii) Clearly laid down authority and responsibility metrics.
(iii) Importance of Vigilance department.
(iv) Tools like Performance, Coaching, and Development systems to control the pockets of lower performance and/or morale before it is too late.
(v) Adherence to Information Governance Policy (information leakage is restricted).

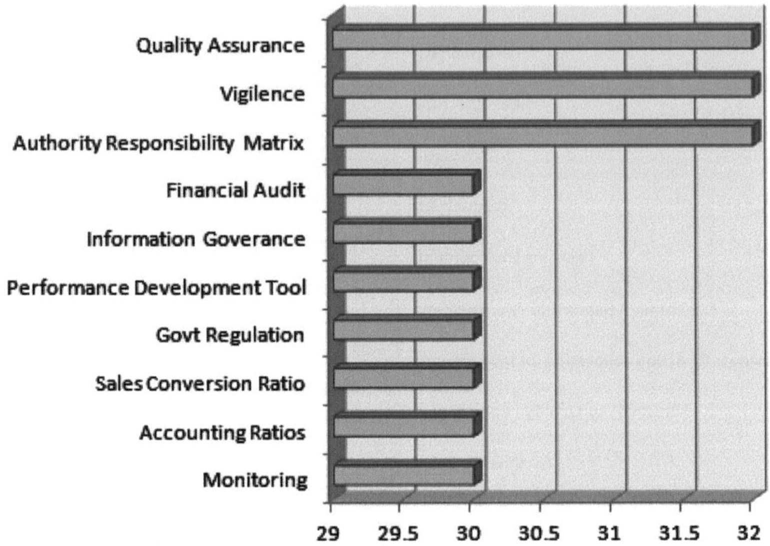

Fig. 11.6 Controllability Parameters bar diagram

(vi) Quality Assurance in purchase.
(vii) Monitoring/measuring aberrations from normal result of process input and output.
(viii) Margins/Accounting Ratios.
(ix) Order book, pipeline, and conversion ratio.
(x) Govt. Regulation (Fig. 11.6).

7 Risk Parameters

The following risk parameters were selected through the Delphi study.

(i) Multitasking may affect output because people may not be good in every area. Expertise may be in one field and may not be that good in other (People Risk).
(ii) Attrition can be termed as loss of knowledge.
(iii) Data Dependency and sanctity of data can be a big threat to the organization.
(iv) Rate of Change of Decisions.
(v) SCM turnover ratio.
(vi) Political uncertainty.
(vii) Monetary policies and cost of finance.
(viii) Risk of Lending because of diversified portfolio.

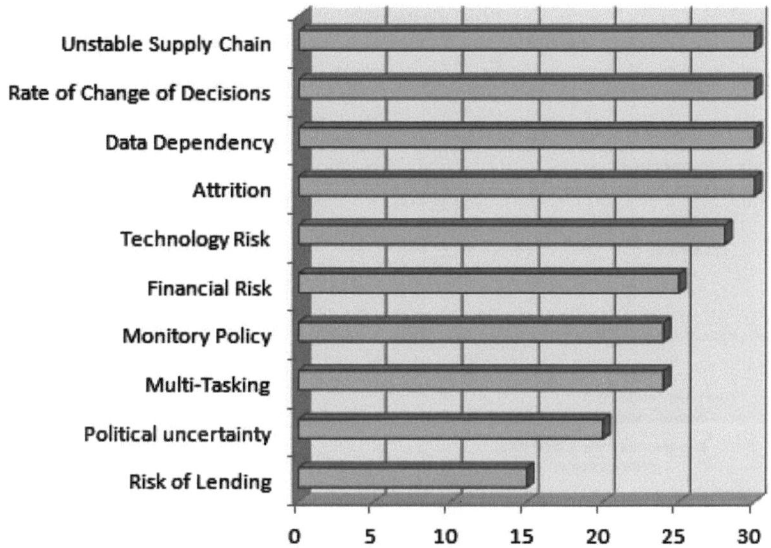

Fig. 11.7 Risk Parameter bar diagram

(ix) Technology Risks – obsolescence of a company's main technology platform.

(x) Financial Risks – these are standard for any company (over leveraged, high debt ratio impacted by high interest rates, etc.) (Fig. 11.7)

8 Inferences from t-Test

Established flexibility, controllability and enterprise risk confluence patterns are as follows:

Flexibility can be measured in three areas – Options, Change Mechanisms, and Freedom of Choice. All risks can be categorized into two major types of risks: risk of not having flexibility and risk of having flexibility. Controllability Parameters can be classified into two groups: (1) internal in the system (known as the self-governance) and (2) external (this is controlled from outside the system).

Established Flexibility Parameters are as follows:

Productivity; Dynamism; Flexi-Structure; Adaptability; Change Management Sensitivity; Flexi, Manufacturing; Flexi, Sales; Economic Indices, Market-side Flexibility; Supply side of people; On-time Delivery; Sensitivity to Quality requirement; Learning Environment; Business Direction, allocation of Investments;

Fig. 11.8 Identified, selected, and established Flexibility Parameters (the number signifies absolute number of respondents agreed to accept the parameters – considerable amount of consensus were achieved after three rounds of Delphi method)

Fig. 11.9 Identified, selected, and established Controllability Parameters (the number signifies absolute number of respondents agreed to accept the parameters – considerable amount of consensus were achieved after three rounds of Delphi method)

Customer Relationship Management; Flexibility in Leadership; Supply Chain Flexibility (Fig. 11.8)

Established Controllability Parameters are as follows:

Financial Audit; Authority Responsibility Matrix; Vigilance; Performance Development Tool; Information Governance; Quality Assurance; Monitoring; Accounting Ratios; Sales Conversion Ratio; Govt. Regulation (Fig. 11.9)

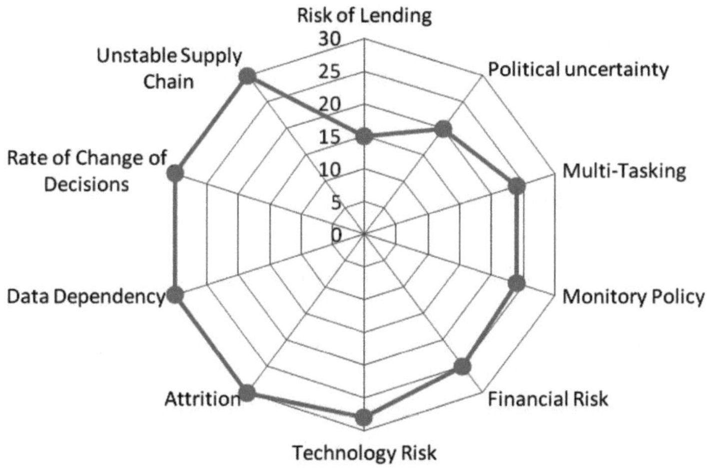

Fig. 11.10 Identified, selected, and established Risk Parameters (the number signifies absolute number of respondents agreed to accept the parameters – considerable amount of consensus were achieved after three rounds of Delphi method)

Established Enterprise Risk Parameters are as follows:

Multitasking; Attrition; Data Dependency; Rate of Change of Decisions; SCM turnover ratio; Political uncertainty; Monitory Policy; Risk of Lending; Technology Risk; Financial Risk (Fig. 11.10)

9 Synthesis of Learning and Proposed Parameters

The need for flexibility in management, both at the theoretical and practical levels, has been emphasized by researchers as well as practitioners. There are multiple connotations attached with the concept of flexibility, in different situations.

It implies openness in thinking, adaptiveness to environment, responsiveness to change, versatility of action, contingency, nonrigidity, variability of parameters and specifications, multiplicity of process setting, freedom, liberalization, informal attitude, adjustment, compromise, autonomy of function, agility in action, resilience in systems, elasticity, looseness, customized or tailor made solutions, and broadening of mind. This is only a representative list and many more connotations of flexibility can be identified.

9.1 Limitation of Research

The research is contextual and covers only some part of the industries. Though more than 25 % of the respondents belong to different countries but most of the respondents and industry experts belong to North India.

To form a comprehensive view of organizational flexibility, controllability, and enterprise risk parameters, the sample size needs to be big and should cover different regions of India and world pertaining to various industries.

9.2 Future Research Area

Literature in organizational flexibility mostly caters to the work done in European Business Environment. The literature is still lacking of comprehensive modeling which explains the relationships between its key variables and consequent side effects of such iterations. Exploring these interactions and the dynamic adaptation processes towards the desired adjustment would lead to frame a model which would explain organizational preparedness to response with the change and its adoption model. This idea of flexibility controllability equilibrium model and its adoption framework are the main motivation of the future research.

10 Concluding Remarks

The main objective of the research work was to identify the organizational flexibility, controllability, and enterprise risk parameters considering the complex paradoxical business scenario. The research reflects dynamic interplay between the thesis and antithesis. The change drivers can be depicted as risk parameters. The continua reflecting the thesis and the antithesis call for synthesis of two extreme business behaviors.

References

Aaker DA, Mascarenhas B (1984) The need for strategic flexibility. J Bus Strat 5:74–82

Abernathy WJ, Utterback JM (1978) Patterns of industrial innovation. Technol Rev 80

Adler M, Ziglio E (1996) Gazing into the oracle: the Delphi method and its application to social policy and public health. Kingsley Publishers, London

Andrew P, Hatum A (2006) Determinants of organizational flexibility: a study in an emerging economy. Br J Manag 17(2): 115–137. ISSN 1467–8551

Ansoff I (1965) Corporate strategy – an analytic approach to business policy for growth and expansion. McGraw-Hill, New York 2:20–26

Anthony RN (1965) Planning and control systems: a framework for analysis, Graduate School of Business Administration. Harvard University, Boston

Anthony RN (1988) The management control function. The Harvard Business School Press, Boston

Anthony RN, Dearden J, Bedford NM (1989) Management control systems, 6th edn. Richard D. Irwin Inc., Illinois

Anthony RN, Govindarajan V (2004) Management control systems. McGraw-Hill, New York

Ashton R (1986) Combining the judgments of experts: how many and which ones? Organ Behav Hum Decis Process 38(3):405–415

Benner MJ, Tushman ML (2002) Process management and technological innovation: a longitudinal study of the photography and paint industries. Adm Sci Q 47:676–706, Benner and Tushman (2001)

Berry AJ, Broadbent J, Otley DT (eds) (1998) Management control theory – history of management thought. Dartmouth Publishing, Aldershot

Bolger F, Wright G (1994) Assessing the quality of expert judgment: issues and analysis. Decis Support Syst 11(1):1–24

Carpenter RD (1995) Grounded theory research approach. In: Streubert HJ, Carpenter RD (eds) Qualitative research and in nursing: advancing the humanistic imperative. J.B. Lippincott Company, Philadelphia, pp 145–161

Carroll JJ (1987) Control methodologies for achievement of strategic objectives. Unpublished Doctoral Dissertation, Nova University, Fort Lauderdale

Chua WF, Lowe T, Puxty T (eds) (1989) Critical perspectives in management control. Macmillan, Basingstoke

Coccia R (2006) ERM plans cut costs, help risk managers bring added value. Bus Insur 40(21):4–4

Daft RL, Lewin AY (1993) Where are the theories for the 'New' organizational forms? Organ Sci 4(4):i–vi (An editorial essay)

Dalkey NC, Helmer O (1963) An experimental application of the Delphi method to the use of experts. Manage Sci 9(3):458–467

Delbecq AL, Van de Ven AH, Gustafson DH (1975) Group techniques for program planning: a guide to nominal and Delphi Processes. Scott, Foresman and Co, Glenview

DuBrin (2000) Fundamentos de administración, Soluciones empresariales, Edition 5. International Thomson Editores, S. A. de C. V.

Ebben J, Johnson A (2005) Efficiency flexibility or both? SMJ 26:1249–1259

Egelkraut TM, Woodard JD, Garcia P, Pennings JME (2005) Portfolio diversification with commodity futures: properties of levered futures. NCR-134 conference on applied commodity price analysis, forecasting, and market risk management, St. Louis

Eisenhardt KM, Martin JA (2000) Dynamic capabilities: what are they? Strategic Manage J 21: 1105–1121

Eppink JD (1978) Planning for strategic flexibility. Long Range Plann 11:9–15

Fink A, Kosecoff J (1985) How to conduct surveys: a step-by-step guide. SAGE, Beverly Hills

Fredman AJ, Wiles R (1998) How mutual funds work. Prentice-Hall, Paramus

Garrison RH, Noreen EW (2000) Managerial accounting. McGraw-Hill, New York

Giddens A (1999) Risk and responsibility. Mod Law Rev 62(1):1

Harrigan (1985) Strategies for joint venture. Lexinton Books, Lexinton

Hartman F, Baldwin A (1995) Using technology to improve the Delphi method. J Comput Civil Eng 9:244–249

Hayes RH, Abernathy WJ (1980) Managing our way to economic decline. Harvard Bus Rev 58:67–77

Helfat C, Finkelstein S, Mitchell W, Peteraf M, Singh H, Teece D, Winter S (2007) Dynamic capabilities: understanding strategic change in organisations. Blackwell Publishing, Malden

Kocourek P, Newfrock J, Van Lee R (2005) SOX rocks, but won't block shocks. Strat Bus 38(Spring)

Kraatz MS, Zajac EJ (2001) How organizational resources affect strategic change and performance in turbulent environments: theory and evidence. Organ Sci 12(5)

Lenckus D (2006) Risk managers name top threats. Bus Insur 3+. ProQuest

Linstone HA, Turoff M (1975) Introduction. In: Linstone HA, Turoff M (eds) The Delphi method: techniques and applications. Addison-Wesley Publishing Company, Reading, pp 3–12

Mason J (1996) Qualitative researching. Sage, London

Merchant KA (1985) Control in Business Organizations. Ballinger, Cambridge, MA, p 161

Merchant KA (1982) The control function of management. Sloan Manag Rev (Summer):43–55

Nadkarni S, Narayanan VK (2007) Strategic schemas, strategic flexibility, and firm performance: the moderating role of industry clockspeed. Strategic Manage J 28(3):243

Otley DT (1989) A strategy for the development of theories in management control. In: Chua WF, Lowe T, Puxty T (eds) Critical perspectives in management control. Macmillan, Basingstoke, pp 27–45

Otley D (1996) Some issues in management control. In: Vagnuer K, Wilkinson C, Berry AJ (eds) Beyond constraint – exploring the management control paradox. The Management Control Association, London

Panning WH (2006) Managing interest rate risk: ALM, solvency, and franchise value. Willis Re White Paper, January. Presented to the international conference of actuaries, Paris, May 2006

Parenté FJ, Anderson JK, Myers P, O'Brien T (1984) An examination of factors contributing to Delphi accuracy. J Forecasting 3(2):173–182

Peterson M (2006) Indeterminate preferences. Philos Stud 130:297–320

Prescott PA, Soeken KL (1989) The potential uses of pilot work. Nurs Res 38:60–62

Rowe, Wright (1999) The Delphi technique as a forecasting tool: issues and analysis. Int J Forecasting 15: 353–375

Sanchez R (2004) Understanding competence-based management: identifying and managing five modes of competence. J Bus Res 57(5):518

Sather (2004) Managerial control of faculty by physical education, Department chairpersons. A dissertation submitted in partial fulfillment of the requirements for the degree of doctorate of philosophy in the graduate school of the texas woman's university health science department

Schmidt R (1997) Managind Delphi surveys using nonparametric statistical techniques. Decis Sci 28(3):763–774

Simons R (1995) Levers of control – how managers use innovative control systems to drive strategic renewal. Harvard Business School Press, Boston

Sommer RA (2003) Business process flexibility: a driver for outsourcing. Ind ManagData Syst 103(3):177–183

Strauss A (1987) Qualitative analysis for social scientists. Cambridge University Press, New York

Strauss A, Corbin J (1990a) Basics of qualitative research: techniques and procedures for developing grounded theory. Sage, Newbury Park

Strauss A, Corbin J (1990b) Grounded theory research: procedures, canons, and evaluative criteria. Qual Sociol 13:3–21

Strauss A, Corbin J (eds) (1997) Grounded theory in practice. Sage, Thousand Oaks

Strauss A, Corbin J (1998) Basics of qualitative research: Techniques and procedures for developing grounded theory, 2nd edn. Sage, Thousand Oaks, CA, Street corner society revisited (1992) J Contemp Ethnogr 21(special issue):3–132

Stoner JAF, Wankei C (1986) Management. Prentice-Hall, Englewood Cliffs

Sushil (1999/2000a) Corporate flexibility. Glob J Flex Syst Manag

Sushil (2000) SAP-LAP models of inquiry. Manag Decis 38:347–353

Teece DJ, Pisano G, Shuen A (1997) Dynamic capabilities and strategic management. Strategic Manage J 18(7)

Verdu Jover AJ, Llorens-Montes JF, Garcia-Morales VJ (2005) Flexibility, fit and innovative capacity: an empirical examination. Int J Technol Manage 30(1,2)

Volberda HW (1998) Building the flexible firm. Oxford University Press, Oxford

Volberda HW (1996) Toward the flexible form: how to remain vital in hypercompetitive environments. Organ Sci 7(4):359–374

Part III
Business Process and Information Systems Flexibility

Chapter 12
Graceful Migration of Agile Systems Across Next-Generation Life Cycle Boundaries

Rick Dove and Garry Turkington

1 Introduction

Something different is happening. Military enterprise, reacting to next-generation warfare, sees the need for a new infrastructure strategy. Net centricity and force transformation encompass that plan (Cebrowski 2004; Research 2003). Business enterprise, reacting to next-generation competition, sees the need for a new infrastructure. Service-oriented architecture and web services encompass that plan (OASIS n.d., W3C 2004).

Both next-generation approaches exhibit a significant distinction from the succession of last generations preceding them: they include the promise of infrastructures that will migrate through continuous change hereafter, putting an end to the traditional scrap-and-replace next-generation progression strategy.

War and competition are situated in a world of continuously increasing complexity. Complexity is a word with many interpretations – here it is used to mean more considerations for a system to deal with, e.g., technologies, interconnections, requirements, situational surprises, and opportunities. What business and military enterprises have recognized is that situational change is an accelerating continuous function, and discreet next-generation realignments, as shown in Fig. 12.1, are now leaving gaps of unacceptable inadequacy.

The value propositions for both force transformation and service-oriented architecture is the realization of an agile enterprise that coevolves with an unpredictable continuously changing future:

R. Dove (✉)
Stevens Institute of Technology, Hoboken, NJ, USA
e-mail: rick.dove@stevens.edu

G. Turkington
Paradigm Shift International, Columbia, MD, USA
e-mail: garry.turkington@gmail.com

Sushil and E.A. Stohr (eds.), *The Flexible Enterprise*, Flexible Systems Management,
DOI 10.1007/978-81-322-1560-8_12, © Springer India 2014

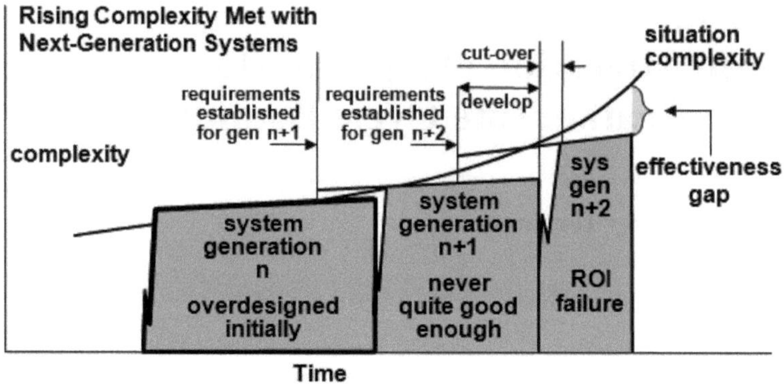

Fig. 12.1 Successive generations of system replacement

- Arthur K. Cebrowski, Director, Force Transformation (Cebrowski 2004): "…we are on course to transform our military into an agile, network-centric, knowledge-based force capable of conducting effective joint and combined military operations against all potential future adversaries.[1]…Transformation is foremost a continuing process. It does not have an end point. Transformation is meant to create or anticipate the future. Transformation is meant to deal with the co-evolution of concepts, processes, organizations and technology."[2]
- NASCIO Research Brief (NASCIO 2006): "Service Oriented Architecture: An Enabler of the Agile Enterprise … Imagine the ability to pick and choose business and technology services. To be able to trade out services based on organizational re-design, new strategic intent, legislative requirements, or business process modifications. It is a whole philosophy about sharing, decoupling business processes from technology, to enable a fluid enterprise that can change and change quickly."

Systems that can migrate across these next-generation gaps seamlessly have clear value. Such systems were the subject of an industry-collaborative study (Nagel et al. 1991; Dove 1992) in the 1990s initially focused on manufacturing enterprise agility and later broadened to encompass agility in enterprises and systems of all kinds. Interest in such systems has continued to grow: most recently with the (Upton and Staats 2008) excellent depiction of a foreign bank's agile business-software infrastructure and (Engel and Tyson 2008) suggesting a new way to value and justify adaptable architecture options.

Some background context on the work reported here is useful. In 2006, the increasing interest in agility as a desired enterprise and system characteristic spawned a four-course graduate certificate in Agile Systems and Enterprises at Stevens Institute of Technology and initiated related research. The Stevens program

[1] Cebrowski 2004, opening page of document: Message from the Director, Office of Force Transformation.
[2] Ibid, p. 8.

emphasizes fundamental domain-independent architecture and design principles that enable agility in systems of any kind, collectively referred to here as Response Ability Principles – or RAP[3] for convenience. Discussed in the next section, RAP encompasses a set of domain-independent architectural principles of structure and strategy that enable agile systems.

The work reported here is a continuation of work reported in Dove and Turkington (2008), which cast agile-system-development methods into the RAP model of domain-independent agile systems and then looked at how the resulting architecture could inform and influence a migration from agile development into agile operations within the system life cycle. That paper concluded by indicating a number of areas for further investigation. One of the areas suggested was to continue the investigation of the RAP migration concept, with a focus on agile systems migrating across next-generation boundaries.

A search for suitable exemplar systems that have migrated successfully across next-generation boundaries was conducted. The principle criteria for suitableness were broad and general familiarity, so that distracting system explanations could be avoided and migration issues and concepts could be the focus. It was also decided that more than one system should be examined and that they should not be in the same domain, in order to help obtain domain-independent abstractions. Three systems ended up on the short list: audio/video home entertainment, the Internet, and a company known to the authors that went through major business model evolutions.

To note is that all three systems fit the general signature of plug-and-play (infrastructure) drag-and-drop (components) characteristic of RAP-based agile systems. No attempt was specifically made to find successful cross-generation migration in systems that do not exhibit this characteristic signature, and no suggestion is made here that such systems do not exist.

Preliminary investigation of all three systems found the company example questionable as a useful migration example – its financial performance has deteriorated recently and it was felt that this fact would obscure the successfulness of its operational migration. Home entertainment and Internet systems fared much better, appearing to provide a sufficiently different system-domain view for effective abstraction while being common enough for broad familiarity. Virtually everybody interacts with both of these systems to some extent, though generally at a more intimate level for home entertainment than Internet for many. A long ongoing migration, home entertainment systems today may contain components that were new technologies 50 years ago, integrated comfortably with new capabilities unimagined 5 years ago. More immediately, the Internet is in early stages of migration to a new packet protocol known as IPv6 (Internet Protocol version 6), which greatly expands urgently needed additional addressing capacity (Beijnum 2007, 2008).

[3] Response Ability Principles encompass research initiated at Lehigh University's Agility Forum in the 1990s and later detailed in *Response Ability* (Dove 2001).

The objective is to employ these two systems as exemplars for migration-enabling purposeful system design. Arguably both of these systems were not designed initially with long-term broad-scale migration, of the magnitude they are delivering, as a specific requirement. This quality materialized, undoubtedly through nurturing, as a fortuitous accident. For sure, the current tools of RAP theory were not formally employed in the design of these systems. How would these systems fair when cast as domain-independent RAP models?

It is one thing to view these systems through the lens of RAP and another to ask if that view illuminates the issues of agile-system migration across next generations usefully. This, then, is the second question to resolve.

Finally, if RAP modeling provides a clear view of migration-enabling concepts, how might that view inform purposeful attempts to build migration-enabled systems, such as force transformation and SOA (service-oriented architecture).

In summary, three questions drove the work reported here:

1. Can RAP tools model and depict the migration of component stereo to today's home entertainment and the migration of the Internet from an IPv4 to an IPv6 infrastructure?
2. Can RAP casting of these two systems inform the understanding of migration in agile systems?
3. Might this RAP viewpoint of agile-systems migration inform the in-process developments of SOA and force transformation as agile systems?

The second section, next, describes the sources and nature of the tools employed in seeking answers to these questions. The third section describes the process and results of pursuing these questions. The fourth section discusses the results and implications. The fifth and final section presents some conclusions and suggests potential further work illuminated by this effort.

2 Experimental Set-up

Answering the three questions was conducted as an exploratory experiment. A suitable set of RAP-modeling tools was selected, the literature was consulted to synthesize an Internet migration characterization, the home entertainment characterization was a refinement of common knowledge, and trial runs were conducted before the sought-after architectural conceptual patterns emerged. This section describes the source and nature of the modeling tools.

Agility as a system behavior is defined here in the broad terms intended by the 1991 Lehigh study (Nagel et al. 1991; Dove 1992; Goldman et al. 1995) that put the word into play: effective response under conditions of uncertainty. Subsequent research recognized that practicing such agility requires at least three aspects: situational awareness, decisive choice making, and the ability to respond. This latter aspect appeared to be the principle stumbling block observed in enterprise systems at that time. This drove a research focus at the Agility Forum on discovering architectural structure and strategy principles that would enable highly adaptable enterprise systems. This aspect of agile systems was later dubbed Response Ability and is detailed in domain-independent terms in Dove (2001). The work here deals only with this third architectural aspect of agile systems.

RAP-based architecture currently encompasses seven thought-guiding frameworks: response requirements categories (2×4 elements), response performance metrics (4 elements), functional design principles (10 elements), design quality principles (3 elements), system integrity responsibilities (4 elements), an overarching architectural philosophy (3 elements), and a conceptual pattern. All except the recent addition of design quality principles are dealt with at length in Dove (2001) and perhaps more accessibly and briefly in Dove (2005).

The conceptual pattern of RAP architecture employed here[4] is one of drag-and-drop components/modules in a plug-and-play infrastructure. The overarching architectural philosophy is reusable components reconfigurable in a scalable infrastructure. Components are encapsulated one-to-one physical and functional units. Infrastructure has two parts: a passive part that provides standards (rules) for connectivity and interaction among components and an active part that consists of four specific integrity responsibilities for maintaining and sustaining readiness for unpredictable system response needs.

Integrity responsibility, the "active" part of the infrastructure, will play a distinguishing role in determining Class 1 or Class 2 characterizations for the systems of interest. The four integrity responsibility elements are:

1. Maintaining sufficient inventory of components ready for use (e.g., in home entertainment: speakers, amplifiers, tuners, tape units, etc.)
2. New component addition and upgrade as new capabilities are needed (DVD units, TIVO-like appliances, Wii, game consoles, etc.)
3. Infrastructure evolution (surround sound, video, wireless, internet, etc.)
4. Assembly of components into on-demand system configurations suitable for changing needs (movement of speakers and tuners to patio, borrowing a DVD player from the family room system for the bedroom system, etc.)

Four of the seven RAP frameworks are employed in the work reported here: the 3-element architectural philosophy, the migration element of the 2×4 response requirements categories, the 4-element integrity responsibilities, and the plug-and-play/drag-and-drop conceptual pattern. In addition, the class distinctions between reconfigurable and reconfiguring agile systems are employed. Thus, system characteristics will be cast in the conceptual pattern of drag-and-drop components in a plug-and-play infrastructure of passive standards and active responsibilities. Exploring application of the other frameworks appears promising but is left to subsequent work.

[4] Dove (2007) distinguishes agile systems as reconfigurable (class 1) and reconfiguring (class 2). The drag-and-drop/plug-and-play pattern is most naturally associated with class 1 (reconfigurable) agile systems, as the four integrity responsibility elements of the active infrastructure are typically peopled rather than systemic.

Table 12.1 Reactive and proactive response requirements categories

Reactive response domains	Proactive response domains
Correction – rectify a dysfunction	Creation – create/eliminate things during operation
Variation – accommodate variable situation parameters	Improvement – improve performance metrics over time
Expansion – add/subtract capacity	Migration – change the infrastructure significantly
Reconfiguration – reorganize internal relationships	Modification – add/subtract capability

The 2×4 response requirements categories are shown in Table 12.1. The purpose of this framework is to stimulate and organize the identification of different types of response requirements a system must be prepared to cope with effectively. Migration is one of the four proactive response domains and is defined in (Dove 2001) as

> *Foreseen, eventual, and fundamental change.* Issues are generally associated with changes to supporting infrastructure or transitions to next generation replacements.[5]

RAP thus characterizes migration as a life cycle concept for systems that hold their own in an environment of continuous situational change. The life cycle of such a system loses much of its traditionally separate stages of life cycle, characterized[6] as a sequential transition through concept, development, production, utilization, support, and retirement, and instead paces situational change with continued augmentation and evolution throughout an extended life cycle, seamlessly crossing traditionally terminal retirement boundaries into next-generation service.

Within a single generation life cycle, we have argued previously (Dove and Turkington 2008) that the distinction between development and operational stages of a system can be one of perspective rather than substance, if both exhibit a continuum of the key agile characteristics of reconfigurable components in an evolvable infrastructure. For a system to realize the benefits of agile development and operational agility, its progression through the intra-system life cycle stages must be a gradual and continuous change as the nature of the components and the agents of integrity responsibility, the active portion of infrastructure, change.

Finally, the conceptual pattern depicting drag-and-drop/plug-and-play functional architecture is shown in Fig. 12.2 for class 1 and class 2 agile systems. Note that the differences are minor and limited to the integrity responsibilities of the active infrastructure.

More and more systems today are experiencing increasingly frequent changes in their environment – be it organizational, market, technical, strategic, or otherwise. The need to respond with improved services quickly and effectively is less tolerant of a retirement and replacement strategy. Agile systems are seen as the facilitator of responsive component reconfiguration as well as infrastructure augmentation, enabling graceful migration into next-generation capabilities.

[5] Dove 2001, p. 88.

[6] INCOSE 2007, p. 3.5.

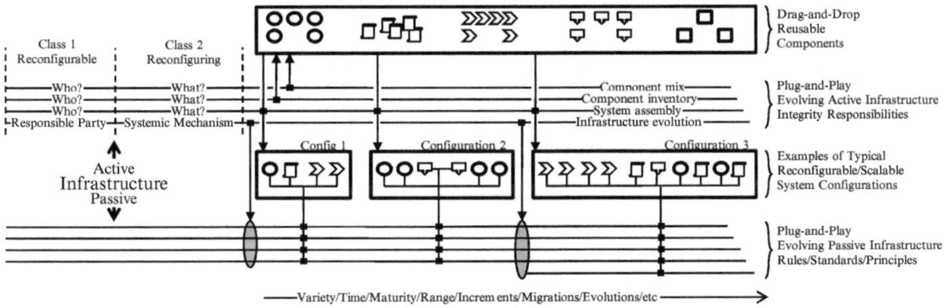

Fig.12.2 Generic drag-and-drop/plug-and-play conceptual pattern for Class 1 and Class 2 agile systems

3 Procedures and Results

To explore this migration concept, we will cast the two chosen systems into the RAP conceptual pattern. The anticipation is that this will identify and provide a clear picture of the migration-enabling elements. This section will address question 1. Questions 2 and 3 will be addressed in the discussion section that follows later.

3.1 Home Entertainment

Since the 1950s, the home entertainment nee component-stereo industry has seen many migration events, but the underlying infrastructure concepts have remained constant throughout. Though technological advances have occurred in all types of components, the fundamental approach to physical and functional connectivity has remained conceptually constant. The core components of home entertainment systems center around the amplifier and speakers, into which multiple content-source components connect. Though vacuum tubes have given way to transistors and vinyl records to cassettes and on to compact discs, the role and nature of the infrastructure and the general method of connectivity have remained constant. Users could upgrade their system largely on their own schedule and according to tastes and budget. Though a new CD player would be used to best advantage with an amplifier and speakers of similar quality, such was not required. This permitted a variety of system configurations ranging from the small and compact bedroom systems to the ultra high-end family room systems to evolve asynchronously and independently of technology developments and the choices made by other system owners.

As depicted in Fig. 12.3, the leading edge migration underway currently is augmenting the infrastructure to accommodate online and multimedia capabilities. Amplifiers began servicing five or more channels with a like number of speakers previously, about the same time as TV integration changed the system designation from HiFi stereo to home entertainment centers. That migration also brought

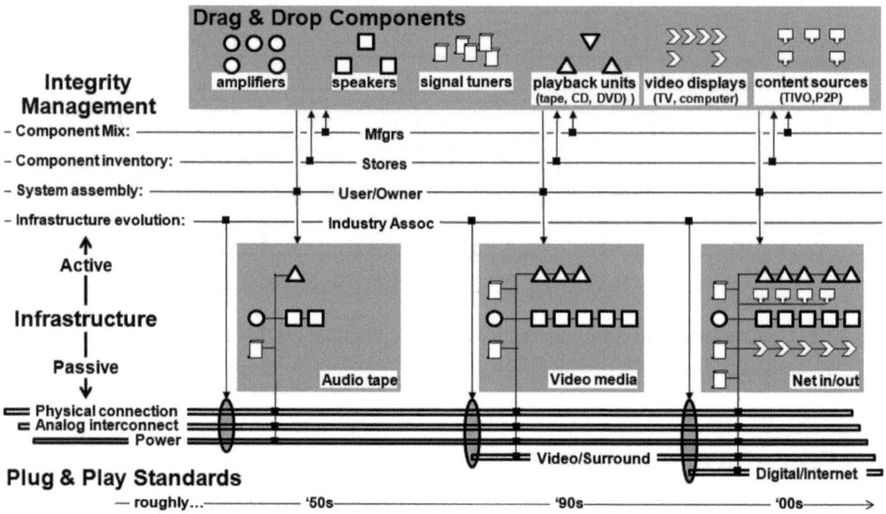

Fig. 12.3 Characterization of home entertainment system migration

component interconnect routing that bypassed the previous central role of the amplifier with direct connections between TV video-input and CD/DVD video sources. For historical purposes the initial generation attempts to depict the reel-to-reel audio tape deck era. Now digital video storage and online Internet content are shown as the new generation of infrastructure accommodation, which also includes gaming consoles, Wii devices, and the current explosion of innovation. Though prior era components may be used as part of the newer systems, it is not possible to accrue the benefits of these new capabilities without augmenting the infrastructure of the previous generation.

Figure 12.3 depicts the casting of the home entertainment system in the RAP conceptual pattern image. Question 1 appears to be answered in the affirmative: Can RAP tools model and depict the migration of component stereo to today's home entertainment?

Pools of component varieties are depicted independent of life cycle or time of employment. As it was not felt germane, no attempt was made to depict the inception of new component pools or the evolution of component technologies and diversity within those pools over time, though such could easily be accommodated by showing perhaps three pools of pools, to roughly coincide with the three time-period configurations. Though no attempt is made to be comprehensive with categories of components, the chosen depictions are representative samples to facilitate the discussion later.

Of most interest to the migration concept, however, is the depiction of both active and passive infrastructure. RAP defines the migration response category as a significant change to infrastructure. The depiction identifies certain augmentations to the passive infrastructure as coincident with the transition across generations. This depiction is of course conceptual and does not pretend to be precise and accurate. Its purpose is to illuminate the fundamental enabling and definitional concepts – contributing toward a pattern language (Alexander et al. 1977; Cloutier 2006) for agile-system architecture.

The active portion of infrastructure identifies the parties responsible for system integrity – notably the actions and sustainment of reconfigurable agility. Available component mix is the responsibility of independent manufacturers, adding new types of components and better technological implementations to the mix. Component inventory is the responsibility of distribution and service channels, such as retail stores, online catalog sales, and repair depots, with responsibility for providing and maintaining ready-to-employ components. System configuration responsibility lies principally with the operational system owner: adding, replacing, upgrading, and reconfiguring components in personal systems as and when desired. Finally, the interoperability standards and evolution of those standards that enable and facilitate plug-and-play are the responsibilities of various standard bodies supported by the industry. In general it is the intent to specifically designate the key responsible parties in the active infrastructure.

The passive portion of infrastructure is conceptually depicted, with no attempt to be comprehensive here. This part of the infrastructure is where augmentation occurs as next-generation capabilities require additional standards.

This extended tour of the home entertainment depiction in Fig. 12.3 will alleviate the need to do the same depth of explanation when we look at Internet Protocol migration next.

3.2 Internet Protocol

The Internet Protocol (IP) is the basis of virtually all Internet traffic. Though most users are unaware of its existence, it enables web browsers to access web sites, online videos to be obtained, and email and text messaging to occur between correspondents. The current version of this protocol has been in place since 1983 when TCP/IP (Transmission Control Protocol/Internet Protocol) replaced the prior NCP (Network Control Protocol) infrastructure. The Internet Protocol version currently dominant is referred to as IPv4, signifying version 4.

The explosive growth of the Internet is quickly approaching the limits of IPv4 addressing capability. The protocol allows every device on the Internet to have a unique address; but as more and more devices are added and new types of devices become Internet-capable, the pool of available addresses dwindled rapidly. In addition to the need for expanded addressing, security has become an issue. The Internet was created in a closed community of academics initially, when security was not critical, and consequently the security aspects of IPv4 are now seen as inadequate.

The next IP version is referred to as Internet Protocol version 6 or IPv6. IPv6 provides a much greater pool of addresses, presumably better security, and other

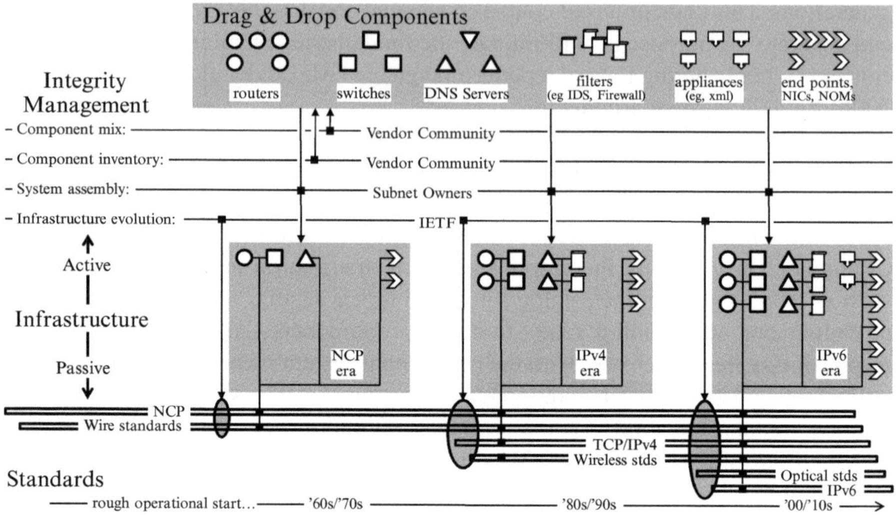

Fig. 12.4 Characterization of Internet system migration

functional advantages as well. The migration to IPv6, depicted in Fig. 12.4, is a massive undertaking and must be achieved without the slightest interruption to existing services or obsolescence of the vast installed device population.

Figure 12.4 depicts the casting of the Internet Protocol system in the RAP conceptual pattern image. Again, question 1 appears to be answered in the affirmative: Can RAP tools model and depict the migration of the Internet from an IPv4 to an IPv6 infrastructure?

For convenience and graphic depiction brevity, we appeal to poetic license and show the migration to TCP/IPv4 approximately at the same time as the migration to wireless standards. Similarly, we show the augmentations of optical standards and IPv6 in time proximity. The depictions of three configuration eras make some attempt to suggest relative sizes of component population, without concern for relative accuracies.

The passive infrastructure is represented simply – with the focus of interest on the NCP to IPv4 to IPv6 migrations – but with the recognition that other elements of infrastructure are migrating as well. The 1980s–1990s time frame indication on the center configuration is an attempt to peg roughly the migration to IPv4 in the 1980s and to wireless in the 1990s. Likewise the other two configurations match paired dates with paired protocol and media migrations.

The interest here again lies in the designation of responsibilities for the active portion of the infrastructure. Unlike the home entertainment designations, where local individuals were designated, here we designate communities for three of the four responsibilities. The difference is recognition that there is more interaction and reaction between the decisions of individual vendors and subnet owners – where decisions by one router vendor, for instance, are likely to precipitate reactive decisions by other router vendors, somewhat like a rebalancing when portions of an ecology undergo a dominance change. As some vendors begin to favor IPv6 product creation and distribution, others are effected competitively and adjust in some fashion. Such is the case among subnet owners as well, as more switch to IPv6 capabilities, others are pressured to respond similarly in a form of self-reorganization or face the potential of becoming a backwater. This is not the case in the individual decisions of home entertainment system owners to nearly the same extent. In contrast, the evolution of infrastructure standards for Internet Protocol is embodied in a single central controlling organization.

4 Discussion and Implications

In this section, we address the two remaining questions: Can RAP casting of these two systems inform the understanding of migration in agile systems, and might this RAP viewpoint of agile-system migration inform the in-process developments of SOA and force transformation as agile systems?

4.1 Informing the Understanding of Agile-System Migration

Components are encapsulated capabilities-based black boxes. In home entertainment, for instance, components can be replaced by different brands or different technological implementations at any time without affecting the serviceability of the rest of the system. Components are encapsulated functionally and physically one to one, allowing them to be inserted and deleted from a system configuration asynchronously and independently of any other component. In some cases, a given component may not be able to manifest usefulness if certain other components are not present, like a DVD player present in an entertainment system without a video display of some type; but such incomplete subgroups do not affect the ability of the rest of the system to provide service.

This encapsulation concept is a key and necessary enabler of RAP-based agile-system migration. Also key and necessary is the concept of augmentation to the passive portion of the infrastructure, as opposed to retirement or incompatible replacement of an infrastructure standard that would render existing components incapable of interoperation.

As illuminated by the modeling exercise, old infrastructure concepts and early vintage components are not forced into retirement and will coexist functionally with the new; and new infrastructure pulls the usage of new capability asynchronously with the allure of benefits, rather than pushing a forced synchronous switch. Owners are free to choose when and which new values make sense to them, rather than being coerced or forced into switching when satisfaction with the status quo, untimely change, or other priorities has precedence.

This architecture has provided the home entertainment industry with a significant level of resilience. The industry has seen numerous so-called format wars where several manufacturers offer competing but incompatible products that provide a new type of capability. Some of these wars have seen a clear winner (Compact Disc vs. Digital Audio Tape) while others have seen the new options fail to gain market traction (Super Audio Compact Disc vs. DVD-Audio). Individual evolution of independent home entertainment systems has virtually no impact on the total global community of home entertainment. A next-generation replacement approach would likely have produced many more make-or-break situations where a single failure could have major negative economic effect.

For the IPv4 to IPv6 migration, similar factors are at play, in that different segments of the Internet have independent life cycles and consequently may be migrated to the new version ahead of others.

The difference between a class 1 and class 2 RAP-based agile system is centrally controlled sustainment vs. self-organizing sustainment. In one case, specific people or committees (for instance) with centralized sustainment responsibilities can be named; in the second case, sustainment is caused by the equilibrium-seeking self-reorganization of decentralized interactions among autonomous agents. It is thought that the home entertainment system fits more the model of class 1, as the owner that configures systems very centrally controls the system configuration, and has little effect or influence on owners of other home entertainment systems. Migration of the Internet Protocol, in contrast, has a greater degree of coupling between the migration-deciding agents. As subnets opt for IPv6 profiles, other interconnected subnets may become shunned for services of lesser security or less optimal interaction.

4.2 Potential for Informing SOA and Force Transformation Adoptions

It is observed that SOA and home entertainment environments share a characteristic that may be useful in guiding SOA adoption plans. Both occur in relative isolation to their greater communities and resemble a class 1 agile system. Force transformation, on the other hand, has an environmental profile more like the Internet Protocol model. Both have sizable subgroups with interdependent couplings – looking somewhat like an ecological system in the large.

Adoption and subsequent migratory evolution of SOA within an enterprise is largely a local decision, with little interdependence on when and what other enterprises choose to do. Though enterprises are increasingly networked to each other electronically as well as strategically, SOA is largely an internal infrastructure for enterprise IT support of business practices. Perimeter gateways of various types are standard methods for reconciling intercompany transactions. The nature of the SOA infrastructure nevertheless must conform to greater community common/universal standards if maximum and sustainable access to component services of benefit is to be realized. This raises a cautionary flag on brand-unique infrastructure employment, as well as enterprise- or brand-unique service interfaces.

Force transformation is a massive undertaking, on many functional fronts within each military force as well as across the many independent but interdependent military forces of Army, Navy, Air Force, Marines, and Coast Guard. Force transformation is predicated on developing far more intimate interoperability than currently exists. The magnitude of the effort necessarily requires an asynchronous adoption for economic, cultural, and technological reasons as a minimum – without any disruption of capability. The military has a tradition of controlled mandated actions that may not serve well in either the initial adoption or the subsequent continual evolution intended. The model of Internet Protocol migration that relies on pulling self-organized adoption with enticing benefit, rather than forcing a change that may be incompatible with the reality of the status quo, might well provide both economic and speed-of-adoption advantages.

These small observations and suggestions are as far as the current work warrants, but they have provided an interesting foundation for further investigation in follow-on work.

5 Conclusion

This work presented a generic conceptual pattern for RAP-based agile systems capable of depicting key agility and migration-enabling elements, independent of the system domain. The nature of, and differences between, class 1 (reconfigurable) and class 2 (reconfiguring) RAP-based agile systems was introduced. It was suggested that the RAP conceptual pattern tool contributes toward the development of a pattern language for agile-system architecture. Migration in a RAP-based agile system was defined as a change to infrastructure facilitating a graceful crossing of next-generation capability boundaries. Two RAP-depicted systems that are successfully providing graceful migration were explored, looking for suggestions of domain-independent fundamental enabling concepts. Finally, it was suggested that the fundamental concepts that appear to enable and facilitate this migration capability might usefully inform purposeful attempts – at designing agile systems for graceful migration across next-generation boundaries.

No claim is made that these observations and suggestions form a sufficient or complete theory of migration in RAP-based agile systems. This work is expected to stimulate further research and application, based on its demonstrated ability to offer a pattern language for exploration and discussion of systems' agility and, specifically, graceful migration across next-generation boundaries.

System life cycle concepts have served us well in system engineering understandings and activities. Clearly there is a time before a system exists, a time when it is created, a time when it is in service, and a time when it no longer exists in any functional capacity. The concepts of investment and return on investment (ROI) are an integral part of life cycle, though usually blurred across the activity boundaries that characterize life cycle stages.

The pace of technology has continued to accelerate, as has the interconnection and interaction of human society and its support systems. All have reached a speed of change that conspires against an ROI for systems not made to freely evolve. The result is a process of natural selection: systems built for evolution will become the dominant concept. Some are already here, more by accident than purposeful design. The need for systems with longer life has reached the conscious system engineering level, and the search for understanding is underway.

Life cycle models will necessarily need updating to recognize continuous revitalization activity. Systems will retain identity across major functional transformations that would have spelled retirement and replacement. ROI will likewise need new math underpinnings as well. All are subjects for research, development, and natural selection.

This work is part of a larger body of research exploring a RAP-based theory of agile systems. It is stimulated primarily by promising masters and doctoral student course-projects that warrant further collaborative development.

References

Alexander C, Ishikawa S, Silverstein M, Jacobson M, Fiksdahl-King I, Angel S (1977) A pattern language: towns, buildings, construction. Oxford University Press, New York

Beijnum I (2007) Everything you need to know about IPv6, ars technica. March, http://arstechnica.com/articles/paedia/IPv6.ars

Beijnum I (2008) The night the IETF turned off IPv4, ars technica. March 2008, http://arstechnica.com/articles/culture/ietf-ipv6-switchoff.ars

Cebrowski AK (2004) Military transformation: a strategic approach. U.S. Department of Defense, Office of Force Transformation

Cloutier R (2006) Applicability of patterns to architecting complex systems. Ph.D. Dissertation, Stevens Institute of Technology, Hoboken

Dove R (1992) What's all this talk about agility – the 21st century manufacturing enterprise strategy, prevision, Japan management association. www.parshift.com/Files/PsiDocs/Rkd92Art6.pdf

Dove R (2001) Response ability – the language, structure, and culture of the agile enterprise. Wiley, New York

Dove R (2005) Fundamental principles for agile systems engineering, Conference on Systems Engineering Research (CSER), Stevens Institute of Technology, Hoboken, www.parshift.com/Files/PsiDocs/Rkd050324CserPaper.pdf

Dove R (2007) SDOE 678 and 683 course materials. Stevens Institute of Technology, School of Systems and Enterprises, available by request to rick.dove@stevens.edu

Dove R, Turkington G (2008) Relating Agile development to Agile operations. Conference on Systems Engineering Research (CSER), University of Southern California, Redondo Beach, April, www.parshift.com/Files/PsiDocs/Pap080404Cser2008DevOpsMigration.pdf

Engel A, Tyson B (2008) Designing systems for adaptability by means of architecture options. forthcoming in Syst Eng 11(2), www.incose.org/symp2008/dmdocuments/paper_example01.pdf

Goldman S, Nagel R, Preiss K (1995) Agile competitors and virtual organizations. Van Nostrand Reinhold, New York

INCOSE (2007) Systems engineering handbook – a guide for system life cycle processes and activities. Version 3.1, International Council on Systems Engineering, Aug www.incose.org/ProductsPubs/products/sehandbook.aspx

Nagel R, Dove R, Goldman S, Preiss K (1991) 21st century manufacturing enterprise strategy, volumes 1 and 2. DIANE Publishing Company, Collingdale, PA

NASCIO (2006) Service oriented architecture: an enabler of the agile enterprise. National Association of State Chief Information Officers, www.enterprise-architecture.info/Images/Documents/NASCIO_SOA_Research_Brief_2006.pdf

OASIS (n.d.) Committee Categories: SOA. www.oasis-open.org/committees/tc_cat.php?cat=soa

Research Evidence Based (2003) Network centric operations conceptual framework. Prepared for John Garstka Office of Force Transformation by Evidence Based Research, Inc., Vienna VA, Nov, www.dtic.mil/cgi-bin/GetTRDoc?AD=ADA457620

Upton D, Staats B (2008) Radically simple IT. Harvard Business Review, March. W3C, Web Services Activities, World Wide Web Consortium

W3C (2004) Web Services Architecture, World Wide Web Consortium, www.w3.org/TR/ws-arch/

Chapter 13
In Pursuit of Workflow Breakthroughs Using "Just Enough Process Management"

Robert Zotti

1 Introduction

As defined by Rummler and Brache (1995), a business process is simply a series of tasks that produce a product or service. They note that "most processes are cross-functional, spanning the 'white space' between the boxes on the organization chart." From a process analysis perspective, these "white space" areas between functional divisions are the most interesting, since they represent not only the areas where processes are most likely to break down but also the areas where there are the most opportunities for process improvement to occur. Organizations, they note, are only as good as their business processes. Successfully achieving organizational goals is largely dependent upon having effective business processes in place.

A classic problem for organizations is how to manage operations in such a way that their infrastructure does not collapse under new demands that inevitably accompany growth. A typical response to such scale-up pressures is the implementation of sophisticated information systems to make it easier for staff members to handle ever-increasing workloads. But one of the fundamental requirements of implementing any large information system is that it should not simply automate existing processes, particularly if those processes are inefficient or obsolete. Numerous authors have also stated a fundamental requirement for any quality and/or process improvement movement: senior management buy-in is essential. But what if, for various reasons, an organization is unable to address large process improvement plans? What if a short-term focus on getting today's work done today dominates the mindset in your organization? What is a manager in a small but growing organization who believes in the long-term benefits of process management to do?

R. Zotti (✉)
Stevens Institute of Technology, Hoboken 07030, NJ, USA
e-mail: rzotti@stevens.edu

Sushil and E.A. Stohr (eds.), *The Flexible Enterprise*, Flexible Systems Management,
DOI 10.1007/978-81-322-1560-8_13,

The Just Enough Process Management concept borrows from the Just Enough Project Management idea put forth by Curtis Cook (2005) in a book by the same name. In the "Just Enough" approach, Cook warns against using more project management practices than a situation calls for, citing examples where complex methodologies were implemented on a scale that were inappropriate to the situation. A simple "initiate/plan/control/close" model of project management, he argues, is enough to get most project managers going.

Similarly, the opening chapter of the *Project Management Book of Knowledge (PMBOK)* ® (2004) notes the fact that practical limitations exist in the application of "good project management practices." Specifically, "good practice does not mean the knowledge described should always be applied uniformly on all projects; **the project management team is responsible for determining what is appropriate for any given project**" (p. 4).

As the name suggests, the concept of Just Enough *Process* Management differs from Just Enough *Project* Management in that it deals with a much higher level of repeatability. As such, Just Enough Process Management is more concerned with promoting a proficiency in operations that have (or can be) largely standardized and ongoing. In contrast, Just Enough Project Management (JEPM) deals with becoming proficient in unique undertakings that have definitive starting and ending times.

This case study will explore the concept of JEPM, and the role of individuals who practice it. JEPM concepts will also be illustrated through the experiences of the WebCampus Division at Stevens Institute of Technology. The concept of JEPM maintains that effective process improvement work can be accomplished by individuals (herein referred to as JEPM managers) without the trappings of most company-wide quality improvement programs. It assumes that, along with normal everyday work, line managers may find it useful to perform process improvement activities without a formal process improvement charter from senior management. These line managers may be obliged to ignore conventional wisdom as they make gradual progress in improving the way work in their organizations gets done. Perhaps the most important aspect of the JEPM is that it can help build a foundation for significant breakthroughs in workflow effectiveness and productivity. The flashpoint for such a breakthrough may be the rare project or initiative, such as the implementation of new business plan, a new information system, or, in the case of WebCampus, the redevelopment of the online learning website.

This case study focuses on the use of a JEPM approach during the transition of the WebCampus division from a "Pioneer Mode," where workflow processes were sometimes implemented in an ad hoc fashion, to a "Settler Mode," where workflow processes became more institutionalized. Significant efforts were made to have more efficient and better documented business processes that are well understood by participants and can be more effectively automated without becoming inflexible. The author, having started in this division in 2003, continues to play a central role in this ongoing transition and the use of JEPM.

2 Limitations

No claim is made that this study has been verified by statistical empirical evidence. The empirical evidence in this chapter comes primarily from a single organization – the WebCampus Division at Stevens Institute of Technology. Further, since the author has himself been the director of operations of this unit for 5 years, a certain level of bias is inevitable. However, it is reasonable to argue that rich insights have been made possible by an up-close and personal familiarity with the business processes and workflow of this unit, from the time it was in a start-up mode through a critical period of growth. Prior experiences of the author in other organizations, though not statistically significant, are nonetheless consistent with the conclusions of this study.

Details about the business processes described in this chapter were gathered by the author through various informal means over a period of several months. These means ranged from simple "water cooler" conversations with workflow participants, to actually creating and documenting workflow processes in response to organizational needs. Brief questionnaires were given to a few key staff members at Stevens who had the most direct exposure to the business processes and workflow described in this study. The questionnaires asked for input regarding how well several core processes have been executed over time, and what might be done to improve them. Answers were not gathered in an ordinal or interval scale, but rather in a rich-text manner.

3 Literature Overview

Obsolete workflow. Enormous backlogs. Angry customers. Overworked staff. Late projects. Unmet objectives.

How big a price does an organization pay when its processes are pushed to their breaking point by the pressure of its own growth? How much scrap and re-work could be avoided? What productivity levels might be possible if things were just done right the first time? These are the types of questions have long been on the minds of managers and executives. A large volume of research has been devoted to the concept of improving core cross-functional business processes and aligning them with organizational goals and objectives. However, relatively little has been written about how workers would go about doing this without a specific mandate from senior management.

The following review of literature goes from a working definition of business process management (BPM) to some of the contemporary views of large-scale BPM. Studies at more granular and smaller-scale BPM are also cited.

Rosemann et al. (2006) summarize business process management as "a holistic organizational management practice that requires top management understanding and involvement, clearly defined roles and decision processes as part of BPM governance, appropriate BPM methodologies, process-aware information systems, educated and well-trained people, and a culture receptive to business processes." They propose a maturity model to help companies assess their BPM proficiency, benchmark their efforts against others, and develop plans for improving their BPM programs. This model is based on both the Software Engineering Institute's CMM framework and a group of six BPM maturity factors: strategic alignment, governance, methods, information technology, people, and culture.

In their landmark publication "Reengineering the Corporation," Hammer and Champy (1993) envision companies achieving 70 % decreases in cycle time; 40 % reductions in costs; 40 % increases in customer satisfaction, quality, and revenues; and 25 % growth in market share resulting from "the fundamental rethinking and radical redesign of business processes to achieve dramatic improvements." Concerned more with "starting over" rather than in "incremental improvement," business process reengineering (BPR) is a drastic top-down approach to improving organizational performance. It drastically changes the way people do their own work and how people work with each other.

Stoddard and Sirkka (1995) classified business process reengineering initiatives into "evolutionary" and "revolutionary" categories. Revolutionary BPR, the type championed by Hammer and Champy, tends to produce adverse and chaotic work environments characterized by secrecy, low employee morale, and resistance to change. Aggressive BPR efforts, rightly or wrongly, became synonymous with cost cutting through downsizing and layoffs. Conversely, evolutionary BPR efforts, though less likely to produce fast "10x" improvements in performance, can help an organization to "get started with a change program that might otherwise seem insurmountable."

Kaplan and Norton (1996) identified business process metrics as one of the four fundamental elements of their "Balanced Scorecard". Once financial and customer goals have been defined, managers identify their most critical processes in their "process value chain" and continually measure their performance. Specifically, this process value chain has three components:

- **Innovation**: Identify current/future customer needs and develop new processes for these needs.
- **Operations**: Build/deliver the product/service.
- **Post-sale**: Offer services after the sale to add to the value a customer receives.

Rather than focusing solely on existing operational processes (which when optimized still won't give distinctive and sustainable competitive advantages), Kaplan and Norton advocate a close examination of the firms' innovation and post-sale processes. This helps to ensure that the organization is adding value for their customers.

Ward Robert et al. (2001) provide a rare analysis of software process improvement efforts in small organizations. They argue that the successful implementation of software process improvement methods in small companies is likely to be vastly different than at larger companies. By way of example, they cited the approach taken by a new COO (Chief Operating Officer) of a 100-person software development company: "His most visible decision early on was to take the company from its creaky ad hoc processes to a company-wide process… He was careful to emphasize a limited number of fundamentals, such as making sure various departments shared their plans – marketing, professional services, engineering, and so forth – with each other and ensuring that everyone understood what the company was trying to accomplish." Concluding that software process improvement initiatives should match the needs and circumstances of the organization rather than being dictated by a theoretical model, Ward offers three simple points:

- A process is a tool, not an end. No process can, by itself, transform an ineffective organization into an effective one.
- Processes must be simple. Complex processes that are hard to follow and difficult to update become quickly irrelevant.
- Processes must be easy to apply and easy to change.

Seacord et al. (2003) describe the long-term impacts that changing business processes and systems can have on existing IS infrastructure. The fact that information systems tend to expand over time to accommodate new features, workflow, and other changes is a major contributing factor to what they call the "Legacy Crisis." As the amount of code that is maintained by some companies can double every 7 years, some experts worry that the pace of an organization's development will exceed its support capacity. This was famously captured in their case study of an effort to modernize a 30-year-old system: "When asked if anyone understood the design of this system, one of the lead engineers quipped: 'Yes, but they are all dead now'" (p. 19). This state of affairs has striking similarities to situations where new business processes are added to an increasingly difficult to understand infrastructure.

Reijers and Mansar (2005) developed a business process redesign model for classifying 29 generic BPR best practices against the dimensions of cost, quality, time, and flexibility (see Fig. 13.1). They noted that any given best practice could improve performance in one dimension but lead to a deterioration of performance in another. Some best practices in BPR actually work against each other. For example, "adding more process controls" to check for completeness is essentially the opposite of removing tasks – particularly redundant tasks. Because of the trade-offs involved in the implementation of any BPR best practice, the authors note that "…BPR is not just about the processes themselves, but about organizational structures, personnel, technology, and communications. Focusing on the processes themselves to the exclusion of this other important factors can lead to missed BRP opportunities."

There appears to be universal agreement in management literature that process improvement involves a certain degree of culture change in organizations – which normally requires the launch of a company-wide initiative. There are numerous studies that deal with the difficulties in implementing the kinds of culture changes that are needed in order to implement process improvement models and techniques in large organizations. For example, Sikkha and Stoddard describe at length the reengineering efforts that took place at CIGNA during the early 1990s. Some attention has even been given to implementing modified process improvement

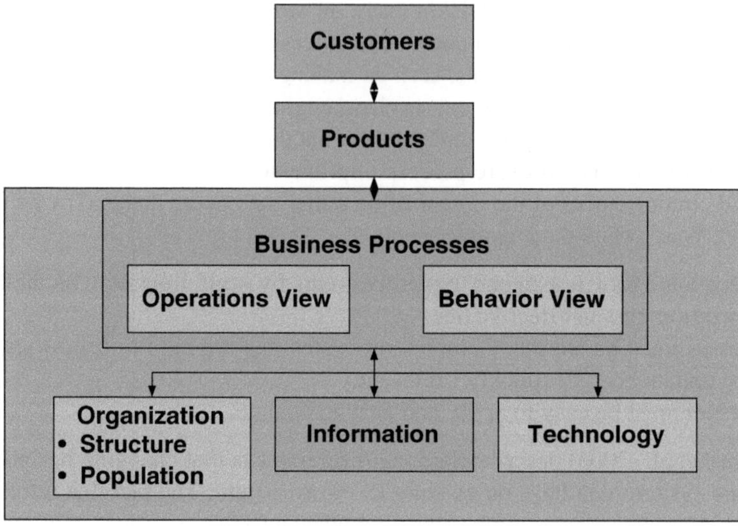

Fig. 13.1 BPR framework for evaluating BRP best practices

models in smaller organizations. However, little or no attention has been given to how process improvement can be implemented in small organizations that simply don't have a process improvement culture.

In some organizations and even entire industries, the commitment to quality improvement programs such as six sigma is now a part of their culture. But the reaction to such movements by managers and employees in other organizations might be characterized as a collective shrug. Some of their comments might include: "That wouldn't work here," "Our business is different," or even "We tried this once and it bombed miserably." Scores of productivity enhancement plans that could not overcome implementation difficulties have been documented. Whether these initiatives fall victim to a lack of executive support or mid-level buy-in, impractical expectations, lack of follow-through, or incompatibility with the established organizational culture, the fundamental questions about lost productivity remain. If the organization cannot or will not change its culture from the top down to focus on improving the way work gets done, what else is left? Reorganization? Downsizing? Unrealistic demands for better results? Lowering expectations?

4 The Theory of Just Enough Process Management

It might not have to be this way. For those who are convinced that the work processes that they are involved in can be made better and who feel empowered enough to make such improvements without a management decree, there remains an option. An approach of "Just Enough Process Improvement," or the gradual adoption of basic process management techniques by individuals, could have both short-term and long-term benefits. This does not call for large implementation efforts that disrupt an already stressed work environment. It does not call for big budgets. It does not even require senior-level managers to declare their support for the effort. Why? Because "Just Enough Process Improvement" can be thought of as a grassroots approach to improving the way work gets done in organizations. It can start with just one person (as a sort of "solo process improvement" program) but will generate enthusiasm in others as time goes on. As processes become better managed (or at least better understood), difficult work becomes more predictable, efficient, and measurable. Even if this is as far as an individual can push things, it still represents a significant improvement. Being able to peer inside the "black box" of a legacy process enables organizational learning. This is essential not only for keeping operations running smoothly during personnel turnovers but for having a better chance at automating and optimizing the process when the opportunity presents itself at some later date. The long-term goal of JEPM is to make itself irresistible for all concerned.

To illustrate how JEPM can be applied, consider the natural tension that exists when a new division is formed inside of a larger organization. New business processes and infrastructure need to be implemented in order to get this division moving. Among other things, this necessitates a certain amount of adjustment by other divisions. As the new division begins to grow, the business processes that were first implemented to support it quickly become obsolete. In order for the new division to achieve its potential, more staff, more resources, and more scalable business processes are needed. This calls for more mutual adjustments to be made by both the new division and the rest of the organization. This evolution is discussed at length by Geoffrey Moore (2002) in his research about the dangers that new high-tech organizations face as they begin to mature.

As Moore puts it, the classic growth challenge for these new organizations hinges on their ability to successfully transition from "pioneer mode" to "settler mode." Pioneers like to do new things, develop new products, and live in very dynamic environments. They trailblaze new territories, move fast, and travel light. Although their accomplishments are often the basis of an organization's future growth, they tend to not spend the majority of their time building scalable business processes that will support long-term growth. In contrast, workers with more of a settler mentality (and who usually arrive after the pioneers) are more concerned with making new and/or current operations as efficient as possible. Innovation does not disappear with the appearance of the settlers, but there is clearly a shift in emphasis. Essentially, this means building an infrastructure with more repeatable business processes and working to bring order to chaos.

Both the pioneers and the settlers perform essential functions. However, they have very different perspectives. This is reminiscent of the differences that Kotter (1990) observed between what managers and leaders do. In the classic sense, leaders concern themselves more with strategic changes. The ever-present challenge for managers is dealing with the complexities that are largely the result of these changes. In the context of business processes, leaders may view business processes

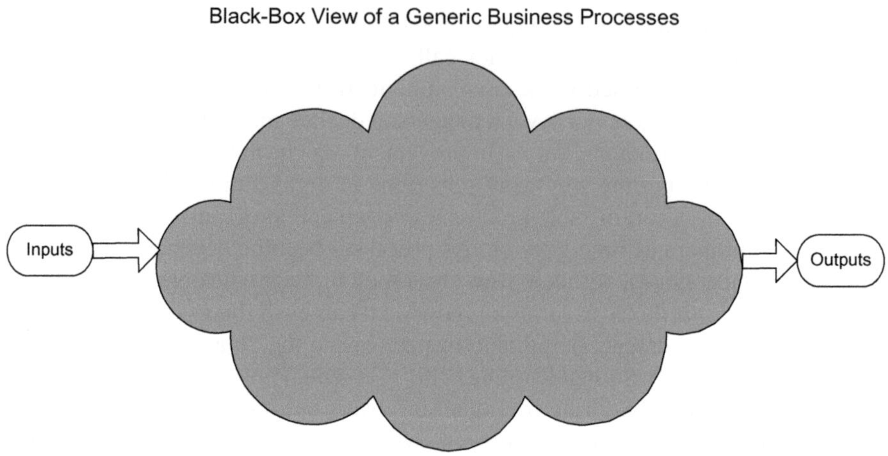

Fig. 13.2 The common view of a single business process. What happens in between the input and output is often unclear

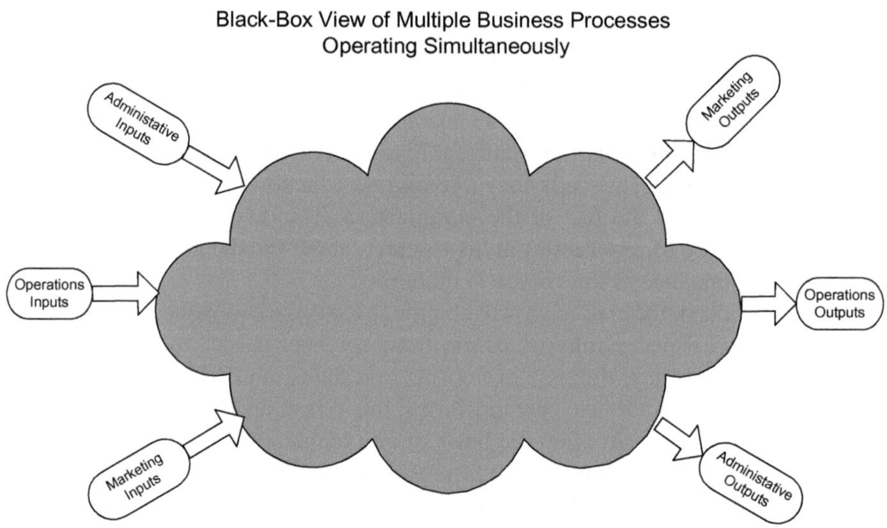

Fig. 13.3 When processes interact, complexities multiply. The *black box* between inputs and outputs is harder to understand

as a black box that generates the appropriate outputs when given the appropriate inputs (see Fig. 13.2).

Compare this view with that of the typical manager, who often sees the interaction of different business processes at a much more detailed level (see Fig. 13.3). In some cases, a business process may need to navigate a complex and even treacherous route of activities, many of which may not be aligned or, worse, may be in conflict with each other (see Fig. 13.4).

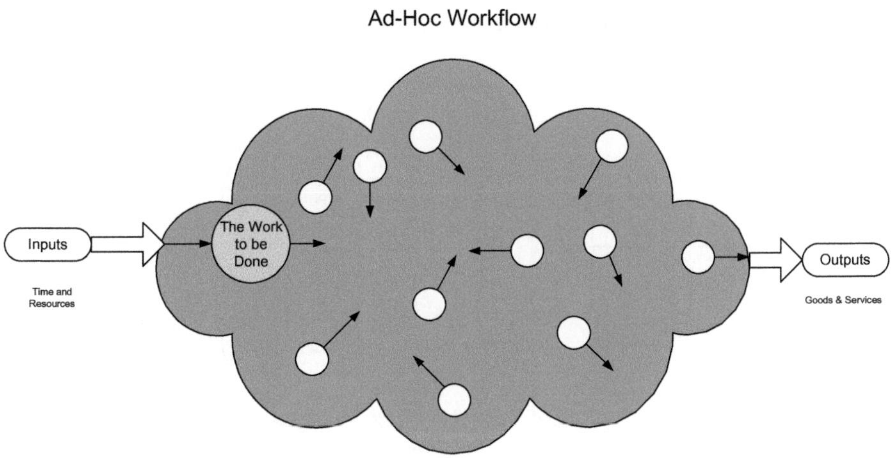

Fig. 13.4 Ad hoc workflows make use of preexisting procedures that are sometimes in conflict with each other

The situation can be likened to a heated container of gas, where the molecules bounce off each other as they move faster and faster and in all directions. In bridging the morass between input and output points, the people who perform the work need to navigate through a labyrinth of red tape. Under such conditions, the wonder is that existing business processes manage to get the required work done at all.

At this point, those with a settler mentality might feel a strong urge to remedy the situation by advocating company-wide business process improvement efforts. But in the world of JEPM, the organization either cannot or will not consider such efforts. At this critical juncture, the initiative falls to individuals who deal most closely with the business process to make whatever improvements that they can. This involves several steps that are neither unique nor revolutionary in and of themselves. The individuals who perform these steps must be prepared to step outside of their comfort zone and look inside of several functional silos. These steps, which can be viewed as the first stage of JEPM, are:

1. Determine the most critical business issues and associated processes.
2. Learn about how these processes currently work and how they address business needs.
3. Determine who all the stakeholders are and what they know (or don't know) about these key business processes.
4. Define a path through the existing processes and infrastructure that makes the most sense to take under the circumstances (see Fig. 13.5).
5. Seek opportunities to utilize existing infrastructure to increase the efficiency and performance of these key processes.

This "tunneling" through the business process landscape involves turning the spotlight on all the things that must happen in order for work to get done. It makes

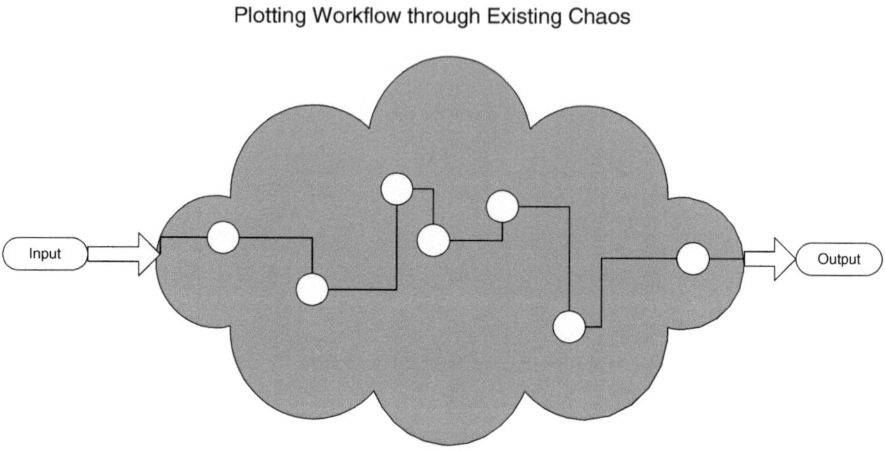

Fig. 13.5 Implementing new workflow involves tunneling through preexisting procedures to find the best possible path from input to output

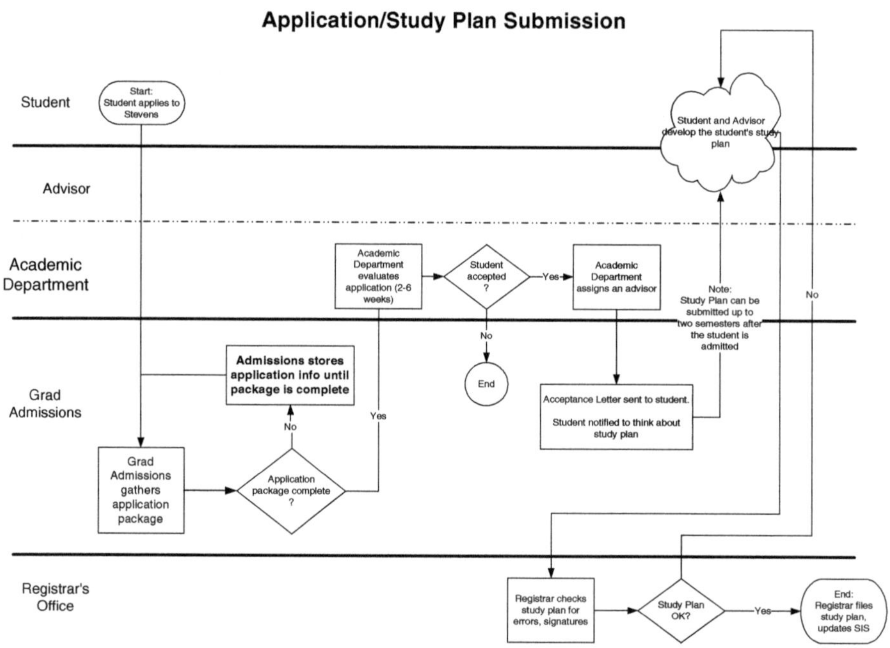

Fig. 13.6 Process chart depicting the order in which tasks are performed and by whom

the path between inputs and outputs more visible. Documenting the existing path with a process chart (see Fig. 13.6) may give many people their first opportunity to see in a holistic manner how the work they do affects others. This tunneling also involves asking the stakeholders if the process in question, whether it is a good one or a bad one, is properly depicted. Finally, feedback about what can be improved can be gathered. Opportunities for incremental improvements should become less challenging to recognize – especially in the "white space" between divisions that Rummler and Brache refer to.

The solitary manager who gets through this stage already has plenty to show for his or her efforts. Work that was ill-defined can now be better understood – especially by new employees who no longer need to learn the hard way about processes that involve them. Process problems can be pinpointed much quicker and dealt with much sooner. Discussing the process at length and in detail over a reasonable period of time with other stakeholders may not eliminate organizational silos, but it should make them less deep. As the results of this kind of analysis are shared, there will be fewer cases where the only people with a deep understanding of critical business processes "are all dead now."

5 From Incremental Improvement to Workflow Breakthrough

JEPM helps to make clear how work currently gets done and paves the way for incremental improvements to be made. Even though JEPM activities are likely to be performed by an individual (often without a mandate from upper management), the results can benefit people in several functional areas. But this is only part of what can be done thru JEPM. Sooner or later, an opportunity to make a bigger difference will present itself. Perhaps the most common type of opportunity can be the deployment of a new information system, such as a website or a workflow management system. If business processes have been managed and improved over a period of time, there is a greater chance that a major productivity breakthrough will result from the implementation of the new system (see Fig. 13.7).

There is one catch in the second stage of the JEPM concept. Owing to the realities of limited time and resources, the JEPM manager realizes that such opportunities

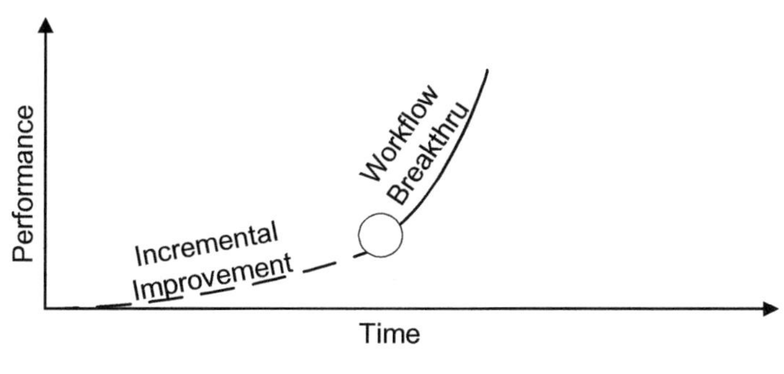

Fig. 13.7 JEPM promotes incremental growth as well as preparedness for a breakthrough in performance

will be few and far between. Hence, the JEPM manager may only get one shot at creating a workflow/productivity breakthrough. The race against time has already begun: if an opportunity to achieve breakthrough results does not occur within a reasonable amount of time, normal career progression will take the JEPM manager to new assignments and perhaps to a new organization altogether. In such an event, unless a new JEPM manager takes up the cause, the effort falls far short of what can be accomplished.

Another challenge for the JEPM manager is that the call of "regular" work will seldom be such that there will be peace and quiet to conduct uninterrupted process improvement efforts. The JEPM manager needs to find some way to integrate this "extra" work into their already busy schedules.

6 JEPM at Work

At this point a valid question to ask is: "how does the daily life of someone engaged in JEPM differ from someone who is not?" At first glance, there is not much of a difference at all. Presumably, the JEPM manager still has a shop to run. Normal operations and projects must be the top priority. In order to have any hope of leading a workflow breakthrough or even incremental process improvements, a JEPM manager must demonstrate a solid record of performance.

The main differentiator is that the JEPM manager takes advantage of opportunities to learn as much as possible about "the way things in the organization work." This involves asking a lot of questions of a lot of people in other divisions – not all of whom the JEPM manager crosses paths with on a regular basis. Thus, the JEPM manager gathers information that includes (but is not limited to):

- Goals and objectives of other divisions
- Important processes and subprocesses of other divisions
- Common bottlenecks in the normal operations of other divisions
- Perspectives of others stakeholders
- The history of how critical pieces of infrastructure were built and why
- Metrics that matter to other stakeholders

When gathering such information from others, it is important to build a non-threatening environment in which to do it in. It may take months to build up informal networks of people who are willing to talk about their work in such detail. Trading non-secret but hard-to-come-by information with stakeholders will help build trust and promote collaborative learning, but information about politically sensitive topics needs to be handled with discretion. As the JEPM manager learns more about the various cross-functional processes that he or she comes in contact with, the information is made available to others as appropriate. Informal discussions about process metrics, procedures, and workflow challenges can lead to incremental changes and lay the groundwork for larger improvements when the right opportunity presents itself.

What is conspicuously absent from this approach are references to company-wide process improvement directives. In the absence of a clear process improvement program backed by senior management, one may rightly wonder how employees can be encouraged to undertake JEPM activities. The answer is often present in employee performance reviews. The kind of skills and behaviors that are commonly assessed in these documents are exactly those that are so important for the JEPM manager. Important skills for the JEPM manager to have include:

- Project management skills
- Presentation skills
- Data collection and analysis skills
- Strategic and tactical planning skills

Additional skills and behaviors that are less commonly found in management performance appraisals but which are important for JEPM managers include:

- Interviewing skills
- Process management and mapping skills
- Works to leverage informal networks (both internal and external) to improve organizational performance
- Demonstrates willingness to collaborate with others
- Demonstrates willingness to learn new technologies
- Takes action to improve inefficient processes rather than just reacting to them

By definition, early-stage JEPM actions are not drastic in nature. The easiest way to get started is to pick a handful of processes and map out the existing workflow. Get input from those closest to it, and have them verify the analysis. Make others aware of the workflow (whether it is good workflow or bad workflow), and help facilitate process improvements to the extent possible.

7 The Case: The Evolution of the Online Learning Unit at Stevens

The evolution of operations in the WebCampus Division at Stevens Institute of Technology can be used to illustrate the concepts of Just Enough Process Management. WebCampus, the online learning unit at Stevens that was founded in 1999, is undergoing a fundamental transformation from a start-up operation, where numerous processes were created on an ad hoc basis, to an operation where processes are better-defined, are understood, and are becoming automated to a significant degree.

From 1999 thru 2003, WebCampus was run primarily in Pioneer Mode. New infrastructure had to be created where little or none had previously existed. Faculty needed to be trained to deliver courses in a way in which few were used to doing. Contracts needed to be developed, deals with partnering organizations needed to be negotiated, and many people inside the school needed to be sold on the concept.

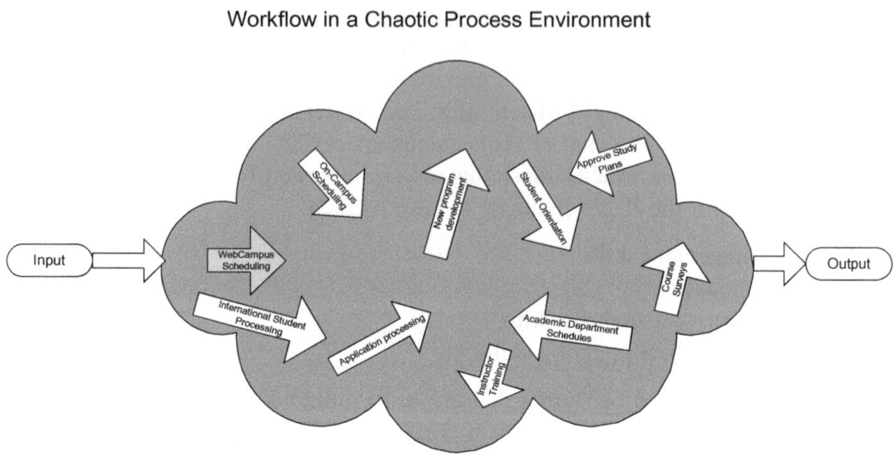

Fig. 13.8 Early WebCampus workflow. Note the conflicting and unaligned subprocesses

As might be expected, WebCampus operations before 2003 had not progressed to a level where process management was the top priority. "There was a general plan to implement the basics," noted WebCampus founder Bob Ubell, "but institutionalization of robust processes would not begin until 2003," (2007). Indeed, during this time, the entire WebCampus administrative staff consisted of Ubell, a secretary, and two graduate student assistants. The workflow situation at this time is shown in Fig. 13.8. Business processes that were created for WebCampus didn't always mesh with existing school operations.

During this time, there were other challenges for the WebCampus Division. The concept of conducting fully online graduate courses ran counter to what some considered a good strategy for the school as a whole. More students online meant less students in the classroom, according to this view. In addition, the quality of online courses was an open question to many. Plans were made to implement processes for course assessments, beef up instructor training, execute marketing efforts to attract students outside the school's traditional territory, and provide more quality services to online students. The alignment of WebCampus operations with those of the rest of the school began to improve, but it was clear that in order to grow, more staff would be needed.

From 2004 thru 2006, WebCampus underwent a classic growth-crunch phase. The number of classes that were made available online increased. The number of students enrolling in online classes increased. The number of online instructors increased. The number of projects (many of which were cross-functional in nature) that the WebCampus unit became involved in had dramatically increased. WebCampus classes became more sophisticated in the technologies they used, integrating web conferencing and anti-plagiarism software, among other things. Revenues climbed steadily, and senior management was happy with the unit's performance. (Significantly, between FY2005 and FY2007, revenues from operations grew between 35 % and 41 %.) But during this time, it became clear that the basic workflow processes which were established when the unit was delivering 20–24 classes per semester were inadequate to support the delivery of over 100 classes per semester. The Summary of WebCampus Operations is provided in Appendix 4.

7.1 Using JEPM at WebCampus

The explosive growth during this period stressed several key processes that had previously created on an ad hoc basis. The staff was able to meet the resulting challenges through a combination of teamwork, collaboration with other divisions, and what might be called low-intensity process management and automation. These key processes were:

1. Managing the semester cycle
2. Attracting and supporting students
3. Supporting and training faculty
4. Supporting the development of new online programs
5. Managing partnerships and client relationships

The proper execution of these essential processes (covered in detail in Appendix 5) largely depended upon the proper alignment between WebCampus and six other groups at Stevens:

1. Registrar's Office
2. Admissions Office
3. Student Services Division
4. Information Technology Division
5. Academic Department Leaders (the Program Directors)
6. Faculty

The first systematic efforts to document these essential workflow processes began in 2003 (see Fig. 13.9).

Since so much about offering classes over the Internet was so new to so many people, the simple act of charting all the players, tasks, and dependencies that were involved proved to be a critical learning experience for both new staff members and existing staff in other divisions. The new Associate Director for WebCampus began this effort through informal interviews with the people that had any exposure to online learning operations. These interviews revealed several themes and issues. For example, which classes should be offered over the Internet? Who decides when they should be offered? Who should conduct these classes? How should they be conducted? How much support can faculty members count on, and who will provide it? How many students can be placed in an online class? How do students actually get into a WebCampus class and learn how to use the online learning technologies once they get there? The details of these and numerous other issues were examined on an ongoing basis. Much was learned through trial and error as operations continued.

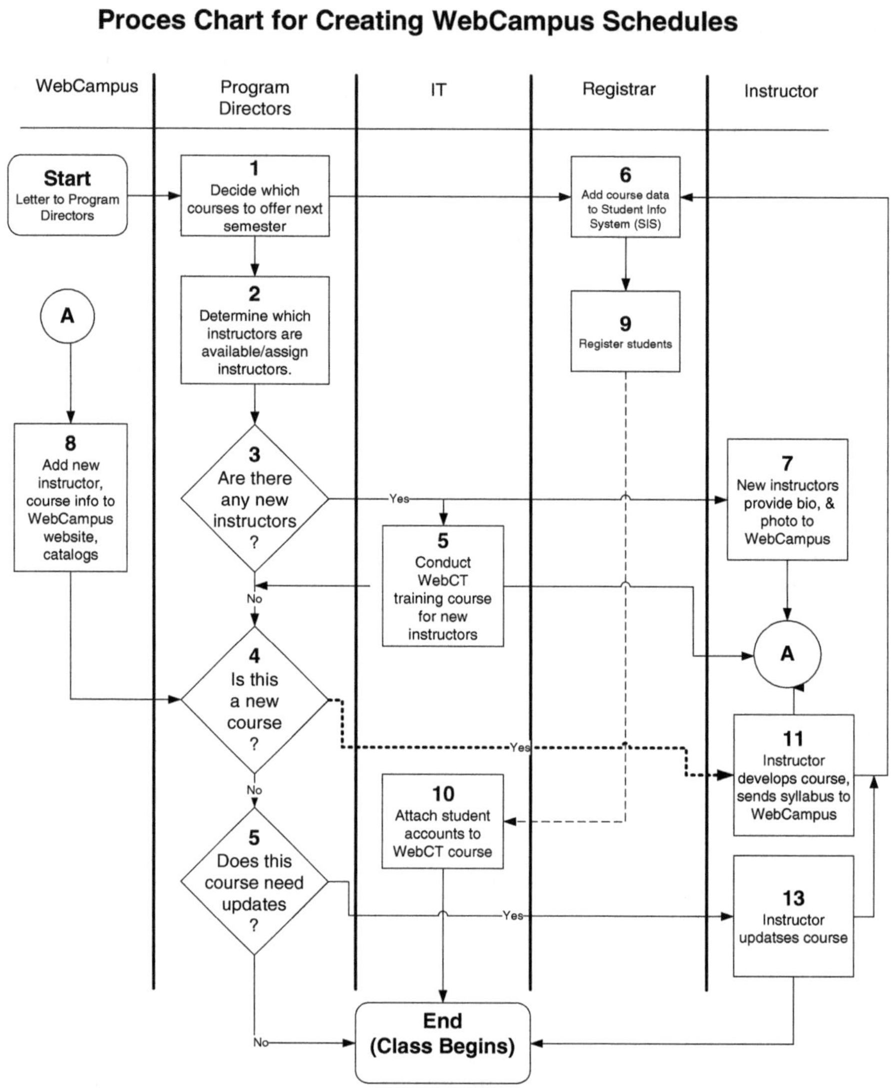

Fig. 13.9 Depiction of essential WebCampus workflow – 2003

In order to perform the kind of work that had been pioneered between 2000 and 2002 on any meaningful scale, it quickly became apparent that a detailed understanding of the way work was accomplished in other divisions was required.

Over time, the process chart depicted in Fig. 13.9 evolved into a 7 feet long by 4 feet high illustration. It was the product of hundreds of mini "learning events." Most of these learning events tended to be conversations with students, faculty, and administrators who had any connections to the five essential WebCampus business processes. (These conversations took place in a variety of formats: meetings, phone

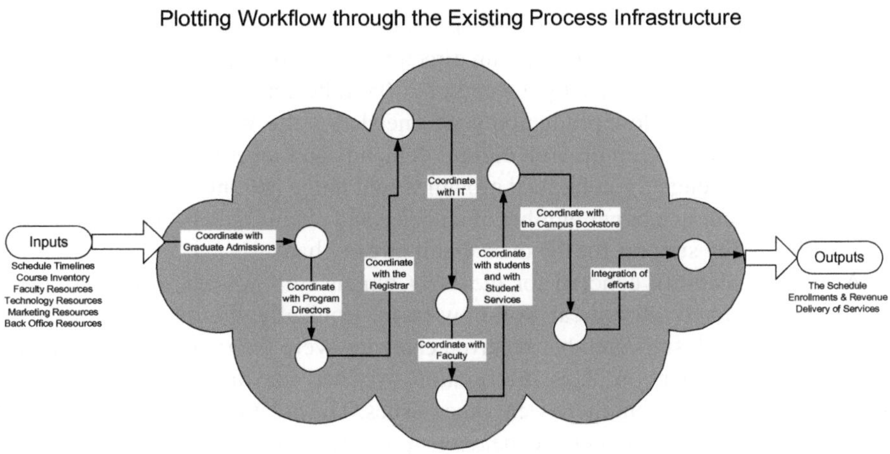

Fig. 13.10 Workflow "tunneling." Analysis of existing cross-unit processes and adapting new workflow accordingly yields the workable route from input to output

calls, email messages, and even chance encounters in the hallways.) Additional lessons were learned through analyzing the results of operations. Some WebCampus processes that were created during the start-up years had to be taken apart and reconstructed in a manner where they were better "plugged in" to the existing process infrastructure of other divisions. As this "tunneling" through existing infrastructure continued, more WebCampus processes became more institutionalized. As illustrated in Fig. 13.10, this tunneling required coordination with numerous areas in order to establish the standard operating procedures or "process tunnels" that would be needed in to accommodate growth.

Significantly, most of this learning occurred not as a separate activity, but along with day-to-day operations. (At no time was there ever an institute-wide push for each area to analyze and document its critical work processes.) With each conversation about how the flow of work should be conducted, and with each small workflow improvement that was made, the overall operation became more robust.

The value of these JEPM activities was demonstrated on numerous occasions. The process charts that were developed were used as a training tool to quickly help bring new staff members up to speed. They were also used to show other players, ranging from members of the Finance Office to representatives of partner organizations, how work was done at WebCampus. Workflows were devised to better manage procedures such as:

- Issuing contracts and signing off on payroll documentation
- Building new course schedules
- Verifying that online course content would be ready and available when needed
- Distributing class rosters to instructors so that they may contact their students
- Maintaining up-to-date content on the WebCampus website
- Increasing communications with students.

By 2005, a predictable and largely reliable rhythm had developed, involving some 100 faculty members, 16 program directors, 30 administrators, and over 1,500 students. Despite these gains, by the end of 2005, it became clear that a significant breakthrough in workflow productivity was needed if the WebCampus staff (now numbering 7) was to keep up with current demands and meet future growth goals. Meeting the challenge for continued growth would hinge not only upon the school's ability for sustaining a larger number of students and clients but also upon its ability to provide quality support for the ones that it already had.

A major scalability concern for the WebCampus staff was the role that email played in practically all critical workflow tasks. Ironically, the hundreds of email messages that each staff member received each day were the root of several breakdowns in communication. This information overload inevitably led to problems with end-user support, but there were other issues. The creation of the all-important WebCampus schedules depended heavily upon the correspondence between the academic program directors and the Director of WebCampus. In fact, getting most work done at all seemed to involve ever-increasing volumes of multi-threaded email conversations.

8 An Opportunity to Achieve a Workflow Improvement Breakthrough

In January 2007, development of a new WebCampus website was authorized. The existing site, built in 1999, contained an impressive amount of useful content: Course schedules, course descriptions, syllabus files, faculty bios and contact information, tuition and fees, admissions forms, newsletters, articles about online learning, and so on. But by 2005 the site was clearly showing its age. In all, there were over 250 individual HTML files, and almost all of them had to be updated manually, one by one, each semester. The updates were all done by a single staff member, the website specialist. As this person was routinely assigned to other projects or otherwise unavailable, the resulting delays in posting up-to-date information were becoming painfully obvious by the 2006–2007 academic year.

Sensing that this project would provide a rare opportunity to vastly improve the operations of the division, the Director of WebCampus spent a considerable amount of time developing a list of business requirements. These requirements, along with all the mission, vision, and goals that were discussed and debated during numerous WebCampus Board of Directors meetings, were poured into a project mission statement and shared with three companies that specialized in website design. After one of the three firms was selected, and after the obligatory journey through the newly enacted Stevens procurement procedures, the project got under way. Requirements management, the very first of CMM's "key process areas," would prove to be a valuable component of JEPM.

Formally released in March 2008, the goal of the new website project was not only to provide a modern end-user experience but to provide the last piece that had

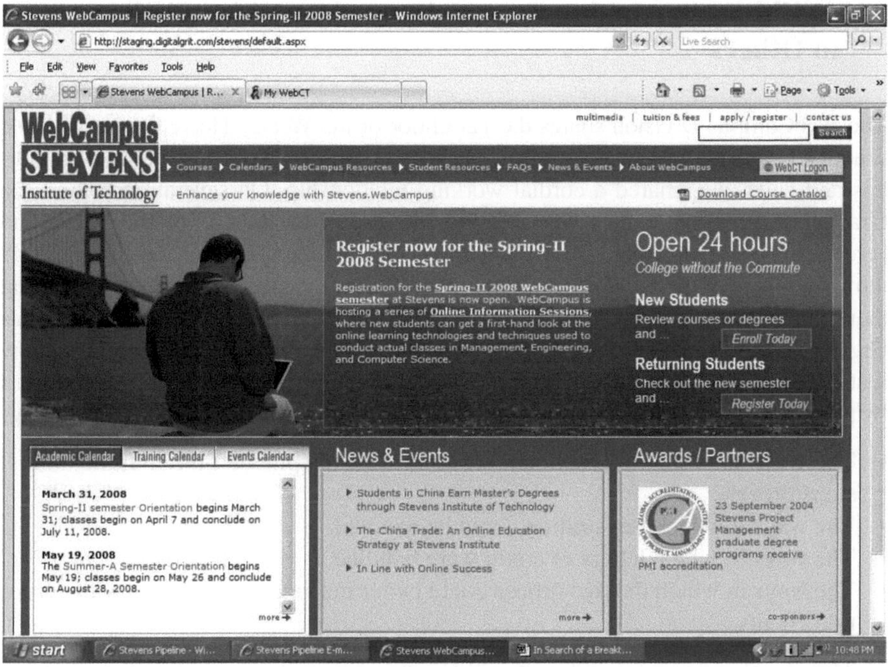

Fig. 13.11 Illustration of the new WebCampus website

been missing from a fundamental breakthrough in the way work is done by the WebCampus division. Among other things, the database-driven content management system at the heart of the new website now allows:

- Non-website experts to quickly and easily make updates that cascade to all appropriate parts of the site.
- Automation of the generation of numerous reports, including enrollment, rebate, commission, and royalty statements.
- Value-added features that will encourage return traffic from prospective, current, and former students. Such features will include an events calendar, and a multimedia section featuring interviews with engineering and management educators and industry leaders (Fig. 13.11).

The new WebCampus website was deployed in late March of 2008. By the end of the Spring 2008 semester, it should become clear whether or not this website will live up to the expectations expressed in the project mission statement and offer some validation to the theory of JEPM. To the extent that the project expectations are met, the staff will have more flexibility to spend additional time on enhancing the quality of online courses, developing new online course offerings, and reaching out to bigger audiences who might be interested in applying to the school's online graduate programs.

9 JEPM V2.0: Making Process Improvement Irresistible to Others

The WebCampus Division shares the 12th floor of the Wesley Howe Center with the school's Graduate Admissions Office. These two units have overlapping responsibilities and have long shared a cordial working relationship. On several occasions, the Graduate Admissions Office was able to make use of the myriad of enrollment and revenue reports that WebCampus staff members maintain. During the Spring 2008 term, members of the Graduate Admissions staff began expressing interest in charting their core processes in the similar manner that had been done at WebCampus. Thus began a joint effort by the two groups to document the many variations in workflow that characterize the process of applying for admission to Stevens. This was followed by plans for charting and improving a variety of other essential procedures, including:

- The ways in which international students were shepherded through the admissions process
- The ways in which registration could be handled
- The ways in which letters of credit were handled
- The ways in which the two offices could better manage relationships with corporate clients

This development is significant in that, once again, there was no mandate from senior management to analyze and improve work procedures in this way. The realities of a high workload and limited resources in the Graduate Admissions unit will necessitate a gradual implementation of business process management. However, the assumption of a gradual implementation is a central part of the JEPM concept. Despite this, incremental improvements may be seen as early as the end of the semester. As the turnover rate of part-time student workers is certain to remain high for the foreseeable future, the JEPM approach should be particularly helpful. The next group of temporary workers should be the beneficiaries of better training on better workflow processes.

As the Graduate Admissions Division and perhaps other units throughout the school begin to formalize their work processes through a JEPM approach, they will also be preparing themselves to take advantage of the next workflow breakthrough opportunity. This next opportunity may very well be the implementation of the PeopleSoft enterprise management system. As with the new WebCampus website, the PeopleSoft implementation can build upon all the JEPM process improvements and vastly improve productivity. But this story will have to wait for another time.

10 Conclusion

To pursue the path of JEPM is to commit to a belief in the value of managing work processes and sharing information. Although there is a fundamental requirement for collaboration with others, the JEPM practitioner may be obliged to go about the bulk of workflow management chores on his or her own accord. To business process

Table 13.1 Suggested JEPM guidelines

JEPM Dos	JEPM Don'ts
Get your own house in order	Call for a company-wide BPR efforts with senior management buy-in
Understand how your own processes affect and are affected by other areas	Complain bitterly about people not understanding critical business processes unless you have something constructive to share
Accumulate knowledge about critical processes over an appropriate amount of time and from a variety of sources	Demand to know everything there is to know about critical processes immediately
Organize the information that you have uncovered	Assume that the information you need about important business processes already exists in an easy-to-use format
Confirm what you have learned from others and share what you have learned as appropriate	Rely too much on unconfirmed or uncorroborated information
Demonstrate the value of what you have learned about critical processes in your day-to-day work	Withhold information to preserve power
Seek ways to help others improve their business processes in low-key ways	Turn business process improvement into a compliance thing
Build on process knowledge over time	Expect quick-hit successes
Prepare for the big improvement opportunity when it finally comes along	Simply automate existing processes when the opportunity finally comes along
(Gently) demonstrate to others the value of your business process improvement activities. Start with small audiences – especially those that are involved in the business processes	Assume that everyone gets it. Or tell everyone that they should get it
Move on to other processes as appropriate	Fixate on only 1 business process or issue

improvement purists, this "solo" brand of process improvement may be considered heresy. But in an environment where business process improvement initiatives are simply not a big priority, the best hope for achieving workflow productivity gains will by default fall to those individuals who are the closest to those business processes and have some level of authority to act. Some suggested guidelines for the solitary process management practitioner are presented in Table 13.1.

A little bit of process management may go a long way. Simply the act of documenting the way work currently gets done in an organization will expose the JEPM practitioners to a wide variety of experiences and give them insights that they would not get inside of functional silos. Work products from JEPM activities (primarily process charts coupled with metrics reports) can be a useful conversation piece that may help open the door for productivity-enhancing projects.

The history of the WebCampus Division at Stevens provides some corroboration for this theory, but to the author's knowledge, it is the only case study that has been analyzed from this angle. In addition, there were some relatively unique factors at work at WebCampus that underscore the need to study JEPM in other contexts. For example, WebCampus was a twenty-first century start-up division in an educational institution that has been around since the 1800s. WebCampus specializes in a

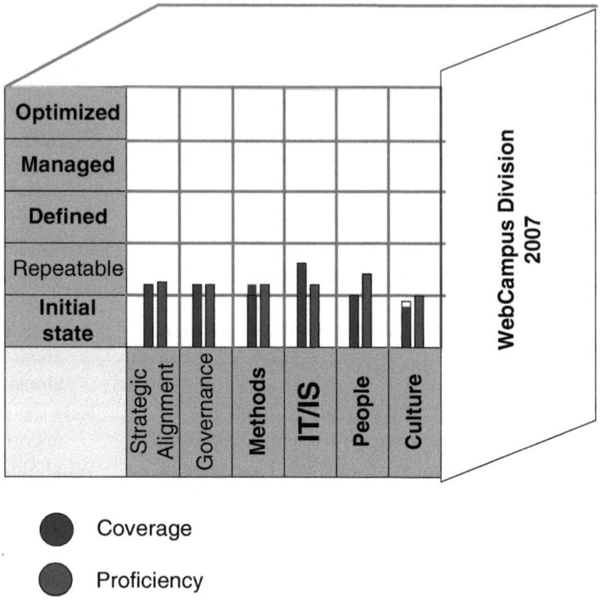

Fig. 13.12 WebCampus business process improvement maturity

service that, for all intents and purposes, was not an option for the masses until the late 1990s. Finally, the Director of WebCampus and author of this chapter had a fairly free hand to pursue JEPM as long as the day-to-day work was completed in an orderly fashion. (The author also had some experience in organizations that had broad process improvement programs.)

If the maturity of business process improvement practices at WebCampus was plotted on the Rosemann et al. (2006) model, it would look very much like the illustration in Fig. 13.12. As JEPM is largely a voluntary proposition taken on by individuals in organizations that don't have big process improvement initiatives, it is probably unrealistic to expect BPI coverage or proficiency to rise far beyond the Initial Level. Even crossing the threshold into the Repeatable Level would be considered a significant long-term achievement.

A follow-up study of the WebCampus and Graduate Admissions operations (presumably after the implementation of PeopleSoft and/or after the current staff has moved on) may provide insights about the long-term viability of the theory of JEPM.

References

Cook C (2005) Just enough project management. McGraw-Hill Companies, New York

Hammer M, Champy J (1993) Reengineering the corporation: a manifesto for business revolution. HarperCollins, New York

Interview with Bob Ubell (2007) Dean of Online Learning, 7 Dec

Kaplan RS, Norton DP (1996) The balanced scorecard: translating strategy into action. Harvard Business School Press, Boston

Kotter JP (1990) What leaders really do. Harvard Business Review, Cambridge, MA. May-June
Moore GA (2002) Crossing the chasm: marketing and selling high-tech products to mainstream customers. HarperCollins, New York
Project Management Book of Knowledge(PMBOK) ® (2004) 3rd Edition (p. 3). The Project Management Institute®
Reijers HA, Mansar SL (2005) Best practices in business process redesign: an overview and qualitative evaluation of successful redesign heuristics. Omega Int J Manage S 33:283–306
Rosemann M, deBruin T, Power B (2006) BPM maturity. In: Jeston J, Nelis J (eds) Business process management. Practical guidelines to successful implementations. Elsevier, Burlingston, MA, pp 299–315
Rummler GA, Brache AP (1995) Improving performance: how to manage the white space on the organization chart. Jossey-Bass, San Francisco
Seacord RC, Plakosh D, Lewis GA (2003) Modernizing legacy systems: software technologies, engineering processes, and business practices. Burlingston,MA: Pearson Education, Inc
Stoddard DB, Jarvenpaa S (1995) Reengineering design is radical; reengineering change is not! Harvard Business Review, 18 July
Ward RP, Fayad ME, Laitinen M (2001) Software process improvement in the small. Comm ACM 44(4):105–107

[illegible]

Chapter 14
Developing Flexible Business Process Management Systems Using Modular Computing Technologies

Minhong Wang and Kuldeep Kumar

1 Introduction

Business process management (BPM) refers to activities performed by organizations to design, implement, operate, manage, and improve their business processes by using a combination of models, methods, techniques, and tools (van der Aalst and van Hee 2002; Melão and Pidd 2000). Most approaches to BPM use information technologies to support or automate business processes in whole or in part, by providing computer-based systems support. These technology-based systems help coordinate and streamline business transactions, reduce operational costs, and promote real-time visibility in business performance.

Traditional approaches to building and implementing BPM systems use workflow technologies to design and control the business process (van der Aalst and van Hee 2002). Workflow-based systems follow highly structured and predefined workflow models and are well suited to applications with standard inputs, processes, and outputs. However, contemporary business processes are complex and dynamic. They evolve and change over time as a result of complex interactions, resource competition, breakdowns and abnormal events, and other sources of uncertainty. Current

This research is supported by a UGC CERG research grant (No. RGC/HKU7169/07E) from the Hong Kong SAR Government, and a Seed Funding for Basic Research (200611159216) from The University of Hong Kong.

M. Wang (✉)
Division of Information & Technology Studies, The University of Hong Kong,
Hong Kong, China
e-mail: magwang@hku.hk

K. Kumar
College of Business Administration, Florida International University, Miami, FL, USA

Rotterdam School of Management, Erasmus University, Rotterdam, Netherlands

Department of Information Systems, City University of Hong Kong, Hong Kong, China
e-mail: kumark@fiu.edu; kkumar@cityu.edu.hk

Sushil and E.A. Stohr (eds.), *The Flexible Enterprise*, Flexible Systems Management,
DOI 10.1007/978-81-322-1560-8_14, © Springer India 2014

research is attempting to support this continuously changing nature of business processes by developing flexible business process management systems using various emerging modular computing technologies, such as Agent-Oriented Computing (AOC), Service-Oriented Architectures (SOA) (Jennings et al. 2000; Leymann et al. 2002; Wang and Wang 2005), Component-Based Development (CBD), and Object-Oriented Programming (OOP) (Kammer et al. 2000; Weske 1998).

There has been a proliferation of studies about the application of agent-, service-, component-, and object-oriented computing solutions to flexible BPM. However, the fundamental questions about their use, such as why we need to introduce these solutions for BPM, how we apply them, and how we integrate them with other solutions, remain unexamined. Most research on technology support for flexible BPM is experience driven, ad hoc, and often lacks a systematic analysis of the rationale for the technology support. Sometimes, the leading edge solutions such as SOA and AOC are proposed without identifying the real rationale for their use in BPM scenarios. There is only minimal work that examines the roots of complexity of business processes, the need of effective approaches for flexible process management, and how this need affects the requirements and technology solutions for flexible process management (Kumar and Narasipuram 2006).

Moreover, as these modular computing concepts and technologies become popular, researchers often attempt to employ and sometimes integrate these modular approaches in creating business process management solutions. However, at present there is considerable ambiguity in differentiating between these overlapping terminologies and consequently their use for flexible BPM systems development. For example, we often hear people discussing their proposed solutions as agent-based systems, whereas they may just be simply using object abstraction. Furthermore, the commonsense understanding of these concepts does not easily map onto each other. Unless we have clarity on these terminologies and the way how to use them, the application and integration of these techniques is likely be problematic.

In this chapter, we first identify the underlying requirements of flexible process management that provide the business rationale for employing these modular technologies in developing BPM systems (Sect. 2). The requirements are examined by investigating the key problems with their solutions in business process management. Next, we examine the similarities and differences between these modular computing technologies to system development: OO, CBD, SOA, and AOC (Sect. 3). Finally, we match these technologies to the requirements of flexible BPM and develop a systemic approach for employing these technologies in developing flexible BPM systems (Sect. 4).

2 How to Deal with Complex Dynamic Business Processes?

A *business process* is a collection of activities that create value by transforming inputs into more valuable outputs (Hammer and Champy 1993). These activities consist of a series of steps performed by actors (either machines or humans) to produce a product or service for the customer. These steps subdivide the business process hierarchically into modular process components (called tasks or subtasks), each component performing a part of the process. The aspiration of most modular computing technologies is to attempt to model the process architecture by a modular software-architecture (objects, components, Web services, and agents), thereby creating an analog of the business process in software.

Real-world processes are often much messier than the typical input-transformation-output view suggests; they are best viewed as networks, in which a number of actors collaborate and interact to achieve a business goal. A business process displays complexity because of multiple interactions of its internal components and interaction of the process with its environment (Melão and Pidd 2000). In this section, we investigate the roots of complexity of business processes as a result of complex structure, interacting components, dynamic environment, and resource coordination. Based on this investigation, we identify the business requirements on technology solutions for BPM in terms of key problems with their solutions in business process management. The requirements include decomposition of complex processes; coordination of interactive activities; an increased awareness of dynamic business environments; and resource selection, integration, and coordination.

2.1 Decomposition of Complex Processes

Business processes are complex systems that are made up of a number of interacting objects with dynamic behavior. To design a complex structure, one powerful technique is to hierarchically decompose it into semi-independent but interrelated set of components (Simon 1981). Thus, a process is decomposed into tasks, task into subtasks, and so on, through many layers in a hierarchy. To reduce complexity, interactions between subtasks within a task are often encapsulated within the task; interactions between tasks are encapsulated within their higher-level process or task.

This raises the issue on how we decompose complex processes. Traditional workflow approaches have selected "task" as the basic module for building process management systems. A business process can be decomposed into a number of semi-dependent, interrelated tasks within an organization. These tasks are then linked to each other in a preestablished, transactional, usually sequential interrelationship, or dependency. With the extension of business processes from intra-organizational to inter-organizational scope, we need to deal with interactions within an organization as well as interactions across different organizations. Moreover, the complexity of business processes is increased by the interweaving of inter- and intra-organizational interactions.

To manage the complexity, we need to distinguish between inter- and intra-organizational interactions and deal with them by isolating one type of interaction from another. We propose "service" as a high-level view of the building block of a process, where a process is composed of a set of services; each service is provided

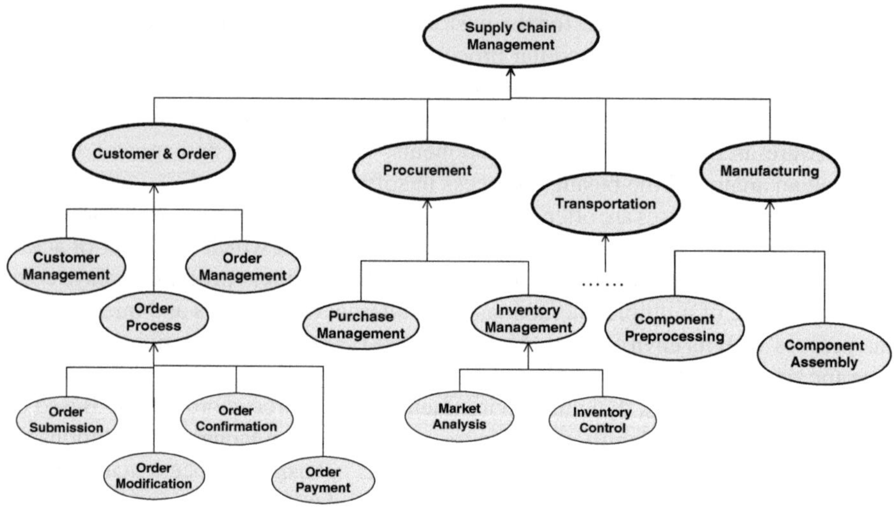

Fig. 14.1 Decomposition of a supply chain process

by a corresponding actor (organization, individual, or computer program) and can be further decomposed into subtasks. For example, a complex supply chain management process is decomposed into customer and order service, procurement service, manufacturing service, and transportation service; each individual service is provided by a corresponding organizational actor and can be further decomposed (see Fig. 14.1).

2.2 *Flexible Coordination of Interactive Activities*

To manage complex interactions in complex processes multiple actors, activities, resources, and goals need to be coordinated. Mintzberg (1979) suggests that every organized human activity gives rise to two fundamental requirements: differentiation, or the division of work into tasks to be performed by various actors, and integration, that is, the coordination of these tasks to accomplish the goals of the activity. After decomposing a complex process into a number of task components, we need to coordinate various interactions between the components at different levels in a network hierarchy. In the context of a hierarchy, a component can be involved in vertical interactions with its subordinates and superordinates and in horizontal interactions with its peers. A component in a complex system, no matter how large or small, may interact with a limited set of superiors, inferiors, and coordinate peers (Simon 1981).

Mintzberg further suggests that environmental uncertainty is an important determinant of the mode for interactions and coordination. The more stable and predictable the situation, the greater the reliance on coordination based on structured and specifiable schedules, such as coordination by plan and coordination by standardization. The more variable and unpredictable the situation, the greater will be the reliance on informal and flexible communication, such as coordination by feedback and coordination by mutual adjustment (Kumar and van Dissel 1996; Kumar et al. 2007). Thus, when faced with increased uncertainties in dynamic environments, organizations need to use more flexible coordination mechanisms to coordinate their business processes. Flexible coordination is portrayed by more bottom-up initiatives and less centralization of decision-making at the top. This requires flatter hierarchies, decentralized autonomy-based units, and decision-based coordination, which in turn reduces direct hierarchical control and encourages greater mutual adjustment and coordination between the work units (Mintzberg 1979; Volberda 1999).

2.3 *Awareness of Dynamism in Business Environments*

As a result of complex interactions, resource competition, abnormal events, and other sources of uncertainty, business processes continuously evolve and change over time. Furthermore, a complex process is usually semi-structured or unstructured; there is an absence of routine procedures for dealing with it. In such situations, we cannot depend on providing the computer system with exact details about how to accomplish a process, but provide the system with guidelines to help it determine how to deal with the process. In other words, problem solving is regarded as an interaction between the behaving organism and the environment under the guidance of a control system. Information and data are input to this system, represented in its memory as declarative knowledge, and then used in problem solving following algorithmic or heuristic steps (Wang and Wang 2006).

A basic idea underlying this viewpoint is the control of complex dynamic systems or situations based on situation awareness. Awareness, according to biological psychology, is a human's or an animal's perception and cognitive reaction to a condition or event. Situation awareness is the perception and understanding of objects, events, people, system states, interactions, environmental conditions, and other situation-specific factors in complex and dynamic environments (Endsley 1995). Situation awareness underpins real-time reactions to environmental changes. In terms of cognitive psychology, situation awareness refers to the active content of a decision-maker's mental model, its purpose being to enable rapid and appropriate decisions and effective actions.

In a dynamic business process environment, an exact execution order of activities is impractical; the interaction or relationship between the environment and activities is more appropriate in determining how to manage and coordinate tasks (Wang and Wang 2006). The dynamicism therefore requires spontaneous decisions and coordination of processes based on situation awareness. We need to be able to coordinate the processes by sensing and comprehending the situation, determining responses to it while, at the same time, taking actions to work towards business goals. In other words, the question of which task to execute and when to execute it is dependent on the current environment and underlying business rules rather than a static process schema.

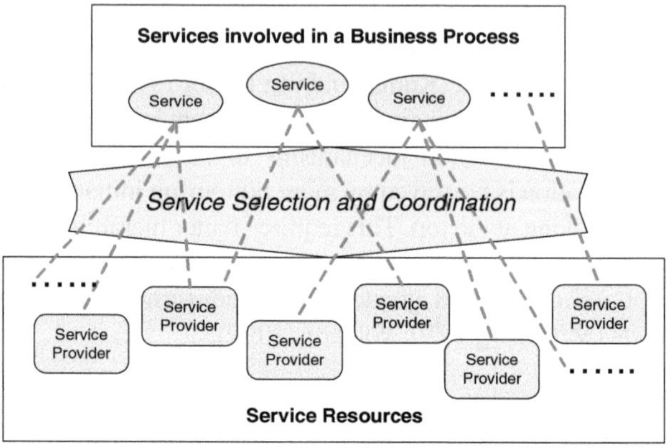

Fig. 14.2 Resource selection and coordination in business processes

2.4 *Flexible Resource Selection, Integration, and Coordination*

Business processes require actors and resources to perform the tasks. These actors and their associated resources may reside either within the organization or, in the case of inter-organizational processes, across a network of multiple organizations. Business networks of resources and actors can be temporarily assembled, integrated, and driven by demands that emerge and operate for the lifespan of the market opportunity (Kumar 2001). In this conception, a firm is not considered as a black box guided by the strategist, but as a bundle of firm-specific resources of use for specific tasks. Along with this conception, new business models have accordingly come into view, such as demand chain, virtual enterprise, and electronic marketplace. They allow companies to operate in dynamically changing environments by quickly and accurately evaluating new market opportunities or new products. The companies may coordinate with potential partners in demand-driven and resource-based soft connections that are made for the duration of the market opportunity.

As a result, a business process can be dynamically established at run-time by connecting or composing several services together from different organizations through alliances, partnerships, or joint ventures. In this situation, attentions on business processes should be extended to other elements in addition to task and procedure, which include resources discovery, selection, integration, and coordination.

What is new in this business process model is reliance on the idea of separating resource requirements from concrete satisfiers (Mowshowitz 1997). This separation allows for crafting process structures that enable management to switch between different resources options for implementing a process (see Fig. 14.2). It creates an environment in which the means for reaching a goal are evaluated and selected for optimized performance. The success of the model is highly dependent on the match between the requirements and satisfiers that deliver the services. One way to ensure this balance is to model the integration or composition of business processes as a management problem which involves (1) the separation of requirements from the means for realization and (2) the dynamic selection and allocation of available resources to requirements (Mowshowitz 1997). In doing it, we model the complex structure of inter-organizational processes by using "service" as the building block, which supports flexible integration and coordination among the services or satisfiers.

3 Clarifying the Terminologies of Technical Solutions

As mentioned above, various modular computing architectures such as *objects, components, Web services,* and *agents* have been proposed to develop systems for flexible process management. In order to use these concepts in business process management, we must first have a clear understanding of their similarities, differences, and relationships. Research employing these concepts has often borrowed from natural language; terms such as agents, autonomous agents, brokers, actors, services, and components are used without precisely differentiating between them. Thus, before we can use these concepts appropriately, we need to understand the similarities and differences between them. Moreover, we also need to understand how these concepts can be used for developing flexible process management solutions. In this section we outline four such concepts: Agents and Agent-Oriented Computing, Services and Service-Oriented Architecture, Objects and Object-Oriented Programming, and Components and Component-Based Development. It needs to be emphasized that the purpose of this section is to clarify the similarities and differences between these approaches and to make explicit some of the underlying assumptions inherent in the use of the terminology, not to redefine them.

3.1 Agent and Agent-Oriented Computing (AOC)

Recently the Agent-Oriented Computing paradigm has gained popularity among researchers attempting to develop complex systems for business process management. Terms such as "autonomous agent" and "agency" are beginning to be commonly used in computer science literature. On the other hand, a rich body of literature on the concept of Agency and the role of agents already exists in the institutional economics and business field. This section is an attempt to reconcile the various terms from the two research traditions.

Actor vs. Agent. Actor is someone who performs an act, that is, does something. An actor may be a person, an organizational unit, or a computer program. An actor may be completely autonomous, that is, it acts of its own volition. If the actor is authorized to do something on behalf of someone else, the actor is an "agent" of the other party.

Agent. Agent is an actor (performer) who acts on the behalf of a principal by performing a service. The agent provides the service when it receives a request for service from the principal. The principal-agent relationship is found in most employer/employee relationships. A classic example of agency relationship occurs when stockholders hire top executives to run the corporation on their behalf. To manage the relationship between a principle and an agent of the principle, agency theory is concerned with various mechanisms used for aligning the interests of the agent with those of the principal such as piece rates/commissions and profit sharing (Eisenhardt 1989).

Agent vs. Broker. A Broker is a special type of agent that acts on behalf of two symmetrical parties or principals – the buyer and seller. A broker mediates between the buyer (service requesting party) and the seller (service providing party). Acting as an intermediary between two or more parties in negotiating agreements, brokers use appropriate mediating techniques or processes to improve the dialogue between the parties, aiming to help them reach an agreement. Normally, all parties must view the mediator as neutral or impartial.

Autonomy. Autonomy is the power or right of self-government. It refers to the capacity of a rational individual to make an informed, uncoerced decision. An autonomous agent therefore is a system situated in, and part of, an environment, which senses that environment, and acts on it, over time, in pursuit of its agenda as derived from its principal. "Autonomous" means that the actor is independent, that is, the actor can decide what to do and how to do it. As an agent acts on behalf of the principal, the agent cannot be fully autonomous. The principal may give the agent different levels of choice in performing the task. For example, the principal can tell the agent what to do, but leave it to the agent to decide as to how to do it.

Software Agent. In computer science, the term "agent" is used to describe a piece of software or code that acts on behalf of a human user or another program in a relationship of agency. It may denote a software-based entity that could enjoy the some properties of autonomy (agents operate without the direct intervention of its principal humans), social ability (agents communicate with other agents), reactivity (agents perceive their environment and respond to changes in a timely fashion), and proactivity (agents do not simply act in response to their environment, but are able to exhibit goal-directed behavior by taking some initiative) (Jennings et al. 2000). The agent-based computing paradigm is devised to help computers know what to do, solve problems on behalf of human beings, and support cooperative working. The behavior of software agents is empowered by human and implemented by software.

Agent-Oriented Computing (AOC). The key idea of Agent-Oriented Computing is the delegation of tasks and responsibility of a complex problem to software agents. It emphasizes autonomy and mutual cooperation of agents in performing tasks in open and complex environments. A complex system can be viewed as network of agents acting concurrently, each finding itself in an environment produced by its interactions with the other agents in the system. AOC is used to model and implement intelligent solutions to semi- or ill-structured problems, which are too complex to be completely characterized and precisely described. AOC offers a natural way to view and describe systems as individual problem-solving agents pursuing high-level goals defined by their principals. It represents an emerging computing paradigm that helps understand and model complex real-world problems and systems, by concentrating on high-level abstractions of autonomous entities (Wooldridge and Jennings 1999).

3.2 Service and Service-Oriented Architecture (SOA)

Service. A service is the work done by somebody (the agent) for someone else (the principal).

Web Service. As defined by W3C (World Wide Web Consortium), a Web service is a software application identified by a URI (Uniform Resource Identifier), whose interfaces and bindings are capable of being defined, described, and discovered by XML and which supports direct interactions with other software applications using XML-based messages via Internet-based protocols. Web services are self-contained and modular business applications based on open standards (Papazoglou 2007). They can share information using standardized communication protocols to ask each other to do something, that is, ask for service.

Service-Oriented Architecture (SOA). Service-Oriented Architecture utilizes Web services as fundamental elements for developing applications. It is an emerging paradigm for architecting and implementing business collaborations within and across organizational boundaries. SOA enables seamless and flexible integration of Web services or applications over the Internet. It supports universal interoperability and location transparency. SOA reduces the complexity of business applications in large-scale and open environments by providing flexibility through service-based abstraction of organizing applications.

AOC vs. SOA. Software agent is a software-based entity that enjoys the properties of autonomy, social ability, reactivity, and proactivity. Web service is a software application in the Web based on open standards. Though both of them are computer applications that perform tasks on behalf of principals (human beings or other programs), the focus of software agents is on their autonomous properties for solving complex problems, while Web services are characterized by their open access standards and protocols over the Internet. While a Web service may only know about itself, agents often have awareness of other agents and their capabilities as interactions among the agents occur. Agents are inherently communicative, whereas Web services are passive until invoked. Agents cooperate autonomously and flexibly and, by forming teams and coalitions, can assemble higher-level and more comprehensive services. However, current standards or languages for Web services do not provide for flexible composing functionalities, such as brokering and negotiation in e-marketplaces (Huhns 2002). Thus, Web services are inherently less autonomous and independent than software agents.

Against this background, there is a movement towards combining the concept of Web services with software agents. W3C introduced a concept, where software agents are to be treated as the foundation for Web services architecture – "A Web service is an abstract notion that must be implemented by a concrete agent." AOC may take SOA into new dimensions to model autonomous and heterogeneous components in uncertain and dynamic environments. The integration of Web services with software agents can function as computational mechanism in their own right, thus significantly enhancing the ability to model and construct complex software systems. It will be a promising computing paradigm for efficient enterprise service selection and integration.

3.3 Object and Object-Oriented Programming (OOP)

Object-Oriented Programming (OOP). Rumbaugh defines OOP as programming in terms of a collection of discrete objects that incorporate both data and behaviors (Rumbaugh 1991). OOP is a software engineering paradigm that uses "objects" and their interactions to design applications and computer programs. It is seen as a collection of cooperating objects, as opposed to a traditional view in which a program is seen as a list of instructions to the computer. OOP was deployed as an attempt to promote greater flexibility and maintainability in programming by strongly emphasizing modularity and reusability in software.

AOC vs. OOP. From a software engineering point of view, Object-Oriented (OO) methodologies provide a solid foundation for Agent-Oriented modeling. AOC can be viewed as a specialization of OOP. OOP proposes viewing a computational system as made up of modules that are able to communicate with one another. AOC specializes the framework by representing the mental states and rich interactions of the modules (agents). While objects emphasize passive behavior (i.e., they are invoked in response to a message), agents support more autonomous behavior, which can be achieved by specifying a number of rules for interpreting the states and governing multiple degrees of freedom of activities.

3.4 Component and Component-Based Development (CBD)

Component-Based Development (CBD) is another branch of the software engineering discipline, with an emphasis on decomposition of the engineered systems into functional or logical components with well-defined interfaces used for communication across the components. CBD includes a component model and an interface model. The component model specifies for each component how the component behaves in an arbitrary environment; an interface model specifies for each component how the component interacts with its environment (Szyperski 2002).

OOP vs. CBD. A component is a small group of objects working together to provide a system function. It can be viewed as a black box at the level of a large system function. At a fine level of granularity, we use objects to hide behavior and data. At a coarser level of granularity, we use components to do the same.

Components inherit much of the characteristics of objects in the OO paradigm. But the component notion goes further by separating the interface from the component model. OO reuse usually means reuse of class libraries in a particular OO programming language or environment. For example, you have to be conversant with SmallTalk or Java to be able to reuse a SmallTalk or Java class. A component, by using public interface, can be reused without even knowing which programming language or platform it uses internally.

SOA vs. OOP and CBD. At a conceptual level, SOA is an extension of earlier OOP and CBD concepts. OOP focuses on the encapsulation of both data and behavior of an object, while SOA also focus on the user's view of a computing object or application, that is, the interface. An interface specifies the services that are provided and contains metadata defining how they behave.

Though CBD goes further than OOP by supporting public interfaces used for communication across the components, the interfaces of a component are easier to change because they are only used by the known clients. In SOA, a service has a published network-addressable interface. A published interface is one that is exposed to the network and may not be changed so easily, because the clients of the published interface are not known. The difference is analogous to an intranet-based site only accessible by employees of the company and an Internet site accessible by anyone.

3.5 Reconciling OOP, CBD, SOA, and AOC

From OOP and CBD to SOA and AOC, the practice of software programming has evolved through different development paradigms. At the conceptual level, these concepts and approaches build upon each other are complementary, and all have a role to play in designing and managing software systems. Each method shift came about in part to deal with greater levels of software complexity. In all cases, the way we manage complexity is by decomposing a complex system or process into smaller modules that can be designed independently, that is, modularity. Modularity ensures easy maintenance and updates of complex systems by separating the high-frequency intra-module linkages from the low-frequency inter-module linkages and limiting the scope of interactions between the modules by hiding the intra-module relations inside a module box (Baldwin and Clark 1997). Based on the idea of modularity, constructs such as objects, components, software agents, and Web services have been continuously invented and evolved for developing software applications.

Object-Oriented (OO) methodologies provide a foundation for software engineering that uses objects and their interactions to design applications and computer programs. CBD provides a coarser grained construct for larger systems and separates interface from the behavior of the construct for supporting public communication between the components which know about each other. SOA goes further by using XML-based and network-addressable interface as well as XML-based messages and standard protocols for open communication among all software applications in Internet. In SOA, a Web service can find and talk with another Web service which is unknown a priori. Compared with OOP, CBD, and SOA, AOC is used to model and implement solutions to semi- or ill-structured problems, which are too complex to be completely characterized and precisely described. In addition to passive behavior, agent is used to perform more autonomous activities in solving complex problems. To achieve this, knowledge or rules for governing the behavior are separated from the behavior of the agent.

In computer science, the terms object, component, software agent, and Web service describe a piece of software that performs some action on behalf of human beings, like an agent or actor. In addition to actor, agent can also be a broker, which mediates between the buyer (service requesting party) and the seller (service providing party). In terms of broker, software agent can be used to search appropriate applications, for example, Web service in the Internet, to perform requested services. This special type of agent works as an intermediary between service requester and service provider, coordinating on behalf of two parties regarding service requirements, qualities, costs, constraints, etc.

4 Applying Technical Solutions to BPM Problems

In Sect. 2, we identified four business requirements on flexible process management (decomposition of complex processes, task coordination, dynamism of the environment, and the resource acquisition and assembly) that provide the business rationale for employing appropriate technologies in developing flexible BPM systems. In Sect. 3, we clarify and explicitly define the similarities and differences between four modular technologies: OOP, CBD, SOA, and AOC. In this section we will show how these technologies can be used to address the challenges outlined in Sect. 2. Table 14.1 below summarizes the relationship between the problem aspects identified in Sect. 2 and solution technologies defined in Sect. 3. Sections 4.1, 4.2, 4.3 and 4.4 expand on this table.

4.1 Decomposition of Complex Processes

Business processes display complexity as a result of interactions of their internal components and interaction of the process with its environment. A process can be

Table 14.1 Technical solutions applied to flexible BPM

Technical solutions	Flexible BPM
OOP, OBD, SOA, and AOC for decomposing complex processes at different level of granularity	Decomposition of complex processes
SOA for decomposing and integrating inter-organizational processes over the Web	
AOC for decomposing and delegating ill-structured tasks to autonomous software entities	
OOP, OBD, and SOA for structured communications among tasks or task components	Flexible task coordination
SOA for open communication among all software applications over the Internet	
AOC for flexible coordination by supporting flatter hierarchies, loosely coupled autonomy-based units and decision-based coordination mechanisms	
Object, component, and service unable to behave in dynamic environments	Awareness of dynamic environments
Agents for reaction to changes in dynamic environments through continuous perception of and interaction with the environment	
Agents for proactive behavior by making prediction of future state of dynamic environments	
Object and component not used for resource coordination	Flexible resource coordination
SOA for seamless and flexible integration of resources across different organizations over the Web	
Agents for coordination among resources	

decomposed into a set of tasks, task into subtasks, and so on, through several layers in a hierarchy. Tasks or subtask components can be delegated to software objects, components, agents, and services, as actors of the tasks, which interact and communicate in performing the process.

To deal with interactions across different organizations, SOA proposes "service" as a high-level view of the building block of a process. A process is composed of a set of services, each of which is provided by an individual organization. By using SOA, the interservice interactions are separated from intraservice interactions; the complexity of both maintained at different layers. Moreover, we can take advantage of reusability, interoperability and extensibility of Web services on the basis of open standards to cater for business process integration and interoperation over the Web.

The highly dynamic and unpredictable nature of business processes makes agent-based approach appealing. AOC assigns business applications' main activities to autonomous agents. Such agents are flexible problem solvers that have specific goals to achieve and interact with one another to manage their autonomy and interdependencies in business processes. AOC is well suited for complex process situations that are not all known a priori, cannot be assumed to be fully controllable in their behaviors, and must interact on a sophisticated level of communication and coordination (Wang and Wang 2005).

4.2 Flexible Task Coordination

A business processes is made up of a number of task components that interact with dynamic behavior. OOP uses objects to hide behavior and data, supporting communications among small objects, for example, functions of tasks. CBD extends OOP by supporting interaction among components, that is, coarser grained constructs, using public communication interface. SOC goes further by using XML-based and network-addressable interface as well as XML-based messages and standard protocols for open communication among all software applications over the Internet.

While OOP, OBD, and SOA mainly support structured communications among tasks or task components, AOC are able to support ill-structured interactions among tasks. To coordinate the interactions in dynamic situations, flatter hierarchies, decentralized autonomy-based units, and decision-based coordination mechanisms are required, where AOC is directly applicable. AOC supports decentralized control and asynchronous operations by a group of autonomous software entities, which are able to perform decision-based coordination of their activities.

In AOC, after decomposing a complex process into a number of loosely coupled tasks in a flat hierarchy, we delegate the tasks to a number of autonomous agents, each working both autonomously and collaboratively throughout the whole process. In complex process management, it is impossible to predefine all activities and interactions at design time. Instead, we define the goal or role of each agent and specify a set of rules for governing the behavior of the agent. Agents operate asynchronously and in parallel. This also results in an increase in overall speed and robustness in BPM. The failure of one agent does not necessarily make the overall system useless, where other agents may adjust and coordinate their behavior reactively and proactively to the change.

4.3 Awareness of Dynamic Environments

The complexity of business processes comes not only from interactions of their internal components but also from interaction of the process with its environment. To manage business processes in a dynamic environment, we need to be able to continuously perceive the environment and make real-time decisions on the process. Objects, components, and services are normally unable to behave in dynamic environments. Agent-based software entity is able to sense and recognize the situation and determine appropriate actions upon the situations. Information about the environment (e.g., events, state of activities, and resources) is sensed and interpreted by the agent on the basis of predefined scheme and rules. In case that information is unanticipated or comes as complete and total surprise, it will be sent to human manager for manual processing.

Unlike the ECA (event-condition-action) rules in workflow systems that make reaction to certain events, AOC goes further by incorporating all environmental information into a mental state that watches over the whole environment. Individual events are put together for a comprehensive understanding; ambiguous information is understood after appropriate interpretation and reasoning (Wang and Wang 2006).

Moreover, AOC supports prediction of future state of the environment for purpose of proactive actions. Different from passive response to current events, proactive behavior has an orientation to the future, anticipating problems and taking affirmative steps to deal with them rather than reacting after a situation has already occurred. It refers to the exhibition of goal-oriented behaviors by taking initiatives.

4.4 Flexible Resource Coordination

As discussed, the rise of Internet-mediated e-Business brings the era of demand-driven and resource-based soft connections of business organizations. A business process can be dynamically established by connecting or composing services provided by different organizations. Against this background, SOA provides a real platform of resource selection and allocation in implementing seamless and flexible integration of business processes over the Web.

However, it is a complex problem to search appropriated services from a large number of resources as well as schedule and coordinate them under various constraints. The complexity arises from the unpredictability of solutions from service providers (e.g., availability, capacity, and price), the constraints on the services (e.g., time and cost constraint), and interdependencies among the services. A service solution to an individual service involved in an integrated process does not have a view of the whole service, very often resulting in incoherent and contradictory hypotheses and actions (Wang et al. 2006).

To deal with the problem, AOC can be used for distributed decision-making and coordination. In process integration, decision-making and coordination among services can be modeled as a distributed constraint satisfaction problem, in which solutions and constraints are distributed into a set of services and to be solved by a group of agents (brokers) on behalf of service requesters and providers. In this context, service-based process integration is mapped as an agent-based distributed constraint satisfaction or optimization problem. Individual services are mapped to variables, and solutions of individual services are mapped to values. A distributed constraint optimization problem consists of a set of variables, each assigned to an agent, where the values of the variables are taken from finite and discrete domains. Finding a global solution to an integrated process requires that all agents find the solutions that satisfy not only their own constraints but also interagent constraints (Wang et al. 2008).

5 Conclusion

In this chapter, we have investigated how relevant modular programming technologies can be applied and integrated in developing flexible BPM solutions. On the one hand, we examine the main problems to be solved in flexible process management.

Based on a theoretical understanding on business processes and the roots of their complexity, we identify and address the main problem with their solutions in flexible BPM. On the other hand, we analyze the overlapping technical concepts and solutions used for flexible BPM systems development. We clarify the differences and relationships between these terminologies and techniques in the context of BPM. Based on the examination of the both sides (BPM requirements and supporting techniques), we have made a clear picture with a systemic approach on how these concepts and technologies can be applied and integrated in developing flexible process management systems. This chapter will benefit professionals, researchers, and practitioners by advanced analysis and theoretical investigations of problems and solutions in developing flexible BPM solutions.

References

Baldwin CY, Clark KB (1997) Managing in an age of modularity. Harv Bus Rev 75(5):84–93

Eisenhardt KM (1989) Agency theory: an assessment and review. Acad Manage Rev 14(1):57–74

Endsley MR (1995) Toward a theory of situation awareness in dynamic systems. Hum Factors 37(1):32–64

Hammer M, Champy J (1993) Reengineering the corporation: a manifesto for business revolution. Brealey, London

Huhns MN (2002) Agents as web services. IEEE Internet Comput 6(4):93–95

Jennings NR, Faratin P, Norman TJ, O'Brien P, Odgers B (2000) Autonomous agents for business process management. Int J Appl Artif Intell 14(2):145–189

Kammer PJ, Bolcer GA, Taylor RN, Hitomi AS, Bergman M (2000) Techniques for supporting dynamic and adaptive workflow. Comput Support Coop Work 9(3–4):269–292

Kumar K (2001) Technology for supporting supply chain management: introduction. Commun ACM 44(6):58–61

Kumar K, Narasipuram MM (2006) Defining requirements for business process flexibility. In: Seventh workshop on business process modeling, development, and support, CAiSE, Luxembourg

Kumar K, van Dissel H (1996) Sustainable collaboration: managing conflict and cooperation in interorganizational systems. MIS Q 20(3):279–300

Kumar K, van Fenema PC, von Glinow MA (2007) Offshoring and the global distribution of work: implications for task interdependence theory and practice. In: First annual research conference and workshop on offshoring, North Carolina

Leymann F, Roller D, Schmidt MT (2002) Web services and business process management. IBM Syst J 41(2):198–211

Melão N, Pidd M (2000) A conceptual framework for understanding business processes and business process modeling. Inform Syst J 10:105–129

Mintzberg H (1979) The structuring of organizations. Prentice Hall, Englewood Cliffs

Mowshowitz A (1997) Virtual organization. Commun ACM 40(9):30–37

Papazoglou MP (2007) Web services: principles and technology. Pearson Education Ltd., Harlow

Rumbaugh J (1991) Object-oriented modeling and design. Prentice Hall, Englewood Cliffs

Simon HA (1981) The sciences of the artificial. MIT Press, Cambridge, MA/London

Szyperski C (2002) Component software: beyond object-oriented programming. Addison-Wesley Professional, Boston

van der Aalst WMP, van Hee KM (2002) Workflow management: models, methods, and systems. MIT Press, Cambridge

Volberda HW (1999) Building the flexible firm: how to remain competitive. Oxford University Press, Oxford

Wang M, Wang H (2005) Intelligent agent supported business process management. In: Proceedings of 38th Hawaii International Conference on System Sciences (HICSS-38), IEEE Computer Society Press, Hawaii

Wang M, Wang H (2006) From process logic to business logic – a cognitive approach to business process management. Inform Manage 43(2):179–193

Wang M, Cheung WK, Liu J, Xie X, Lou Z (2006) E-service/process composition through multi-agent constraint management. In: Fourth international conference on Business Process Management (BPM), LNCS 4102, Vienna, pp 274–289

Wang M, Liu J, Wang H, Cheung W, Xie X (2008) On-demand e-supply chain integration: a multi-agent constraint-based approach. Expert Syst Appl 34(4):2683–2692

Weske M (1998) Object-oriented design of a flexible workflow management system. In: 2nd East-European symposium on advances in databases and information systems. Lecture notes in computer science, Poznan, Poland, vol 1475. pp. 119–130

Wooldridge M, Jennings NR (1999) Software engineering with agents: pitfalls and pratfalls. IEEE Internet Comput 3(3):20–27

Chapter 15
Rapid Deployment Approach Through Flexible System Design: Breakthrough in Technology Innovation and Process Optimization for eClinical Trials

MaryAnne Rizk

1 Introduction

Managing trials of new drugs is a major undertaking for pharmaceutical companies. The pharmaceutical industry witnesses increasing competitive and regulatory pressures. In this fast-paced market, being the most efficient in identifying viable new compounds is not just a means of achieving growth but also a key to survival. The first company to market with a new drug can enjoy a virtual monopoly for years, generate tremendous profits, and possibly transform the lives of millions of people. The second gets very limited benefits:

> Approximately, 10,000 compounds synthesized, only ten will be advanced to clinical development, of which on average, only one will be approved for commercial introduction. It is reported that US pharmaceutical companies spend an average of over 1 billion over ten to twelve years to bring a new product to market. Once on the market seven out of ten products fail to return the cost of the company's investment. – Journal of Health Economics 22 (2003) 151–185 (refer Fig. 15.1)

Drug discovery is not only costly and risky but there are additional uncertainties over whether the process can be managed correctly, and the benefits from new drug discovery can be appropriated through technology. The pharmaceutical industry competitive challenge is the struggle for speed, as a single day of delay in getting a new product to market can cost millions of dollars in sales:

> "An additional reason for speed is, of course, the cost of the new drug development process itself: currently $30,000 per day, which is rising by 10–12% per year." – Journal of Health Economics 22 (2003) 151–185

Adopting technology innovation to optimize the clinical trials management has become an increasingly growing priority for the pharmaceutical industry. With the pharmaceutical industry under increasing pressure to raise productivity and cut drug

---

M. Rizk (✉)
Stevens Institute of Technology, Hoboken, NJ 07030, USA
e-mail: mrizk@stevens.edu; rizkmanagement@gmail.com

Sushil and E.A. Stohr (eds.), *The Flexible Enterprise*, Flexible Systems Management,
DOI 10.1007/978-81-322-1560-8_15, © Springer India 2014

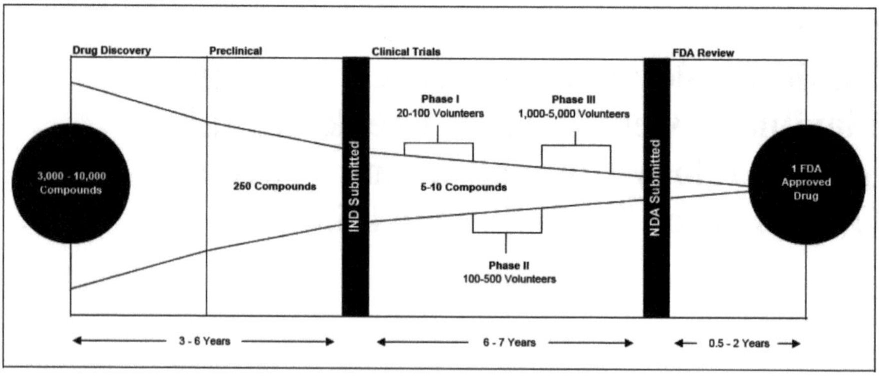

Fig. 15.1 Number of compound to produce a new drug

development costs, technology innovation is critical to maintain market competitiveness for pharmaceutical companies.

Clinical trials are the backbone for the success within the pharmaceutical product pipeline. Ensuring the success of clinical trials by rising to the challenge of regulatory demands and getting a product into clinical trials on time can play a pivotal role in the launch of a new drug. Automation of the clinical trials workflow could speed up the process that would allow companies to be first to market with new drugs and increase profitability. Technology innovation introduces entirely new possibilities for drug development perhaps not possible before.

New product development has strategic importance for a firm's success. In the pharmaceutical industry, attention to new product development is especially critical. The long lead time to develop new drugs and the high costs of development mean that drug companies cannot afford failure. Moreover, new drugs reaching the market often have a rather short time span left for patent protection. Generic versions, off-label use of established drugs, and intense competition worldwide for "blockbuster" drugs create additional pressures on the R&D capabilities of a pharmaceutical company.

By inducing technology innovation and process optimization through flexible systems, pharmaceutical and biotech firms can accelerate the clinical and data management process, be first to market with new drugs, and increase profitability. Success in clinical development is key to the long-term success of pharmaceutical and biotech companies. This chapter focuses on the implementation effects of technology innovation to streamline clinical trials processes to give pharmaceutical companies competitive advantages for early new product development.

2 Problem Statement

The clinical data is the heart of clinical trial process. The challenge for pharmaceutical companies is to quickly expedite the handling of the clinical data. The quality of the data is extremely important for pharmaceutical executives to make earlier decisions about the future direction for a drug to market. Through proven case studies, clinical trials can be designed in less time using EDC systems than managing the trial using paper case report forms.

3 Emerging Technologies

Enabling technology adoption for an eClinical solution allows EDC to hold the key to far-reaching competitive advantages for drug and medical-device companies. Pharmaceutical companies that are bringing EDC in-house are doing so because they recognize EDC as a strategic weapon in their pursuit of more efficient, cost-effective clinical trials. Choosing an EDC technology that is flexible and scalable is the ideal goal as it gives corporations control over how much of the system can be implemented and tailored to clinical protocol studies based on their corporate strategies. To further accelerate this implementation, flexible EDC systems coupled with this next-generation process model breakthrough will change the landscape for clinical trials development. The technology and process combination of this potent formula can allow pharmaceutical and biotech firms to accelerate the clinical and data management processes, be first to market with new drugs, and increase profitability.

4 Research Method

This chapter focuses on the enabling technologies that will be the catalyst for changing the paradigm of eClinical process implementation. There will be an evaluation on the Waterfall Software Lifecycle (SLC) comparing the origin of the eClinical study development lifecycle and the contemporary catalyst for rapid deployment. EDC systems providing intuitive and ultraefficient study configuration coupled with the process optimization to take the final transition from development to configuration. Supporting details will be elaborated on the issues encountered by pharmaceutical companies during their configuration stages and what the steps are to overcome them. The SAP–LAP framework (Sushil 2001) is used to outline the framework consisting of the situation, actor, process, learning, action, and performance criteria.

5 Systemic Flexibility

The integration point where technology innovation meets process optimization will require flexibility for corporations to continuously analyze, adopt, and refine. Through the SAP–LAP framework model, principles from the situation, actor, process, learning, action, and performance will require different types of flexibility as shown in Fig. 15.2.

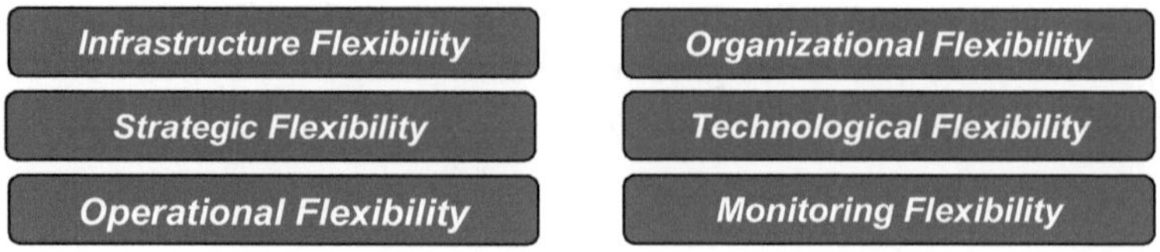

Fig. 15.2 Types of flexibility

The SAP–LAP framework consists of situation, actor, process, learning, action, and performance as illustrated below:

Situation	**Pharmaceutical companies need to find ways to reduce the time from discovery through approval. The rapidly increasing costs and risks of developing drugs have led to the creation of a fast-growing business within the pharmaceutical industry: finding ways to improve the efficiency of the R&D process** **Streamlining clinical development through technology and process efficiency is on the rise given the highly competitive regulated industry. It takes ~8 years on average for new chemical entities (NCEs) to reach the market, leaving less than ~12 years of patent protection** **One of the primary factors to aid in this problem is expediting the data collection of the real-time results of clinical trial testing**
Actors	Internal stakeholders **Biopharmaceutical/pharmaceutical**: data managers, clinical programmers, site coordinators, investigators, site monitors, site manager, CRF designers, database designers **Clinical research organizations (CROs)**: data managers, clinical programmers **Technology vendors** (EDC providers, 3rd party providers) External FDA and regulatory approvals
Process	Business process reengineering and integration of eCRF design using adaptive trial approach. SDLC Lifecycle mapped to the clinical trial development cycle Phase I, Phase II, Phase III, and Phase IV Impacted clinical processes Program/study design Database design Study start-up Ongoing study/site management Data analysis and CSR preparation Study closure/database lock
Learning	Training, education of electronic data capture (EDC) tools, continuous improvement in process implementation
Action	Combined process efficiency, adaptive clinical trial design, and full integrated global EDC technology
Performance	Reduce number of days to configure clinical trial case report forms for data collection and analysis

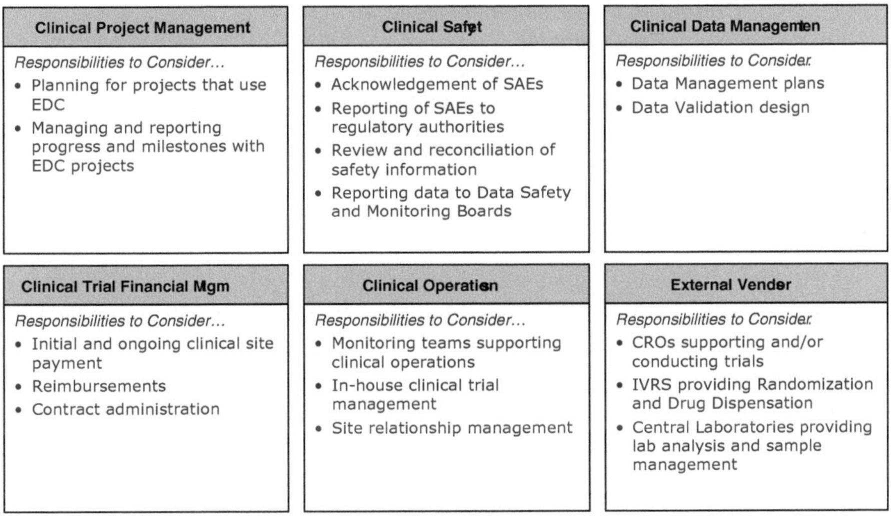

Fig. 15.3 Actors involved in process optimization

The actors shown in Fig. 15.3 will impact the flow of the process optimization. The clinical development teams will play a significant role in the adaptive trial process optimization.

6 Traditional Approach: Waterfall SLC (Software Life Cycle)

Typically the clinical development process (Fig. 15.4) for configuring system study trial design has followed the waterfall model. The standard waterfall model for systems development is an approach that goes through various cycles and steps. The actors listed in Fig. 15.3 go through the linear processes which can elongate the clinical development process into a 12-week implementation.

6.1 Current Specification Document Design Approach

The current process lifecycle uses paper specification to communicate EDC configuration requirements between all key stakeholders including data management, clinical operations, statistics, program, and project managements. This iterative lifecycle is cycled back to the technical teams to interpret the design of the trial. As changes occur, this cycle moves back in the process, thus adding delays to the

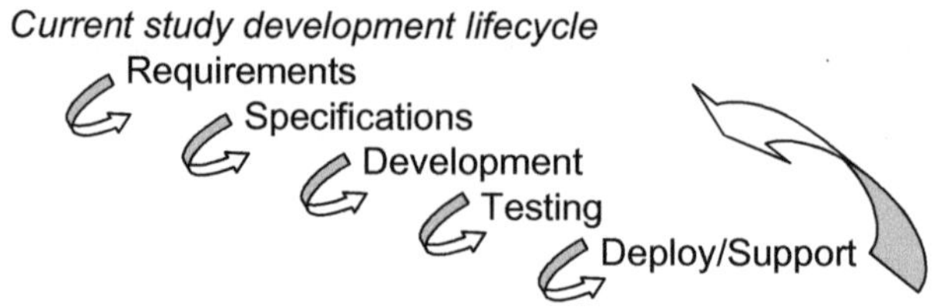

Fig. 15.4 Waterfall model

timelines, cascading a domino effect to timelines. A delay in development leads to late enrolment for subjects on a trial, pushing the delays to monitor the results of the study and thus the ripple effect to close the trial and submission to the FDA. In the height of competition to be first to market, every day counts.

Process steps that clinical developers and data managers go through with sponsors include this linear process that includes the following:

1. Document the concept.
2. Identify system requirements and analyze them.
3. Break the system into pieces (architectural design).
4. Design each piece (detailed design).
5. Code the system components and test them individually (coding, debugging, and unit testing).
6. Integrate the pieces and test the system (system testing).
7. Deploy the system and operate it.

7 Next-Generation Model: Rapid Deployment Approach

The future model requires behavior changes for the key clinical stakeholders to move away from the traditional waterfall SDLC and take a leap into the accelerated approach. This alterative design approach will take EDC system configuration environment as the combined specification and configuration tool.

The size and complexity of clinical programs are increasing disproportionately faster than available resources. To succeed, clinical organizations must find new, more efficient ways of operating. That requires reviewing (and often revamping) current work processes, organizational structures, and technologies. Clinical development leaders are seeking to improve the efficiency and effectiveness of their operations. Experts are desired to help drive change initiatives so that their key staff can remain focused on producing clinical results. To succeed, clinical organizations must find new, more efficient ways of operating.

By replacing design and requirements specifications and turning them into human readable definitions, development is the heart of this breakthrough for eClinical Trials deployment. Rapid deployment strategies will be outlined during the chapter to address the needs of various protocols and therapeutic areas. Additionally,

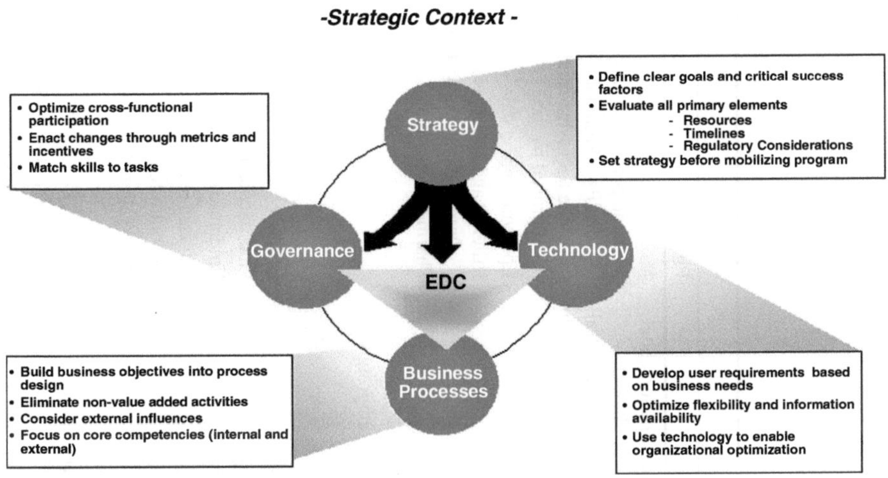

Fig. 15.5 EDC strategy model

discussions on the ability to reduce process workflows through the utilization of a flexible system and process designs will be broached.

8 Strategic Flexibility

The implementation strategy will encompass change to processes and methodologies, integrating technologies and revising the supporting organizational infrastructure within a defined time frame. The impact of the strategic flexibility on a corporation will encompass implementation strategy, people, process, and technology (Fig. 15.5).

9 Infrastructure Flexibility: Breakthrough in Clinical Design

The design of the clinical trial dictates how the system configuration will be constructed to support the data collection for the study. This essential step is pivotal for leveraging emerging technologies and advancing the business process reengineering. Below is a comparison table of the clinical trial phases (Table 15.1).

Traditionally, clinical trials can run 14–24 months. At the end of the trial during database lock, the data is reviewed to determine the results of the study. Performing interim analyses can increase speed and accuracy from the data analysis. In the design of the clinical trial, organizations need to map out the expected data flow, identify and validate required technology integrations, and determine the appropriate edit checks to fire queries.

Table 15.1 Clinical trials matrix

Comparison of Clinical Trial Phases

	Phase I	Phase II	Phase III	Phase IV
Objectives	Determine the metabolic and pharmacological actions and the maximally tolerated dose	Evaluate effectiveness, determine the short-term side effects and identify common risks for a specific population and disease	Obtain additional information about the effectiveness of clinical outcomes and evaluate the overall risk–benefit ratio in a demographically diverse sample	Monitor ongoing safety in large populations and identify additional uses of the agent that might be approved by the FDA
Factors to be identified	Bioavailability Bioequivalence Dose proportionality Metabolism Pharmacodynamics Pharmacokinetics	Bioavailability Drug–disease interactions Drug–drug interactions Efficacy at various doses Pharmakodynamics Pharmakokinetics Patient safety	Drug–disease interactions Drug–drug interactions Dosage intervals Risk–benefit information Efficacy and safety for subgroups	Epidemiological data Efficacy and safety within large, diverse populations Pharmacoeconomics
Data focus	Vital signs Plasma and serum levels Adverse events	Dose response and tolerance Adverse events Efficacy	Laboratory data Efficacy Adverse events	Efficacy Pharmacoeconomics Epidemiology Adverse events
Design features	Single, ascending dose tiers Unblinded Uncontrolled	Placebo controlled comparisons Active controlled comparisons Well-defined entry criteria	Randomized Controlled 2–3 treatment arms Broader eligibility criteria	Uncontrolled Observational
Duration	Up to 1 month	Several months	Several years	Ongoing (following FDA approval)

Population	Healthy volunteers or individuals with the target disease (such as cancer or HIV)	Individuals with target disease	Individuals with target disease	Individuals with target disease, as well as new age groups, genders, etc.
Sample size	20–80	200–300	100–1,000	1,000
Example	Study of a single dose of Drug X in normal subjects	Double-blind study evaluating safety and efficacy of Drug X vs. placebo in patients with hypertension	Study of Drug X vs. standard treatment in hypertension study	Study of economic benefit of newly approved Drug X vs. standard treatment for hypertension

Research Coordinator Orientation, University of Pittsburgh, 2002

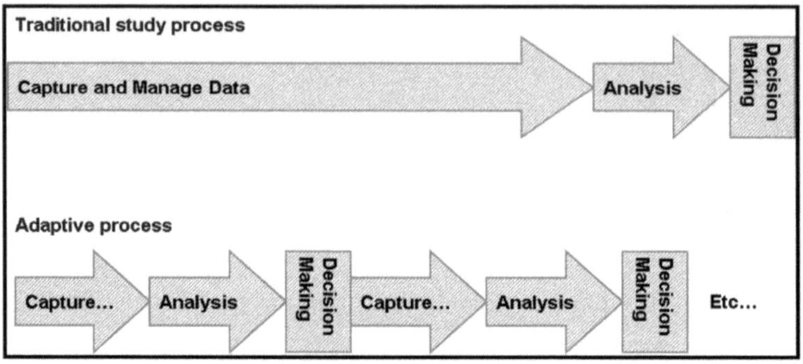

Fig. 15.6 Clinical trial process: traditional versus adaptive

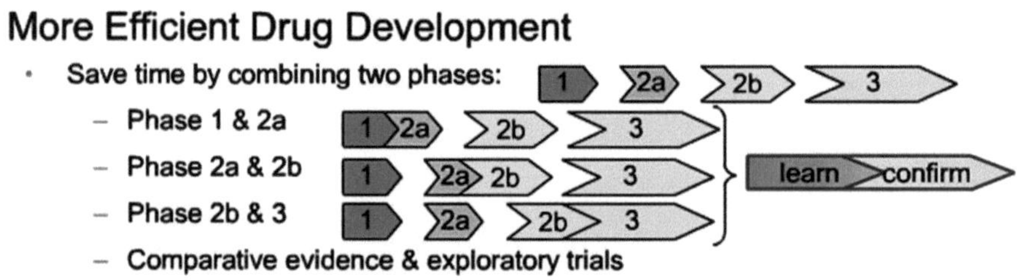

Fig. 15.7 Combining clinical trial phases

Interim analysis can lead to real-time data collection, cleansing, and monitoring. It gives the ability to review and analyze the data often. The simulations and modeling maintain the statistical validity of the data.

Adaptive Clinical Trial Design allows interactive data collection, analysis, and earlier decision making. By adopting the adaptive process, organization can access real-time data for early decision making. Clinical monitors can assess results from subject's response to a drug. Interim analysis phase allows pharmaceutical companies to utilize real-time data and determine whether to keep the treatment arm running for a trial or dismiss and kill the clinical study (Fig. 15.6).

Adaptive trials allow more efficient drug development. By combining and blending phases in a trial, the data can be comparative and the learning factor can confirm the direction for the drug development. Designing a study using the adaptive trials approach can save time by combining two phases: Phases 1 and 2a, Phases 2a and 2b, and Phases 2b and 3 (Fig. 15.7).

9.1 Process Optimization Through Design on Trial Management

Primary benefits of applying adaptive process include better ethics since adaptive randomization will favor effective treatments. Depending on the early warning signs, determination can be identified if a drug is ineffective or toxic, which may avoid serious adverse events within the clinical trial. This adaptive process will also lead to better science as more dosages will be introduced and leanings about dosage respond model and toxicity into a pivotal trial. This is a significant breakthrough as this response and reducing failure rate in that phase can lead to an early termination of a trial and reduce failure risk of those volunteer subjects.

Adaptive trial design can lead to a more efficient drug development by combining phases and accelerating the "learn and confirm" methodology but applying immediate leanings to the next steps within the trial, therefore possibly shorting development process for later trials.

10 Process Change

Pharmaceutical companies that have had EDC experience have already discovered that they cannot automatically switch from a pilot project to full-scale implementation because major process changes are often required to support the software. It is the equivalent of taking a square peg and forcing it into a round hole. There needs to be the right process identified that specifically match the supporting technology for a seamless implementation that "fits" the organization.

Breaking down the high-level process into activities, organizations can measure their flexibility (Table 15.2).

11 Organizational Flexibility

When introducing EDC into an organization, the following factors needs to be considered:

I. **Ensure EDC becomes an integral part of the organization's strategic plan**. EDC must be leveraged into the organization's strategy of process, people, and overall technology. An organization must measure how well the enterprise technology performs against its strategic objectives Oracle Whitepaper (2006).

According to an executive sponsor from an experienced EDC pharmaceutical company, *"EDC is not an IT project. It has an IT component and it uses contemporary technology, but successful implementation requires that responsibility reside elsewhere. In my opinion, effective leadership and change management are the most critical success factors with technology playing a vital, but smaller role."*

The clinical development process are broken down into three main categories: study design, study conduct, and study close. These areas have impact across all clinical processes (Fig. 15.8).

II. **Align organizational roles and map to the specific functionality that can be preformed within the technology.** Through the advancement of graphical user interface (GUI) available in today's configurable technologies, there may be less of

Table 15.2 Process mapping EDC implementation tasks: Matrix to provide the crossroad where technology meets the impacted organizational processes

High-level process	Activities	Considerations
Program/study design	Protocol authoring	How will EDC timelines affect protocol development?
		How will EDC-specific language be incorporated?
	Study planning	How will protocol team members be trained on how to use the EDC tool?
		What should be updated in existing clinical development SOPs and templates (e.g., input/output plan, data review plan, statistical analysis plan)?
		How will the use of EDC affect study start-up timelines?
Database design	CRF design and database development	How will CRF layout and validation checks be designed now that they will be done directly in EDC?
		Who will design and configure the eCRFs and data validations?
		How will defining global standards for CRFs and reusable nonstandard modules fit into the process?
		How will CRF completion instructions be affected with the use of EDC?
		How will CRF design merge with data extraction design into one process?
		How will the organization be affected now that database design is no longer required?
		Who will require workflow administration training?
		How will usability of EDC screens and online validations from the site's perspective be tested?
		How will EDC affect timing of project configuration relative to First Patient First Visit?
Study start-up	EDC account creation	Who will be responsible for the creation and maintenance of EDC accounts?
	Country/site selection	How will use of EDC technology (connectivity, Internet, etc.) affect site selection?
		How will sites be evaluated for connection and provisioning requirements?
	Provisioning	How will provisioning sites with EDC hardware (i.e., laptops) and connectivity impact the current process?
		If hardware is provided to a site, how will the expense be handled?
	Clinical supplies	How will randomization and drug supply be handled in an EDC study?
		How will the IVRS system work/integrate with the EDC tool, if at all?
	Investigator/site training	How will initial and ongoing EDC trainings (e.g., EDC tool, site initiation, processes) be delivered to sites and investigators?
		How will EDC affect the relationship between the sponsor and investigator?
	Clinical trial agreement	How will EDC considerations (e.g., site assessments, provisioning) affect the clinical trial agreement process?

Ongoing study/site management	Data entry workflow	How will workflow in EDC affect the data entry process?
		How will sites entering data directly from source documents into eCRFs using EDC fit into the process?
		How will automated edit checks impact the process?
Study closure	Database lock	How can EDC be utilized to lessen the time to database lock?
		How will interim locks for EDC sites impact the resolution of discrepancies?
		How will site access be removed (e.g., deleting accounts, locking all data, shutting down the URL)?
		How will the decreased need to audit the database for EDC sites affect the database lock process?
	Site closure visits	How will incorporating EDC-related items (e.g., provisioning, records retention, patient data archival) affect the current sit closure process?
	Archiving	How will investigators receive a record of their study data?
		When will archiving activities begin relative to database lock?
		How will sites access to EDC change once the study is closed?

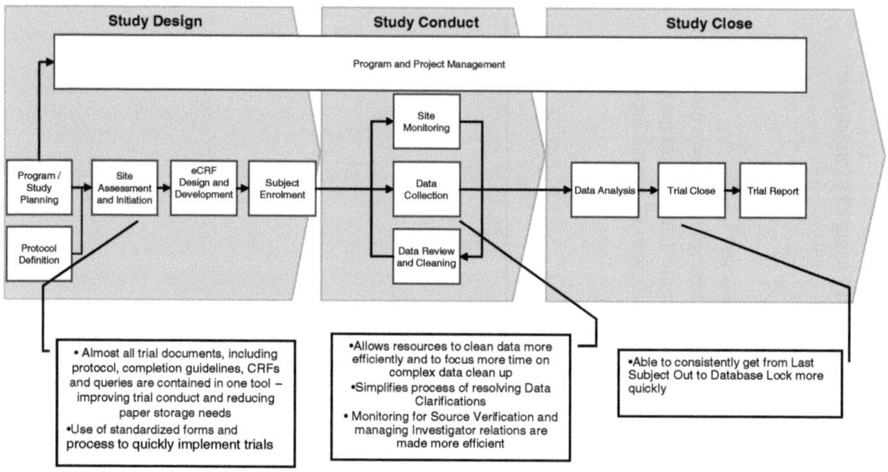

Fig. 15.8 Study phases approach *Flexible impact of responsibilities per phase based on technology and process optimization*

CRF / Database Designer	Site Coordinator	Investigator
Responsibilities to Consider... • Input / Output Plan • CRF and eCRF Design • CRF and eCRF Development and Testing • Data Validation Development and Testing	*Responsibilities to Consider...* • Data Entry • Data Review / Correction • Alerting Principal Investigator of eCRF status • Query resolution	*Responsibilities to Consider...* • Data Entry • Data Clarification • Signatures • Site Staff Compliance with Federal Regulations on Electronic Records and Signatures
Site Monitor	**Data Manager**	**Site Manager**
Responsibilities to Consider... • Data Review and Verification (SDV) • Creating Discrepancies • Reviewing and Closing Discrepancies • Site's First Point of Contact for Study Questions • Protocol deviations	*Responsibilities to Consider...* • Ongoing Data Review to Identify Inconsistencies • Creating, Routing, and Discrepancies Appropriately • Locking Data • Protocol deviations	*Responsibilities to Consider...* • Early Process Control of Data Entry, Verification, and Cleaning Processes • Identifying and Communicating eCRF / Protocol Compliance Issues to Site • Performance or Data Quality

Fig. 15.9 Selection of actors by a pharmaceutical company

a need to have a higher technical resource to configure a piece of the application. Whereas there may have been a need for a technical clinical developer to design an electronic case report form (eCRF), this now can be configured by a data manager who may not need an application development skill set.

Depending on the EDC technology that a pharmaceutical company selects, various actors will be determined as indicated in Fig. 15.9.

Fig. 15.10 Technology flexibility: Divisions of how technology impacts the sum of parts that equal a greater cohesive whole. Measurement areas include organizational and operational processes

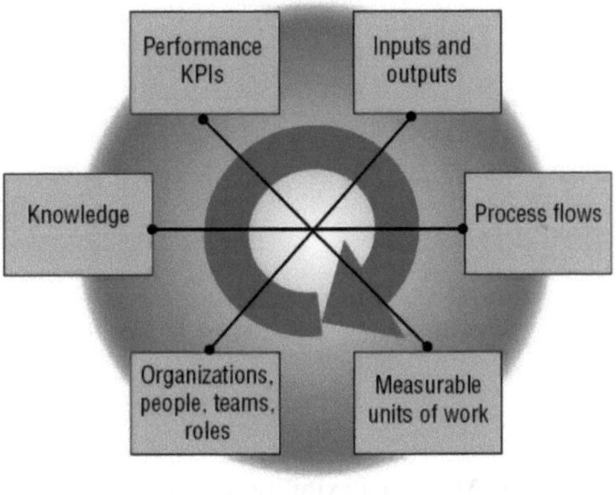

III. **Develop goals and establish metrics to evaluate and maximize the return on investment**. Key performance indicators (KPIs) are the measurement scale to determine the success rate of the organizational flexibly. Measurement variables that organizations can use to confirm effectiveness of EDC adoption include number of days of database lock and number of days of study start-up (Fig. 15.10).

IV. **Execute standard implementations globally**. Organizations that can work through challenges and adaptations on a global scale will be highly efficient. Management executives that can align consistency of implementation globally are paramount. Establishing global standards for role harmonization and consistent use of EDC.

To be faster and quicker to market requires companies to focus on establishing enterprise standardization on clinical research globally. This standardization trend in the clinical research is occurring at an accelerating rate. The ability to have a consistent manner of handing data unfolds to additional areas for how the clinical data is managed that includes every aspect of data collection, management, manipulation, storage, dissemination, and submission in clinical research.

The benefits of standards are exponential not just to the immediate pharmaceutical company internally, but it establishes a common language and common reference points so the data can measure and communicate technology solutions to third-party companies and regulatory bodies. Standards drive compatibility and create new ways the community measures and communicates their impact.

Pharmaceutical and biotech companies are now mandating technology solutions and tools to comply with a certain amount of standardization. The force behind the drive is the FDA wanting companies to use submission standards. That sends a very strong signal to sponsor companies: in order to comply with federal guidelines, we need to enforce these standards, ensure adoption, and improve compatibility.

V. **Recognize where new processes are required and whether existing processes can be streamlined using EDC.** Flexibility Monitoring measures

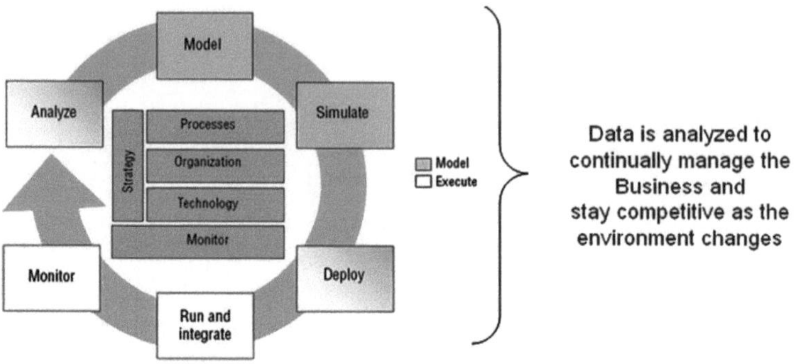

Fig. 15.11 Monitor flexibility: Continuous measurement to improve the process through learning knowledge gained through cycle implementations

performance and allows the automotive company to sense and *respond to changes* and react accordingly. The Learning Factor plays a significant role to the incorporation of new process added to the overall implementation (Fig. 15.11).

VI. **Identify the correct roles and responsibilities for the corresponding task**. It is a highly import process to create the ideal role to map to the process. The goal is to consolidate roles where possible since there will be overlap in activities.

12 Conclusion

For pharmaceutical and biopharmaceutical companies to succeed in the race for the cure, there must be both enterprise and strategy flexibility within the organization to introduce new methodologies in tradition clinical trial design phases. The more flexibility a pharmaceutical company allows, the more resilient and resistant to market threats – and responsive to opportunities – it becomes.

References

Journal of Health Economics 22 (2003) 151–185. The price of innovation: new estimates of drug development costs. October 2002
Oracle Whitepaper (2006) EDC in clinical trials – benchmark analysis of Oracle RDC, June 2006
Sushil (2001) SAP – LAP framework. Glob J Flex Syst Manage 2(1):51–55

Chapter 16
Information Systems Flexibility in Organizations: Conceptual Models and Research Issues

Ramaraj Palanisamy

1 Introduction

Information systems (IS) departments in organizations have experienced great difficulties in coping with the rapid changes and high complexity characteristic of today's business and technological landscapes (Murray 2000; Hopper 1996; Scott 1998). Both the academic and practitioner literature suggests that flexibility is the key for coping with such dynamic, uncertain, and complex environments (Alter 2000; Chakravarthy 1997; Evans 1999) and this need is well recognized by IS executives (Overby 2001). Increasing information system flexibility with flexible information technology infrastructure and adaptable application systems has been a critical issue for IS managers (Duncan 1995; Prahalad, and Krishnan 2002; Sambamurthy et al. 2003). Information systems must be flexible to satisfy user requirements, particularly in changing environments. Business environments are very dynamic and volatile in nature. The information system has to constantly deal with the volatile nature of the business requirements. As a result, the information system in an organization can be easily outdated and irrelevant. In addition, the IS environment is changing at an ever-increasing rate (Benamati and Lederer 2001). The technology, which is apparently current, becomes obsolete at an increasing speed.

However, while IS flexibility seems to be increasingly important from both academic and practitioner perspectives, knowledge about the concept is limited. This chapter explores the concept of IS flexibility by presenting the different components for building flexibility in information systems. Based on a review of the literature, four conceptual models are presented and the different components of the models are discussed.

R. Palanisamy (✉)
St. Francis Xavier University, Schwartz School of Business and IS, Antigonish, NS B2G 2W5, Canada
e-mail: rpalanis@stfx.ca

Sushil and E.A. Stohr (eds.), *The Flexible Enterprise*, Flexible Systems Management, DOI 10.1007/978-81-322-1560-8_16, © Springer India 2014

2 Information Systems Flexibility

IS flexibility can be viewed as the capability of an information system to respond to the changing technology and business environments. A definition encompassing organization and environment is given by Duclos et al. (2003). They define IS flexibility as "the ability to align information system architectures and systems with the changing information needs of the organization as it responds to changing customer demand." Mensah (1989) defines MIS flexibility as "the ability to respond and adapt to changing business conditions both within and outside the organization." Similarly, Palanisamy and Sushil (2003) define IS flexibility as "the capacity of the information systems to change or to adapt and adjust in response to new conditions, demands, or circumstances from the organization." Since the concept of flexibility is complex, multidimensional, and hard-to-capture construct (Sethi and Sethi 1990; Bahrami 1992; de Leeuw and Volberda 1996), flexibility has been denoted with different connotations. Building flexibility is developing ways and means of change across a range of options, and providing freedom of choice to various actors to make this change happen with minimum time and efforts (Sushil 1997, 2000, 2001). As a result, several different dimensions and types of flexibilities have been proposed. For instance, distinctions had been made between product and process flexibilities (Athey and Schmutzler 1995), resource and coordination flexibilities (Sanchez 1995), operational, structural, and strategic flexibilities (Volberda 1996), internal and external flexibilities (Upton 1994), realized and potential flexibilities (Dixon 1992), offensive and defensive flexibilities (Evans 1991), and speed and variety flexibilities (Volberda 1996).

The challenge of improving the flexibility of an information system is compounded by the multidimensional nature of the flexibility concept and the lack of widely accepted measures. Within an information systems context, a number of researchers have explored the multidimensional nature of flexibility. For example, Duncan (1995) highlights that IT infrastructure flexibility consist of three components: technological components, flexibility characteristics, and types of indicators. The technological components consist of platform technology, network and telecommunication technologies, key data, and core data-processing applications. The flexibility of each component is measured by three types of indicators: component characteristics, resource management practice, and IT capabilities. Flexibility characteristics are indicated by compatibility, connectivity, and modularity.

Byrd and Turner (2000, 2001) measure IT infrastructure flexibility in terms of technical and human IT infrastructures. The technical side of IT infrastructure flexibility is measured by such dimensions as IT connectivity, application functionality, IT compatibility, and data transparency. The human side of IT infrastructure flexibility is measured by technology management, business knowledge, management knowledge, and technical skills dimension. To operationalize IS flexibility, Byrd and Turner identified three categories: (i) personnel (refers to the flexibility of the IT personnel, as the variety of skills and attitudes of the IT staff), (ii) integration of data and functionality, and (iii) modularity of system components provided by reusable software modules, vendor-independent database connectivity, and object-oriented development tools.

Based on Soh, Sia, and Tay-Yap's (2000) general scheme, Gebauer and Schober (2006) give factors/measures for the built-in flexibility of information systems: system functionality, scope of the underlying database, user interface, and processing capacity. Functionality refers to the range of functional modules or the different features provided to the user. The examples of system functionality are the range of functional modules in an enterprise system, the various interactions provided between an organization and its business partners in an inter-organizational system, models, and techniques provided by a DSS. The scope of the database refers to the capacity of the database to produce a number of reports and to conduct various analyses. The user interface refers to the various features and methods available for a user to interact with an IS. For instance, user interface includes the type of access channels such as desktops, mobile access, range of input schemes, and output presentation formats. Information processing capacity refers, for instance, to the number of users that could be accommodated or concurrently accessing an information system, number of transactions that could be processed, and others.

3 Proposed Models

Given the multidimensional nature of IS flexibility, identifying and assessing the required levels of flexibility needed to respond to change is especially challenging for organizations. As a starting point for managing IS flexibility within organizations, this research presents a number of conceptual models of the relationship between IS flexibility and various aspects of an IS, such as IS requirements, IT staff, and end-users.

4 External Environment

Figure 16.1 is a conceptual model for the degree of fit between an ideal IS and its capability. The environment is conceptualized with uncertain forces such as more complex, increased competition, global challenges, and market shifts together with rapid technological developments including World Wide Web, electronic commerce, and mobile communication (Behrin et al. 1994). Environmental dynamism is defined as unexpected, hard to predict, and continuous changes of the environmental forces (Dess and Beerd 1984). The environmental dynamics make an impact on the organization resulting into volatility of net sales and the volatility of operating income to name a few (Boyd 1995). Powell (1993) measured this construct using five items to capture environmental dynamism. The items are (i) rapid growth in the demand, (ii) more need for R&D innovation compared to other industries, (iii) the growth stage of the industry, (iv) industry characterization such as high tech, and (v) more unstable industry changing more quickly and unpredictably.

The changes in the environmental forces are increasingly turbulent and the changes need to be addressed to deal effectively with the opportunities presented by

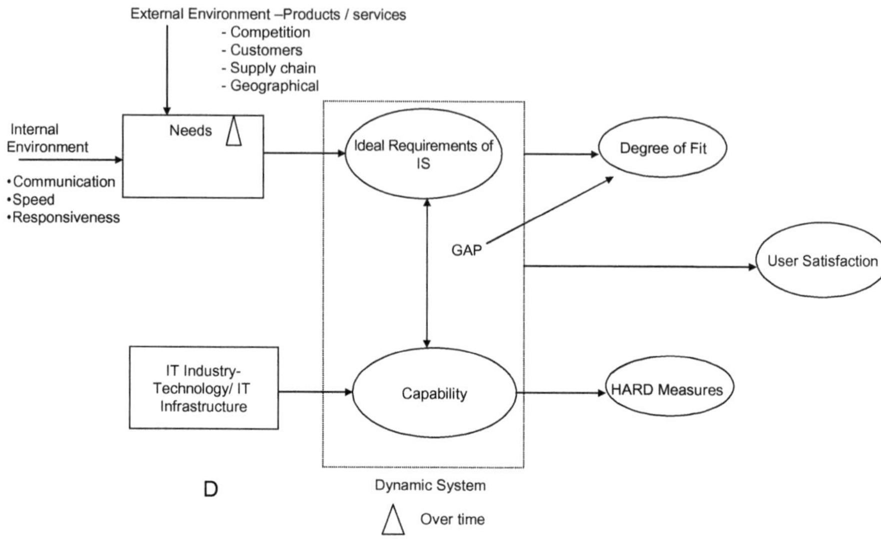

Fig. 16.1 Conceptual model for showing the degree of fit between ideal requirements of IS and its capability

the changes (FitzGerald and Siddiqui 2002). There is an increasing pressure on organizations to respond to and deal with environmental changes more effectively. It is important that the organization needs to be flexible and adaptable in the face of environmental discontinuities (Ciborra 1993). The flexible information system is one of the elements of organizational flexibility and IS must be able to adapt to new circumstances in the organization quickly and inexpensively (Frazelle 1986). For example, the severity of environmental changes such as the deregulation of the electricity industry in the UK caused a disruptive effect on the enterprise information system implemented in the Global Energy Development PLC (GE) (Kanellis and Paul 2005). The implemented ERP systems had been vulnerable in turbulent environments and found unable to adapt to the new and constantly changing organizational realities. Research studies were conducted to address the impact of IS on organizational flexibility and efficiency (Robey and Boudreau 1999; Palanisamy and Sushil 2003). Accordingly, the environmental changes are to be handled by the system developers during and after the implementation of information systems.

IS environmental changes include changes in both internal and external business requirements as well as changes in IT during and after the implementation of information systems. Environmental dynamism consists of rate of change and unpredictability of change has been found to moderate the relationship between flexibility and performance (Lee 2003). The changes such as unstable environment, changes in the business and technological requirements, changing scope/objectives, introduction of new technology, and instability of technical architecture are listed as the major risks in implementing information systems (Schmidt et al. 2001). When carrying out the changes are difficult, time consuming, and expensive, then the IS has

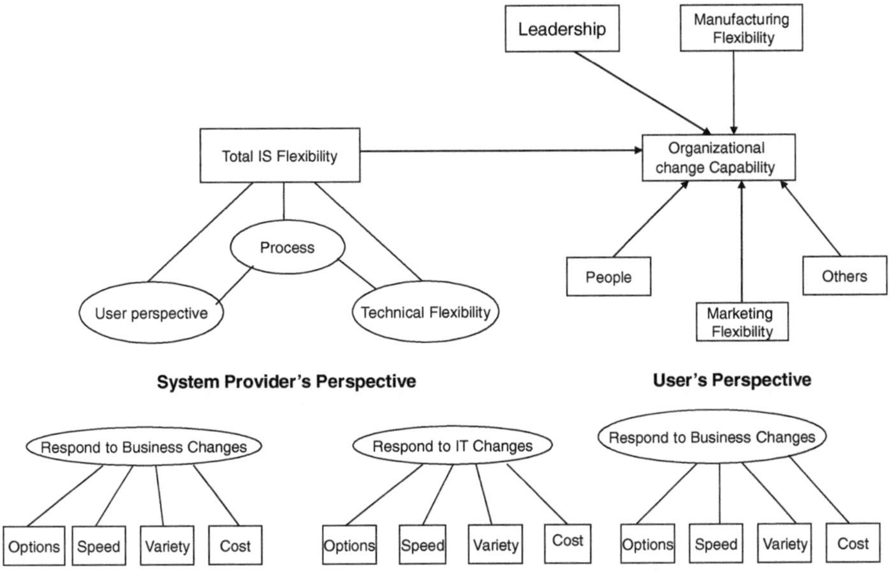

Fig. 16.2 Conceptual model for total IS flexibility and different perspectives for building flexibility in IS

the potential to obstruct organizational flexibility (Hedberg and Jonsson 1978). Eardley, Avison, and Powell (1997) explained that the rigid information systems have restricted the organizational capability to exploit business opportunities by not allowing changes in business strategy. Accordingly, IS/IT must share responsibility for the rigidity and inflexibility of organizations (Lambert and Peppard 1993).

4.1 Fit

The congruence or fit between two components is the degree to which the needs, demands, goals, and objectives of one component are consistent with that of the other (Nadler and Tushman 1979) and "fit" is defined as "matching" (Harrington et al. 2004). In the context of IS, the fit refers to the matching of IT infrastructure/IS capability with the ideal requirements of an IS. This is the matching between information systems and organizational needs (Kannellis et al. 1999). Accordingly, the concept of "fit" is the congruence between the capability shown by the different components of an information system and organizational information requirements. The organizational fit of IS depends on contextual factors (environment, technology, structure, and others) and IS characteristics (database, reports, applications, architectures, and others) (Iivari 1992). In case of an existence of gap between the ideal requirements and the capability of an IS, user satisfaction may be hampered.

Figure 16.2 is a conceptual model for total IS flexibility and different perspectives for building flexibility in IS. In general, information systems and IT are held to be the keys to flexible organizations. Total IS flexibility refers to the capability to respond to unanticipated changes or to adjust to the unexpected changes. Total IS flexibility is a resource in enabling organizations to compete more effectively by integrating various information systems. IS and IT offer opportunities to improve customer services by moving an organization and its product offerings more closer to the customer thereby increasing the change capability of the organization (Ives and Mason 1990). Besides, development of IS capabilities enhances the flexibility of organizations and increases the change capability to respond to customer needs (Levy and Powell 1998).

5 Actors in IS Flexibility: User Perspective and System Provider Perspective

The important actors who have to carry out the task of building flexibility of IS/IT are users, planners (system providers), and top management whose viewpoints and conceptual frameworks are different (Moynihan 1990). Accordingly, the three elements to flexibility of IS/IT are user view, IS department/system provider view, and business view (Rochester 1989). Business view (top management) aims for increasing the capability to build or adapt information systems in response to organizational changes; user view expects intuitive and adaptable interfaces; and the IS department (system provider) view means IT infrastructure flexibility in terms of portability, connectivity, maintainability, and others. Building flexibility in IS is not just the task of a system provider but that the top management has a major role to play by encouraging the philosophy rather than constraining the concept (FitzGerald and Siddiqui 2002).

6 Responding to Business and Technological Changes: System Provider's Perspective

In the presence of uncertainty in business and technological requirements, flexibility has more value. The information systems department/system provider must continuously sense and respond to business as well as technological changes. The system providers have to react to constant changes in the business environment. Within that context, it is hard for them to predict what the system is capable of doing and what its limitation is. This depicts the practical difficulties faced by the system developers in order to cope with the changes in the IS environment. The changes in business strategies, business processes, organizational structure, and other changes will make changes in user requirements from the IS. Adapting to the business and technological changes requires adequate/relevant resources, knowledge, competence, and capabilities. Based on the nature of change, system provider requires different types of skills. Technology changes may occur at various levels including the IT infrastructure and tools/methods. The IS must adapt to these changes taking the existing technology under consideration.

6.1 Responding to Business Changes

The system providers can build the built-in flexibility so that the IS can prepare in advance for unpredictable future changes or should make provisions in the IS so that the IS can make adjustments after an unpredictable event has occurred. Sometimes the events, which trigger the need to change, can be predicted beforehand. More often than not, nonetheless, IS needed to respond to expected as well as unexpected changes. The business changes result in changes in the user requirements (Jalotc 2000; Whitten et al. 2001) such as changes in technical and nontechnical requirements (SEI 1994), system inputs/outputs, logical internal files, interface files, and external inquiries (Low and Jeffrey 1990). Lee and Xia (2005) give three groups of business changes: (i) changes in the setup of an IS development project such as system delivery date and budget for the project; (ii) changes in the functional requirements such as system objectives, system scope, input data, output data, business rules/processes, data structure, and user interface; and (iii) changes in nonfunctional or operational requirements, such as system throughput, system response time, system reliability, and documentation. Gebauer and Schober (2006) give a model for IS flexibility, in which the emphasis is given on the IS capability to accommodate a certain amount of variation regarding the requirements of the supported business processes. Gebauer and Karhade (2004) give a framework to assess the impact of IS flexibility on the performance of business processes.

6.2 Responding to Technological Changes

Besides business changes, technology also changes during and after the implementation of information systems. System developers deal with changes in software development tools and infrastructure technologies (Cooprider and Henderson 1991). The examples of software development tools are programming languages/tools, systems analysis/design methodologies, systems development tools, IT architecture, computer-aided software engineering (CASE) tools, databases, packaged software, and others. Infrastructure technologies include hardware, operating systems, platform technology, network/telecommunication technologies, key enterprise data, and core enterprise applications (Duncan 1995). Lee and Xia (2005) give three groups of technological changes: (i) changes in software programming languages/tools, systems analysis/design methods, and CASE tools; (ii) changes in technology architecture, hardware platform, operating systems, network/telecommunication, and infrastructure; and (iii) changes in the other systems that the application under development will interface with and in the enterprise master data that the application will use.

7 Responding to Business Changes: User's Perspective

Traditionally, based on the user's business requirements, information systems are designed, built, and tested to those requirements. However, the business requirements are dynamically changing during and after the implementation of information systems. Internal and external business environments are continuously changing. For instance, users experienced "disappointment" due to imposed changes on the ERP systems that had not been designed to incorporate them (Kanellis and Paul 2005). Since the IS success is measured in terms of user satisfaction over the IS, information requirements determination must be based on the users' use to which the information systems is meant for.

User's information needs are determined by changes from both external environment and internal environment (Kanellis and Paul 2005). The business needs are arising when the organization is interacting with its external environment (externally generated changes) and the interaction of various organizational components themselves (internally generated changes). The examples for external environmental changes are privatization process, expansion into new and unfamiliar international markets, change in customer taste and preferences, competitors' actions, and others. The examples of internal environment changes are radical reorganization of business processes, change in strategies, introduction of new working practices, procedural change to produce at the lowest possible cost, and others. The changes from external and internal environments have a direct impact on the fit of existing capabilities of IS with the ideal requirements.

The nature of these changes can be organized into steady and permanent, ad hoc and temporary, slow and fast, and predictable and unpredictable. These changes make serious repercussions on the IS. Kanellis and Paul (2005) give examples of difficulties experienced by users in responding to future business changes because of change in the organizational structuring from centralization to decentralization. To overcome such difficulties, users may get complete freedom regarding the development of applications that fit their own requirements. When multiple users started using this autonomy for adding value to the business, managing infrastructure could be a difficult task for system providers. Further, organizations may go through a period of major changes in their IT investments for developing a multiuser system.

Figure 16.3 is a conceptual model for interfacing change requests from users.

7.1 *System Provider's Perspective*

Assessing the existing capability of the information systems in organizations in terms of its adaptive capability to respond to business and technological changes helps the system providers to identify the areas of strengths and deficiencies in the

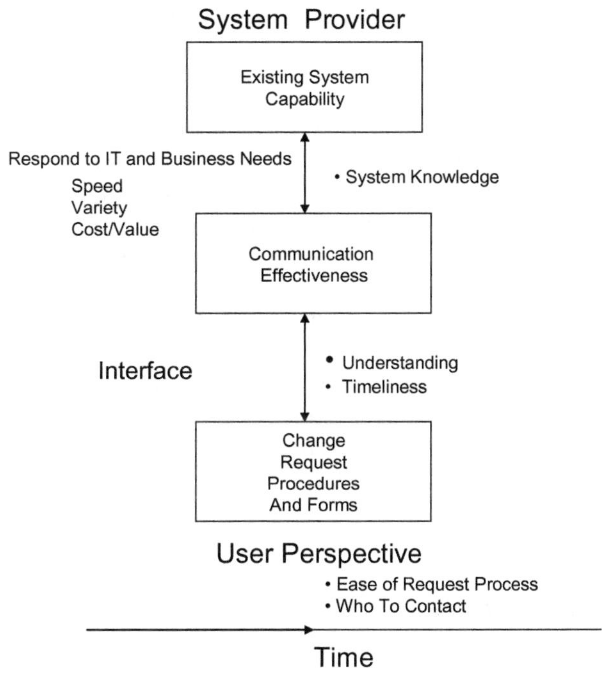

Fig. 16.3 Interfacing change requests from users

existing information systems. The information system may be flexible in one area and may not be capable of adapting to the changes in the other end.

The strengths and deficiencies could be identified in terms of the various dimensions of flexibility such as speed, variety, ease, options, cost, effort, and time. The system providers address the deficiencies by building more capability with the information system. The capabilities could be built by strengthening the different dimensions of flexibility identified in the conceptual model. The following are examples of building capabilities. More options could be created for users for their usage, decisions, and business tasks; an increasing number of provisions are made for handling special/unusual requirements in organizational functions such as sales, finance, production, and other functional areas; an increasing variety of user interfaces such as icons, and menus could be built into the system. New technologies provide more flexibility for usage. For instance, new technologies such as component-based and service-oriented software architectures (Bieberstein et al. 2006), Web-based services (Whiting 2003), autonomous computing concepts (Horn 2001), and mobile applications (Siau et al. 2001) assure greater flexibility compared to the legacy, mainframe, client/server, and non-mobile systems.

7.2 System Provider's Knowledge About Changes, Capabilities, and Responses

The system providers need to maintain a growing body of knowledge about both business as well as technical changes. Besides, the knowledge is required on the existing capabilities of the information system to assess the abilities of IS. Further, the knowledge about the ways of responding to the changes in a more effective and efficient manner adds more value to the systems professional.

For these reasons, the management has to build an IT talent base that provides a solid internal pool of skilled IS/IT professionals trained in various technologies. Further, the pool of talent base needs to rapidly absorb new skills by considering the retirement of obsolete skills. The value system practiced by the IS staff needs to be more entrepreneurial in nature so that the expertise of the IS providers can be rapidly and economically leveraged across different projects. The skills and capabilities of the IS/IT personnel led directly contributing to IS flexibility in organizations.

7.3 User Perspective

Business requirements keep changing continuously over time. Business goals, business processes, and operations change continuously to match with changing market needs and stay competitive (Lee 2003). Users may not precisely articulate their needs at the time of implementing information systems. Further, based on the user's individual requirements, there could be different ways of defining flexibility.

The system developers need to address the individual and changing business requirements of the users. The flexibility to change an information system is particularly important to support business and technological needs that are characterized by high uncertainty regarding future requirements. Some of the changes could be known beforehand (deterministic), some are probabilistic, and some are unknown (Gebauer and Karhade 2004).

Information systems are being developed and used in a variable or changing organizational environment. The change in IS requirements is often superseded by change in organizational events such as objectives, policies, and procedure which also change the information needs for users (Patel and Irani 1999). To cope with organizational variability, users are to be involved in IS design decisions, as it is difficult for system developers to capture all required information (Trigg et al. 1987), and thus, IS become responsive to user's situational needs. The increasing pace of business changes forces the users to contact the system providers for making changes in the existing information systems. The procedure for making changes needs to be easy, convenient, simple, and straightforward. The procedures for submitting change requests are to be reasonable.

As a result of the changing business environment, system providers must constantly respond to new or changing user requirements. Further, who to contact for requesting changes should be clear to the users. Users feel comfortable for having a single point of contact for making requests for changes.

Accordingly, users expect the IS/IT personnel to handle their requests promptly regardless of its nature. Prompt response from the system providers create some kind of trust between the users and IS/IT personnel, which may increase the dependability over the system providers. When the changes are difficult to implement/incorporate, the systems personnel need to explain to the users the reasons of difficulty. The systems personnel need to keep accurate records on users' change requests for future analysis and reference.

The existing information systems should have built-in flexibility for handling the business changes. For instance, the existing IS should easily let the users create new reports and new ways of presenting information. Nonetheless, in some cases, the business requirements may demand unrealistic changes like trying to "fit" a square in a rounded hole.

In a turbulent environment, the numbers of requests for changes to the system may increase exponentially in a nonstop manner. Failure to incorporate the changes may end up with "misfit" referring to the incapability of IS to keep providing the consistent services to business processes. The "misfit" in the long run may cause the organization to make inappropriate decisions.

7.4 Interface Between the User and Systems Developer: Communication Effectiveness

In general, when there is incongruence between ideal requirements of IS and the existing capabilities, system providers need to understand and gain knowledge regarding the deficiencies/misfits which require corrective action. At the same time, any possible restrictions in attaining the goals of proposed actions are to be clearly understood. Further, when the change requests are submitted, the communication between the users and system providers needs to be meaningful. The system provider needs to understand the change request from the users. Paying personal attention to the users will enhance the trust with the IS/IT department. The existing communication procedure to request a change should be easy to understand.

Timely response to the change requests is essential for increased effectiveness in user-developer communication. Some changes are easy to make and some are not. Depending on the nature of the changes, the duration for incorporating the change will vary. The reaction to user request for changes creates a lot of learning opportunities for the system providers to know about the deficiencies of the existing system. However, they are more concerned about trading off the IS/IT resources and the number of users and their requests.

Figure 16.4 is a conceptual model for communicating technical changes to system.

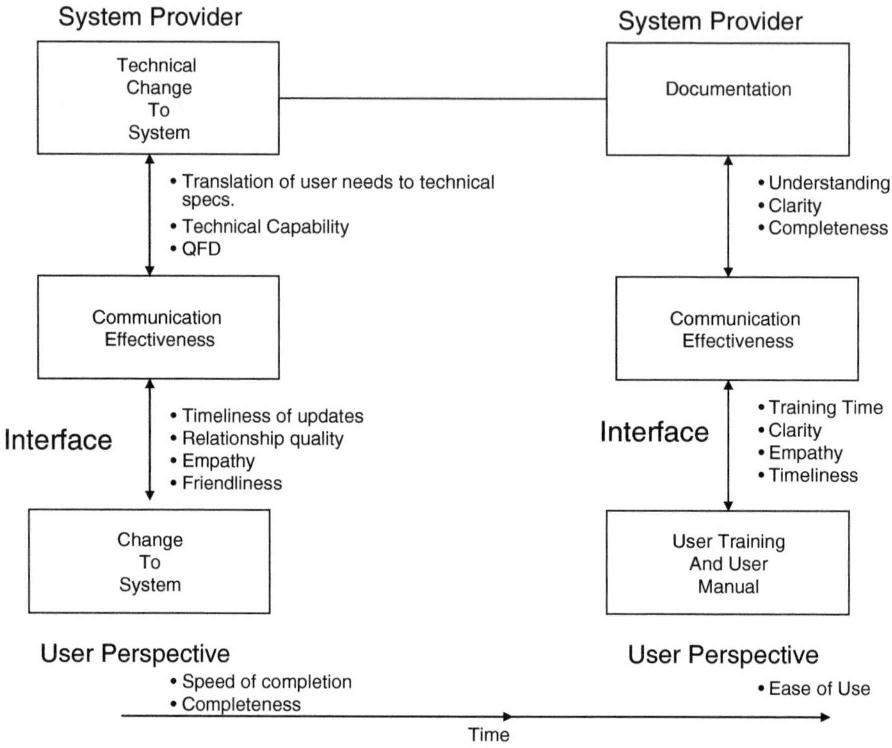

Fig. 16.4 Communicating technical changes to system

7.5 Technical Changes to System: System Provider's Perspective

It becomes necessary to design procedures to identify and remove deficiencies of an information system, and thus the IS needs to be continuously adaptive (Ackoff 1967). Accordingly, technological changes are to be carried out with the existing information systems. Lee (2003) gives the following reasons for adapting new technologies: (i) a better technology becomes available in the market, (ii) the current technology needs to be replaced by a newer version of the technology, and (iii) the current technology is incapable of meeting the user needs. Rapidly identifying the required changes in the system and developing them facilitate speeding of products to markets and add value to the customers. In incorporating technological changes, the system providers need to work toward establishing the current requirements and based on prediction work toward what might be needed tomorrow. For this purpose, the user's current and potential requirements are to be translated into technical specifications. Failure to do the forward planning may end up with dissatisfaction of the users. To alleviate this problem, users are to be involved in proposing proactive systems with respect to future systems and the ways in which the new technologies should be developed/changed. Besides, changes in users' business requirements also affect both current and ongoing development efforts. Eventually, business drives the technical changes.

Supporting resources to enable the changes is an important consideration to be made by the system developers. In most of the cases, the IS/IT budget and other available resources are constraints for the fast implementation of the proposed changes. Technological changes are to be done in compatible with whatever else was going on in the organization. For making changes in the system, Fitzgerald (1990) has proposed a technique known as "flexibility analysis." This technique is used to ascertain the likely future changes needed for an IS. To apply this technique, potential changes are identified together with the probability of occurrence and the cost of accommodating the change in the current IS. The changes are ascertained when the probability is high and the cost is low. According to this rule, not all changes can be made, but if some can, it should improve the level of flexibility. The changes, which are disregarded, have to be considered and traded off for the cost and the benefits/growth in the long term. Further, IT on its own does not inherently adapt to changes and it has to be planned, predicted, and designed to provide flexibility (FitzGerald and Siddiqui 2002). The flexibility analysis needs to be carried out with an IS to analyze the ways of changing the system in the future. In the long run, some of the changes may be small so that the IS can adapt without any extra efforts or cost. At the same time, some changes can be major ones where the resources need to be committed enormously. Obviously, not all potential changes can be handled. Some may be too difficult to accommodate and some may be not worth doing. However, the potential changes are to be considered and addressed for possible accommodation.

Over a period of time, system providers need to develop systems that will have a good fit. The changes made with any IS should fit into the overall business strategies, goals, objectives, and business processes (Kanellis and Paul 2005). The system providers make changes to the system as quick fixes in a more cost-effective way. Nonetheless, in the long run "fit" at the various levels is only a temporary phenomenon because the business is changing continually. Another problem mostly experienced by users is "technological misfit," which is referring to fast changes in technology itself making the existing technology obsolete for the users.

7.6 Changes to System: User Perspective

The changes to be made in the system need to "freeze" on the mutual agreement between the developers and users. Nonetheless, no new requirements could be introduced while system development is underway. Accordingly, the proposed technical changes are to be implemented in a speedy and in a more compete way. Though many managers welcomed the idea of applying IT for competitive advantage, they have been found that IT is often a barrier to change rather than enabler of change (FitzGerald and Siddiqui 2002). For example, with the problem of year 2000, the legacy systems were found to be disruptive. Normally, the cycles of business changes are happening much faster than the IS/IT changes. For instance, the problem of accommodating the Euro (European currency) with the existing financial systems is well known. These are a very few exceptions where IT failed to accommodate the business changes. IT has been identified as a major component of organizational flexibility and IT has been identified as a means to provide a whole range of options and possibilities to achieve the objectives of an organization (Darnton and Giacoletto 1989). Accordingly, IT plays the role of enabler as well as barrier of organizational flexibility.

7.7 Communication Effectiveness Between the User and Systems Provider

When technological changes are required, the system providers should make timely updates. Completeness in making the update in technical changes is also required. Because updating only one part of the system can lead to problems in technical performance such as compatibility. The changes made to the system, business processes/strategies supported by the system, are to be clearly communicated to the users. The problems of the users need to be understood with empathy and the communication between the user and the system provider has to take place in a friendly manner.

8 Communicating Technical Changes to System: Documentation and Training

8.1 Documentation from System Provider's Perspective

The technical changes made in the system are to be communicated clearly to the users for effective and efficient use of the technology. A clear emphasis of the technological change is the need for documentation. The steps associated with the changes and the instructions to operate the changed technology are to be clearly documented without any ambiguity. The new operating instructions about the changes made in the technology are to be given in a more understandable manner. The user documentation manuals need to be accurate, timely, easy to understand, meaningful, and helpful. In order to handle the changes, an online document system should be also developed. The changes in the documentation are to be reviewed and approved by the concerned IS/IT staff who made the changes. The instructions are to be stated clearly and controlled by a group of systems people.

Another problem faced by the users is the choice of the technical language in the documentation. When the users do not understand or are not aware of the changes, one is handicapped in the process of using the information system. There is a need to have improved tidiness with less ambiguity in instructions. Provisions are to be made to modify the document for future changes. The electronic documentation is more preferred for the reasons for easy searching, fast distribution, and consistent documentation.

8.2 User Training and User Manual in the User Perspective

In the user's perspective, a general training is required in how to use the new system. Another source of support is through user manuals where users could look up how to perform the various procedures in the newly changed technology. To supplement user training, the user manual (that could be provided upon request) could be used as reference materials, an easy-to-use and a step-by-step approach to instruct the users for using the changed system. The sequence of using the new system could help the user for effective and efficient use of the system.

9 Effectiveness in Communicating Technical Changes to Users

In preparing the users to operate the new system, creation of appropriate training programs is important. When the trail run is complete and to ensure that the system work, users are to be properly and timely instructed about the new changes. The training should take place at least few weeks in advance before the changed system/technology goes live. User manuals are to be available well in advance of going live. If necessary, the system provider should offer a help line to answer additional questions. Users need training to understand how the changes made in the system will change their routine tasks and business processes.

To alleviate this problem, a support unit such as help desk is also critical to clarify the changes after installation. Though user manuals could address all possible changes made for completeness, based on the frequently asked questions by the users, the manuals could be improved based on the experiences of the users. Online help and user manual with full tutorial with voicemail, modem support, on- and off-site trainings, and other modern support should be available to address the questions from the users. Innovative and creative approaches to user training are demanded for implementing technological changes. Since pictures are reputed to be worth a thousand words, a pictorial form of a user manual is another solution to most of the problems faced by the users. When the users are not comfortable, even the best-prepared training/user manual may face failures.

10 Conclusion

The changing environment in which an organization operates changes the information requirements of users. Organizational change capability may be inhibited if the information system cannot respond to these changing needs. The external flexibility of an information system is provided by the business and technological changes. If the environment is stable, then the information system hardly needs to be flexible and emphasize the sustainability of the current operations. On the other hand, if the business and technological changes are turbulent, then the need for realizing the flexibility will be increased. Expecting the turbulence and learning about the business and technological changes would be a first step to build flexibility in information systems.

This chapter begins to address the issue of building flexibility in information systems. Based on the review of literature, four conceptual models are given with the consideration of two different perspectives: user perspective and system provider perspective. The different components of the models are discussed. The dimensions of flexibility that can possibly measure flexibility of information systems are defined. The interface between the system provider and the user is the highlight of the conceptual models. The conceptual framework described in this chapter is intended to understand the information systems flexibility in organizations. The models will serve as a basis (i) to assess the impact of total IS flexibility on organizational change capability, (ii) to assess the capability of the existing IS in response to business and technological changes, (iii) to measure the different dimensions of IS flexibility and thereby the measurement for the IS flexibility construct, and (iv) to develop managerial guidelines on how to manage flexibility in IS in the perspectives of users and systems providers.

From these models, researchers can proceed through the testing of these models empirically for the purpose of comparing them with the reality. Thus, the models could be refined as studies built upon one another. There are several research questions that can be raised to advance the understanding of information systems flexibility for practice. Some of these questions are suggested below:

- Are the components of information systems flexibility as defined in the models relevant? Since the communication effectiveness between the user and the system provider is the highlight of these models, have all the relevant sub-components of communication effectiveness been identified?
- The proposed models assume the external environmental changes for IS are coming from business and technological requirements. An information system, which addresses only these two types of changes, can it be totally flexible? If not, what are the other types of changes hampering flexibility in information systems?
- How can dimensions of flexibility be measured as the ongoing researchers might be interested in developing measurement for the IS flexibility construct? What specific items can be used to measure the dimensions? What is the importance of these dimensions in engendering total flexibility in information systems?

- How do the dimensions relate to one another? Making changes in one dimension, does it affect the performance of the other dimension? For example, if more options are added with the information system for the improved flexibility, will it improve any other dimension of flexibility?
- What are the facilitators and barriers of building flexibility in information systems? How should they be overcome in different organizational setups? What are the facilitators and barriers of involving users in the process of building flexibility in information systems?
- How can the communication process between the user and system providers be improved? What are the barriers of the effective communication between the two?
- Empirical research is needed which gives deeper insights into what constitutes IS flexibility in various organizations and industries. Industry size, will it be a determinant for deciding the level of flexibility in information systems? For instance, the facilitators and barriers of building IS flexibility, are they same or different for SMEs and large organizations?
- The results from these studies should give implications for managers in various organizations and industries. Research must be conducted in understanding how flexibility can be managed in total and in different dimensions as business and technological changes are happening in a continuous manner. The studies could be conducted in the context of various IS types such as enterprise systems, SCM, CRM, EIS, and DSS.
- Research is needed to study the cost of building flexibility in IS for different degrees of environmental dynamism. For instance, when the uncertainty in environmental dynamism is high, there is a need for high capability in built-in flexibility in IS. What about the degree of flexibility requirement for various degrees of environmental dynamism such as risky situation? At the same time, too much flexibility is expensive. How do we optimize the cost of building flexibility in information systems? By applying this economic approach for managing flexibility in IS, what are the guidelines for practicing managers for their investment decisions for building flexibility in information systems?
- How do managers assess the flexibility of existing IS? How are managers actually addressing the question of built-in flexibility vs. flexibility to change? Future research can evolve an instrument/methodology for assessing the existing system capability. In making technical changes to IS, there is a need for developing a methodology to analyze the kind of changes that might be required over time and how those changes can be accommodated in the IS/IT.
- What are the flexibility issues in the interfacing of user and systems provider? How do we address these issues in favor of building flexibility in information systems?

This chapter has attempted to examine the question of building flexibility in information systems in organizations. The results from the above research questions have implications for managers in various organizations. Many companies are beginning to understand the concepts of managing flexibility in various types of information systems and started using the flexibility for the strategic advantage of the organization. Research must be conducted that can help in understanding how flexibility in information systems can improve strategic advantage.

References

Ackoff RL (1967) Management misinformation systems. Manage Sci 14(4):147–156
Alter AE (2000) IT leaders require strategy, flexibility. Computerworld 8(6): 36. May 8
Athey S, Schmutzler A (1995) Product and process flexibility in an innovative environment. Rand J Econs 26(4):557–574
Bahrami H (1992) The emerging flexible organization: perspectives from Silicon Valley. Calif Manage Rev 34:33–52
Behrin M, Mason G, Sharpe T (1994) Reshaping IT for business flexibility. McGraw-Hill, London
Benamati J, Lederer AL (2001) Coping with rapid changes in IT. Commun ACM 44(8):83–88
Bieberstein N, Bose S, Fiammante M, Jones K, Shah R (2006) Service-oriented architecture compass. Pearson, Upper Saddle River
Boyd BK (1995) CEO duality and firm performance: a contingency model. Strategic Manage J 16(3):301–312
Byrd TA, Turner ED (2001) An exploratory analysis of the value of the skills of IT personnel: their relationship to IS infrastructure and competitive advantage. Decis Sci 32(1):21–54
Byrd TA, Turner DE (2000) Measuring the flexibility of information technology infrastructure: exploratory analysis of a construct. J Manage Inf Syst 12(3):187–205
Chakravarthy BS (1997) A new strategy framework for coping with turbulence. Sloan Manage Rev 38(2):69–82
Ciborra CU (1993) Teams, markets, and systems, business innovation and information technology. Cambridge University Press, Cambridge
Cooprider JG, Henderson JC (1991) Technology-process fit: perspectives on achieving prototyping effectiveness. J Manage Inf Syst 7(3):67–87
Darnton G, Giacoletto S (1989) Towards an enterprise information model, DEC. GD&SD, Geneva
Dess GG, Beard DW (1984) Dimensions of organizational task environments. Adm Sci Q 29:52–73
Dixon JR (1992) Measuring manufacturing flexibility: an empirical investigation. Eur J Oper Res 60(2):131–143
Duclos LK, Vokurka RJ, Lummus RR (2003) A conceptual model of supply chain flexibility. Ind Manage Data Syst 103(5/6):446–457
Duncan NB (1995) Capturing flexibility of information technology infrastructure: a study of resource characteristics and their measure. J Manage Inf Syst 12(3):187–205
Eardley A, Avison D, Powell P (1997) Developing information systems to support flexible strategy. J Organ Comput Electron Commer 7(1):57–77
Evans JS (1991) Strategic flexibility for high technology maneuvers: a conceptual framework. J Manage Stud 28(1):69–89
Evans N (1999) Flexibility, adaptability are key to e-business. Internet Week 16(6):16.
Fitzgerald G (1990) Achieving flexible information systems: the case for improved analysis. J Inf Technol 5(1):5–11
Fitzgerald G, Siddiqui FA (2002) Business process reengineering and flexibility: a case for unification. Int J Flex Manuf Syst 14(1):73–86
Frazelle EH (1986) Flexibility: a strategic response in changing times. Ind Eng 18(3):17–20
Gebauer J, Karhade P (2004) A framework to assess the impact of information systems on the flexibility and performance of business processes. 38th Hawaii international conference on systems sciences (HICSS-38), Maui, Hawaii

Gebauer J, Schober F (2006) Information systems flexibility and the cost efficiency of business processes. J Assoc Inf Syst 7(3):122–147

Harrington RJ, Lemak DJ, Reed R, Kendall KW (2004) A question of fit: the links among environment, strategy formulation and performance. J Bus Manage 10(1):15–38

Hedberg B, Jonsson S (1978) Designing semi-confusing information systems for organizations in changing environments. Account Organ Soc 3(1):47–64

Hopper MD (1996) Complexity: the weed that could choke IS. Computerworld 30(28):37, Framingham, Jul 8

Horn P (2001) Automatic computing: IBM's perspective on the state of information technology, IBM white paper. T.J. Watson Research Center, Yorktown Heights

Iivari J (1992) The organizational 'fit' of information systems. J Inf Syst 2(3):3–29

Ives B, Mason R (1990) Can information technology revitalize your customer service? Acad Manage Exec 4(4):52–69

Jalote P (2000) CMM in practice: processes for executing software projects at Infosys. Addison-Wesley, Reading

Kanellis P, Paul RJ (2005) User behaving badly: phenomena and paradoxes from an investigation into information systems misfit. J Organ End User Comput 17(2):64–91

Kannellis P, Lycett M, Paul RJ (1999) Evaluating business information systems 'fit': from concept to practical application. Eur J Inf Syst 8(1):65–76

Lambert R, Peppard J (1993) Information technology and new organizational forms: destination but no road map? J Strateg Inf Syst 2(3):180–205

Lee G, Xia W (2005) The ability of information systems development project teams to respond to business and technology changes: a study of flexibility measures. Eur J Inf Syst 14:75–92

Lee G (2003) The flexibility and complexity of information systems development projects: conceptual frameworks, measures, and empirical tests. Published Ph.D. thesis, University of Minnesota

Leeuw AD, Volberda HW (1996) On the concept of flexibility: a dual control perspective. Omega Int J Manage Sci 24(2):121–139

Levy M, Powell P (1998) SME flexibility and the role of information systems. Small Bus Econ 11(2):183–196

Low GC, Jeffrey DR (1990) Function points in the estimation and evaluation of the software process. IEEE Trans Softw Eng 16(1):64–71

Mensah KE (1989) Evaluating information systems projects: a perspective on cost-benefit analysis. Inf Syst 14(3):205–217

Moynihan T (1990) What chief executives and senior managers want from their IT departments. MIS Q 14(1):15–35

Murray JP (2000) Reducing IT project complexity. Inf Strateg Exec J 16(3):30–38

Nadler DA, Tushman M (1979) A congruence model for diagnosing organizational behaviour. In: Kolb DA, Rubin IM, Mclntyre JM (Eds.) Organizational psychology, 3rd ed. Prentice Hall, pp 442–458

Overby S (2001) Quick change artists. CIO :90–98

Palanisamy R, Sushil (2003) Achieving organizational flexibility and competitive advantage through information systems flexibility: a path analytic study. J Inf Knowl Manage 2(3): 261–277

Patel NV, Irani Z (1999) Evaluating information technology in dynamic environments: a focus on tailorable information systems. Logist Inf Manage 12(1):32–39

Powell P (1993) Information technology and business strategy: a synthesis of the case for reverse causality. J Strateg Inf Syst 2:320–334

Prahalad CK, Krishnan MS (2002) The dynamic synchronization of strategy and information technology. MIT Sloan Manage Rev 43(4):24–33

Robey D, Boudreau MC (1999) Accounting for the contradictory organizational consequences of information technology: theoretical directions and methodological implications. Inf Syst Res 10(2):167–185

Rochester JB (1989) Building more flexible systems. I/S Analyzer 27(10):1–12

Sambamurthy V, Bharadwaj A, Grover V (2003) Shaping agility through digital options: reconceptualizing the role of information technology in contemporary firms. MIS Q 27(2):237–263
Sanchez R (1995) Strategic flexibility in product competition. Strateg Manage J 16(5):135–159
Schmidt R, Lyytinen K, Keil M, Cule P (2001) Identifying software project risks: an international Delphi study. J Manage Inf Syst 17(4):5–36
Scott K (1998) Battle complexity to add profitability. Information Week 700, Sept 14 18ER
SEI (1994) The capability maturity model: guidelines for improving software process. Addison-Wesley, New York
Sethi AK, Sethi SP (1990) Flexibility in manufacturing: a survey. Int J Flex Manufac Syst 2:289–328
Siau K, Lim E, Shen Z (2001) Mobile commerce: promises, challenges, and research agenda. J Database Manage 12(3):4–14
Soa C, Sia SK, Tay-yap J (2000) Cultural fits and misfits: is ERP a universal solution? Communic ACM 43(4):47–51
Sushil (1997) Flexible systems management: an evolving paradigm. Syst Res Behav Sci 14(4):259–275
Sushil (2000) Situation-actor-process options: mapping and enhancing flexibility. Syst Res Behav Sci 17(3):301–309
Sushil (2001) Flexibility metaphors. Syst Res Behav Sci 18(2):569–575
Trigg RH, Moran TP, Halasz FG (1987) Adaptability and tailorability in note Cards. In: Bullinger HJ, Shackel B (eds) In: Proceedings of the second IFIP conference on human-computer interaction (Interact '87), Stuttgart, North Holland, 1–4 Sept
Upton DM (1994) The management of manufacturing flexibility. Calif Manage Rev 36(2):72–89
Volberda HW (1996) Toward the flexible firm: how to remain vital in hypercompetitive environments. Organ Sci 7(4):359–372
Whiting R (2003) Money machines. Information Week 96(2): 34–44
Whitten JL, Bentley LD, Dittman KC (2001) Systems analysis and design methods. McGraw Hill, Boston

Part IV
Operations Flexibility

Chapter 17
Flexibility via Virtual Cellular System for Variability

Jainarine Bansee and Boppana V. Chowdary

1 Introduction

The manufacturing industry produces a large variety of products in order to satisfy the diverse needs of markets. This is due to the dynamic environment in which we live, informed customers who desire goods with closer tolerances (DeGarmo et al. 1997) and demand additional features (Evans and Lindsay 2005). Hence, customer satisfaction (Mason-Jones et al. 2000) is of utmost importance. As a result, manufacturing operations must be flexible to accommodate varying needs of customers. Flexible operations are responsive; they are able to react when customers make unexpected demands (Szwejczewski and Cousens 2007). It has become one of the most sought after properties in modern manufacturing systems (Shewchuk 1999) in order to handle uncertainties and variations (Ramaseh and Jayakumar 1991) in both internal and external environments.

Customers require goods and services which must be easily available with short lead time and of a high quality at competitive prices. Field trips were undertaken and discussions held with members of Trinidad and Tobago Manufacturers Association and the above is apparent within the manufacturing industry in Trinidad and Tobago (TT). The product variety which is produced in the manufacturing industries within TT is accomplished through Job Shop (JS), Flow Shop, Project, and Continuous Processes. Customers demand small quantities and in most cases one of a kind from a large variety (DeGarmo et al. 1997); hence, in today's environment the JS manufacturing operation becomes critical.

J. Bansee
The University of Trinidad and Tobago, Pt. Lisas, Trinidad and Tobago, West Indies
e-mail: jainarine.bansee@utt.edu.tt

B.V. Chowdary (✉)
The University of the West Indies, St. Augustine, Trinidad and Tobago, West Indies
e-mail: boppana.chowdary@eng.uwi.tt

Sushil and E.A. Stohr (eds.), *The Flexible Enterprise*, Flexible Systems Management,
DOI 10.1007/978-81-322-1560-8_17, © Springer India 2014

Manufacturers must be competitive and flexible in all aspects for their survival due to the turbulent environment in which they operate. They are encountering extreme difficulties (Nomden and Van Der Zee 2008; Tay and Ho 2008) such as product reliability, quality assurance, and on-time delivery (Karim et al. 2008). The competitive market place of varying demand and product mix from one period to another requires manufacturers to improve their operations and decrease their manufacturing cost (Khilwani et al. 2011; Kesen and Gungor 2011). They must improve at a faster rate if they are to become leaders in the industry. The key to their survival is getting the right product, at the right price and at the right time to the consumer (Mason-Jones et al. 2000). There has to be a shift to meet market requirement with respect to flexibility, quality, and delivery performance due to an increase in global competition. Hence, it is critical for the success of any manufacturing organization to maximize the utilization of workers, materials, and machines (DeGarmo et al. 1997).

As a result, the elimination of waste (Evans and Lindsay 2005) is a major strategy being pursued by manufactures globally. Ohno (1998) postulated that waste is what drives up cost. Waste is anything which does not add value to the product or manufacturing activity and which the customer is not willing to pay for (Womack et al. 1990), for example, jobs on a machine to be processed while major setup is being undertaken or products waiting in a queue to be processed or inspected. The elimination of these wastes is being undertaken by a culture of continuous improvement (kaizen, kanban), "pull" production, mistake proofing (poka-yoke), just in time, value stream mapping, cellular manufacturing (CM), and virtual cellular manufacturing (VCM).

Additionally, to bring about competitive advantage, flexibility together with cost, quality, and time (Szwejczewski and Cousens 2007) is now a strategic objective being pursued by international manufacturers. More so, flexibility through reconfiguration of manufacturing systems can be accomplished with low additional cost (Kesen and Gungor 2011). Therefore, for longevity and profitability of the local manufactures, more so for the JS manufactures, this practice of flexibility must be incorporated within their respective plants. It must be embedded in their operational plan and diligently followed as a strategic objective. VCM as outlined by Chowdary et al. (2005) and Slomp et al. (2005) demonstrated this flexibility and now in this research it will be further tested through a case study.

Therefore, the objective of this research is a comparison of the JS performance with the traditional CM and the new concept of VCM. This will be evaluated against shop performance measures, such as waiting time (WT), setup time (ST), and flow time (FT). This reconfiguration for flexibility will be accomplished during the shortest time and at the lowest cost, by varying the methods of production with a minimum interruption to the manufacturer.

In order to meet the objective of this research, the remainder of this chapter is arranged as follows: Sect. 2 gives a brief synopsis of manufacturing systems – JS and VCM. An overview of the manufacturing industry is highlighted in Sect. 3. A case which widely represents JS manufacturing sector in TT is evaluated in Sects. 4 and 5 adopts strategies to alleviate the problems identified. A discussion follows in Sect. 6 and the chapter ends with a conclusion in Sect. 7.

2 Manufacturing Systems

2.1 *Job Shop*

When manufacturers are required to produce a large variety of products, a number of different machinery are essential. The JS distinguishing feature is when similar production machines are grouped together according to their functionality and arranged into different departments within a plant layout (Irani and Huang 1998; Herage 1994; Shafer and Charnes 1993). Maximum flexibility can be achieved with JS layout. This is evident when products of small lot sizes are required to be manufactured from a large variety. However, during major setup on the machines, waste is incurred in the form of time when dissimilar parts are manufactured utilizing the same machine. Based on a review (Bansee 2012), the advantages and disadvantages associated with JS layout are identified beneath.

Advantages associated with JS are:

- Production of large variety of products in small quantities
- High utilization of machines through overlapping
- High flexibility in allocating operations to alternative machines
- Flexibility to adapt to changes in customer requirement
- Quick adjustment to the manufacturing of new products

However, the disadvantages associated with JS are:

- Long wait time (WT)
- Long setup time (ST)
- Long flow time (FT) due to material flows through complicated routes
- High work-in-process (WIP) levels
- High material handling costs

2.2 *Virtual Cellular Manufacturing*

VCM follows on from CM; hence, it utilizes the principles and philosophy of group technology (GT) (Chang et al. 1998) for the formation of families of parts. In the formation of these families, there should be the avoidance to the addition of new machinery while at the same time the existing machinery within the JS should be efficiently utilized. VCM affords us to minimize job ST through pooling synergy of machines (Kesen and Gungor 2011; Suresh and Meredith 1994). Implementation of the VCM layout will resemble the traditional JS layout which still exists in majority of companies globally. There is no reconfiguration of the machines and departments; they remain in the same physical location (Kesen and Gungor 2011; Chowdhary et al. 2005). That is, the machines within the existing department are retained. Accessibility to machines is available to more than one cell, hence, the efficient utilization of resources through machine overlapping (Khilwani et al. 2011).

Based on the processing requirements for the family of parts, the appropriate machinery will be identified for the virtual cells. Remember these cells configuration will only be in the minds of the workers. The machines are only temporarily dedicated to the cells. Once the part family processing has been completed, the cells are disbanded and are free to associate themselves with other cells for the processing of other families. This reformatting of cells facilitates quick changes in customer's requirement at relatively no cost to the manufacture in terms of plant layout, thus affording them the benefits of volume and mix flexibility (Szwejczewski and Cousens 2007). The VCM concept utilized the steps within the model by Bansee and Chowdary (2007).

3 Industry Overview

In order to assist in the identification of common problems and a basis for the generation of common solutions, interviews and discussions were held. Additionally, observations were made to the actual way in which firms operated in TT. As a result of the various processes which were being undertaken by the respective manufacturers, it was observed that wastage was being incurred on the shop floor. We can conclude that the majority of customers were not satisfied due to delays, to which the customers are asked to pay more prices. This conclusion is further reinforced by the first author who has over 20 years of personal experience working in a JS environment at a state company. However, based on an extensive literature search and field visits, factors which contribute to a number of difficulties inclusive of delays are categorized as management and operational levels issues and are listed below.

3.1 Management Issues

- No documented or adopted policy that is strictly followed in terms of job scheduling (Flynn and Jacobs 1987)
- Lack of strategic planning for machinery replacement and upgrades (Shafer and Charnes 1993)
- Low reliability of plant and machinery due to lack of any scientific maintenance program which results in equipment breakdown and unavailability and leads to additional waiting time (Conner 2001)
- Insufficient training pertaining to new operational techniques and advancement of skills for employees (Conner 2001)
- No strategic succession program for continuity of effective and efficient operations
- A low level of employee moral due to an absence of motivation and compensation (Shafer and Charnes 1993)

3.2 Operational Issues

- Due to implementation of the nonscientific methods of material handling and the arrangement of facilities within JS, delays in movement of materials occur.
- Due to insufficient information on the job sheet, consequently operators often seek clarification, resulting in delays.
- The amount of time taken to setup jobs is resulting in further job delays and leads to high WIP inventory.

All these delays lead to a high FT and low system utilization. An evaluation of the above issues within the local manufacturing industry demonstrates that there is wastage in resources, inclusive of time. All of the above contribute to the frustration which customers have to incur – when they have to suspend their individual operations. This results in difficulties to their own consumers and intricacy in retaining them. Additionally, there is loss of revenue and profit to both customers and manufacturers. Hence, to mitigate these issues an alternative mode of JS operation like VCM which facilitates configuration flexibility is taken up in this research for investigation purposes. Recognizing across the manufacturing industry that most of the customer's order delays occurred at the operational level, it will be a good starting point to reduce such delays at this level, in order to improve the shop performance through machine scheduling flexibility.

4 Evaluation of Case Study

4.1 Job Shop Layout

For this research, a manufacturer operation, which widely represents the JS manufacturing sector in TT, is evaluated. The manufacturing operation within the existing JS is accomplished by 21 machines arranged in nine (9) functional departments. Eight (8) machines are currently not in operation and are not included in this research. Table 17.1 identifies the quantity of machines to each department and a schematic layout of the arrangement of the existing machines is shown in Fig. 17.1.

4.2 Processing Operation

All jobs are held in a waiting queue when they arrive in the JS. The jobs are then accessed in order to determine their operational requirements. Thereafter, the jobs are sequenced through the appropriate departments based on their operational requirements. The scheduling of the jobs is determined on the basis of first in, first out (FIFO), otherwise on job criticality.

Table 17.1 Machine allocation to departments

	Machine type		
Departments (D)	Name	Number	Machine code used in the study
1	Lathe	10	M3, M4, M5, M6, M7, M8, M9, M10, M11, M12
2	Drills	1	M15
3	Milling	3	M17, M18, 19
4	Boring	2	M20, M21
5	Grinding	1	M25
6	Shapers	1	M26
7	Band saw	1	M27
8	Slotting machine	1	M28
9	Reblading machine	1	M29
Total		21	

Legend: M3, M4... M29 – Machine3, Machine 4... Machine 29

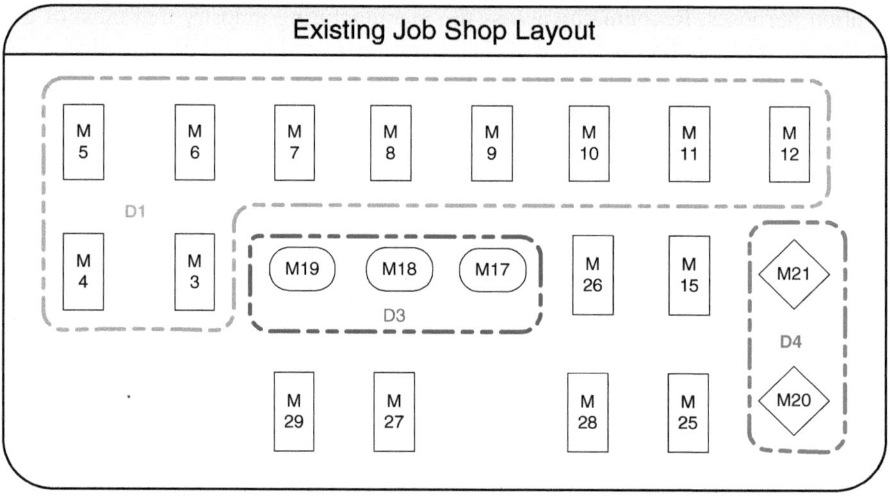

Fig. 17.1 Job Shop layout (Departments 1, 2 ...9, and M3, M4... M29, corresponds to Table 17.1)

The first available machine within a department is utilized for jobs which have been sequenced for manufacturing operation. If required, the job then proceeds to the next sequence department for its second operation and again uses the first free machine which is available in that department and continues so until all the manufacturing operations are completed. When a second operation is required and a machine is available, scheduling is based on the initial job which was scheduled to the first operation, and not necessarily the job which arrive to JS first. However, this does not apply if a latter schedule job can be completed in its second processing department before the earlier job arrives in that department.

Prior to any processing operation, some ST is encountered as jobs enter a department. However, if the same machine is used for a subsequent job which is similar to the first job, no major setup is required. On the other hand if the job is dissimilar to the first one, a major setup is required prior to processing. This continues for all jobs, using a range of machines within the functional departments. For the jobs considered in this research, job setup times and processing times are given in Appendix 6. In this research no minor setup time is considered and job handling time is ignored.

4.3 Data Acquisition and Analysis

Job requests were acquired from the company records which were placed by clients from October 1, 2010, to September 30, 2011. A 12-month period was chosen because it is most likely that the company will receive similar type of jobs in the following 12 months. For the period identified, 1,325 job requests were made by clients. This data was filtered to represent the jobs that were specifically assigned to the JS. The number of jobs that were assigned to the JS was 696.

The company management emphasized that efforts should be concentrated where the most financial benefit can be derived. Hence, the jobs were ranked according to their Annual Revenue Value (ARV). Eighteen jobs, which contributed more than $50,000 of revenue towards the company, were chosen for evaluation purposes. These jobs are identified as J-1 to J-18 in Appendix 6 and will form the basis of this research.

The 18 jobs to be manufactured required processing in 1–3 departments. The sequences of processing through their respective departments are shown in Appendix 6. For example, for J-1 the number of processing departments is three and the sequence of departments at which processing takes place is from 7 to 1 to 4. The progression of events follow the same format as described. For the 18 jobs selected, the ST and PT are given in Appendix 6. The JS under review operated 5 days per week for 8 h per day and 1 day for 4 h. The resulting calculation gives jobs inter-arrival time of approximately 3 h. The 18 jobs will be rearranged based on their actual arrival order for scheduling within the JS, as shown in Appendix 6.

These 18 jobs under study are scheduled through the existing JS system at an inter-arrival rate of three hours and the processing activities are presented in Appendix 6. A sample description of these activities is at row 4 and column 14 for J-3: the cell represents that at 20 h J-3 setup and processing is completed on M27 in department 7 and move to department 4 and loaded on M20; and at row 7 and column 1, J-6 is loaded on M3 in department 1. The progression of activities follow the same format as described. The results (the average times in hours) for the 18 jobs that were processed through the existing JS system are shown in Table 17.2.

In order to improve the existing system, two cellular strategies will be adopted and analyzed for the data in the next section.

Table 17.2 Results of the existing JS system

Description	Average time (hours)
Wait time	11.11
Setup time	5.67
Processing time	18.72
Flow time	35.5

5 Adoption of Strategies

The company's operational efficiency must increase for improvement of customer satisfaction. In order to achieve this and the objectives previously set, there must be adoption of new strategies. These strategies will be explained and then evaluated.

5.1 Cellular Manufacturing

CM involves the processing of jobs within dedicated cells. As a result the existing JS layout at the company will have to be reconfigured to a cellular layout. Utilizing the principles and philosophy of GT, the individual jobs will be classified. This classification into families will be based on similarities in the processing requirement for the jobs. The machines required to accomplish the processing requirement will be determined. Hence, the requirement for the cell configuration will be established.

Within the physical layout, the various cells location will be identified, and the previously established cell configuration will be installed. That is, the existing JS layout will be reconfigured to accommodate the cells. With CM the machines are permanently dedicated to the assigned cell. Based on the scheduling policy, the various jobs will be dispatch to the appropriate cells for manufacturing utilizing the concept of processing families of parts. The scheduling policy adopted is FIFO; therefore, this will be used in this research.

In analyzing the data, the 18 jobs were grouped into four families and were assigned into four cells. For the families of parts, the machines have been identified based on the departments at which processing takes place. It will be considered that all machines within the same category have the same capability. This will avoid variation in cycle time and prevent the desire to duplicate machines of the same category of various capabilities within the same cell.

Based on the configuration developed, it is recognized that there is a need for additional machines. However, there will be excess machines within some department. In order to create the cells with the appropriate machines, where additional machines are required, they will be introduced. By following this methodology, the four families and machines were allocated to four cells as shown in Table 17.3.

The three (3) additional machines which will be needed to facilitate the formation of the respective cells are Cell-B one band saw and Cell-C and Cell-D one boring machine each. These additional machines are referred as M32, M30, and M31.

Table 17.3 Allocation of families and machines to cells

Family	Cell	Machines
A	Cell-A	M27, M3, M20
B	Cell-B	M21, M32, M4
C	Cell-C	M30, M5
D	Cell-D	M6, M17, M31, M15

Legend: M3, M4… M29 – existing machines
M30, M31, M32 – new machines

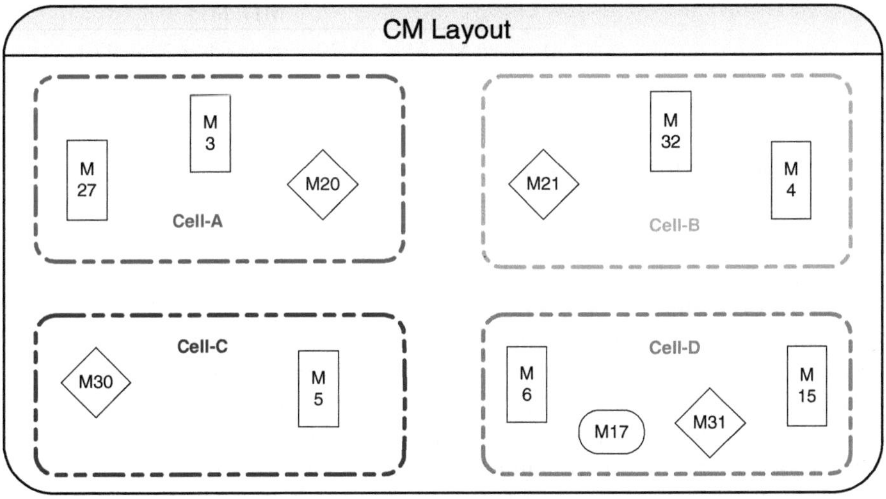

Fig. 17.2 Machine allocation in cellular layout

The seven (7) unutilized machines in the cell formation are six lathes (M7, M8, M9, M10, M11, and M12) and one milling machine (M11). These machines can be used for other purposes. The cellular layout with the respective machines assigned to cells is shown in Fig. 17.2.

Using the data for ST and PT and with an inter-arrival time for the jobs of three hours, these 18 jobs will be scheduled through the cellular layout based on the strategy adopted in the preceding section and the result are observed. Again, this scheduling will be based on the actual arrival pattern of the jobs. It should be recalled that ST only occurs the very first time the part family is processed on the machine within a cell. These results for the processing activities for the CM system for the jobs are shown in Appendix 7. A sample description of these activities is at row 2 and column 8 for J-1; the cell represents that at 3 h J-1 setup and processing is completed on M27 in Cell-A and move to M3 in Cell-A; and at row 5 and column 1 for J-4, the cell represents that at 9 h J-4 is loaded on M30 in Cell-C. The progression of activities follow the same format as described. The results (the average times in hours) for the 18 jobs that were processed through the CM system are shown in Table 17.4.

Table 17.4 Results for the CM system

Description	Average time (hours)
Wait time	9.5
Setup time	1.44
Processing time	18.72
Flow time	29.67

Table 17.5 Allocation of families and machines to virtual cells

Family	Virtual cell	Machines
AB	VC-AB	M27, M3, M4, M5, M6, M7, M20
CD	VC-CD	M21, M8, M9, M10, M11, M12, M17, M15

Legend: M3, M4..., M29 corresponds to Table 17.1

5.2 *Virtual Cellular Manufacturing*

The utilization of the concept of VCM affords us with a number of options for the formation of families for the various jobs to be process. These options can be based on the number of families, pooling time of families, size of families, similarities in the processing requirement, due date, and family releasing mechanism. For this research, the formation of families is based on similarities in the processing requirement.

Since VCM follows CM, the family formation used for CM will initially be the same for VCM. However, as it pertains to pooling synergy of machines, the 18 jobs were classified only into two families of parts, as our strategy, compared to CM where four families have been created. These two families resulted from the merging of the families of parts. Family type B were merged with A to form virtual cell AB (VC-AB), and family type D were merged with C to form virtual cell CD (VC-CD). This resulted in two families and two virtual cells. The reduction in families with VCM affords us to minimize job ST. Also, the configuration risk will be reduced due to minimum disruption to the JS operations. By following this methodology and with the emphasis on maximum utilization of machinery, these families will be assigned to VC-AB and VC-CD, as shown in Table 17.5.

The layout with the respective machines assigned to VC-AB and VC-CD is shown in Fig. 17.3.

Families will be released to the JS virtual cells for processing when they are formed. That is, when jobs arrive into the shop, they are evaluated to determine which family they belong to and are assigned to their respective family queue. The minimum size of the family considered for this study is two jobs. The company consented for the size of the family to have a minimum of two jobs. However, the maximum WT for the formation of a family from when the job first arrives in the shop until it is released to the JS is 9 h.

The initial order of arrival will be used together with the ST and PT for the manufacturing of jobs. As it pertains to the addition of jobs to the formed family – if a family has been scheduled and is processing within the virtual cells and another family

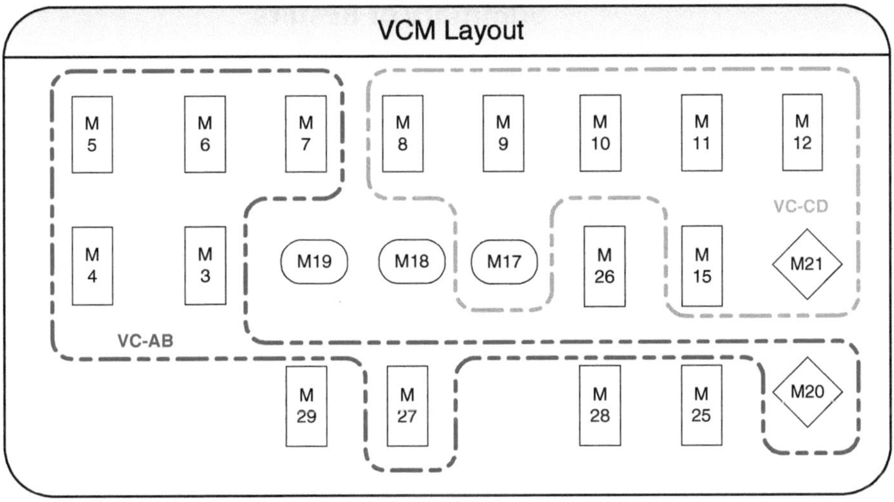

Fig. 17.3 Virtual cellular layout (Departments 1, 2 …6 and M3, M4… M29 corresponds to Table 17.1)

Table 17.6 Results for the VCM system

Description	Average time (hours)
Wait time	7.89
Setup time	1.28
Processing time	18.72
Flow time	27.89

part arrives in the shop – it joins the family for processing to save ST. With respect to re-routing – if a latter job can be completed in the second process before the earlier job arrives to the workstation within the cell – the latter job can be processed.

For the VCM system the processing activities is presented in Appendix 8 for the 18 jobs. A sample description of these activities is at row 3 and column 9 for J-2; the cell represents that at 19 h J-2 setup and processing is completed on M8 in VC-CD and move to M17 within the same cell; and at row 5 and column 6, J-4 is loaded on M21 in VC-CD. The progression of activities follow the same format as described. The results (the average times in hours) for the 18 jobs that were processed through the VCM system are shown in Table 17.6.

6 Discussion

A summary of the results derived from an assessment of the strategies adopted, together with the present strategy being followed by the company, is shown in Fig. 17.4. This summary is based on the following shop performance measures:

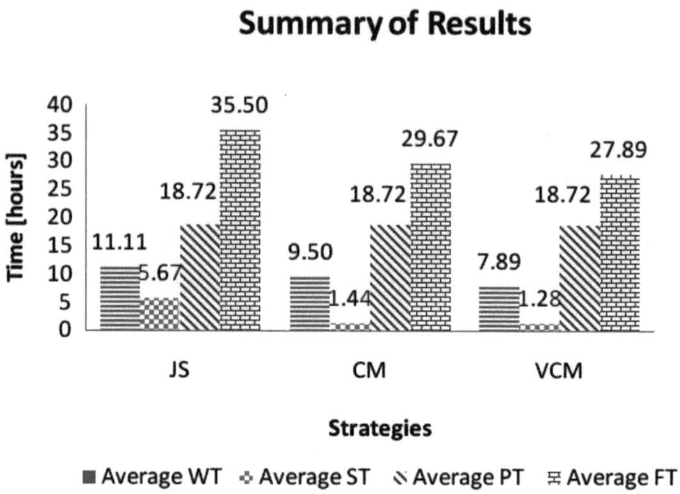

Fig. 17.4 Summary of results

Table 17.7 Analysis of results in terms of percentage

Items	Shop performance measures	Strategies		
		CM vs. JS	VCM vs. JS	VCM vs. CM
1	Waiting time	14.5 % decrease	29 % decrease	17 % decrease
2	Setup time	74.5 % decrease	77.5 %	11.5 %
3	Processing time	Same	Same	Same
4	Flow time	16.4 % decrease	21.4 % decrease	6 % decrease

WT, ST, PT, and FT. Corresponding to Fig. 17.4, the average WT for the 18 jobs for the existing strategy is 11.11 h, whereas for the adopted strategies of CM, 9.5 h and VCM 7.89 h, respectively.

An analysis of the above results is shown in a tabulated format in Table 17.7. Both ST and WT showed a decrease of 74.5 % and 14.5 % for CM when compared with the JS. The effect of this resulted in a decrease of the FT by 16.4 % with the CM strategy. However, as described previously, there are problems with the implementation of CM strategy. Foremost is a considerable amount of capital which must be invested. This will be used for shop reconfiguration and the purchase of additional machines. With CM the machines are permanently dedicated to the cells (Irani and Huang 1998). Every time the products mix changes, the CM layout will have to be reconfigured. Therefore, this type of manufacturing system is impractical (Flynn and Jacobs 1987).

The VCM system showed a decrease with the ST and WT of 77.5 % and 29 %, respectively, when compared with JS. The cumulative effect of this resulted in a decrease of the FT by 21.4 % with the VCM strategy. With VCM there is no reconfiguration of the JS. The existing JS layout remains the same when implementation of VCM occurs. No new machinery is purchased and added to the current shop. Comparing the VCM system with the CM system, as the data shows, also resulted in decreases in ST, WT, and FT by 11.5 %, 17 %, and 6 %, respectively. These results verify that between the VCM and the CM layouts, the VCM layout is superior as supported by Bansee (2012). As a result, the existing strategy must clearly be changed in order to enhance customer satisfaction.

7 Conclusion

Due to delays in the delivery of customer's orders by JS manufacturers, the customers are dissatisfied. This is felt in terms of inconvenience to their respective customers and in their balance sheet in terms of profit. The main driver of the economy of TT is the energy sector. They are the major revenue earners for the JS manufacturers. As a result, the JS manufacturers must change their existing strategy and adopt an alternative mode of JS operation, such as VCM for their survival.

As a study, a JS setup was analyzed and two cellular strategies were adapted. The results were compared. The comparison revealed superior results for both the CM and VCM strategies in terms of ST when compared against the existing JS strategy. Additionally, there was a reduction in WT and hence an overall decrease in FT for the CM and VCM. Furthermore, the results also revealed that the VCM strategy was better than the CM strategy and which makes it very attractive for manufacturers to adopt.

Successful implementation of VCM to an existing JS layout brings benefits such as reduction in WT, ST, and FT. The effects of this reduction result in a drastic decline in WIP and afford the availability of the system, that is, increase in system utilization. Furthermore, reliability with customer due date delivery is enhanced. Additionally, the existing JS layout is retained. There is no capital investment for reconfiguration of the shop as compared to CM. VCM is flexible in assigning jobs and the virtual cells can be rearranged very rapidly. Additionally, this system affords the quick adaptation to changes in both product mix and volume.

References

Bansee J (2012) Flexibility with virtual cellular systems – improvement to job shops. LAP LAMBERT Academic Publishing, Germany

Bansee J, Chowdary BV (2007) A new concept of cellular manufacturing: a case study. Fifth LACCEI International Latin American and Caribbean Conference for Engineering and Technology, LACCEI, Tampico, pp 1–10

Chang T-C, Wysk RA, Wang HP (1998) Computer aided manufacturing, 2nd edn. Prentice Hall, Upper Saddle River

Chowdhary BV, Slomp J, Suresh NC (2005) A new concept of virtual manufacturing. West Indian J Eng 28(1):45–60

Conner G (2001) Lean manufacturing for the small shop. Soc Manuf Eng, Dearborn

DeGarmo PE, Black JT, Kohser R (1997) Materials and processes in manufacturing, 8th edn. Prentice Hall, Upper Saddle River

Evans JR, Lindsay WM (2005) The management and control of quality, 6th edn. Thomson South-Western, Mason

Flynn BB, Jacobs FR (1987) Applications and implementation: an experimental comparison of cellular (group technology) layout with process layout. Decis Sci 18(4):562–581

Herage SS (1994) Group technology and cellular manufacturing. IEEE Trans Syst Man Cybern 24(2):203–214

Irani SA, Huang H (1998) Layout modules: a novel extension of hybrid cellular layouts. ASME international mechanical engineering congress and exposition, Anaheim, pp 15–20

Karim MA, Smith AJ, Halgamuge S (2008) Emperical relationships between some manufacturing practices and performance. Int J Prod Res 46(13):3583–3623

Kesen SE, Gungor Z (2011) How important is the batch splitting activity in scheduling of virtual manufacturing cells (VMCs). Int J Prod Res 49(6):1645–1667

Khilwani N, Ulutas BH, Islier AA (2011) A methodology to design virtual cellular manufacturing systems. J Intell Manuf 22(4):533–544

Mason-Jones R, Naylor B, Towill DR (2000) Lean, agile or leagile? Matching your supply chain to the marketplace. Int J Prod Res 34(17):4061–4070

Nomden G, Van Der Zee DJ (2008) Virtual cellular manufacturing: configuring routing flexibility. Int J Prod Econ 112:439–451

Ohno T (1998) Toyota production system. Production Press, Cambridge

Ramaseh RV, Jayakumar MD (1991) Measurement of manufacturing flexibility: a value-based approach. J Oper Manag 10(4):446–468

Shafer SM, Charnes JM (1993) Cellular versus functional layouts under a variety of shop operating conditions. Deci Sci 24(3):665–681

Shewchuk SM (1999) A Set of generic flexibility measures for manufacturing applications. Int J Prod Res 37(13):3017–3042

Slomp J, Chowdary BV, Suresh NC (2005) Design of virtual manufacturing cells: a mathematical programming approach. Robot Comput Integr Manuf 18(3):273–288

Suresh NC, Meredith JR (1994) Coping with the loss of pooling synergy in cellular manufacturing systems. Manag Sci 40(4):466–483

Szwejczewski M, Cousens A (2007) Increasing flexibility: what is your options? Manage Serv 51(1):17–20

Tay JC, Ho NB (2008) Evolving dispatching rules genetic programming for solving multi-objective flexible Job-shop problems. Comput Ind Eng 51(1):17–20

Womack JP, Jones D, Roos D (1990) The machine that changed the world. Free Press, New York

Chapter 18
Role of Manpower Flexibility in Lean Manufacturing

T.P. Singh

1 Introduction

In today's highly competitive market, survival of a manufacturing organization depends upon its ability to introduce new and improved products while containing their prices within competitive range. Cost cutting through process improvement has assumed a great importance in all kinds of manufacturing organizations. Minimizing wastage of resources and moving towards implementation of lean manufacturing have become key strategies to achieve cost cutting. Lean manufacturing encompasses five interdependent principles: value definition, value stream analysis, flow, JIT/pull, and perfection. "Value definition" involves finding out the customer requirements, giving due weights to these requirements, and bringing them into product designs. "Value stream analysis" takes care of the design of the process to add value to the product in accordance with the customer requirements in the intended products. This value stream or production process is designed for transformation efficiency and effectiveness. The emphasis is on the performance of value-added activities and minimizing non-value-added activities. "Flow" demands that the processes are so reliable that the transformation process goes on uninterrupted. "JIT or pull" requires that the production is carried out only when there is a confirmed customer order. The last principle of lean manufacturing, "perfection," ensures that all four aforementioned principles are perfectly implemented.

Successful implementation of lean manufacturing requires sophisticated flexible numerically controlled machines; use of latest technology, systems, and procedures of work; standardization; multi-skilled flexible work force; and so on. In this chapter, the importance of manpower flexibility for implementing lean manufacturing is highlighted.

T.P. Singh (✉)
Symbiosis Institute of Technology, Symbiosis International University,
Pune, Maharashtra, India
e-mail: tp_malik@yahoo.com

Sushil and E.A. Stohr (eds.), *The Flexible Enterprise*, Flexible Systems Management,
DOI 10.1007/978-81-322-1560-8_18, © Springer India 2014

In traditional mass manufacturing, there were specialized workers who were managed. The objective was to use their physical strength. They needed a great deal of supervision. Lean manufacturing, on the other hand, needs flexible workforce who have multiple skills and are responsible. The aim is to use their intellect along with their physical strength. The workers need to be empowered and supervision reduced, and officers need to devote time to high-end jobs. In lean manufacturing, the jobs are broader and the workers can derive pleasure and pride by performing these jobs.

While trying to find the reasons why Japanese flexible manufacturing system outperforms its counterpart in the USA, Jaikumar (1989) discovered that labor flexibility has proved the key to the success of flexible manufacturing systems in Japan. Browne et al. (1988) also note that in search of flexibility, Western countries are often technology driven, while Japanese not only strive for technological improvements but also utilize flexible workforce. Labor flexibility can be enhanced through the management of workers' intellectual development such as multidiscipline training and job rotation.

Labor flexibility refers to the ability of the workforce to attain new skills and change jobs as and when required. Chen et al. (1992) define labor flexibility as the ability of the workforce to perform a broad range of manufacturing tasks effectively. Labor flexibility is the ease of moving personnel to different departments of an organization, and it is achieved by the aptitude of multi-trained staff to carry out a wide variety of tasks (Tsourveloudis and Phillis 1998). A flexible workforce is especially valuable in responding to the design changes and new product introduction. With labor flexibility, well-trained multifunctional operators can be allocated to different work centers or redeployed to practice setups and other maintenance tasks. Higher labor flexibility provides enhanced productivity and quality (Hung 1993; Franchini et al. 2001; Zulch et al. 2004).

Labor flexibility has been recognized as a tool for enhancing manufacturing performance in manufacturing systems, since it provides several strategic advantages (Nagarur and Azeem 1999). The use of a multifunctional workforce allows the firm to respond quickly to unexpected and unbalanced demands that may arise in the concern. Such flexibility helps the firm to reduce manufacturing flow times and work-in-process inventories and improves their customer service while providing an efficient use of both labor and equipment (Polakoff 1991). In general, firms pursuing high divisions of labor, and therefore fostering specialized skills in their workers, will tend to be less flexible than firms relying on a more broadly trained worker that can adapt more quickly to new products or product changes or to new technologies. Treleven (1989), Jaikumar (1989), Chen et al. (1992), and Bobrowski and Park (1993) have discussed various dimensions of labor flexibility like multiple skills and range of manufacturing tasks. Labor flexibility can be measured from various indicators in the organization (Koste and Malhotra 1999; Koste et al. 2004).

Gupta et al. (2001) carried out a study to assess the role of labor flexibility in improving productivity in engineering industry. In this study, a questionnaire survey of engineering industry was carried out which was followed by detailed case studies in some selected organizations. The information collected from the industry was used to calculate the values of labor flexibility and productivity. Correlation analysis depicted strong correlation of labor flexibility with productivity. Another study by Khamba et al. (2001) demonstrated a positive contribution of improving various kinds of flexibilities, including labor flexibility, towards technology management. Garg et al. (2002) analyzed the role of manpower in the management of change and concluded that improvement in manpower flexibility facilitates management of change. Chauhan and Singh (2011) presented a comprehensive review of literature on labor flexibility, lean manufacturing, and their relationship.

Based on these and many other studies on manpower flexibility, it can be hypothesized that manpower flexibility has a strong correlation with lean manufacturing. The present study is undertaken to test the hypothesis and to ascertain the strength of relationship.

2 The Study

The study was carried out in small-scale auto parts industry of Punjab in India. The methodology adopted includes the following:

(a) Preparation of a questionnaire covering various aspects of labor flexibility and lean manufacturing and its pretesting
(b) Collection of data through personal visits
(c) Analysis of data and assessing the following:

   i. Status of each aspect of labor flexibility
   ii. Status of each aspect of lean manufacturing
   iii. Status of each company in all aspects of labor flexibility taken together
   iv. Status of each company in all aspects of lean manufacturing taken together
   v. Correlation between various parameters of labor flexibility and lean manufacturing

A questionnaire was specially designed to collect data on various aspects of labor flexibility and lean manufacturing. These aspects are given in Tables 18.1 and 18.2. The tables also contain the codes given to the aspects. The codes have been used for carrying out statistical analysis of the collected data.

Considering the nature of various kinds of wastes to be measured to assess the status of lean manufacturing, it was decided to collect data from various industrial firms by personal visits and observations. The number of firms from where the data was collected was restricted to only ten. The questionnaire contained in all 30 questions on various aspects of labor flexibility. There were 18 questions on various types of wastes. In addition to the questions, data collected through personal observations and descriptions given in the questionnaire was made use of for determining the status of various major aspects of labor flexibility and lean manufacturing.

Status of lean manufacturing was found out from the levels of seven kinds of wastes. Table 18.2 depicts these seven categories along with the codes given to each category.

Table 18.1 Various aspects of labor flexibility

S. No.	Aspect	Code
i	Ability of the workers to work on various machines	LF1
ii	Skill levels of workers to perform on different jobs	LF2
iii	Cooperation of workers in achieving production targets	LF3
iv	Attitude of workers towards change	LF4
v	Training of workers	LF5
vi	Changes in the workforce strength over a period of time	LF6
vii	Ability of production workers to perform inspection jobs	LF7
viii	Extent of autonomous maintenance carried out by workers	LF8
ix	Job designs	LF9

Table 18.2 Various aspects of lean manufacturing

S. No.	Aspect	Code
i	Correction, that is, repairs or rework	LM1
ii	Motion, any wasted motion to pick up parts or stack parts	LM2
iii	Overproduction, producing more than needed, before it is needed	LM3
iv	Conveyance, wasted effort to transport materials, parts, or finished goods into or out of storage or between processes	LM4
v	Inventory, maintaining excess inventory of raw materials, parts in process or finished goods	LM5
vi	Processing, doing more work than is necessary	LM6
vii	Waiting, any non-work time, waiting for tools, supplies, parts, etc.	LM7

Each question on labor flexibility and lean manufacturing had five options and, thus, a score from one to five. From these scores the percentage score achieved by each broader aspect of labor flexibility and lean manufacturing has been worked out.

Tables 18.3 and 18.4 depict the percentage scores of various aspects of labor flexibility as well as lean manufacturing, respectively. These scores have been worked out from the raw scores collected from the response of the questionnaire using the following formula:

$$\text{Percentage score} = \frac{\sum Sa_i}{nSm} \times 100$$

where Sa_i is the average score of a subarea which is further equal to $\frac{\sum S_i n_j}{N}$, Si is the score of a company in a subarea (i varies from 1 to 5), nj is the number of companies securing that score where $\sum nj = N$ is the total number of companies, and Sm is the maximum score of a subarea, that is, 5.

From the percentage score of each aspect of labor flexibility and lean manufacturing for each of the ten companies, the following have been worked out:

i. Average score of each aspect of labor flexibility in all the ten companies taken together
ii. Average score of each aspect of lean manufacturing in all the ten companies taken together.

Table 18.3 Percentage scores of companies in various aspects of labor flexibility

	Percentage score									
Firm/company	LF 1	LF 2	LF 3	LF 4	LF 5	LF 6	LF 7	LF 8	LF 9	LF
1	45	49	68	64	68	65	52	28	67	56.22
2	47	52	65	60	65	64	53	28	63	55.22
3	65	67	81	67	77	74	60	44	69	67.11
4	39	44	70	60	69	62	50	29	64	54.11
5	55	56	77	67	74	72	57	42	70	63.33
6	57	59	80	68	78	75	56	43	72	65.33
7	57	58	83	59	76	70	50	41	61	61.66
8	64	66	80	58	80	74	61	47	71	66.44
9	53	56	78	60	72	63	52	27	62	58.33
10	38	41	68	57	61	61	49	24	61	51.11
Avg	52	55	75	62	72	68	54	35	65	59.7

Table 18.4 Percentage scores of companies in various aspects of lean manufacturing

	Percentage score							
Firm/company	LM 1	LM 2	LM 3	LM 4	LM 5	LM 6	LM 7	LM
1	72	67	75	68	62	76	60	68.5
2	70	63	71	69	60	70	56	65.57
3	78	73	83	76	61	84	65	74.28
4	69	62	70	67	58	68	55	64.14
5	75	71	80	73	57	80	67	71.86
6	73	69	82	77	61	82	70	73.42
7	72	68	75	69	55	78	68	69.28
8	77	72	84	77	58	80	64	73.14
9	74	70	70	74	60	78	63	69.85
10	64	58	65	60	52	63	54	59.57
Avg.	72.4	67.3	75.5	71	58.4	75.9	62.2	68.96

iii. Average score of each company in all aspects of labor flexibility taken together
iv. Average score of each company in all aspects of lean manufacturing taken together

From these average scores, the status of each aspect of labor flexibility and lean manufacturing and the status of each company with regard to labor flexibility and lean manufacturing have been worked out. A brief explanation of these is given in the subsequent sections.

3 Labor Flexibility

In this section, status of each aspect and that of each company in labor flexibility have been discussed.

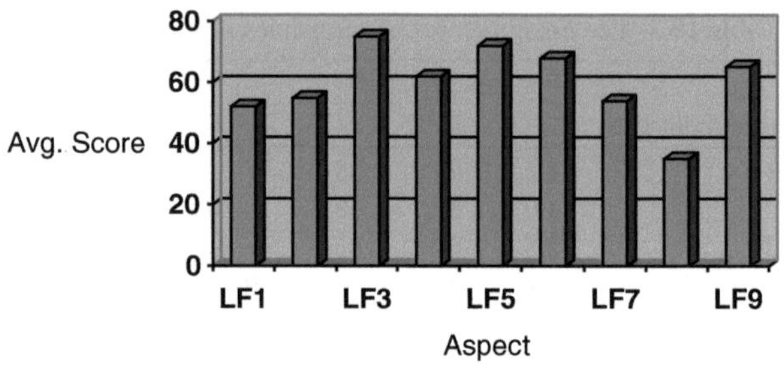

Fig. 18.1 Average scores of various aspects of labor flexibility

3.1 Status of Each Aspect

Figure 18.1 depicts the status of various aspects of labor flexibility pictorially. A close look at percentage score of various companies in labor flexibility depicts that workers try to cooperate in general in achieving production targets (75 %) but this cooperation is limited to the activities to be carried out within the mutually agreed upon rules and regulations. Low scores of "Ability of the worker to work on various machines" (52 %) and on various jobs (55 %) amply support this view. Although a fair amount of training is being imparted (72 %), multi-skilling of workers does not look to be of a good order.

Two other important aspects which have become very crucial in today's industry, that is, "Ability of production workers to perform inspection jobs" and "Extent of autonomous maintenance carried out by workers," are found to be at a poor level with scores of 54 % and 35 %, respectively. This dictates the need to reorient education and training and carefully implementing techniques like Total Productive Maintenance (TPM) and Total Quality Management (TQM). By giving equal weightage to all above major aspects, an average percentage score for manpower flexibility has been worked out to be 59.7 %. Further, scores of all the 10 companies in various aspects of manpower flexibility and lean manufacturing have been worked out. Table 18.3 presents the details.

3.2 Status of Various Companies

Scatter diagram of Fig. 18.2 shows the status of various companies in labor flexibility. It is observed that the variation in the average scores of the companies is not very large, the lowest score being 51.11 % and the highest 67.11 %. In case of the average score of various aspects in all the companies taken together, the variation between the lowest score (35 %) and the highest (75 %) is very large. This phenomenon depicts that all the companies have made efforts to improve manpower flexibility. In all the companies, some aspects of labor flexibility, particularly extent of autonomous maintenance and skill levels, have not been taken care of very well.

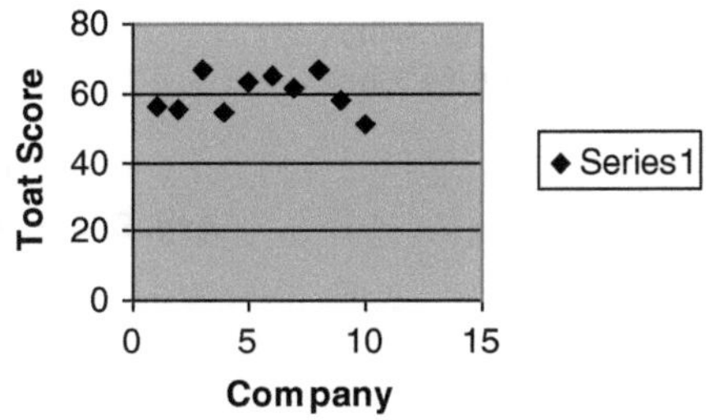

Fig. 18.2 Status of various companies in labor flexibility

Further, it is seen that out of ten companies from where detailed information was collected, three have scores of above 65 % which can be termed as good, two have scores between 60 % and 65 % which is fair, and the remaining have a score of less than 60 % which should be termed as poor in today's scenario. Overall, it can be said that labor flexibility in our industry is below satisfactory level (59.7 %). Even the companies getting the highest scores are not at a very good or excellent level, and there is a large scope for improvement which needs concerted and sustained efforts.

4 Lean Manufacturing

4.1 Status of Each Aspect

Table 18.4 shows the average scores of each of the ten companies in various aspects (kinds of wastes) of lean manufacturing. Overall average score of each aspect and the average score obtained by each company in all aspects taken together are also shown in the table. Figure 18.3 gives a comparison of the average scores of various aspects. The figure represents a very interesting phenomenon.

Four aspects, that is, correction (72.4 %), overproduction (75.5 %), conveyance (71 %), and doing more work (75.0 %), have scores of above 70 % which can be termed as good. It shows that companies have paid attention to these areas and put in efforts to reduce wastes of these four types. They have been successful in reducing the amount of rework produced. In other words, they try to produce the product of right quality in first attempt itself. A higher score of overproduction depicts that the concept of Just in Time production is being implemented. Companies are producing only when there is a firm customer order. The old practices of producing in advance and keeping inventory in the finished goods stores is being replaced by producing only against confirmed orders. Further, the companies have improved their material flow within the organization to optimize on material handling. This has reduced unnecessary transport of material within the work areas. The highest score has been achieved by "doing more work than required" depicting thereby that now only those features of the product are taken care of which have their functional

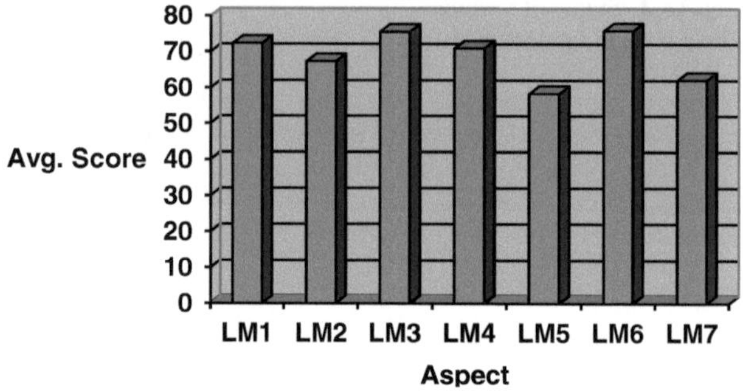

Fig. 18.3 Average scores of lean manufacturing aspects

utility and are demanded by the customers. Unnecessary work done on the product which will not add value has considerably come down.

The remaining three aspects of lean manufacturing, namely, "unnecessary motions" on work centers (67.3 %), "waiting due to various kinds of shortages" (62.2 %), and "higher inventories" (58.4 %), got comparatively low scores. Still there are unnecessary movements and efforts to pick up parts or place parts on the work centers. There is thus a need of a proper work place design through application of the principles of motion economy. Waiting due to various reasons got a considerably low score. It shows that various kinds of shortages like material shortages, unavailability of tooling, and breakdowns are still on quite a higher side. The lowest score has been received by "inventory." Inventories of raw materials, in-process goods, and finished products are still on the higher side. This shows that processes are not so reliable and inventories have to be kept higher to take care of the flaws and shortcomings of the production processes.

4.2 *Status of Various Companies in Lean Manufacturing*

Table 18.4 depicts the average score of each company in all aspects of lean manufacturing taken together. Figure 18.4 is a scatter diagram showing the total average score of the companies and their status with regard to lean manufacturing. The scatter diagram depicts that four companies have scores between 70 % and 75 % which can be termed as good with regard to lean manufacturing status. Another four companies have scores between 65 % and 70 % and fall in the category of "fair." The remaining two companies have scores less than 65 % and fall in the "unsatisfactory" category.

5 Relationship of Labor Flexibility and Lean Manufacturing

Table 18.5 shows the coefficient of correlation between various parameters of labor flexibility. The table depicts that the relationships within all parameters of labor flexibility are significant. This shows that all factors are complementary to one

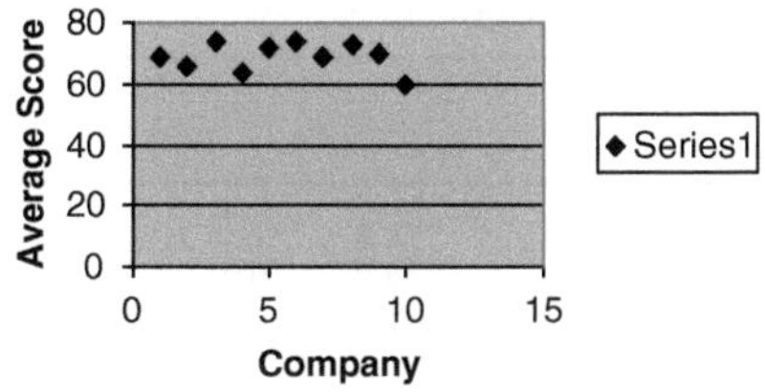

Fig. 18.4 Status of various companies in lean manufacturing

Table 18.5 Correlation among various aspects of labor flexibility

Parameters	LF 1	LF 2	LF 3	LF 4	LF 5	LF 6	LF 7	LF 8	LF 9	LF
LF1	1	.992	.847	.390	.900	.885	.822	.880	.588	.961
LF2	.992	1	.798	.381	.887	.859	.840	.851	.592	.946
LF3	.847	.798	1	.293	.900	.766	.509	.809	.383	.847
LF4	.390	.381	.293	1	.413	.591	.481	.447	.699	.550
LF5	.900	.887	.900	.413	1	.885	.720	.913	.661	.948
LF6	.885	.859	.766	.591	.885	1	.823	.970	.804	.964
LF7	.822	.840	.509	.481	.720	.823	1	.793	.842	.854
LF8	.880	.851	.809	.447	.913	.970	.793	1	.726	.950
LF9	.588	.592	.383	.699	.661	.804	.842	.726	1	.750
LF	.961	.946	.847	.550	.948	.964	.854	.950	.750	1

Table 18.6 Correlation among various aspects of lean manufacturing

Parameters	LM 1	LM 2	LM 3	LM 4	LM 5	LM 6	LM 7	LM
LM1	1	.979	.859	.913	.565	.929	.712	.951
LM2	.79	1	.848	.904	.501	.969	.818	.968
LM3	.859	.848	1	.847	.440	.876	.767	.919
LM4	.913	.904	.847	1	.616	.904	.757	.949
LM5	.565	.501	.440	.616	1	.545	.247	.573
LM6	.929	.969	.876	.904	.545	1	.898	.987
LM7	.712	.818	.767	.757	.247	.898	1	.863
LM	.951	.968	.919	.949	.573	.987	.863	1

another. If one becomes better, it has a positive effect on other factors and vice versa.

Similarly, the complementary nature of all parameters of lean manufacturing is evident from the significant relationships between them as shown in Table 18.6.

Table 18.7 also shows the relationship of labor flexibility with all the parameters of lean manufacturing. It is seen that all relationships are positive and significant. This shows that labor flexibility contributes towards the achievement of lean manufacturing by reducing wastes of various resources.

The study concludes that there is a very strong relationship between labor flexibility and lean manufacturing. The firms where the labor flexibility is higher are

Table 18.7 Correlation between lean manufacturing and various aspects of labor flexibility

Parameters	LF 1	LF 2	LF 3	LF 4	LF 5	LF 6	LF 7	LF 8	LF 9	LF
LM1	.901	.918	.701	.509	.853	.771	.840	.762	.665	.892
LM2	.912	.909	.783	.535	.879	.794	.783	.773	.645	.908
LM3	.865	.862	.671	.618	.879	.960	.894	.928	.885	.950
LM4	.870	.893	.705	.539	.881	.796	.822	.756	.731	.895
LM5	.317	.399	.916	.585	.366	.458	.412	.712	.484	.347
LM6	.906	.897	.803	.654	.893	.854	.738	.799	.679	.930
LM7	.814	.764	.876	.579	.864	.850	.526	.809	.559	.865
LM	.915	.917	.771	.639	.914	.879	.812	.832	.752	.951

generating less amount of waste of resources and are closer to the implementation of lean manufacturing. It is also brought out that a successful lean manufacturing implementation program should address the human aspect first of all, particularly in Indian context.

6 Conclusion

The study has shown that almost all the manufacturing units have put in efforts to reduce wastes of various kinds and move towards lean manufacturing. One of the strategies used for this purpose is to bring in labor flexibility. It has been shown that variations between the companies with regard to their overall standing in labor flexibility is not much but some aspects of labor flexibility are in a poor stage in almost all the organizations. It is also revealed that overall standing of the companies in labor flexibility needs improvement. Regarding wastages of various kinds considered under lean manufacturing, it is shown that some obvious areas have really improved, but few areas like “higher inventories” are at a poor level and need immediate attention. Further, the study revealed that there is a strong correlation among all parameters of labor flexibility and lean manufacturing. It can be concluded that improving labor flexibility will certainly contribute towards achievement of lean manufacturing. The results go very well with the hypothesis as well as the studies appearing in the literature on the role of labor flexibility with productivity, technology management, management of change, and other areas.

References

Bobrowski PM, Park PS (1993) An evaluation of labour assignment rules when workers are not perfectly interchangeable. J Oper Manag 11(3):257–268

Browne J, Harhen J, Shivanan J (1988) Production management systems: a CIM perspective. Addison Wesley, Reading

Chauhan G, Singh TP (2011) Lean manufacturing through management of labour and machine flexibility: a comprehensive review. Global J Flex Syst Manag 12(1&2):69–90

Chen IJ, Calantone RJ, Chung C-H (1992) The marketing – manufacturing interface and manufacturing flexibility. Omega Int J Manage Sci 20(4):431–443

Franchini L, Caillaud E, Nguyen P, Lacoste G (2001) Workload control of human resources to improve production management. Int J Prod Res 39(7):1385–1403

Garg R, Singh TP, Sushil (2002) Managing change for competitiveness. Global J Flexi Syst Manag 3(4):13–22

Gupta AB, Singh TP, Sushil (2001) Flexibility in an automobile manufacturing enterprise. Global J Flex Syst Manag 2(1):43–50

Hung R (1993) Improving productivity and quality through workforce scheduling. Utility and energy industries: quest for quality and productivity conference, Charlotte, 8–9 Mar

Jaikumar R (1989) Postindustrial manufacturing. Harv Bus Rev 64(6):69–76

Khamba JS, Singh TP, Sushil (2001) Flexible management of new technology. Global J Flex Syst Manag 2(4):41–53

Koste LL, Malhotra MK (1999) A theoretical framework for analyzing the dimensions of manufacturing flexibility. J Oper Manag 18(1):75–93

Koste LL, Malhotra MK, Sharma S (2004) Measuring dimensions of manufacturing flexibility. J Oper Manag 22(2):171–196

Nagarur N, Azeem A (1999) Impact of commonality and flexibility on manufacturing performance: a simulation study. Int J Prod Econ 60–61:125–134

Polakoff JC (1991) Reducing manufacturing costs by reducing cycle time. Corp Contr 4(2):62–64

Treleven M (1989) A review of the dual resource constrained system research. IIE Trans 21(3):279–287

Tsourveloudis NC, Phillis YA (1998) Fuzzy assessment of machine flexibility. IEEE Trans Eng Manag 45(1):78–88

Zulch G et al (2004) A simulation approach for planning and re-assigning of personnel in manufacturing. Int J Prod Econ 90:265–277

Chapter 19
Supply Chain Flexibility: Some Perceptions

Bibhushan, Anuj Prakash, and Bharat Wadhwa

1 Introduction

Supply chain flexibility (SCF) is a relatively new area with a growing number of publications appearing during recent times. Literature indicates the existence of several definitions and perceptions on flexibility in the domain of manufacturing systems as well as supply chain systems. Wadhwa and Rao (2000) define flexibility as the ability to deal with change by judiciously providing and exploiting controllable options dynamically. The developments in manufacturing flexibility stimulated efforts on flexibility at the level of systems and enterprises as well. For example, Sushil (2000) defines flexibility as the exercise of free will or freedom of choice on the continuum to synthesize the dynamic interplay of thesis and antithesis in an interactive and innovative manner, capturing the ambiguity in systems and expanding the continuum with minimum time and efforts. Wadhwa and Rao (2003) examined the concept of flexibility in relation to the concept of agility, highlighted certain commonalities and differences, and suggested a possible vision for future evolution of these two important concepts. Tang and Tomlin (2008) explore that flexibility enhances supply chain resiliency but in a limited manner. Chan et al. (2009) define that flexibility could reduce the impact of under demand and also reduce holding cost for unsold items, whereas Prakash (2011) defines the flexibility for all the system in such manners as flexibility as an ability, which can collect the environmental changes, experience the changes, and control the system according to changes. It is the multifactor, multidimensional approach in each context (manufacturing or supply chain), and these factors and dimensions

Bibhushan (✉)
JDA Software, Banglore, India

A. Prakash (✉)
The Hong Kong Polytechnic University, Hung Hom, Hong Kong, China

B. Wadhwa
Indian Institute of Technology Delhi, Hauz Khas, New Delhi, India

Sushil and E.A. Stohr (eds.), *The Flexible Enterprise*, Flexible Systems Management,
DOI 10.1007/978-81-322-1560-8_19, © Springer India 2014

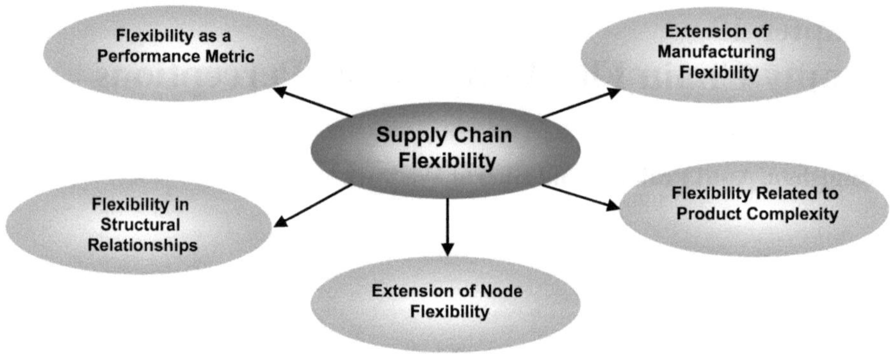

Fig. 19.1 Some perceptions of supply chain flexibility

will be described on the basis of particular context. Wadhwa and Browne (1989) define the different action points in a flexible system.

Researchers as well as practitioners agree that, to be competitive in a dynamic business environment, supply chains must be sufficiently flexible. Hence, there is considerable interest to enrich this domain. However, there have been multiple perceptions of flexibility within the research community (see Fig. 19.1). While some authors view supply chain flexibility in terms of manufacturing flexibility, several other authors view supply chain flexibility as an extension of the flexibility concept from individual entities to the entire supply chain. Many authors view flexibility as an important performance parameter of a supply chain, just like time, cost, and quality. In addition, several authors view supply chain flexibility in terms of the product customization. A number of other authors view supply chain flexibility in terms of supply chain structural relationships. Supply chain flexibility is also being discussed in relation with product complexity that arises in the case of short life cycle products. For such products, IT is needed for quickly identifying the customer requirements, making suitable product designs, and manufacturing the customized products. A firm in the downstream market can choose between irreversibly committing to an early order and postponing ordering until after better demand information is available. In our view, such growth in complexity in supply chain structures highlights the research and industry motivation to focus on supply chain flexibility. As complexity increases, a variety of outcomes become possible, and a more detailed modeling would be required with a greater number of contingencies to deal with the added dimensions. This chapter explores different perceptions of supply chain flexibility (shown in Fig. 19.1).

2 SCF as an Extension of Manufacturing Flexibility

Many of the publications on flexibility focus on the manufacturing flexibility dimension (Wadhwa and Rao 2003). One of the most accepted frameworks for manufacturing flexibility is the framework proposed by Browne et al. (1984). This

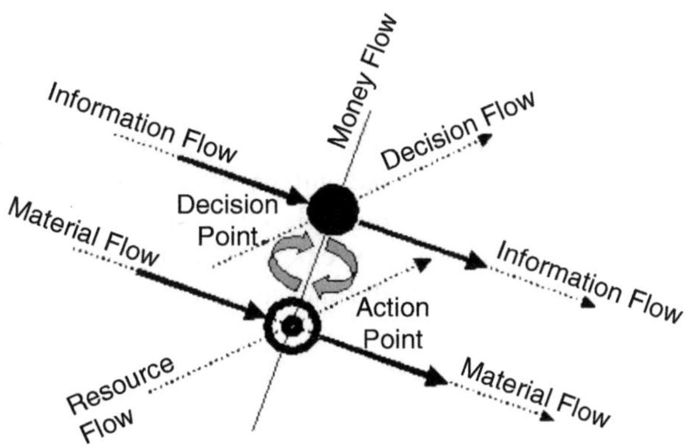

Fig. 19.2 Multiple-entity flow perspective (Wadhwa and Rao 2003)

framework identifies and defines eight types of manufacturing flexibilities: machine, routing, product, process, operation, volume, expansion, and production flexibilities. The interrelationships among these flexibility types have also been identified in this framework. The flexibility in manufacturing environments, particularly computer-integrated manufacturing systems (CIMS), can be intelligently exploited by judicious use of IT (Wadhwa and Rao 2000). In his research, Wadhwa (1988) suggested a focus on interaction delays caused by processes involving the control on flow of multiple entities. He also proposed three types of decision points linking the decision (direction of status change) and information (system status) to exploit available flexibility in flexible manufacturing systems. In a later work, Wadhwa and Aggarwal (1993) suggested flexibility, integration, and automation as three key dimensions of computer-integrated systems based on this framework.

Wadhwa and Rao (2003) also highlight the importance of supply chain flexibility while proposing a multiple-entity flow perspective to understand and exploit different types of flexibilities within the supply chain. They view supply chain in terms of five entity flows: *information flow*, *decision flow*, *material flow*, *resource flow,* and *money flow*. In this framework, shown in Fig. 19.2, information flow and decision flow were viewed as constituting the control system, which controls the material flow and resource flow. The information and decision flows meet at discrete points called the decision points, and the material and resource flows meet at discrete points called the action points. The decision points and the action points interact with each other to ensure smooth functioning of the system.

A number of authors consider supply chain flexibility as an extension of manufacturing flexibility. For instance, Koste and Malhotra (1999) feel that the presence or absence of manufacturing flexibility in supply chains and its relationship with performance should be explored, and the effect of supply chain integration on the development of manufacturing flexibility in supply chains should be examined. Similarly, Duclos et al. (2001) argue that supply chain flexibility, which includes manufacturing flexibility, should further improve the performance of supply chain. In a recent work, Ozbayrak et al. (2006) highlight that flexible systems like MTO are required for meeting diverse and customized orders in a supply chain. Boute et al. (2009) emphasized on modeling capacity structure in flexible manner to achieve the flexibility in supply chain to cope with the uncertainty of the market and customer demand. Ivanov et al. (2010) viewed that in supply chains, different structures (functional, organizational, informational, financial, etc.) are (re)formed. These structures interrelate with each other and change in dynamics. They provide a new vision of adaptive supply chain. These examples clearly highlight that the idea of the flexibility can be extended from the manufacturing domain into the supply chain domain, since the underlying concepts of manufacturing and supply chain flexibility are very similar.

3 SCF in Relation with Product Complexity

Supply chain flexibility is also being discussed in relation with product complexity that arises in the case of short life cycle products. In their survey, De Meyer et al. (1989) identified that product range flexibility is viewed as a core competence for competitive success by managers. Similarly, while reviewing the evolving business environment, Beamon and Ware (1998) observe that today's changing industry dynamics have influenced the design, operation, and objectives of supply chain systems by increasing emphasis on flexibility of product customization to meet customer needs. However, this added flexibility may come at an additional investment cost and higher logistics cost, as identified by Randall and Ulrich (2001) while investigating a bicycle industry supply chain. Alshawi (2001) observes that flexibility to offer business partners the ability to make changes in their operations or products is more important than providing visibility over materials, information, and money. He mentions an example where the members of the potato-crisp supply chain might decide to produce potato sticks as an alternative snack food. Viswanath and Gilbert (2002) examine the trade-off between strategic commitment and operational flexibility as it arises in a supply chain when a supplier offers competing buyers opportunities to make early purchase commitments for a product with a short life cycle. In their model, a firm in the downstream market has two options: irreversibly committing to an early order and postponing the ordering until better demand information is available. Suppliers are able to manipulate the trade-off between flexibility and strategic commitment by offering early purchasing opportunities.

In a recent work, Chandra et al. (2005) modeled a major automotive company in terms of capacity planning, flexibility, and part commonality. Their experimental results showed that increasing level of flexibility and part commonality yielded improvements in production profitability. Similarly, Wu et al. (2007) assert that manufacturers and suppliers need to be flexible in the product range they offer and in the volumes they supply in order to adapt to uncertain and unpredictable changes from customers. This discussion brings out an important perception of flexibility as an option available to a customer.

4 SCF as an Extension of the Flexibility of Each Entity

Several authors view supply chain flexibility as an extension of the flexibility within individual supply chain nodes to the entire supply chain. For example, Taylor (2000) highlights the need for developing systems capable of coordinating the supply chains, while emphasizing flexible response in a supply chain. Chandra and Kumar (2000) feel that the agility realized through flexible organization is an important attribute for any enterprise. They feel that a flexible organization of a firm supports plant and distribution networks by achieving operational efficiency through quick line changeovers as well as savings realized by avoiding back hauling and enhanced product realization. Similarly, Simatupang et al. (2002) observe that a firm needs to develop effective coordination within and beyond its boundaries in order to maximize the potential for converting competitive advantage into profitability. Along similar lines, Garavelli (2003) argues that networked enterprises like supply chains need coordination among many plants, which produce and deliver goods to customers located in different places, and suppliers, who provide each plant with the required components. Krajewski et al. (2005) propose a "reduce uncertainty" strategy, and they argued that the "cope with uncertainty" strategy emphasizes flexible supply contracts, relatively frequent schedule revisions, and low levels of form postponement. The idea that the supply chain as a whole should work in a coordinated manner indicates an important direction of research.

5 SCF in Terms of Structural Relationships

A number of authors view supply chain flexibility in terms of supply chain structural relationships. For example, Jordan and Graves (1995) introduced the concept of "chaining" as an effective flexibility strategy. They define a "chain" as a group of products or plants, which are all connected, directly or indirectly, by product assignment decisions. Literature indicates that such complex supply chain structures may be a common feature in the future. For example, Ritchie and Brindley (2000) predict that the extant linear supply chain relationship model that dominates most sectors will rapidly be replaced by a more amorphous supply chain relationship model. The amorphous relationship reflects that the structures may be difficult to map, and they may be subject to a process of continuous change and reformulation depending on the strategies of the individual partners, both present and prospective. They suggested the ability to build flexible alliances quickly as a critical management skill required for these emerging business models. Similarly, while discussing the importance of buyer–supplier relationships, Hoyt and Huq (2000) observe that buyer–supplier relationships play an important role in an organization's ability to respond to dynamic and unpredictable change. If the relationship is too restrictive, flexibility will be difficult to achieve. Some authors view supply chain flexibility as an ability to restructure the supply chain. For example, Mello (2001) views supply chain flexibility as the ability to restructure the system quickly and inexpensively. Similarly, Marquez and Blanchar (2004) consider flexibility regarding supplier contract in their paper. They have defined, characterized, and simulated three generic types of supplier contracts to accomplish varying degrees of security and flexibility. Gosling et al. (2010) have proposed two new type of flexibility: vendor flexibility and sourcing flexibility. They observe that supply chain flexibility can be achieved by developing vendor flexibility, sourcing flexibility, or by mixing the two types of flexibility. They further argue that vendor and sourcing flexibility are key dimensions for considering supplier selection and supplier relationship development.

6 SCF as a Performance Metric in Supply Chains

A number of authors view flexibility as an important performance parameter of a supply chain, just like time, cost, and quality. For example, while discussing the appropriateness of various performance measures for supply chains, Beamon (1999) identified flexibility, perceived as how well the system reacts to uncertainty, as a vital component to supply chain success. They argue that a supply chain performance measurement system must place emphasis on flexibility measures such as volume flexibility, delivery flexibility, mix flexibility, and new product flexibility. However, they caution that each type of flexibility may not be appropriate for every supply chain. The work by Bruniaux (2000) considers flexibility as one of the important parameters for event management in supply chains. Similarly, while reviewing the evolving business environment in the context of supply chain management, Barratt and Oliveira (2001) observe that the battle commands of today are flexibility, speed, and productivity. Gunasekaran et al. (2001) also argue that flexibility should be an important metric for measuring supply chain performance. They argue that the previous research established a strong correlation of supply chain response time and flexibility. Hence, by defining flexibility as a metric and by evaluating it, companies can achieve what was previously impossible: rapid response to meet individual customer requirements. Similarly, Chan (2003) considered flexibility as one the seven performance metrics in their AHP-based framework for supply chain performance measurement. Along the similar lines, Chan and Qi (2003) consider manufacturing flexibility, delivery flexibility, transport flexibility, and order flexibility as some of the important constituents of supply chain performance measurement.

Some authors perceive supply chain flexibility as an essential requirement for functioning of supply chains in real life. For example, Lamming (1996) argues that for supply chain to function in a real situation, certain basic flexibility is necessary. This flexibility might take the form of "time to think" or "space to experiment." He observes that a workforce which has no "time to think" might not deliver innovation through suggestion schemes and might dislike their jobs so much that their organization would derive no benefit from their motivation. While reviewing the role of supply chains in the economic development, Bateman (1998) emphasizes that dynamic, flexible, and quality-conscious local supply chains are now considered a critically important feature in an industrial structure. He observes that in Italy and Germany, regional success largely came about because of the efficient operation of regionally based supply chains involving dynamic and highly flexible groups of small- and medium-sized manufacturing enterprises. This clearly indicates that supply chains play an important role in economic development, and they are of vital importance for developing countries.

Many authors have considered flexibility as an important parameter for designing supply chains decision support tools. For instance, Sadeh et al. (2001) also focused on flexibility as an important constituent in their reconfigurable agent-based planning tool called MASCOT. Similarly, Janssen (2005) considered flexibility as an important parameter for improving supply chain responsiveness while presenting a multi-agent system for supply chain management. Mangina and Vlachos (2005) considered flexibility as an important dimension in their agent-based framework for supply chain management and demonstrated that agents can enhance the flexibility in the supply chain. Along similar lines, Ding et al. (2005) developed a discrete event simulation package to achieve modeling flexibility and simulation efficiency, based on generic modeling and simulation framework for supply chain design. Hung et al. (2006) scrutinized the flexibility in supply chain as an important factor, and they emphasized on managing it on supply chain level rather than operational level due to an axiom: "a 1-cent reduction in supply-chain costs can have as much as a 5-cent improvement on operating profits." In a recent paper, Liu et al. (2007) exploited flexibility for modeling events and event rules for supply chain event management.

A number of authors view supply chain flexibility as a way of dealing with this growing complexity. For example, Hobbs and Young (2000) observe that supply chain complexity leads to transaction complexity. As complexity increases, a variety of outcomes become possible, and a more detailed contract would be required with a greater number of contingencies to deal with the added dimensions of the transaction. They visualize that a strategic alliance, which allows sufficient flexibility in the relationship to deal with the complexities, should be a possibility. In the context of steel stock supply chain, McAdam and Brown (2001) consider flexibility as the ability to meet one-off needs. Similarly, Wu et al. (2007) are of the view that manufacturing industry is suffering from an increasing requirement for more flexibility and agility to deal with the variety and uncertainty in the markets it serves. A supply chain should have enough built-in flexibility in order to handle such changes without the need for interrupting activities or major restructuring. Wadhwa and Rao (2003) provide a detailed literature review on the interrelationships between these two important concepts. Swafford et al. (2008) argued that being responsive (agile) is an increasingly important skill in today's global economy. Naturally, it follows that an organization's agility depends on its supply chain being agile. Chan and Chan (2010) argue that supply chains need to be flexible and adaptive because their operations are always subject to a variety of uncertainties like customer demand and supplier capacity, particularly for Make-to-Order (MTO) supply chains since their

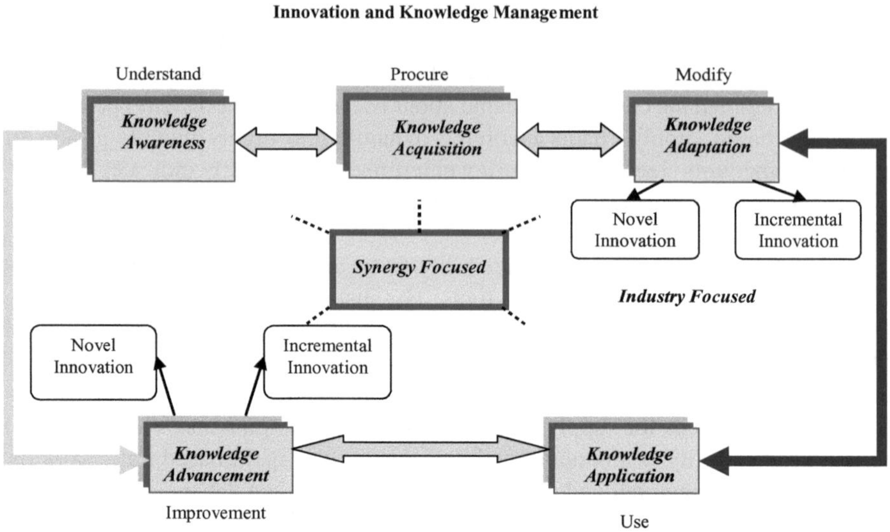

Fig. 19.3 Vision for promoting innovation and KM in supply chain frameworks

flow of materials is only triggered by customer orders. They proposed a coordination mechanism between flexibility and adaptability in delivery quantity and due date. A number of authors discussed supply chain flexibility in relation to the concept of agility.

Some authors feel that increasing flexibility is not sufficient to cope with the variety and uncertainty inherent in the supply chain. For instance, Upton (1995, 1997) observed that 40 % of flexibility-improvement projects were unsuccessful due to "failure to identify precisely what kind of manufacturing flexibility was needed, how to measure it, or which factors affected it most". Jordan and Graves (1995) found that offering limited flexibility yielded most of the benefits to be obtained from being flexible. Similarly, Garavelli (2003) proposed the adoption of limited flexibility to improve supply chain performance. They considered partial flexibility as a particular configuration of product assignments to plants and components to suppliers, which can yield many benefits without dramatically increasing the flexibility costs. In a recent work, Wu et al. (2007) observed that although flexibility or agility is widely accepted as a core competence in coping with variety and uncertainty, being flexible is not, by itself, the whole answer to coping with the variety and uncertainty inherent in a supply chain. They further suggest that adaptability of the suppliers to demand changes and adaptability achieved by implementing appropriate planning and scheduling procedures is essential. Figure 19.3 summarizes the role of promoting innovation and knowledge management in the supply chain. These ideas can improve the performance of supply chain and can be implemented in the industrial contexts (Wadhwa and Saxena 2006). They have discussed the web-based supply chain and also promote the role of knowledge management in web-based supply chain.

7 Conclusion

This chapter discussed supply chain flexibility in terms of five different perceptions, as viewed by different researchers. Firstly, supply chain flexibility was viewed as an extension of manufacturing flexibility. Subsequent discussion focused on the flexibility in the supply chain, which is discussed as a method of dealing with product complexity. The view of supply chain flexibility as composed of the flexibilities within each entity within the supply chain was presented next. This was followed by a discussion on supply chain flexibility in terms of structural relationships within the supply chain. Finally, the role of flexibility as an essential component and as a performance metric of supply chain was presented. The chapter clearly highlights the importance of flexibility in the supply chain framework. Hence, there is a need to model supply chain framework with flexibility, which can give more profit, customer satisfaction, etc. Simultaneously, the role of knowledge management is also very important, and it will help to achieve the goals of the supply chain.

References

Alshawi S (2001) Logistics in the internet Age: towards a holistic information and processes picture. Logist Inf Manag 14(4):235–242

Barratt M, Oliveira A (2001) Exploring the experiences of collaborative planning initiatives. Int J Phys Distrib Logist Manag 31(4):266–289

Bateman M (1998) Local supply chain development in the transition economies: the case of Kazakhstan. Supply Chain Manag 3(2):79–88

Beamon BM (1999) Measuring supply chain performance. Int J Op Prod Manag 19(3):275–292

Beamon BM, Ware TM (1998) A process quality model for the analysis, improvement and control of supply chain systems. Logist Inf Manag 11(2):105–113

Boute RN, Disney SM, Lambrecht MR, Van Houdt B (2009) Designing replenishment rules in a two-echelon supply chain with a flexible or an inflexible capacity strategy. Int J Prod Econ 119:187–198

Browne J, Dubois D, Rathmill K, Sethi SP, Stecke KE (1984) Classification of flexible manufacturing systems. The FMS Magazine, April, 114–117

Bruniaux R (2000) Simulation Continue de re'seaux de Sites Industriels. Application aux chaînes logistiques dans le secteur Automobile. Ph.D. Dissertation in French; Universite' Blaise Pascal, Clermont-Ferrand

Chan FTS (2003) Performance measurement in a supply chain. Int J Adv Manuf Technol 21(7):534–548

Chan FTS, Qi HJ (2003) An innovative performance measurement method for supply chain management. Supply Chain Manag: An Int J 8(3):209–223

Chan HK, Chan FTS (2010) Comparative study of adaptability and flexibility in distributed manufacturing supply chains. Decis Support Syst 48:331–341

Chan HK, Wang WYC, Luong LHS, Chan FTS (2009) Flexibility and adaptability in supply chains. Supply Chain Manag An Int J 14(6):407–410

Chandra C, Kumar S (2000) Supply chain management in theory and practice: a passing fad or a fundamental change? Ind Manag Data Syst 100(3):100–114

Chandra C, Everson M, Grabis J (2005) Evaluation of enterprise-level benefits of manufacturing flexibility. Omega Int J Manag Sci 33(1):17–31

De Meyer A, Makane J, Miller J, Ferdows K (1989) Flexibility: the next competitive battle, the manufacturing futures survey. Strateg Manag J 10(2):135–144
Ding H, Lyès B, Xiaolan X (2005) A modeling and simulation framework for supply chain design. Supply Chain Optim 219–232. doi:10.1007/0-387-23581-7_16
Duclos KL, Lummus RR, Vokurka RJ (2001) A conceptual model of supply chain flexibility. In: Proceedings of the 2001 annual meeting of the Decision Sciences Institute, San Francisco, California
Garavelli AC (2003) Flexibility configurations for the supply chain management. Int J Prod Econ 85:141–153
Gosling J, Purvis L, Naim MM (2010) Supply chain flexibility as a determinant of supplier selection. Int J Prod Econ 128:11–21
Gunasekaran A, Patel C, Tirtiroglu E (2001) Performance measures and metrics in a supply chain environment. Int J Op Prod Manag 21(1/2):71–87
Hobbs JE, Young LM (2000) Closer vertical co-ordination in agri-food supply chains: a conceptual framework and some preliminary evidence. Supply Chain Manag An Inter J 5(3):131–143
Hoyt J, Huq F (2000) From arms-length to collaborative relationships in the supply chain. Int J Phys Distrib Logist Manag 30(9):750–764
Hung WY, Samsatli NJ, Shah N (2006) Object-oriented dynamic supply-chain modeling incorporated with production scheduling. Eur J Op Res 169:1064–1076
Ivanov D, Sokolov B, Kaeschel J (2010) A multi-structural framework for adaptive supply chain planning and operations control with structure dynamics considerations. Eur J Oper Res 200:409–420
Janssen M (2005) The architecture and business value of a semi-cooperative agent-based supply chain management system. Electron Commer Res Appl 4:315–328
Jordan WC, Graves SC (1995) Principles on the benefits of manufacturing process flexibility. Manag Sci 41(4):577–594
Koste LL, Malhotra MK (1999) A theoretical framework for analyzing the dimensions of manufacturing flexibility. J Oper Manag 18:75–93
Krajewski L, Wei JC, Tang LL (2005) Responding to schedule changes in build-to-order supply chains. J Oper Manag 23:452–469
Lamming R (1996) Squaring lean supply with supply chain management. Int J Op Prod Manag 16(2):183–196
Liu R, Kumar A, Aalst W (2007) A formal modeling approach for supply chain event management. Decis Support Syst 43:761–778
Mangina E, Vlachos IP (2005) The changing role of information technology in food and beverage logistics management: beverage network optimization using intelligent agent technology. J Food Eng 70:403–420
Marquez AC, Blanchar C (2004) The procurement of strategic parts. Analysis of a portfolio of contracts with suppliers using a system dynamics simulation model. Int J Prod Econ 88:29–49
McAdam R, Brown L (2001) Strategic alignment and the supply chain for the steel stockholder sector: an exploratory case study analysis. SCM An Int J 6(2):83–95
Mello A (2001) Bulletproof your supply chain, ZDNet Tech Update. http://techupdate.zdnet.com/techupdate/stories/main/0,14179,2821506,00.html. Accessed 31 Oct 2001
Özbayrak M, Papadopoulou TC, Samaras E (2006) A flexible and adaptable planning and control system for an MTO supply chain system. Robot Comput Integr Manuf 22:557–565
Prakash A (2011) Performance improvement of manufacturing system by using knowledge based Meta-Heuristics. Ph.D. Thesis, IIT Delhi
Randall T, Ulrich K (2001) Product variety, supply chain structure, and firm performance: analysis of the US bicycle industry. Manag Sci 47(12):1588–1604
Ritchie B, Brindley C (2000) Disintermediation, disintegration and risk in the SME global supply chain. Manag Decis 38(8):575–583
Sadeh NM, Hildum DW, Kjenstad D, Tseng A (2001) MASCOT: an agent-based architecture for dynamic supply chain creation and coordination in the internet economy. Prod Plan Control 12(3):212–223

Simatupang TM, Wright AC, Sridharan R (2002) The knowledge of coordination for supply chain integration. Bus Process Manag J 8(3):289–308

Sushil (2000) Concept of systemic flexibility. Glob J Flex Syst Manag 1:77–80

Swafford PM, Ghosh S, Murthy N (2008) Achieving supply chain agility through IT integration and flexibility. Int J Prod Econ 116:288–297

Tang C, Tomlin B (2008) The power of flexibility for mitigating supply chain risks. Int J Prod Econ 116(1):12–27

Taylor DH (2000) Demand amplification: has it got us beat. Int J Phys Distrib Logist Manag 30(6):515–533

Upton DM (1995) What really makes factories flexible? Harv Bus Rev, July-Aug:74–84

Viswanath C, Gilbert SM (2002) Strategic commitment versus postponement in a two-tier supply chain. Eur J Oper Res 141:526–543

Wadhwa S (1988) Development of generalized simulators for design evaluation of Robot Based Flexible Assembly System. Ph.D. Thesis, National University of Ireland

Wadhwa S, Aggarwal A (1993) Modeling computer integrated manufacturing systems using systems dynamics. In: Proceedings of the 5th national conference on systems dynamics. Indian Institute of Technology, New Delhi

Wadhwa S, Browne J (1989) Modeling FMS with decision petri nets. Int J Flex Manuf Syst 1:253–280

Wadhwa S, Rao KS (2000) Flexibility: an emerging meta-competence for managing high technology. Int J Technol Manag 19(7–8):820–845

Wadhwa S, Rao KS (2003) Flexibility and agility for enterprise synchronization: knowledge and innovation management towards flexagility. Stud Inform Control 12(2)

Wadhwa S, Saxena A (2006) A KM motivated web based supply chain simulator: facilitating e-learning for SMEs. Int J Bus Perform Manag 8(2/3):207–228

Wu Y, Frizelle G, Efstathiou J (2007) A study on the cost of operational complexity in customer–supplier systems. Int J Prod Econ 106:217–229

Chapter 20
Marketing Flexibilities: Lessons from the Corporate

Nripendra Singh

1 Introduction

The phenomenon of liberalization, privatization, and globalization (LPG) has literally changed the way business is being done. As a result of LPG, boundaries are now eroded, competition has become fierce, and customers have become the real king. The very basic assumptions of somewhat stable environment has almost become irrational now as things are changing at a very fast pace, so fast that sometimes it becomes almost impossible to predict what next will happen in the marketplace. In the backdrop of all these uncertainties, flexibility has taken a center stage on the horizons of business environment. The importance of flexibility as a strategic tool has been well recognized by practitioners as well as academicians. Flexibility in organizations not only improves the performance but also helps to adapt early according to newly evolved paradigm. According to Drucker (1980), a business needs to be able to both ride out sudden hard blows and avail itself to unexpected opportunities in turbulent times. This implies that business should be flexible enough to handle both the unexpected threats and opportunities posed by an uncertain future and unstable environment.

In 1980s and 1990s, Indian companies like Royal Enfield's – Bullet Motorcycle and Hindustan Motor's – Ambassador Car could not understand the benefits of flexibility and lost market share and profits to companies like Hero MotoCorp (erstwhile Hero Honda) and Maruti Suzuki, as they believed on the importance of being flexible.

The role and importance of flexibility in the survival and success of organizations, in the fast-changing environment, has been well recognized by several

N. Singh, Ph.D. (✉)
Faculty – Marketing Area, Jaypee Business School, A Constituent of JIIT University, A-10, Sector-62, 201307 Noida, India
e-mail: singhnripendra@hotmail.com; nripendra.singh@jiit.ac.in

Sushil and E.A. Stohr (eds.), *The Flexible Enterprise*, Flexible Systems Management, DOI 10.1007/978-81-322-1560-8_20, © Springer India 2014

authors in management theory. Peter (1991) in his 45 prescriptions of successful business mentions the relevance of flexibility. Pasmore (1994) maintains that flexible organizations can respond to change in a much better way as compared to rigid or non-flexible organizations.

Majority of them have focused on giving the classification framework for the construct of flexibility. The purpose was to identify how flexibility can be created, implemented, utilized, and measured in the organization. From the literature, it is evident that a large number of experts have talked on creation of flexibility, but implementation, utilization, and measurement are still left to be touched.

Flexibility in marketing has also been discussed from strategic angle, but the implementation part has not been explored due to the complexity of the issue. This chapter tries to delve into the details of marketing flexibility and its construct by taking examples/cases of successful organizations, being more flexible than their competitors.

2 Literature Review on Flexibility

The construct for flexibility is given in the pioneer work of Ansoff (1965). He defined the concept of flexibility in the context of its external and internal aspects. He described external flexibility by the maxim of not putting all of one's eggs in a single basket, while internal flexibility, according to him, seeks to provide a cushion for response to catastrophe. Bahrami (1992) defined the flexibility as a multidimensional concept – demanding agility and versatility; associated with change, innovation, and novelty; coupled with robustness and resilience: and implying stability, sustainable advantage, and capabilities that may evolve over time. One of the most comprehensive definitions of flexibility was provided by Volberda (1996) which says that flexibility is the degree to which organizations have a variety of managerial capabilities and the speed at which they can be activated, to increase the control capacity of management and improve the controllability of the organization.

Aaker and Mascarenhas (1984) propose a framework that is based on the approaches available to companies for the creation of flexibility. They identified six functions in which flexibility can be created, namely, R&D, finance, operation, marketing, international, and managerial/structural areas. Three methods for increasing flexibility are identified, namely, diversification, investment in underutilized resources, and reducing commitment of resources to specialized use.

Ansari and Bell (1997) suggested three strategic aspects, namely, quality, cost, and time. Slack (1983) identified another strategic aspect, namely, range. In majority of the work on flexibility a functional approach is adopted, like Aaker and Mascarenhas (1984), but Hamel and Prahalad (1989) noted that creating labor flexibility by adjusting the size of the workforce may not lead to the creation of flexibility at all, rather serve to maintain inflexibility. It is therefore important not to view the flexibility process as being restricted to only certain aspects or functions of an organization.

Johnson (1992) defines flexibility from the perspective of customer satisfaction, by adopting a functional perspective and identifying the concept of flexibility as producing immediately or within a period that satisfies the customers, exactly what the customer requests. He perceives that the flexibility in the long run can be achieved by changing lifestyles and ways of thinking. Harrigan (1985) used the term strategic flexibility to define flexibility from market perspective. Strategic flexibility refers to firm's ability to reposition itself in market, change its game plan, or dismantle its current strategies. Eppink (1978) used the term competitive flexibility and defined it as the ability of the enterprise to read to competitive changes caused by a major transformation of the market position, through the introduction of a new market or the entry of new competition. According to Rich Freeman, finance teams and sales and marketing organizations rely on the IT department to make them more efficient and keep their companies flexible.

Flexibility is not to do as you like, but freedom of choice within a framework. It refers to options, change mechanisms, and freedom of choice (Sushil 1999, 2000). One of the key characteristic of flexibility is the continuity. It is not a onetime change but the process of continuous change as per the changing needs (Singh and Sushil 1997). A comprehensive review of literature on flexibility is reported by Sharma et al. (2010).

3 Literature Review on Marketing Flexibility

Though the roots of the concept of flexibility can be traced back to 1921 when Lavington established connection between variability and flexibility, its application in the context of marketing system is not addressed comprehensively (Lavington 1921). Literature says that marketing flexibility refers to the ability of an organization to enter and leave markets and to position itself within existing and new markets. An organization with marketing flexibility gains competitive advantage as a result of its ability to change and reposition itself rapidly within competitive global markets.

Prahlad and Hamel (1990) maintain that such organizations search new markets quickly, penetrate emerging markets, and are also able to change patterns of customer choice. It is said that such capability allows them to do so (enter or leave market) as customer preferences, cost barriers, compositions, attributes, and competition within the industry. Second capability which creates marketing flexibility originates from the competitive strategies adopted within existing markets like overall cost leadership, differentiation, and focus (Porters – 3 Generic Strategies). The four strategic elements of time, cost, quality, and range (Ansari and Bell 1997; Slack 1983) also apply to marketing flexibility. The wider the range of options (size, feasibility) available to respond to market changes, the more flexible it is deemed to be.

Another concept of mobility barrier was given by Porter (1977), which was referred as a constraint to marketing flexibility. Harrigan (1985) argues that barriers to entry and exit of markets represent mental baggage of managers, and therefore, marketing flexibility can also be achieved by overcoming physical and mental constraints.

4 Concept

Marketing has inherent relation with the market which in turn is characterized by the buyers and sellers involved in the transaction process. Sellers offer the products at some price to cater the need of the buyers. Though the ultimate transaction phenomenon looks simple, there is a complex web of interrelated activities that make this transaction possible. Grewal and Transtutaj (2001) related marketing flexibility with the ability of transnational corporations to recalibrate the marketing efforts in a short-changing environment context, while Abbot and Bannerji (2003) described marketing flexibility as the ability to have a high market share/strong market presence. Flexibility, in the context of marketing, refers to the ability of the company to meet the challenge of globalization as well as varying needs of the customers within the overall framework of its business strategy (Sharma et al. 2010).

Marketing flexibility, thus, has been broadly explained from strategic point of view. This chapter tries to delve into the details of marketing flexibility, by taking lessons from select successful organizations which are much more flexible than their competitors. Apart from the 4 Ps of marketing, it also includes areas like consumer satisfaction, employees (sales people), organizational structure (structural design), R&D, New Product Development (NPD), information technology, logistics and operations, competition, marketing research, and branding and training. It is imperative to understand the pressures created by them for the purpose of flexibility. The major areas that create pressures for flexibility are shown in Table 20.1.

Therefore, in order to balance all these pressures amid the newly evolving business paradigm, there is a need of a more holistic and complete approach to the marketing – Systems of System (SoS) approach. A system with its inherent capability to produce whole which is greater than the sum of individual contributions has been widely accepted as a solution of many complex problems. Systems perspective to marketing is the key to remain competitive amid all this environmental dynamism. Lee Adler talked explicitly about the benefits related to systems approach to marketing in 1967. The advantage of considering the marketing as a system is that it allows the analysis of the various cross impacts that affect their subsystems and vice versa. As customer satisfaction is the ultimate aim of any organization, considering of only four Ps of marketing is not enough, especially keeping in view today's competitive environment. Singh and Kumar (2011) argued that the rationale behind these arguments is that successful organizations (discussed here) do not have narrow functional approach of marketing as 4 Ps, but follow SoS approach, to have flexible marketing system in their organization.

Systems approach, in contrast to functional one, will help the organizations not only to understand the customer requirements in a better way (including NPD and

Table 20.1 Pressure for flexibility by marketing domains

Domain	Causes
Product	Want to satisfy the customers by more models while keeping cost low
Place	Want to place the product closest to customer
Consumers	Want lower prices with instant delivery
Competitors	Want to strive to satisfy more customers
Sales promotion	Want to increase the sales without loss of margin
Advertising	Want to reach out to maximum
Industrial buying	Want to supply nonstop; long-term association
Marketing research	Want to achieve precision but depend upon sampling
Segmentation	Want to target customers to increase revenue
Branding	Want to position the product and increase the volumes
Pricing	Want to minimize the price and maximize the revenues
Sales force	Want high salary, service, and flexible work hours
Personal selling	Want to maintain relationship by putting minimum time and maximum reach
Retailing	Want more commission and to satisfy customer demand
Direct marketing	Want to maximize coverage by alternate channels
CRM	Want loyalty and commitment from customers
Marketing strategy	Want long-term and sustainable strategy
Global marketing	Want global reach in diversified tastes and preferences
Rural marketing	Want deeper penetration at substantial margins
Service	Want to provide the customer satisfaction by being consistent
Physical evidence	Want to tangible the intangibles to provide the quality to customers
Process	Want to differentiate through service delivery process
People	Want to control emotions while encountering customers

information system) but also to satisfy them in a better way by acting speedily on the distribution and logistics aspects of value proposition. This holistic approach will help the organizations to multiply their growth prospects as a result of the increased customer satisfaction.

5 Marketing Flexibility Construct

As marketing flexibility is an intangible concept, its measurement can be done with the help of a construct. The concept of marketing flexibility is embedded in various subsystems of marketing. As these subsystems collectively constitute the marketing system of an organization, measurement of their individual flexibility will lead to the overall flexibility of marketing system. The intensity or the degree of flexibility of the marketing system of any organization can be assessed with the help of the dimensions and their attributes. Lee Adler (1967) gave the model of marketing subsystems and total system, which has been adapted to further the study on marketing flexibility (Fig. 20.1). From the existing literature and corporate/business case studies, there is an effort to find out the dimensions of such a marketing system to be

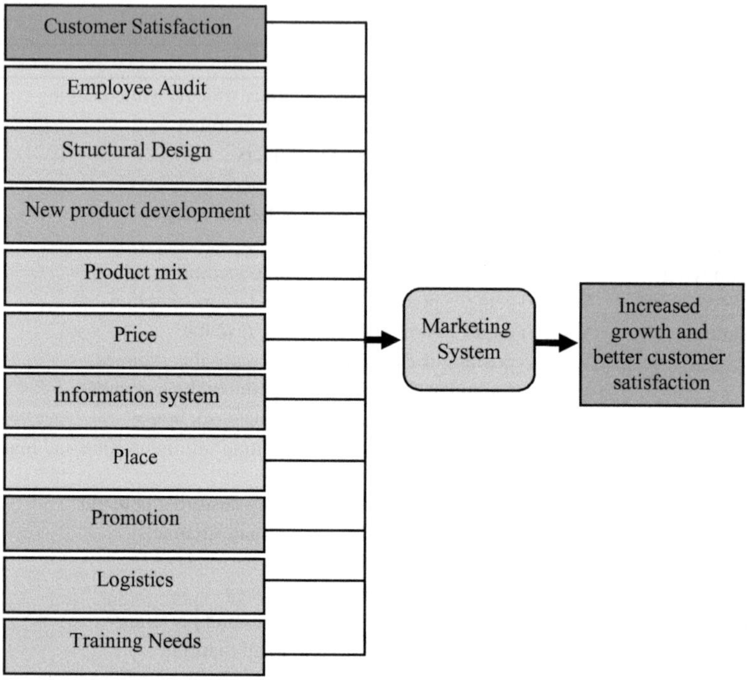

Fig. 20.1 Marketing flexibility construct (Adapted from: "Systems Approach to Marketing," Alder (1967))

developed into a construct. In a recent work of the author (2011), a scale named FLEXMARK is provided for measuring the marketing flexibility in any organization for sustained profitability, which was possible using the construct mentioned in this chapter.

Importance of marketing flexibility can be assessed from the corporate cases as discussed below (in "Lessons from the Corporate"). It is clearly visible from these cases how organizations use different types of marketing flexibilities strategically which are derived from one of the constructs/dimensions of marketing flexibility. Organizations having flexibility in its marketing system are more successful than its competitors because of its ability to adapt quickly to changing circumstances. It can satisfy its target customers in a much better manner by equipping itself with better combating power in order to deal with the competition.

6 Lessons from the Corporate

Nokia vs Micromax (Developmental (NPD), Distribution, and Price Flexibility): Although Nokia is still a major player of Indian mobile handset segment, it has lost its tremendous share to competitors because of inflexibility like developmental

(NPD), distribution, price, logistics, and IT flexibilities in developing new products (NPD). Due to this flexibility or rigidity, Nokia lost touch of its market, which gave the competition enough space to seize the market share of low-income consumer segment. Micromax, which is currently ranked third in the mobile handset industry, took a large chunk of market share away from Nokia because of the developmental flexibility. New innovative features like dual sim and wireless radio were offered by Micromax in its products. Nokia, however, failed to arrest its market share, because it could not add such innovative features in its handsets. Due to this, Micromax zoomed to third position in the market, while it started as a small trader/dealer of Nokia products in India.

Although Nokia has lost some of its share to its rivals, it still enjoys the market share to the tune of 30 % in 2011 quarter of October–December (Report on). Along with other factors, what has also contributed to the success of Nokia is its price and distribution flexibility. Various authors Ariga and Okusha 1998 give the essence of price flexibility. Price flexibility relates to the number of price points companies have on offer according to the customer preferences. Distribution flexibility is another success factor that proved crucial in the case of Nokia. Ron Ashkenas (2000) has talked about the place flexibility which is closely associated with the Nokia's success. Study reveals that the success of the firm is related to its ability to add or subtract the place according to opportunity or threat arising out of the environmental conditions. It is estimated that there are about 90,000 mobile sales outlets in India, and out of which 50,000 have only one brand to sell, i.e., Nokia. Further distribution flexibility of Nokia endowed company to include some other non-traditional formats for mobile-handset sales like Mom & Pop stores, stationary shops, STD booth owners and cloth merchants (India Knowledge@Wharton 2007).

Wal-Mart/Big Bazaar vs Subhiksha (Promotional, Distribution, Logistics, and IT Flexibility): Wal-Mart, founded in 1962, is the world's largest public corporation, in terms of revenue. The company employs 2.2 million people for its 8,970 locations (Wal-Mart/wiki). One of the critical success factors of Wal-Mart is its IT flexibility. MacKinnon et al. (2008) talked about the importance of information flexibility in providing the competitive edge to the firms. EDI system has been implemented by Wal-Mart which has made it possible for the company to connect to its thousands of partners on real-time basis (Wal-Mart/Cisco). No wonder Wal-Mart is reaping rich benefits due to its IT flexibility.

Similarly in Indian context, biggest retailer Big Bazaar of the future group has reaped the benefit by using IT flexibility and promotional flexibility. Raju et al. (1990) observed that the companies use the promotion tool in order to get the larger share of the market. Promotion can also be a very useful tool in spurring up the demand, and this is exactly what Big Bazaar does. Founded in 2001, Big Bazaar is the largest chain of hypermarket in India. It has 214 stores in 90 cities and towns covering around 16 million sq. feet of retail space (Big Bazaar/wiki). Along with its humongous size and depth of assortment, promotional flexibility has played a crucial role in ensuring the success of this hypermarket chain in India. Every Wednesday, as well as end of season, and festival sales are used as special promotional campaigns for low price of its merchandise. The company usually clears all the backlog of the inventory that is piled up in the stock of the company. Big Bazaar is able to lower its prices also due to its ability to negotiate special prices from its vendors, use of effective methods of supply chain, and efficient utilization of its other resources like distribution and logistics. As a result of this constellation of measures, it has been able to promote and offer the low prices to its customers.

In contrast, Subhiksha, another Indian retailer, also started very well with its first store in Chennai in 1997. Initially, everyday-low-price strategy in its food and grocery stores went well, but IT inflexibility proved fatal for the company. The company went on the expansion spree from 2006. Just in a short span of 2 years, the numbers of stores went from 150 to 1,600 with a humongous growth rate of 1,100 % (subhiksha-retail-phenomenon-which.htm). But it failed miserably to effectively integrate and manage the stores with no proper information system in place and was out of the business in 2009 (Subhiksha/retailbrains).

Bajaj, Kinetic Honda vs Honda (Developmental and Pricing Flexibility): Way back in the 1970s and 1980s Bajaj was the leader in scooter market. Bajaj met with phenomenal success with its geared scooter. Kinetic Honda entered Indian market with gearless scooters. However, with the changing aspirations and technical efficiency, scooter market started losing to motorcycle/bike market. With average of around 50–55 km/l, motorcycles came in sync with the customer expectations. Both Bajaj and Kinetic could not keep pace with the changes and failed to upgrade the scooter technology to make it more efficient in order to get the customers' faith back in scooter segment. As a result, Bajaj added motorcycles to their business, while Kinetic kept struggling for its existence. Also, even after the split between Honda and Kinetic in 1998 (Kinetic Honda Case-Study), Kinetic continued to price its products ambitiously, which added to its debacle. As a result, today the company is struggling to get the things back on track. Honda, on the other hand, with its world-class four-stroke technology entered the gearless scooter market in 2000. With its ultrarefined engine and continuous improvement in technology, Activa today dominates the gearless scooter category in India. *Developmental flexibility* has emerged as one of the critical success factors for Activa as the new model claims even 15 % more mileage than the previous one (honda2wheelersindia.com).

Zee TV vs Star TV (Customer Satisfaction and Positioning Flexibility): In contrast to early foundation of Zee TV in 1993, Star TV was born in 2001. Initially, Star Plus was not able to cater a wide customer base simply because it could not relate to customer expectations. So the company finally decided to change its positioning strategy and repositioned itself with viewer-oriented soaps and dramas (The-Failure-of-Zee). This positioning flexibility is at the root of the success of channel that it is enjoying today. Similarly, Star launched a new reality game show *"Kaun Banega Crorepati"* hosted by the legendary Amitabh Bachhan, while Zee failed miserably with its reply in the form of *"Sawaal Dus Crore Ka"* hosted by another Bollywood actor Govinda. Thus, Star showed better understanding of viewers' interest (*customer satisfaction flexibility*) with domestic soap operas and garnering the highest television rating points.

Hindustan Motors – Ambassador vs Maruti Suzuki – 800 (Product Flexibility): Till the 1980s, more than 70 % of the market share was with the Ambassador, while 30 % remained with the Fiat's Premier Padmini. Until the advent of Maruti, Hindustan Motors ruled the market with its Ambassador. The car was built tough and sturdy in nature. However, the situation changed after Maruti Suzuki launched its 800 car in the market. In order to arrest the falling market share, the company approached McKinsey & Co. to provide them with consultancy about how to get out of the problem situation. One of the major loopholes McKinsey found was inflexible product proposition, as there existed little margin for product up-gradation. (Hindustan Motors/marketingpractice.blogspot). Ambassador underwent some upgrades between 1958 and 2000, named Mark II, Mark III, and Mark IV. These were cosmetic in nature with no real value addition (ambassador-marketing-myopia.html). This inflexibility is due to the constraints led by shop floor or production units. Consultancy report in its recommendations gave the suggestion to reengineer the shop floor in order to increase the *product flexibility*. Maruti, on the other hand, continuously upgraded the technological as well as aesthetic aspects of the car. Many value additions were done, and all these value additions were perceived very well by the customers. No wonder Maruti Suzuki still holds nearly 40 % share in Indian four-wheeler market.

McDonald's vs Pizza Hut (Developmental (NPD) and Customer Satisfaction Flexibility): Though both the companies belong to the category of fast-food restaurants, McDonald's insights about the customer preferences have made it a leader in the fast-food market with its product development ability according to tastes and preferences of the customers across the geographical regions. Along with the new product development (NPD), flexibility and price flexibility also added to the volume of sales. Happy price menu starting from as low as Rs. 20 is an example of price flexibility that stemmed from the efficient and effective operational capabilities of organization. In contrast to McDonald's, Pizza Hut is not doing very well because of the high pricing and non-customized offerings. Also the pricing strategy of Pizza Hut is not as flexible as that of McDonald's.

Ford Motor Company (Product Flexibility): Product flexibility equips the manufacturer with the ability to make multiple products on same capacity and the ability to relocate the capacity between different products in response to realized demand as observed by Goyal and Netessine (2011). With the investment of the tune of $550 million, Ford has achieved wonderful product flexibility. This huge investment led the Michigan assembly plant to become one of the most flexible plants of the company capable of producing gasoline-powered, battery-electric, hybrid, and plug-in hybrid electric vehicle on the same production line (Ford Motor Company, News Center). It can now readily adjust the production of the vehicles according to increase or decrease in the overall demand of the product. This product flexibility is sure to hedge Ford against the ill effects of demand–supply fluctuation on the health of automobile industry.

Apple's iPhone (Developmental Flexibility): Unveiled by Steve Jobs in 2007, iPhone has met with unprecedented success all over the world. After its inauguration till now, Apple has added numerous features as well as applications to iPhone. The continuous upgradation of the features on iPhone made iPhone one of the biggest players in smartphone industry. Sales of around 35.10 million units in the second quarter of 2012 (iPhone/wiki) was achieved due to distinctive competence.

Harley-Davidson (*Information System Flexibility)*: Flexibility in information system not only helps to disseminate the information in a quick way but also helps in finding the correct relevance of this information in changed scenario. For this, a seamless integration of the components is required. Service-oriented architecture (SOA) is one such technique that helps in integrating the primary resources of organization in a seamless way (Erol et al. 2009). HD is one such company which implemented the SOA and reaping rich benefits due to its implementation. With the help of SOA, the company is able to make its credit and loan facility more flexible and adaptable especially in the peak season of its demand. New system implemented has the SOA in middle, and with the help of key changing indicators, which takes care of rest of the system automatically, HD is now more responsive to change and sell motorcycles more than before (Harley-Davidson/service-oriented/born-to-be-service-oriented).

7 Conclusion

With the cut-throat competition and uncertainties in the market, flexibility, as a strategy for sustained profitability, has gained wide acceptance in the corporate. With its three underlying principles of options, change, and freedom of choice in the corporate, flexibility helps organizations to remain competitive in the long run. Flexibility ensures quick adaptation to the changing environmental conditions and helps companies in gaining competitive edge over its competitors. In normal situation, flexibility ensures competitive edge to the firm, while in case of turbulent times, it ensures sustainability.

Similarly, realization of marketing as the backbone of any organization and its role in increasing profitability and overall revenue generation, successful corporates do not view it as mere function. SoS approach with its essence of whole is definitely far better in order to satisfy the customers too. Holistic view and the ability to better analyze the interrelations that exist among various subsystems are distinctive competencies of the systemic approach. Hence, considering marketing as a system will bring necessary competence in the organization to sustain and survive in the long run.

Marketing system of the organization with the attributes of flexibility embedded within will help organizations by equipping them with ability to quickly learn and adapt according to changing conditions. This directly means that a flexible marketing system helps the company by ensuring sustainability aspect of growth and competitiveness by satisfying both customers and stakeholders in a much better way. A case example of Punjab National Bank, which started operations for long hours, can be taken in this regard. Flexibility in this example is achieved by two ways: first by providing the service/product to customer for long hours and second by use of technology, i.e., Internet. Similarly, movie theaters offer tickets at lower price during low rush hours, i.e., in mornings to attract more people during low peak time. Therefore, flexibility here is achieved by discounted price methods. Example of flexibility in terms of extended hours of working can be quoted by taking the case of retailers who work for extended time period during festive seasons. Pantaloons India Ltd., Shoppers Stop, and Spencer's follow this strategy. Also by employing extra human resources or paying increased wages to the existing employees, companies meet the demand of human resources in peak seasons. Offering variable products or customizing preferences is another method of achieving flexibility. Credit card companies like American Express or Barclays offer more than one type of card (variable products), while GM produces cars for various purposes and personalities (customization); a similar strategy has been adopted by GE. Through the Internet, customers can put their specifications at the design stage along with recommendations about the materials. GE plants then adjust their manufacturing operations quickly as the customer makes a change in their choice of design. Eureka Forbes with its general pattern of meeting the clients individually creates the flexibility by overcoming the location constraint (meeting at customer's desired location) as well as risk perceptions of customers (explaining about the product).

Managerial implication of marketing flexibility is to have enhanced understanding of the business even at the basic levels. With the increased competition, marketing system flexibility has become an inevitable strategy today. Diversifications of strengths and developing capabilities along with maintaining presence in several markets can be used in order to develop the flexibility of marketing system. This requires to perceive the holistic view of marketing as a system in any organization, and also it entails to study the relationships with other subsystems for customer satisfaction. Marketing flexibility, once created, is sure to increase the market share of the organizations by positively affecting its brand equity. This will also help in evolving all the entities in such a way that maximizes the satisfaction proposition for all the stakeholders involved.

The managerial implication of the marketing flexibility is to enhance understanding and importance of flexibility in day-to-day business practices. With the fast-changing business models and standardization of the products, it is detrimental for any business to skip marketing as an integral part of their strategy. Diversifications of strengths like participating in multiple product markets, developing capability of using multiple distribution channels, and maintaining a presence in several countries, and investment in underutilized resources like developing "excess" customers' loyalty to buffer competitive actions, and designing operating procedures to handle environmental change can be used to increase marketing flexibility in the organizations.

The chapter is based on the literature available in this field, which itself is not sufficient to do comprehensive analysis. Therefore, for further study, empirical data especially taking live cases may be considered. Limitation of adopting functional approach only in a classification framework (previous studies) is that the functions may be viewed as discrete parts, rather than a whole – the organization. It is also observed from the literature survey and the corporate examples that there is a need to understand the flexibilities in functional areas, especially to highlight the implementation and utilization of these flexibilities in the organization. At the same time, specific study on particular industries and sectors may be considered for better understanding of the concept, also generic model may not be applicable to all organizations in different sectors.

References

Aaker DA, Mascarenhas B (1984) The need for strategic flexibility strategic flexibility. J Bus Strateg Flex Syst Manag 5(2):74–82

Abbot A, Banerji K (2003) Strategic flexibility and firm performance: the case of US based transnational corporations. Glob J Flex Syst Manag 4(1&2):1–12

Adler L (1967) Systems approach to marketing. Harv Bus Rev 45:105–118

Ansari S, Bell J (1997) Target costing core group, target costing: the next frontier in strategic cost management. A CAM-I, CMS model for profit planning and cost management, Irwin, Chicago, IL

Ansoff HI (1965) Corporate strategy: business policy for growth and expansion. McGraw-Hill, New York

Ariga K, Okusha Y (1998) Price flexibility in Japan, 1970–1992: a study of price formation. Int J Ind Organ Neth 16(5)

Ashkenas R (2000) Management: how to loosen organizational boundaries. J Bus Strateg 21(2):11–12

Bahrami H (1992) The emerging flexible organization; perspectives from silicon valley. Calif Manage Rev 34(4):33–52

Big Bazaar http://en.wikipedia.org/wiki/Big_Bazaar. Retrieved 10 Apr 2012

Drucker P (1980) Managing in turbulent times. Harper and Row, New York

Eppink DJ (1978) Planning for strategic flexibility. Long Range Plann 11(4):9–15

Erol O, Sauser BJ, Boardman JT (2009) Creating enterprise flexibility through service oriented architecture. Glob J Flex Syst Manag 10(1):11–16

Ford Motor Company, News Center http://corporate.ford.com/news-center/press-releases-detail/pr-ford-opens-flexible-green-michigan-34225. Retrieved 11 May 2012

Goyal M, Netessine S (2011) Volume flexibility or product flexibility or both. Manufacturing service operation management 13(2):180–193

Grewal R, Tanshuhaj P (2001) Building organizational capabilities for managing economic crisis: the role of market orientation and strategic flexibility. J Mar Sci 65:67–80

Hamel G, Prahalad CK (1989) Strategic intent. Harv Bus Rev 67:63–76

Harley-Davidson http://www.zdnet.com/blog/service-oriented/born-to-be-service-oriented/615?tag=content;siu-container. Retrieved 07 June 2012

Harrigan KR (1985) Strategies for joint ventures. Lexington Books, Lexington

Hart AG (1940) Anticipations, uncertainty and dynamic planning. University of Chicago, Chicago

Hindustan Motors http://marketingpractice.blogspot.in/2008/05/ambassador-marketing-myopia.html. Retrieved 07 May 2012

Hindustan Motors http://www.authorstream.com/Presentation/bharatsoni007-250363-hindustan-motors-4928421-case-study-ppt-business-finance-powerpoint/. Retrieved 07 May 2012

India Knowledge@Wharton 2007. http://knowledge.wharton.upenn.edu/india/article.cfm?articleid=4220. Retrieved 05 Apr 2012

iPhone http://en.wikipedia.org/wiki/I_Phone. Retrieved 17 May 2012

Johnson G (1992) Managing strategic change, strategy, culture and action. Long Range Plann 25(2):28–36

Kinetic Honda http://www.scribd.com/subhendu_mukherjee/d/40549295-Kinetic-Honda-Case-Study. Retrieved 13 Apr 2012
Lavington F (1921) The English capital market. Methnen & Co. Ltd, London
MacKinnon W, Grant G, Cray D (2008) Enterprise information systems and strategic flexibility, international conference on system sciences. In: Proceedings of the 41st annual. Hawaii, pp 402–402
Pasmore WA (1994) Creating strategic change; designing of flexible high performance organization. Wiley, New York
Peter T (1991) Thriving on chaos; handbook for management revolution. Harper Perennial Edition, New York
Prahalad C, Hamel G (1990) The core competence of the corporation. Harv Bus Rev 68:79–91
Raju JS, Srinivasan V, Lal R (1990) The effects of brand loyalty on competitive price promotional strategies. J Mar Sci 36(3):276–304
Report on Nokia http://www.livemint.com/2012/05/14214221/Nokia-fights-back-as-Samsung-e.html. Retrieved 05 Apr 2012
Sharma MK, Sushil, Jain PK (2010) Revisiting flexibility in organizations: exploring its impact on performance. Glob J Flex Syst Manag 11(3):51–68
Singh N (2011) FLEXMARK: scale for testing the flexibility in the marketing system. In: 11th Global Conference on Flexible Systems Management, IIM Kozhikode, 09–12 Dec
Singh N, Kumar S (2011) An approach towards marketing SoS. In: 11th Global Conference on Flexible Systems Management, IIM Kozhikode, 09–12 Dec
Singh TP, Sushil (1997) Management of system waste using flexible system methodology. In: Proceedings of the ICMOT, New Delhi, 21–24 Dec, p. 803
Slack N (1983) Flexibility as a manufacturing objective. Int J Op Prod Manag 3(3):4–13
Subhiksha http://retailbrains.blogspot.in/2009/11/subhiksha-retail-phenomenon-which.html. Retrieved 11 Apr 2012
Sushil (1999) Flexibility in management. Global Institute of Flexible Systems Management/Vikas Publishing House, New Delhi
Sushil (2000) Systemic flexibility. Glob J Flex Syst Manag 1(1):77–80
Volberda HW (1996) Towards the flexible form: how to remain vital in hypercompetitive environments. Organ Sci 7(4):359–387
Wal-Mart http://en.wikipedia.org/wiki/Walmart. Retrieved 07 Apr 2012
Wal-Mart http://www.cisco.com/warp/public/779/ibs/vertical/retail/Wal-Mart.PDF. Retrieved 07 Apr 2012
Zee TV http://www.scribd.com/doc/36575597/The-Failure-of-Zee. Retrieved 27 Apr 2012

Appendix 1: List of Identified Forces of Change and Continuity in E-Government

S. No.	Forces of change	Explanation
1	*Globalization*	Globalization has placed strong pressures on states to compete for trade flows, investments, and resources and is a strong force outside the control of government. It is affecting stakeholder's perception of service delivery and seems to be the basic imperative to change the way governments relate to the citizens
2	*New opportunities*	"E-government is not just about forms and services online," it brings about new and unique opportunities like enhanced efficiency, transparency, accountability, participation, and effectiveness for all stakeholders
3	*Pressures of good governance*	Governments are under continual pressure from the society to increase their effectiveness and efficiency, competing with their peers to provide electronic services to the citizens
4	*Stakeholders' needs and expectations*	Citizen's expectations for better government services change with changing times. They expect a similar level of service from government as customers expect from e-business and hence e-alignment of e-government with the needs of the primary stakeholders is called for
5	*New technology*	Adoption of information and communication technologies (ICT) to deliver government services has become a global trend in public administration. Proliferation of such new technologies has thus become the underpinning driver and enabler of e-government
6	*The e-platform*	With citizens increasing comfort level with the e-platform, the pressure to adopt e-government increases. E-government offers the potential to reform the public sector, just as e-commerce is driving change in the business sector
7	*Government policies and legislation*	Changes in government policies and legislation are expected to pave the path for e-government implementation. Institutional infrastructure and apt legal framework have been identified by the researchers as critical success factors for national e-strategy
8	*Public-private partnership*	Public-private partnership has emerged as a viable alternative towards faster and sustainable growth of e-government initiatives and hence can be considered as a significant driver for change in the domain

(continued)

Sushil and E.A. Stohr (eds.), *The Flexible Enterprise*, Flexible Systems Management,
DOI 10.1007/978-81-322-1560-8, © Springer India 2014

(continued)

S. No.	Forces of continuity	Explanation
1	*Large number and heterogeneity of citizen base*	The challenge of addressing a large and heterogeneous citizen base affects the implementation of e-government projects. Governments, however, have to focus on training the existing citizen base to use the new delivery mechanism rather than strategize to retain them, as is the case with business organizations where the inertia creeps in due to the fear of losing large customer base
2	*Established traditional infrastructure*	E-government projects inherit huge traditional infrastructure, which may become redundant with the implementation of e-government technology, and are expected to experience greater continuity
3	*Existing process of service delivery*	A preexisting network of supply chain/delivery process leads to a greater continuity in the current offering and could pose a major challenge for e-government implementation, if not adequately managed
4	*Manual records or legacy databases*	From manual records to computerized databases and now networked databases, changes in governance have largely been technology driven, which, if not leveraged, can pose serious problems in e-government implementation
5	*Existing culture*	*E-government requires change in the processes, attitude, and mind-set of the government which is a big challenge. In fact the problem of change management in e-government implementation largely revolves around managing the existing culture*

Source: Adapted from Nasim and Sushil 2010

Appendix 2: Strategic Factors with Brief Description

S. No.	Project factors: ten strategic factors/deliverables from project perspective with brief description
1.	**Financial performance of the project**
	Cost savings from the project (infrastructure, operational, personnel cost) to the government
	Increase in revenue earned from the project
	Adequate mechanism to recover capital cost
	Volume of service delivered (number of citizens using the service)
2.	**Replication and sustainability of the project**
	The extent of replicability (technical/commercial) of the project
	The extent of innovation in service delivery
	Sustainability of the project
	Adequate organizational structure to support the project for continuous functioning
3.	**Top management commitment**
	Top management (administration) support
	Project champion commitment to the project
	Continuity of project cha mpions from conceptualization to roll-out phase of the project
4.	**Employee training and involvement**
	Adequate level of employee training is carried out
	Employees are quite clear about their roles in the project
	Employee involvement in design and implementation
5.	**Vendor relationship and user group reviews (if any)**
	Private vendors involvement in the project
	Service levels measures defined for the private partners
	Assessment of vendors on a regular basis
	There are user groups conducting service reviews
6.	**Strategy and policy**
	The roadmap/plan for the project is clearly laid out
	Proper documentation policy for the project is adopted
	There is a policy for customer feedback
	Policies/strategies for project assessment (third-party audit) are in place

(continued)

DOI 10.1007/978-81-322-1560-8,

(continued)

S. No.	Project factors: ten strategic factors/deliverables from project perspective with brief description
7.	**Technological process**
	Technology architecture is compatible with international standards
	The degree of scalability of the project is quite high
	Extent of compliance with security standards is satisfactory
	The technology is easy to install and operate
	There are alternative arrangements in case of breakdown
8.	**Internal efficiency**
	There is substantial increase in productivity in handling transactions
	The interaction between government employees across local, state, and central levels is seamless (uninterrupted/smooth)
	There is high level of process automation at the back end
	It is easy for the internal stakeholders (employees, administrators, etc.) to adopt the e-government process
9.	**Interaction with external stakeholders**
	E-government has facilitated seamless interaction with its customers (citizens and business)
	The process of interaction with vendors or other e-government solution providers is quite effective
	Government partnership with special interest groups (NGOs, CSOs, international organizations like OECD and UN) is facilitated by e-government strengthening social development
10.	**Political will and e-government readiness**
	There is a strong political will and leadership to implement e-government projects
	The level of infrastructure (ICT) development and contracting undertaken for deploying e-government projects is adequate
	Substantial capability development has been undertaken to facilitate e-government
	Convergence in technology is paving way for greater maturity in e-governance
Citizen factors: Five performance parameters from citizen perspective with brief description	
1.	**Service efficiency (user time, money saved)**
	Total user time saved
	Total user money saved
	Number of citizens using the services
	Number of services offered to the citizens
2.	**Availability and convenience**
	Availability of the system 24×7
	Accessibility through multiple channels (PCs, kiosks, mobile phones, etc.)
	Convenience of location/single-window interface
3.	**Ease of use**
	Simple to understand and use
	Ease of use due to local language interface
	Easy to use due to usefulness of help menus
4.	**Transparency**
	Increase in transparency
	Decrease in corruption

(continued)

(continued)

S. No.	Project factors: ten strategic factors/deliverables from project perspective with brief description
5.	**Accuracy and privacy of information**
	Accuracy of information
	Security/privacy of information provided by the citizens
6.	**Citizen participation**
	Increase in government citizen interaction
	Keeps citizens informed/build up knowledge
	Helps citizens communicate effectively with the state
	Makes citizens feel part of an active democracy

Appendix 3: Result of Grounded Theory Methodology

The factors identified after conducting the study are as follows:

General pattern

1. Flexibility can be measured in three areas – options, change mechanism, and freedom of choices.
2. All risks can be categorized into two major types of risks – risk of not having flexibility and risk of having flexibility.
3. Controllability parameters can be classified into two groups – (a) internal in the system (known as the self-governance) and (b) external (this is controlled from outside the system).

Statements on flexibility

4. Multitasking ability can be considered as flexibility parameter.
5. Network-based approach can be considered as flexibility parameter.
6. Productivity can be considered as flexibility parameter.
7. Dynamism can be considered as flexibility parameter.
8. Teamwork can be considered as flexibility parameter.
9. Information technology proficiency can be considered as flexibility parameter.
10. Flexi-timings can be considered as flexibility parameter.
11. Flexi structure can be considered as flexibility parameter.
12. Flexi compensation can be considered as flexibility parameter.
13. Flexi appraisal can be considered as flexibility parameter.
14. Adaptability to change can be considered as flexibility parameter.
15. Change management procedure can be considered as flexibility parameter.
16. Manufacturing process flexibility can be considered as flexibility parameter.
17. Sales flexibility measured by time to respond to a change in the market can be considered as flexibility parameter.
18. Outsourcing/third-party engagement can be considered as flexibility parameter.
19. Data center has to be flexible to accommodate skewed data flux due to seasonality in business – can be considered as flexibility.
20. Market-side flexibility can be measured by economic parameters.

Sushil and E.A. Stohr (eds.), *The Flexible Enterprise*, Flexible Systems Management,
DOI 10.1007/978-81-322-1560-8, © Springer India 2014

21. Supply side of people – the variability is in the general economic conditions.
22. Exchange rate generally has an impact on organization in deploying flexible measures.
23. HR policies can be considered as flexibility parameters and can be measured by attrition rate.
24. Measure of on-time delivery can be considered as flexibility parameter.
25. Sensitivity to the quality requirement can be considered as flexibility parameter.
26. Learning environment measured by the number of initiatives taken to create the learning environment can be considered as flexibility parameters.
27. Key aspects of the business model are (a) on-site and offshore mix and (b) support and maintenance vs. new projects.
28. Flexibility may work in a negative way for a bureaucratic government setup which is involved in certifying electronic transactions.
29. Flexibility lies in business direction, i.e., allocation of investments across new and old product portfolio, flexibility in business direction (e.g., make vs. buy).
30. Flexibility is resilience in customer handling, i.e., openness to customer queries and complaint management across channel (e.g., services handled equally when request placed telephonically, on the web-channel, at the retail store).
31. Flexibility in leadership (in a complex case) can be a flexibility parameter.
32. Supply chain flexibility – demand and supply lines should have sufficient flexible capacity to absorb business demands – should be considered as flexibility parameter.

Statements on controllability

33. Financial system (triple-audit system – internal, external, and statutory) can be considered as controllability parameter.
34. Clearly laid down authority and responsibility metrics can be considered as controllability parameter.
35. Legal competency of an organization can be considered as controllability parameter.
36. Importance of vigilance department can be considered as controllability parameter.
37. Tools like performance, coaching, and development systems to control the pockets of lower performance and/or morale before it is too late – can be considered as controllability parameter.
38. HR policies can be considered as a control measure – can be measured by attrition rate.
39. Adherence to information governance policy can be considered as control parameter (information leakage is restricted).
40. Mind control can be considered as controllability parameter – can be measured by the initiatives taken by the organization.
41. Quality assurance in purchase may be considered as controllability measure.
42. Monitoring/measuring aberrations from normal result of process input and output can be considered as controllability parameter.

43. Growth strategy – focus on domain, strategy, and investment decisions can be considered as controllability parameters.
44. Margins/accounting ratios can be considered as controllability parameters.
45. Order book, pipeline, and conversion ratio can be considered as controllability parameters.
46. New customer acquisition vis-à-vis repeat order generation can be measured as controllability parameters.
47. Policies and procedures of the enterprise can be considered as controllability parameters.
48. Government regulation can be considered as controllability parameter.

Statements on risk

1. Multitasking may affect output because people may not be good in every area. Expertise may be in one field and may not be that good in other fields (people risk).
2. Attrition can be termed as loss of knowledge and can be considered as risk parameter.
3. Too much of dynamism may end up with decision-making processes without evaluating the situation – can be considered as risk parameter.
4. Conflict can be considered as risk parameter.
5. People-centric organization may have skewed performance over the corporate landscape.
6. Data dependency and sanctity of data can be a big threat to the organization.
7. Rate of change of decisions can be considered as risk parameter.
8. Vertical monitoring can be considered as risk parameter.
9. Emotional risk – when you are too deeply involved into your work – can be considered as risk parameter.
10. Physical risk can be considered/should be considered as risk parameter in a production system.
11. SCM turnover ratio can be considered as risk parameter.
12. Political uncertainty can be considered as risk parameter.
13. Currency fluctuations can be considered as risk parameter.
14. Prices of natural resource can be considered as risk parameter.
15. Monetary policies and cost of finance can be considered as risk parameter.
16. Inflation can be considered as risk parameter.
17. Transparency in information flow can be considered as risk parameter.
18. Risk of lending because of diversified portfolio can be considered as risk parameter.
19. Too many touch points (project based) can be considered as risk parameter.
20. Technology risks – obsolescence of a company's main technology platform – can be considered as risk parameter.
21. Financial risks (over leveraged, high debt ratio impacted by high interest rates, etc.) – these are standard for any company and can be considered as risk parameter.
22. Organization's risk appetite measured by investments towards R&D (or innovation).
23. Organization culture of risk reward in the compensation structure can be considered as risk parameter.

Appendix 4: Summary of WebCampus Operations

Online Graduate Programs
Through the WebCampus division, courses for 15 Masters Degrees, 39 Graduate Certificates, and the school's MBA are offered online.

Corporate Campus Programs
Through the WebCampus division, numerous programs at off-site locations have been initiated and supported. Significantly, the amount of new activity at existing corporate campus sites has dramatically increased.

International Programs
The WebCampus division has also demonstrated the capability to exploit new international opportunities. Through the WebCampus division, the school has begun offering classes in Beijing via partnerships with Chinese universities. These partnerships make use of a hybrid and innovative approach in offering programs, with some classes run online and others conducted in conventional classrooms. The first Chinese cohorts started in 2003. The experience gained from this undertaking was instrumental for Stevens, when IBM awarded special training contracts for their Chinese employees. The school's second award from the prestigious Sloan Foundation can be traced to these efforts.

Training Programs
Through the WebCampus division, the school has been able to run a limited number of special training programs for corporate clients. The model involves leveraging current faculty members and existing course content in the development of customized materials based on client needs.

The WebCampus division has also developed a blended PMP Exam Preparation training course. Originally developed for the "retail market," this course has been successfully run for corporate clients.

It has been the experience of the WebCampus division that developing and deploying training programs are very labor-intensive, with low margins. Despite the benefits that a training arm would bring to the WebCampus portfolio, a lack of

Sushil and E.A. Stohr (eds.), *The Flexible Enterprise*, Flexible Systems Management,
DOI 10.1007/978-81-322-1560-8, © Springer India 2014

resources gave the division no choice but to suspend further development of training programs at the beginning of FY08.

Proposed Undergraduate Degrees

Finally, discussions are under way to deploy two online undergraduate degrees. (This is not to be confused with the Euclid program, which consists of four online courses designed for incoming freshmen that WebCampus has offered since 2003.) The online undergraduate degrees under consideration are likely to be targeted towards people who have been in the workforce for several years but have reached a plateau in their careers.

Appendix 5: Essential WebCampus Processes

1. ***Managing the Semester Cycle***: Managing the schedule of offerings is perhaps the single most important and time-sensitive process that the WebCampus team is involved in. This process has several critical milestones that cannot be missed under any circumstances. The schedule of courses and instructors must be built and posted at least 2 months before the start of the registration period. Although some aspects of the schedule are somewhat routine, many schedule elements can change radically from semester to semester. Opportunities for automation exist; however, a fully automated scheduling process will not be practical for the foreseeable future. If the posting of the schedule is delayed for any reason, it would have a cascading effect upon sales and marketing activities and hence enrollments and revenues.

   Apart from scheduling, there is a myriad of sub-processes that are executed each semester: distributing instructor contracts, filling out faculty payroll requisitions, ensuring course content is loaded and ready for orientation week in all WebCT shells, distributing rosters to instructors, performing web conferencing directory maintenance, calculating cosponsor commissions and developer royalties, making routine website updates, synchronizing the ACE student survey systems, collecting operational performance metrics, and numerous cases of technical and administrative troubleshooting that are inevitable in every semester.
2. ***Attracting and Supporting Students***: Managing the student experience from "inquiry" thru graduation and beyond involves a complex and often changing mixture of sales, marketing, and operations activities. For attracting new students, WebCampus uses a mixture of marketing approaches, which can involve any combination of corporate (B2B) sales and outreach efforts, on-site and online information fairs, email blasts to existing lists of prospective students, and various forms of online advertising. Due to budget constraints, most online advertising approaches such as banner ads, search engine optimization, and paid "lead generation" programs have not been consistently pursued. Some work has been done in website analytics, though the link between this activity and increased enrollments has not yet been demonstrated at Stevens. Finally, printed catalogs and

Sushil and E.A. Stohr (eds.), *The Flexible Enterprise*, Flexible Systems Management,
DOI 10.1007/978-81-322-1560-8, © Springer India 2014

public relations efforts (such as writing articles and networking at conferences) also round out the list of marketing activities at Stevens. None of these activities are nearly as routine as the schedule-building process. However, there are frequently work products from previous iterations that can be recycled, as is the case of creating catalogs and revising information session presentations.

In contrast, sub-processes for supporting incoming and existing students are more well established. Naturally, the various student support processes can be quite complex and involve many staff members. For example, application processing starts with the student, who may be "coached" by either faculty or Admissions staff members. Application components (including transcripts and letters of recommendation) are gathered by the Admissions department, logged in the record-keeping system, and then sent to the appropriate academic department for evaluation. The academic department renders an admissions decision and forwards the application package back to Admissions. Admissions takes the appropriate admit or reject documentation and enters this additional data into the school's record-keeping system. Students who are accepted are informed of how to log on to their accounts, who their advisors are, and are then required at some point to submit study plans. The study plan process itself ironically has highly structured and non-structured components. Students have a wide time window in which to work with their advisors and get their study plans on file. Some parts of the application process are semiautomated, and some opportunities for further automation exist in study plan processing. Yet these two support processes are still highly prone to error and/or delay.

Most situations where students withdraw from courses are handled in a routine matter. But numerous petitions for Incompletes and full refunds are evaluated on a case-by-case basis. Similarly, handling student complaints about course content, quality, delivery technologies, or faculty are handled on a case-by-case basis. Often, intervention by other areas, such as the Registrar, Student Services, or the appropriate academic department, is required.

The process of giving course surveys is largely automated – at least from the student perspective. Unfortunately, there is a large amount of non-automated and semiautomated work (primarily data management) that goes into maintaining the ACE survey system. This, in turn, makes the course assessment process prone to errors that require manual intervention to correct.

With the redevelopment of the WebCampus website, some services for online students will be vastly improved. More content that is of general interest to both on-campus and off-campus will be made available. Much work has been done in improving library service for WebCampus students as well. Other services have not been addressed. For example, providing career services specifically for online students is a largely unexplored area. Other than contingency planning mechanisms such as compiling a list of frequently asked questions, the opportunities for automating many of these tasks are limited.

3. ***Supporting and Training Faculty***: Nearly 150 faculty members have taught online courses at Stevens. WebCampus staff members have been available to

assist online professors in a wide range of topics, ranging from administrative, technical, and course quality matters.

Since 2000, WebCampus and the IT division have coordinated WebCT training sessions, and more recently Interwise training sessions. (WebCT is the learning management system where most virtual classroom activities are performed. Interwise is a web conferencing system that is used to supplement the capabilities of WebCT.) In addition to traditional classroom-based or one-on-one sessions, training on the use of these technologies can now be taken in real-time web conferences or through prerecorded self-paced modules. Promoting student participation in ACE surveys, distribution of student contact information, and even assisting in the uploading of course content are just some of the things that the WebCampus division does to aid instructors.

Perhaps most significantly, WebCampus offers advice to new and current online faculty members regarding matters of pedagogy. WebCampus staff members, some of which have taken online courses, routinely advise instructors on effective methods for conducting various class activities. From grading strategies to advice on how to structure exams and team assignments, the WebCampus staff is constantly sharing knowledge that is gleaned from past experience, current student feedback, and the latest research in the online teaching profession. Instructors are expected to attend WebCampus colloquium meetings every year to discuss best practices. Topics such as effective virtual teaming, fostering active discussions, the effective use of standard course materials and templates, and plagiarism detection are some of the topics that have been covered in previous faculty colloquia.

Finally, the WebCampus staff often intervenes when students are having administrative or technical difficulties that may be related to registering for, logging onto, or sometimes exiting from an instructor's online courses. These interventions are important not only for helping students out of difficult situations, but also to allow faculty members to concentrate on what their mission is providing top quality instruction for their class. As with many forms of student support, these activities are largely addressed on a case-by-case basis.

4. ***Supporting the Development of New Online Programs***: In all, there are over 150 courses in the WebCampus inventory. About 130 of them are given on a regular basis; approximately 105 of them are given each semester. Whenever a course is to be developed, the WebCampus and IT divisions will jointly coordinate the training of the course developer on the appropriate technologies and offer assistance and advice to the developer regarding how to course content should be deployed.

   For cases where other faculty members teach the course using the developer's materials, a process has been set up for calculating and distributing royalty payments. This process should be largely automated when the new WebCampus website is released.

5. ***Managing Partnerships and Client Relationships***: This is an extremely high-touch set of activities, many of which are not conducive to automation. Examples of these activities include holding frequent discussions about the status of existing

agreements, plans for future engagements, providing customer services, and analyzing the effects of various events upon the partnership. Specific tasks might range from the development of client/partner Internet landing pages to attending partner/client conferences and education fairs. These activities help to build trust and credibility with the client, which in turn opens the door for additional opportunities such as cross-selling programs and/or recruiting additional students. However, this activity can greatly benefit from process improvements and automation in the reporting of various metrics.

Metrics reporting is handled as a separate process (or perhaps more accurately described as a sub-process). It entails monitoring, controlling, reporting, and improving upon these five basic processes. It is an activity that has grown in importance with each passing semester. In this regard, WebCampus faced many of the same challenges that other divisions at Stevens did. As in many organizations, the appetite for reports by senior management seemed insatiable. Though the infrastructure at Stevens made broad real-time reporting impractical, there was an ever-present demand to provide the most up-to-date information as possible during weekly departmental meetings. These metrics normally included such things as enrollments new student applications, revenues generated, comparisons with data from the previous year, and forecasts for the following year. With help from the Registrar's Office, WebCampus developed a system of metrics and reports that were able to satisfy the most common inquiries from senior management. The major problem with this activity was that it was enormously time-consuming. The enormous complexity of the raw data in the Registrar's system has led to numerous cases of misinterpretation. Sifting the data and formatting it into easy-to-understand reports was largely a manual process. (The planned replacement of the Registrar's Sunguard/SCT Student Information System with a PeopleSoft information management system will eventually make this kind of reporting much easier. However, no date has been set for this transition project to begin.)

Results of operations	FY2004	FY2005	FY2006	FY2007
Total enrollments	1917	2469	2896	3607
Graduate enrollment	1391	1853	2310	3138
Sections conducted	178	209	263	315
Students per section	10.77	11.81	10.99	11.45
Graduate students per section	7.81	8.87	8.77	9.96
Revenues	\$3,316,000	\$4,467,000	\$6,007,000	\$8,457,000[a]
Percent revenue increase over previous year		34.7 %	34.5 %	40.8 %[b]

[a] New accounting schedule adopted in FY 2007 changed the way Summer-A revenues are booked. Accounting for this change, booked FY 2007 revenues were \$9,288,000

[b] Allowing for the new Summer-A accounting rules adopted in FY2007, this percentage is actually 54.6 %

Appendix 6: Existing JS System: Processing Activities

Sushil and E.A. Stohr (eds.), *The Flexible Enterprise*, Flexible Systems Management, DOI 10.1007/978-81-322-1560-8,

		Activity					Out	Activity					Out	Activity						Total			
Jobs	IAT	D	WT	Mc	ST	PT	IN	D	WT	Mc	ST	PT	IN	D	WT	Mc	ST	PT	Out	WT	ST	PT	FT
J-1	0	7	0	M27	1	2	3	1	0	M3	4	16	23	4	0	M21	1	8	32	0	6	26	32
J-2	3	1	0	M4	2	8	13	3	0	M17	1	2	16						16	0	3	10	13
J-3	6	1	0	M5	3	8	17	7	0	M27	1	2	20	4	0	M20	2	6	28	0	6	16	22
J-4	9	4	0	M20	1	4	14	1	0	M4	1	4	19						19	0	2	8	10
J-5	12	4	0	M21	2	6	20	1	0	M3	1	5	26						26	0	3	11	14
J-6	15	1	0	M3	1	4	20	4	12	M21	2	6	40						40	12	3	10	25
J-7	18	4	10	M20	4	12	44	1	0	M4	4	16	64						64	10	8	28	46
J-8	21	7	0	M27	1	5	27	1	0	M3	4	16	47	4	0	M20	4	8	59	0	9	29	38
J-9	24	1	0	M4	4	16	44	4	0	M21	4	12	60	2	0	M15	1	3	64	0	9	31	40
J-10	27	4	13	M21	1	2	43	7	0	M27	2	5	50	1	0	M8	4	8	62	13	7	15	35
J-11	30	7	0	M27	2	4	36	1	0	M5	4	16	56						56	0	6	20	26
J-12	33	4	26	M20	4	16	79						79						79	26	4	16	46
J-13	36	7	0	M27	2	4	42	1	0	M6	4	12	58	4	2	M21	3	12	75	2	9	28	39
J-14	39	7	11	M27	2	4	56	1	0	M7	4	12	72	4	3	M21	4	8	87	14	10	24	48
J-15	42	4	37	M20	4	12	95	7	0	M27	1	1	97	1	0	M9	1	2	100	37	6	15	58
J-16	45	7	11	M27	1	2	59	1	0	M3	2	14	75						75	11	3	16	30
J-17	48	4	39	M21	2	12	101						101						101	39	2	12	53
J-18	51	7	8	M27	2	6	67	4	28	M20	4	16	115						115	36	6	22	64
																			Average	**11.11**	**5.67**	**18.72**	**35.50**

Legend: *IAT* inter-arrival time; *D* department's numbers; *WT* waiting time; *Mc* machine; *ST* setup time; *PT* processing time; *FT* flow time

Appendix 7: CM System: Processing Activities

Sushil and E.A. Stohr (eds.), *The Flexible Enterprise*, Flexible Systems Management,
DOI 10.1007/978-81-322-1560-8, © Springer India 2014

			Activity				Out	Activity				Out	Activity					Total			
Jobs	Cell	IAT	WT	Mc	ST	PT	IN	WT	Mc	ST	PT	IN	WT	Mc	ST	PT	Out	WT	ST	PT	FT
J-1	A	0	0	M27	1	2	3	0	M3	4	16	23	0	M20	1	8	32	0	6	26	32
J-2	D	3	0	M6	2	8	13	0	M17	1	2	16					16	0	3	10	13
J-3	B	6	0	M4	3	8	17	0	M32	1	2	20	0	M21	2	6	28	0	6	16	22
J-4	C	9	0	M30	1	4	14	0	M5	1	4	19					19	0	2	8	10
J-5	C	12	2	M30		6	20	0	M5		5	25					25	2	0	11	13
J-6	C	15	10	M5		4	29	1	M30		6	36					36	11	0	10	21
J-7	C	18	18	M30		12	48	0	M5		16	64					64	18	0	28	46
J-8	A	21	0	M27		5	26	0	M3		16	42	0	M20		8	50	0	0	29	29
J-9	D	24	0	M6		16	40	0	M31	4	12	56	0	M15	1	3	60	0	5	31	36
J-10	B	27	1	M21		2	30	0	M32		5	35	0	M4		8	43	1	0	15	16
J-11	A	30	0	M27		4	34	8	M3		16	58					58	8	0	20	28
J-12	D	33	23	M31		16	72					72					72	23	0	16	39
J-13	A	36	0	M27		4	40	18	M3		12	70	0	M20		12	82	18	0	28	46
J-14	A	39	1	M27		4	44	26	M3		12	82	0	M20		8	90	27	0	24	51
J-15	B	42	0	M21		12	54	0	M32		1	55	0	M4		2	57	0	0	15	15
J-16	A	45	0	M27		2	47	35	M3		14	96					96	35	0	16	51
J-17	D	48	24	M31		12	84					84					84	24	0	12	36
J-18	B	51	4	M32		6	61	0	M21	4	16	81					81	4	4	22	30
																	Average	**9.50**	**1.44**	**18.72**	**29.67**

Legend: *IAT* inter-arrival time; *WT* waiting time; *Mc* machine; *ST* setup time; *PT* processing time; *FT* flow time

Appendix 8: VCM System: Processing Activities

Sushil and E.A. Stohr (eds.), *The Flexible Enterprise*, Flexible Systems Management,
DOI 10.1007/978-81-322-1560-8, © Springer India 2014

	V.		Activity					Out	Activity					Out	Activity						Total			
Jobs	Cell	IAT	D	WT	Mc	ST	PT	IN	D	WT	Mc	ST	PT	IN	D	WT	Mc	ST	PT	Out	WT	ST	PT	FT
J-1	AB	0	7	6	M27	1	2	9	1	0	M4	4	16	29	4	0	M20		8	37	6	5	26	37
J-2	CD	3	1	6	M8	2	8	19	3	0	M17	1	2	22						22	6	3	10	19
J-3	AB	6	1	0	M3	3	8	17	7	0	M27		2	19	4	0	M20	2	6	27	0	5	16	21
J-4	CD	9	4	0	M21	1	4	14	1	0	M9	1	4	19						19	0	2	8	10
J-5	CD	12	4	2	M21		6	20	1	0	M9		5	25						25	2	0	11	13
J-6	CD	15	1	0	M10	1	4	20	4	0	M21		6	26						26	0	1	10	11
J-7	CD	18	4	8	M21		12	38	1	0	M8		16	54						54	8	0	28	36
J-8	AB	21	7	2	M27		5	28	1	0	M3		16	44	4	0	M20		8	52	2	0	29	31
J-9	CD	24	1	0	M10		16	40	4	0	M21		12	52	2	0	M15	1	3	56	0	1	31	32
J-10	AB	27	4	0	M20		2	29	7	0	M27		5	34	1	0	M4		8	42	0	0	15	15
J-11	AB	30	7	4	M27		4	38	1	0	M5	4	16	58						58	4	4	20	28
J-12	CD	33	4	19	M21		16	68						68						68	19	0	16	35
J-13	AB	36	7	2	M27		4	42	1	0	M4		12	54	4	0	M20		12	66	2	0	28	30
J-14	AB	39	7	3	M27		4	46	1	0	M3		12	58	4	8	M20		8	74	11	0	24	35
J-15	AB	42	4	32	M20		12	86	7	0	M27		1	87	1	0	M4		2	89	32	0	15	47
J-16	AB	45	7	1	M27		2	48	1	0	M6	2	14	64						64	1	2	16	19
J-17	CD	48	4	20	M21		12	80						80						80	20	0	12	32
J-18	AB	51	7	0	M27		6	57	4	29	M20		16	102						102	29	0	22	51
																				Average	**7.89**	**1.28**	**18.72**	**27.89**

Legend: *IAT* inter-arrival time; *D* department's numbers; *WT* waiting time; *Mc* machine; *ST* setup time; *PT* processing time; *FT* flow time

Index

Sushil and E.A. Stohr (eds.), *The Flexible Enterprise*, Flexible Systems Management, DOI 10.1007/978-81-322-1560-8, © Springer India 2014

MIX
Papier aus verantwortungsvollen Quellen
Paper from responsible sources
FSC® C105338

If you have any concerns about our products,
you can contact us on
ProductSafety@springernature.com

In case Publisher is established outside the EU,
the EU authorized representative is:
Springer Nature Customer Service Center GmbH
Europaplatz 3, 69115 Heidelberg, Germany

Printed by Libri Plureos GmbH
in Hamburg, Germany